Unequal Cities

This seminal edited collection examines the impact of austerity and economic crisis on European cities. Whilst on the one hand the struggle for competitiveness has induced many European cities to invest in economic performance and attractiveness, on the other, national expenditure cuts and dominant neo-liberal paradigms have led many to retrench public intervention aimed at preserving social protection and inclusion. The impact of these transformations on social and spatial inequalities – whether occupational structures, housing solutions or working conditions – as well as on urban policy addressing these issues is traced in this exemplary piece of comparative analysis grounded in original research.

Unequal Cities links existing theories and debates with newer discussions on the crisis to develop a typology of possible orientations of local government towards economic development and social cohesion. In the process, it describes the challenges and tensions facing six large European cities, representative of a variety of welfare regimes in Western Europe: Barcelona, Copenhagen, Lyon, Manchester, Milan and Munich. It seeks to answer such key questions as:

- What social groups are most affected by recent urban transformations and what are the social and spatial impacts?
- What are the main institutional factors influencing how cities have dealt with the challenges facing them?
- How have local political agendas articulated the issues and what influence is still exerted by national policy?

Grounded in an original urban policy analysis of the post-industrial city in Europe, the book will appeal to a wide range of social science researchers, PhD and graduate students in urban studies, social policy, sociology, human geography, European studies and business studies, both in Europe and internationally.

Roberta Cucca is Marie Curie Fellow at the Department of Sociology, University of Vienna. Her main research interests are oriented to: economic competitiveness and social inequalities in contemporary cities; deliberative and participatory democracy; environmental crisis and social vulnerability.

Costanzo Ranci is Full Professor in Economic Sociology at the Polytechnic of Milan, Italy. He is Director of Social Policy Research Unit (LPS) and of the International PhD programme in Urban Studies at the Polytechnic of Milan. He has published extensively on social inequality and welfare policy.

Unequal Cities

The challenge of post-industrial transition in times of austerity

Roberta Cucca and Costanzo Ranci

Routledge
Taylor & Francis Group

LONDON AND NEW YORK

First published 2017
by Routledge

2 Park Square, Milton Park, Abingdon, Oxfordshire OX14 4RN
52 Vanderbilt Avenue, New York, NY 10017

Routledge is an imprint of the Taylor & Francis Group, an informa business

First issued in paperback 2019

British Library Cataloguing-in-Publication Data
A catalogue record for this book is available from the British Library

Library of Congress Cataloging in Publication Data
Names: Cucca, Roberta, editor. | Ranci, Costanzo, editor.
Title: Unequal cities : the challenge of post-industrial transition in times of
austerity / edited by Roberta Cucca and Costanzo Ranci.
Description: Abingdon, Oxon ; New York, NY : Routledge, 2016.
Identifiers: LCCN 2016022144| ISBN 9781138919464 (hardback) | ISBN
9781315687865 (ebook)
Subjects: LCSH: Cities and towns–Europe. | Sociology, Urban–Europe. |
Equality–Europe. | Europe–Economic conditions–Regional disparities. |
Europe–Social conditions.
Classification: LCC HT131.U535 2016 | DDC 307.76094–dc23
LC record available at https://lccn.loc.gov/2016022144

ISBN: 978-1-138-91946-4 (hbk)
ISBN: 978-0-367-87328-8 (pbk)

Typeset in Times New Roman
by Wearset Ltd, Boldon, Tyne and Wear

Contents

Figures

Tables

Contributors

Hans Thor Andersen is Director of Research at the Danish Building Research Institute (SBi), Aalborg University. His main areas of interest are social geography, housing and urban politics. His recent work includes socio-spatial changes as preconditions and outcomes of political-economic transformations.

Irina Auernhammer, Architect and Urban Planner ByAK, graduated in architecture from the University of Stuttgart, Faculty of Architecture and Urban Planning, and co-founded the Munich-based studio Auernhammer Wohlrab Architektur. After working as Chair of Urban Development at the Munich University of Technology, she teaches as Academic Associate at the Institute for Lightweight Structures and Conceptual Design (ILEK), Professor Werner Sobek, at the University of Stuttgart.

Ana Belén Cano Hila is Adjunct Lecturer at University of Barcelona and member of the research group CRIT UB. She holds a PhD in Sociology, University of Barcelona. She has collaborated in the management of regional and national projects of research on social innovation and governance; social cohesion, culture and participation; immigration and education.

Rémi Dormois has a "hybrid" profile of Practitioner and Researcher. He works for the French housing ministry in county level administration as Head of the Housing Department. With a PhD in political science, he is Fellow Researcher in the UMR 5600 EVS "Environment, City and Society" (Lyon University). His research topics deal with urban governance and regeneration policies implemented in cities facing demographic and economic crisis.

Yvonne Franz is an urban geographer and Postdoctoral Researcher at the Institute for Urban and Regional Research at the Austrian Academy of Sciences. She has been working on two international JPI Urban Europe projects dealing with gentrification from a relational approach and super-diversity at neighbourhood level. She is also co-organizing the Vienna Summer School in Urban Studies and teaching at the University of Vienna.

Deborah Galimberti holds a PhD in political science from Lyon University and Bicocca University of Milan. She is currently member of Triangle UMR 5206 research centre. Her research interests include the comparative analysis of local and regional politics in Europe, in particular of the relationships between public and private actors, and lie at the intersection of the sociology of public action and comparative political economy. She is currently working on the regulation of regional innovation systems.

Marisol Garcia is Professor of Sociology at the University of Barcelona and member of the CRIT Urban Research Group. She has been a visiting professor at Oxford University, Royal Institute of International Affairs, European University Institute, University of Amsterdam, University of Bielefeld, University Milano Bicocca and Fulbright Visiting Scholar at University of Illinois at Chicago. Her main research interests are: comparative analysis on issues that challenge social citizenship, such as unemployment, shortage of social housing and poverty as well as social innovation in cities.

Nicola Headlam is Urban Transformations and Foresight Future of Cities Knowledge Exchange Research Fellow at COMPAS, School of Anthropology, University of Oxford. She is an urbanist with expertise in city governance, economic development and urban policy. She is also a researcher at the Heseltine Institute for Public Policy and Practice at the University of Liverpool and is a founding member of the Urbanista UK network for women involved in positive urban change.

Nathalie Kakpo is an Administrative Officer in the French Ministry for Economy (Directorate of Competition Policy, Consumption and Fraud Control). Her PhD in sociology showed how the French second generations' trajectories at school, on the labour market and in the state institutions shaped their attitudes towards Islam. Her research also tackled urban segregation and the inclusion of immigrants in big cities.

Lara Maestripieri holds a PhD in Sociology and Social Research. She is Postdoctoral Fellow at the Department of Social and Political Sciences at the University of Pavia, where she is member of the Italian team involved in 7FP CRESSI – Creating Economic Space for Social Innovation. Her main research interests are: knowledge workers and professional identity; gender and social vulnerability; young workers and precariousness.

Agostino Petrillo, PhD in Sociology, is Associate Professor of Urban Sociology at the Polytechnic University, Milan. His main fields of research are: history of the sociological thought, city theory, comparative metropolitan studies, migrations, urban movements and conflicts.

Gilles Pinson is a Professor of Political Science in Sciences Po Bordeaux and a Researcher in the Centre Emile Durkheim (Université de Bordeaux, Sciences Po Bordeaux, CNRS). His research deals with urban policies and politics, urban and metropolitan governance and the transformations of the relationships between territorial states and cities. He is currently working on the politicization of inter-municipal bureaucrats in French metropolis and the construction of the local markets of the "smart city".

Marc Pradel Miquel is Assistant Professor of Sociology at the University of Barcelona and member of the research group CRIT UB. He has been visiting researcher in the Centre for Metropolitan Studies (Tecnische Universität, Berlin) and in Centre d'études Européennes (Sciences Po, Paris). His research field involves multi-level governance, social inequalities and citizenship. He has participated in Spanish and European research projects on citizenship, social innovation and local economic development.

Alain Thierstein is a Full Professor for Urban Development at the Munich University of Technology, department of architecture. Also he works as senior consultant and partner with EBP Ltd, Zurich/Berlin. He holds a PhD in Economics and a master's degree in Economics and Business Administration from the University of St Gallen/Switzerland. Current research includes impact of the knowledge economy on urban and mega-city-regions development, polycentric urban structures, accessibility infrastructure, and impact studies on policy measures.

Rossana Torri is an Architect with a PhD in Sociology. She currently collaborates with the municipality of Milan (Comune di Milano), where she is responsible for projects relating to innovation in urban policies. She teaches at the Politecnico di Milano, where she trained and has conducted research for many years in the field of urban sociology.

Fabian Wenner, MSc, is a Research and Teaching Associate at the Chair of Urban Development at Munich University of Technology. He holds a bachelor's in Spatial Planning and a master's (LSE) in Regional and Urban Planning Studies. His research interests include regional and urban economics as well as urban development in international and historical perspectives.

Acknowledgements

The seed for this book was planted more than seven years ago, in 2009, when the Milan Chamber of Commerce, Industry, Handicraft and Agriculture decided to finance the *Third Social Report on Milan*, which represented the first step of the long process that has led to the final publication of this volume. This institution has provided most of the financial resources required for this comparative study, funding the investigation over different consecutive steps. We would like to acknowledge Pier Andrea Chevallard, Vittoria De Franco, Lidia Mezza and Aurora Caiazzo for supporting our ideas and plans for the investigation.

This project evolved over three different stages: the first one in 2009–2010 involved researchers based mainly at the Polytechnic of Milan (Viviana Andriola, Nathalie Kakpo, Daniele Pennati, Agostino Petrillo, Rossana Torri), who conducted fieldwork investigations in Barcelona, Copenhagen, Lyon, Milan, Manchester and Munich; the second step in 2011–2012 involved a group of international scholars with expertise in the institutional contexts studied (Hans Thor Andersen, Irina Auernhammer, Ana Belén Cano Hila, Rémi Dormois, Deborah Galimberti, Marisol Garcia, Alan Harding, Nicola Headlam, Gilles Pinson, Marc Pradel, Alain Thierstein); finally, the last step in 2015–2016 involved all the researchers participating in the project and a few more authors who updated and revised the manuscript for publication (Yvonne Franz, Lara Maestripieri and Fabian Wenner).

The results of this work have been presented and discussed in preliminary versions at many international conferences organized by the RC21 of ISA (Conferences and Forums in Goteborg, Amsterdam, Berlin and Urbino), EURA (Copenhagen), Sciences Po Lyon and Sciences Po Paris, and the Urban Affair Association (New Orleans). We are extremely grateful to all the scholars who took part in these conferences and helped us to improve the manuscript with their comments. We also want to thank the scholars who discussed with us the main results of this complex investigation, in the setting of formal or informal seminars taking place during the whole cycle of the research project: Massimo Bricocoli, Sandro Cattacin, Enrico Gualini, Chris Hamnett, Mauro Magatti, Marc Oberti, Gabriele Pasqui, Carolina Pacchi, Edmond Préteceille, Guido Sapelli, Lanfranco Sen.

The concluding chapter of the book was written at the Department of Sociology of the University of Vienna – a very supportive and welcoming context.

We especially thank Yuri Kazepov and Christoph Reinprecht for the highly productive discussions we had about the final draft of the chapter. However, the major part of this research was carried out at the Social Policy Research Laboratory of the Polytechnic of Milan. We want to thank all the scholars who have been working in this group (Stefania Cerea, Giuliana Costa, Lara Maestripieri, Stefania Sabatinelli), and especially Laura di Maria who has supported us during the whole process leading to this final publication. Finally, Alyson Claffey (our editorial assistant at Routledge) has been very helpful and patient during all the stages that lead to the final publication of this volume.

From these few notes it emerges quite clearly that this study is a result of a collective effort, carried out by a multidisciplinary research group composed of sociologists, political scientists, geographers and urban planners. The authors of the chapters of the book worked together in different phases trying to follow a common analytical perspective. We really wish to thank all of them for their invaluable contribution to the final result. However, the final responsibility for the aggregate outcomes belongs, as usual, to the editors.

1 Introduction

European cities between economic competitiveness and social integration

Roberta Cucca and Costanzo Ranci

1.1 The crisis of the "European city model"

European cities have been historically characterized by a strong association between social integration and economic competitiveness. Levels of social inequality and spatial segregation are generally much lower in European cities than in cities of a similar size and with the same economic potential located in other continents (Kazepov, 2005). And in many of those cities, the search for equity and spatial integration have been accompanied by significant economic performances demonstrating that social integration and economic competitiveness have been handled as interdependent aspects in European urban policies (Bagnasco and Le Galès, 2000; Buck *et al.*, 2005).

Specific factors have contributed to this result. First, welfare state intervention and the activism of local authorities in meeting the population's social needs have played a very important role (Hamnett, 1994; Kazepov, 2005). Second, in Europe, the occupational structure of the urban population has exhibited the dominant role of the middle class and therefore less room for dualization processes (Hamnett, 2003; Préteceille, 2000). Third and finally, whilst in other continents recent migration flows have strongly exacerbated a marked dualism in skills and income conditions, in Europe the composition of the migrant population reflects fewer social disparities (Cassiers and Kesteloot, 2012). As a consequence of these factors, the "European city" model (Bagnasco and Le Galès, 2000; Le Galès, Vitale, 2013) is considered to be crucially linked to lower levels of inequality in income distribution.

This model is today under strong pressure due to the impact of the current crisis and of austerity policies. However, the crisis has only revealed a long-run trend of *disconnection* between economic growth and social integration already at work for many years. In the Fordist period, competition and social integration were two elements in a kind of equilibrium. Cities were the principal places of both production and consumption. Economic growth was fuelled by strong demand for consumption, to a large extent concentrated in the cities. At the same time, if the production functions were to be efficient and stable, they required the organization of social reproduction through stable industrial relations, housing policies able to make residing in the city affordable, and measures to protect the vulnerable groups and to support consumption (Kazepov, 2005). The strong need for the stability of economic systems found its pivot in the industrial city, and it was supported by high growth rates and by the generosity of welfare systems. Today, by contrast, social stability is less economically important than flexibility, and the search for greater competitiveness no longer requires a high level of social integration. Indeed, the latter becomes an obstacle, a social superstructure that hampers the development of the new, post-industrial economy.

In fact, since the 1990s, the historical balance between competitiveness and inequalities founded on this particular compromise between economic interests in the city and social responsibility (Le Galès, 2002) has begun to waver. Two research studies conducted for the European Commission (Rheinisch-Westfälisches Institut für Wirtschaftsforschung, 2010; European Commission, 2011) reported trends towards increasing social dualization. As a report of the European Commission stated:

> European cities have traditionally been characterized by less segregation and less social and spatial polarization compared to, for instance, US cities. This has been especially true for cities in countries with strong welfare systems. However, there are many signs that polarization and segregation are increasing. The economic crisis has further amplified the effects of globalization and the gradual retreat of the welfare state in most European countries.
>
> (European Commission, 2011: 22)

This process has been the result of an entanglement of factors. But it has been especially fostered by the globalization and financialization of the economy largely driven by a neo-liberal approach that has led to a strong rhetoric relative to the role of cities as economic actors in the global arena, and which are supposed to compete among themselves (Taylor, 2003). From this perspective, urban policies have been even more oriented to economic competitiveness through different "neo-liberal tools of urban government" (Halpern *et al.*, 2014), such as the promotion of international events, infrastructures for connectivity, urban renewal, sustainability policies, cultural interventions. However, although these measures have often been quite successful in attracting the creative class, talents, foreign investments and new populations to cities (Musterd, 2010), they have also fostered new forms of inequality, especially in terms of labour market structure and spatial inequalities between social groups able to afford very expensive housing and other populations evicted from the city or concentrated in the most deprived areas of the urban context.

At the same time, at national and local levels, welfare policies have exhibited a trend towards inertia or retrenchment, especially in the current situation of economic crisis. Austerity policies have even exacerbated, and not reduced, the social dualization taking place in the labour and housing markets (Emmenegger *et al.*, 2013). Although in this regard European cities still largely differ since welfare services are still mainly provided at the national level of government, they have undergone a general trend of decreasing financial support provided by national governments in order to protect the most disadvantaged groups (Ranci *et al.*, 2014). Even cities more dependent on their own revenue base have not been able to afford social and redistributive policies because higher taxation to support welfare would have driven out capital investment (Fainstein, 2010). For this reason, European cities once known as the "cities of welfare", like Copenhagen, have progressively adopted more neo-liberal policies oriented to economic competitiveness (Andersen and Winther, 2010).

In this framework, the aim of this book is to describe the tensions among factors related to economic competitiveness and social inequalities in European cities and to discuss their implications for urban policy, thereby furnishing a new understanding of the transformations affecting the European social model at an urban level. The book is based on original research carried out in six large European cities characterized by high levels of globalization and a leading economic role in their respective national contexts: Barcelona, Copenhagen, Lyon, Manchester, Milan and Munich. The cities considered have a number of characteristics in common: they play a central, if not dominant, economic role in their respective national economies; with the exception of Copenhagen, they are not the capitals of the nation-state in which they are situated; they are of large urban size (being the second or third largest cities in their respective countries); they exhibit a strong tendency to globalization and are embedded in transnational urban networks. Their selection makes it possible to control for one of the decisive factors of social integration identified in previous research (Kazepov, 2005; Ranci, 2011): the coverage and generosity of welfare programmes. The six cities considered pertain in fact to different welfare models: the Social-Democratic regime (Copenhagen), the Liberal regime (Manchester), the Corporatist regime, including both the Francophone (Lyon) and the German (Munich) variants, and the Mediterranean regime, with its two variants: Spanish (Barcelona) and Italian (Milan).

Finally, these cities are highly globalized and competitive in their own national contexts and within the European scenario. At the same time, they are peculiarly different from global mega-cities and capitals, such as London and Paris, on which research on global cities has mainly focused (Sassen, 1991; Hamnett, 2003; Fainstein, 2010; Maloutas and Fuijita, 2012; Tammaru *et al.*, 2016). Not only is their size significantly smaller than that of a mega-city, but also their multilevel interdependence, both at local and regional–national scales, is noticeably more relevant. While mega-cities have become relatively independent bodies within national configurations and have developed a relatively high autonomy in respect of their urban regions, our "second national cities" are still entrenched within their national or regional settings and have built up their own economic success on assets that are mainly based on their local context. This book intends, therefore, to contribute to re-balancing the dominant scholars' consideration of urban globalization, providing a better understanding of the impact of globalization occurring in medium-to-large cities.

To sum up, our investigation aims to answer some key questions: What are the main challenges faced by medium-to-large cities for developing competitiveness and preserving social integration? What have been the main economic trends in these cities, and how have they impacted on social and spatial inequalities? How have these problems been defined in the public discourse on these cities? To what extent have the issues of social integration and economic competitiveness been combined in local political agendas? What has been the impact of the current crisis, and what have been the reactions at the city level?

Four crucial aspects of the interconnection between economic performance and social integration will be considered: increasing social inequalities within the cities in relation to the specificity of their local production regime; the trade-offs between local interests protection and the capacity to attract global flows of financial and human resources; new social morphologies emerging in these cities as a consequence of their globalization; the integration of immigrants and ethnic minority groups (EMGs) in the labour market.

All these cities have undertaken large-scale urban projects and policies intended to promote their international functions and to attract foreign invest-ments and high-quality human resources. We will consider the extent to which globalized economic functions have been performed independently of the social context, and we will show how these impacts have differed among the cities con-sidered, and how they essentially depend on the distinctive development pattern of each city. The role played by local policies will be examined in this context by focusing on policy fields in which cities play a crucial role. In this regard, two policy issues will be investigated as crucial, both for the impact on the social integration of cities, and for the importance of the role played by local actors: how to deal with housing affordability problems arising as a consequence of increased land value, and how to create new employment of good quality in terms of pay and stability.

1.2 Disconnected cities

Over the past decade, the study of the disconnection between competitiveness and social integration has been a major issue in urban studies (Ranci, 2011), and with a particular focus on: socio-economic inequalities related to income distri-bution and the labour market structure (Hamnett, 2003); spatial inequalities in terms of residential segregation and access to a decent home (Musterd, 2005); inequalities between genders (Kutsar and Kuronen, 2015) and among ethnic groups in relation to the chances of upward social mobility. These investigations have mainly shown, from several points of view, the limits of the neo-liberal rhetoric stating that fostering economic competitiveness is of general benefit for the entire population, and that

> the fundamental mission of neo-liberal state is to create a "good business climate" [...] because it will foster growth and innovation and that this is the only way to eradicate poverty and to deliver, in the long run, higher standards to the mass of the population.

(Harvey, 2006: 25)

Indeed, this entrepreneurial style of government has had results in terms of socio-economic inequality and spatial justice (Ache *et al.*, 2008; Buck *et al.*, 2005) rather distant from the assumption implicit in the neo-liberal approach to urban policies.

As far as socio-economic inequalities are concerned, the pattern of economic growth over the past decade has been considered to foster trajectories of social polarization or increasing inequalities among social groups. According to Castells (1996) and Sassen (1991, 2000), the rise of global financial markets and the introduction of IC technologies have exposed cities to increasing competition from other cities. This has given rise to greater social polarization as a consequence of the parallel growth of a low-paid, low-qualified service industry, attracting masses of immigrant workers as well as high-skilled workers. Authors such as Hamnett (2003) have instead argued that whilst the economic growth of the past decade has been extremely beneficial to the upper class, it has not been completely detrimental to the lower class. For this reason, European cities, according to Hamnett, may be represented as social contexts affected more by increasing inequality than by polarization. Finally, more recent research has highlighted different patterns of inequality affecting European cities – patterns consistent with social phenomena characterizing national contexts, such as demographic trends and innovation in welfare states, and the different patterns of economic development adopted to foster economic competitiveness at an urban level (Buck, 2005; Cucca, 2011). To sum up, European cities exhibit a broad mosaic of possible interrelationships between economic competitiveness and social inequalities that only recently have been categorized (D'Ovidio and Ranci, 2014).

Increasing social inequalities have spatial impacts as well. Although European cities are still less divided than North American ones (Préteceille, 2000; Musterd, 2005), there has been a more general agreement among scholars on the increase in spatial inequalities and residential segregation (Cassiers and Kesteloot, 2012). Since segregation is mainly the projection of a social structure onto space (Häussermann and Siebel, 2001), it reflects the pattern of social polarization or increasing inequalities discussed above. Segregation affects social groups particularly subject to social exclusion, such as recent immigrants, refugees and unemployed people, as well as social groups that have benefited most from the economic growth of the past decade, such as the urban elite living in gated communities or gentrified areas (Cousin and Chauvin, 2014).

Furthermore, spatial segregation is not only a mirror of the social structure; it may itself act as a driver of social inequalities. In European cities, social exclusion is less the result of a presumed *neighbourhood effect* (Massey and Denton, 1992) than the consequence of the concentration of disadvantaged people or homogeneous ethnic communities in places not supported by adequate social and physical infrastructures (Arbaci and Malheiros, 2009; Cattacin, 2006). This situation makes segregated areas wholly disconnected from the places where there are social resources and opportunities. Two factors – the recent retrenchment of the public housing sector in many countries and the decline in affordable housing solutions driven by the market – have jointly pushed most of the disadvantaged groups to the social and physical boundaries of cities. Moreover, a large part of the urban middle class has been induced by the same factors to spend a large part of their family income in order to have decent housing in the city or in suburban areas. Within this framework, the scientific debate on spatial segregation is divided not so much on the analysis of the phenomenon as on the specific solutions to adopt (Musterd and Andersson, 2005). Two alternatives are generally discussed: (a) area-based interventions in deprived areas in order to develop better infrastructures; (b) sectorial policies intended to combat social inequalities and provide more affordable housing solutions. In a context of retrenchment of the public funds available for housing policies, area-based policies have achieved considerable success among local institutions, although a large body of empirical evidence shows that these policies have been rather ineffective in reducing spatial inequalities (Musterd, 2005).

Whilst these investigations have clearly contested the existence of positive impacts of urban competitiveness on social inequalities, still lacking is a general understanding of the possible positive effects of a social structure characterized by fewer inequalities as a component of urban competitiveness. A large part of the literature usually correlates low levels of inequalities to more secure and cohesive communities, offering an attractive social environment for post-industrial, non-material economic activities (Begg, 1999; Cheshire, 1999; Buck *et al.*, 2005). However, research carried out in the United Kingdom in the 1990s (Buck *et al.*, 2005) found no empirical support for this supposed interdependence. Changes in the levels of economic performance of British cities during the 1990s were much better explained by traditional economic factors (level of deindustrialization, spatial deconcentration) than by positive correlations between economic competitiveness and low levels of inequality. Furthermore, investigations carried out on German cities (Panebianco, 2008) and Spanish cities (Lopez *et al.*, 2008) found a positive correlation between social integration and competitiveness. According to Panebianco, the beneficial impact of increasing competitiveness among cities on their social integration was mainly exerted via the labour market, and it consisted in a significant decrease in the unemployment rate. However, this analysis did not investigate further crucial aspects of social integration such as income inequality (Ranci, 2011).

To sum up, research states that the conventional or academic wisdom of the "natural" complementarity between competitiveness and social integration does not have adequate empirical support. If this weak interdependence demonstrates the unrealistic assumptions of conventional liberalist wisdom (Buck *et al.*, 2005), it should be considered an important empirical result in itself. It may be hypothesized, indeed, that a lack of necessary interdependence between competitiveness and social integration *is* the actual condition under which the economic growth of cities comes about in the global era. Empirical analysis of 50 Western European cities exploring the relationship between inequality and social inclusion, on the one hand, and global competitiveness (including measures of productivity and transnational connectivity) on the other, showed that there was no statistical interdependence between these two dimensions: cities performing well on one dimension did not necessarily perform in the same way on the other dimension (Ranci, 2011). Further investigations found a very low correlation between economic performances and equity in social opportunities in European cities, and wide differences among cities in this relationship (d'Ovidio and Ranci, 2014). More than a European urban model, therefore, a plurality of models seem to emerge as a result of differentiated patterns of urban development.

Whether or not, and to what extent, economic growth is combined with social integration is therefore not a matter of normative assumption; rather, it is merely one possibility among a broad range of options. In this book we argue that policy implementation at an urban level still may play an important role in this regard, although, as stated by Häussermann and Haila (2005), the influence of public decisions on the socio-spatial organization of cities has been diminishing dramatically and there is a tendency towards the dissolution of the city as a public good through the privatization of housing, the selling of public land, the selling of public enterprises and the commodification of public and social services.

As we will show, differences among urban contexts are still huge, both in terms of the strategies adopted to foster economic development and in terms of the social impacts of such transformations on the different social groups. These differences are the result of an entanglement of factors: on the one side the variety of welfare regimes as well as of national capitalistic pattern; on the other hand the impact of strategic choices operated by local governments.

1.3 The role of urban policies

In the current economic and social crisis, these trends raise an additional challenge against the European urban model. As recently reported by Stone (2013) on the American context, conditions today do not hold out much promise of replicating the degree of power convergence found around growth through land valorization (Molotch, 1976) in an earlier age. In various respects, today's alternative appears to be a piecemeal agenda fragmented by both function and geography. This can also be applied to the European context, where urban policies have weaker local fiscal bases but receive more state funding and support than American cities, and where the multilevel institutional infrastructure is much thicker and more interdependent than in the United States.

Our empirical question is therefore this: how have European cities combined measures to enhance urban competitiveness and public programmes aimed at preserving their internal social integration? Urban policies have become crucial testing grounds for the capacity of cities to bring these two aspects together. The lack of standard solutions due to the crisis of Keynesian approaches has paved the way for innovation and differentiation in urban initiatives. Moreover, the retrenchment of the welfare state in many European countries has exacerbated dilemmas and trade-offs, reducing state financing to local municipalities and correspondingly increasing the need for local integration policies.

In this multifaceted scenario, urban policies have had to deal with social problems aggravated by the financial crisis and with the greater need to support local competitiveness. Inequalities, therefore, are the result not only of economic and social trends but also of urban policies targeted on inter-city competitiveness and attractiveness. In particular, as we argue in this book, cities have taken different approaches to this issue independently from national welfare regimes and from the political orientation of urban governments, but as the result of a complex entanglement of diverse factors such as the overall system of governance and the specific distribution of power among institutions on specific policy areas (local development, labour market, urban planning and housing policies).

Within this framework, our hypothesis is that the main trade-offs between local competitiveness and social integration are found in two traditional fields of urban policy where European cities have traditionally played an important role: (a) economic strategies aimed at fostering competitiveness with expected positive impacts on local employment; and (b) urban renewal projects intended to sustain real estate markets combined with housing affordability measures. In the past two decades, both these fields have been characterized by increasing trade-offs and dilemmas between the goal of promoting attractiveness and market mechanisms, on the one hand, and the need to fight unemployment, poverty and housing deprivation on the other. They therefore constitute two large-scale testing grounds for the directions and capabilities of current urban policies in our six European cities.

1.3.1 Economic competitiveness and social inequalities: do "good jobs" matter?

Determining the role of cities in fostering economic competitiveness and the effects of these policies on social inequalities is a complex task. The economic trajectories of the European cities appear extremely heterogeneous, since urban contexts are embedded in different production regimes and because they seem to have responded differently to globalization dynamics (Gallie, 2007; Hall and Soskice, 2001). To date, however, only few attempts have been made to understand and categorize the patterns of economic development followed by European cities (Ache *et al.*, 2008, Kazepov 2005, Musterd and Murie, 2010, Fainstein, 2010) and their effects in terms of social inequalities, and to evaluate the role played by urban policies in this regard. Our investigation attempts to fill this gap, first by proposing an analysis of the impacts of cities' patterns of economic specialization on the labour market structure; and second by analysing the urban policies adopted in order to foster economic competitiveness and their effects in terms of "good-quality employment".

Cities have exhibited different trends in their general transition from a Fordist economic structure to a service-based economy. In our investigation we seek to capture the features of this transition and propose a categorization. Cities have experienced different patterns of urban economic specialization, especially by attracting global capital through investments in infrastructures for connectivity, urban renewal and sustainability policies, cultural and housing schemes oriented to the creative class or tourists. The spatial division of labour within firms' production processes (Massey, 1984) has reinforced the diverse occupational structures of cities, and this has also fostered dissimilar patterns of inequality in the labour market structure and income distribution among urban contexts (Cucca, 2011; Pratschke and Morlicchio, 2012).

Within this framework, the occupational structure is a mechanism important for understanding the relations between the economic and social dimensions of urban development. Our investigation studies the economic performances of cities in terms of effects on the labour market, with reference to the level of employment achieved, as well as the quality of the jobs created and the impact of the current economic crisis. The notion of job quality is a complex one, but its investigation is of crucial importance. According to the International Labour Organization, job quality encompasses numerous aspects: protection and income security, quality of participation in the labour market and inclusion in society.[1] Although this is a concept complex to analyse, our investigation takes account of the quality of the jobs created through urban policies fostering the city's economic growth in order to determine whether these interventions have been able to promote a labour market that positively affects economic and social inequalities, or conversely generates processes of polarization.

A second step of the investigation presented in this book is the examination of the role of urban policies in this transition, studying both how competitiveness is promoted at an urban level today and the role of municipal governments in preserving social integration. Usually, when social and economic scientists have analysed economic competitiveness, they have mainly paid attention to the national level, largely ignoring the local level of analysis. Furthermore, economic competitiveness is a goal that the public sector cannot achieve alone (Stone, 1993; Molotch, 1976). Therefore our analysis focuses not only on direct public intervention by local municipalities but also on various forms of negotiation and partnership with private actors (Buck *et al.*, 2005).

Conversely, the role of the local and municipal levels of government in fighting social inequalities has been investigated (Buck *et al.*, 2005). Our hypothesis in this case is that during the past decade the capacity of urban policies to affect social inequalities has been greatly weakened by the inertia or retrenchment of national welfare state intervention, but that social innovation at the local level has recently increased to fill the gap between a growing need for social intervention at the local level and a shortage of financial resources at the central level. We shall show how social integration policy has entered the public agenda of most of our cities, making social policy one of the most interesting fields of urban policy development.

1.3.2 *Planning for the competition: the effects on housing affordability*

As already mentioned, the main policy strategies employed by urban and local institutions in order to promote local growth are: (a) investments in infrastructure, subsidies and regulatory relief to property developers and firms (such as office-led development, malls, sport facilities, clustering of related companies), often providing expensive housing solutions for the high-middle class; (b) large-scale urban renewal projects in deprived neighbourhoods or brownfield redevelopment strategies able to provide the right urban environment for the creative class "wanted" for the city's new economic development. However, the consequences of these projects for spatial equity have been relevant.

As argued by Fainstein (2010), the first important effect of such policies in terms of social equity has been the use of public funds in favour of private investments, contributing more to market processes than to collective goals. This shift in urban policy has been an important reason for the decreasing investment in municipal and social housing interventions, with negative effects in terms of social redistribution. Although these strategies may mainly depend on the national level of government, disparities in the levels of affordable housing among cities within the same country show that urban patterns of local development have a certain degree of autonomy (Arbaci and Malheiros, 2009). Furthermore, since the 1970s, policies of this kind have been accused of fostering gentrification (Smith, 1979) by increasing the value of properties and attracting the presence of middle-class groups to central areas. As final result, these processes have led not only to the displacement of the most disadvantaged social groups but also to a general lack of affordable housing solutions for the remaining part of the lower and lower-middle class population.

Urban policies intended to deal with these "unexpected consequences" have been quite rare, and those implemented have achieved uncertain results. In some cities, private developers of large housing estates have been asked to include a proportion of units for low income residents, in order to increase the availability of affordable housing. This has seemed also a shrewd way to create more "mixed and balanced communities" (Bridge *et al.*, 2011); however, some scholars (Arbaci and Rae, 2010) have argued that this has generated a huge process of urbanization with a low production of affordable housing. Moreover, it has led to more severe stigmatization and segregation for low-income social groups concentrated in small communities (Arbaci and Rae, 2010).

Other public interventions have been oriented to supporting social housing associations, instead of the direct (and more expensive) involvement of public authorities in housing provision; public subsidies to non-profit organizations or to private developers are now the principal means by which new affordable housing is provided (Van Kempen *et al.*, 2005). However, private homeowners usually have greater freedom to discriminate against more problematic tenants, such as former criminals or mentally disabled people, as well as to define "quotas" for recent immigrants (Bricocoli and Cucca, 2016).

Moreover, strategies for rent control and rent support have been introduced to avoid strong processes of displacement of the population from gentrified neighbourhoods (soft gentrification). However, these strategies have often produced limited effects owing to a shortage of public funds available for these programmes. Also support for home-ownership, in this period of financial and housing market crises, has generated huge economic problems for people unable to afford the mortgages and other property expenditures.

Because policies addressing this issue have not reversed the dominant trends towards gentrification and displacement of the poorest population from city centres, in some cities public institutions have decided to re-start support for municipal housing provision, or they have introduced new mechanisms with which to make some of the interventions already mentioned more effective. Within this area of analysis, the aim of our research is to determine how local governments have dealt with this challenge and what the most important effects have been.

1.4 Plan of the book

The book is organized into three parts.

The first part examines social trends occurring in our six cities through a comparative, transversal perspective. The second chapter by Roberta Cucca and Lara Maestripieri examines the trajectories of social inequality characterizing the six cities investigated in this research, with the focus on the relations between the economic specialization of cities and transformations of the labour market. In fact, there is a need for analysis to understand the different patterns of social development characterizing European cities. In particular, the chapter describes some patterns of transition from Fordism to post-Fordism at an urban level in Europe and how they have affected inequalities in the occupational structure.

The third chapter by Agostino Petrillo shifts the discussion from social to spatial trends. Starting from the main theories on the social impact of globalization and the growing competition among cities, the chapter's aim is to identify the principal mechanisms working in the cities selected, in particular by highlighting the territorial and spatial dimensions of the transformations. The cities are analysed by taking the wider "urban regions" as references. All the cities studied are affected, with different intensities, by far-reaching changes that imply, on the one hand, the progressive movement of economic and political sectors on a supranational/global level, and on the other, the strengthening of subnational/regional institutions. The chapter addresses some key questions: What is the role of cities in this scenario? How are these opportunities and restrictions distributed or concentrated according to economic reorganization at a regional level? What have been the main hard and soft factors used by cities in their strategies towards higher competitiveness? And what have been the main implication in terms of residential mobility and working conditions of the inhabitants?

The fourth chapter by Yvonne Franz and Rossana Torri analyses how the changes in the cities' economic bases, and particularly in their local labour markets, have influenced urban property dynamics. It highlights the mechanisms of these changes and their impacts on the spatial distribution of the population, by using gentrification as a key-notion.

The fifth chapter by Nathalie Kakpo and Roberta Cucca focuses on how immigrant groups integrate in the changing labour markets of the six cities considered in this book. The key question is: does a knowledge-based economy imply an exclusion of immigrants from the labour market and their massive concentration in the low employment sectors, or rather are we witnessing complex processes involving different groups' trajectories? How do factors such as ethnicity and social classes affect the ways immigrants EMGs settle in the local labour markets?

The second part of the book is based on case studies investigating urban policies implemented in Barcelona, Copenhagen, Lyon, Manchester, Milan and Munich in order to foster economic development and to preserve social integration in two fields (housing and employment), with especial attention paid to local actions to combat the effects of the current crisis. This part of the book is centred on city-based case studies investigating urban policies addressing the two crucial political issues just mentioned: providing affordable housing in the context of rising land values and supporting employment in a phase of economic depression. Chapter 6, by Ana Belén Cano Hila, Marc Pradel and Marisol García, describes the situation of Barcelona. Among the cities selected for this research, Barcelona has been the most successful in terms of economic growth before 2007, as well as being the urban context most affected by the crisis. On the side of social integration, unemployment has followed a markedly fluctuating trend, while housing conditions have been characterized by affordability problems for middle-class families especially, and more recently by increasing evictions. However, in terms of urban policies, before the crisis Barcelona had a balanced approach to development: although the priority has always been the city's economic growth, the local governments have at the same time fostered programmes explicitly aimed at promoting jobs of good quality and housing policies intended to enlarge the affordable stock.

Also Copenhagen went through a period of economic development over the decade before the crisis. As described by Hans Thor Andersen in Chapter 7, unemployment was very low in the 1999–2007 period due to the high demand for high-skilled jobs in business services, media, info tech, consultancy and finance. Social integration was also preserved by the still very high level of public employment. In Copenhagen, the crisis has increased the unemployment rate and the labour market segregation of migrants/refugees. However, at the same time it has also sharply decreased housing prices and made it possible for middle-class workers to purchase decent housing in central Copenhagen. Nevertheless, a large number of households have become insolvent as prices have generally dropped by a third; their purchase of housing before the crisis has given them huge debts and they will be trapped in their present property for years. This situation has been also the result of local policies strongly oriented to economic competitiveness after the risk of municipal bankruptcy in the 1990s and which have given rise to an increase in spatial inequalities and residential segregation.

In Chapter 8, Deborah Galimberti, Rémi Dormois and Gilles Pinson describe the case of Lyon, a city that experienced strong economic growth in the 1990s, which was followed by a stop-and-go process. This came with a large increase in the city's population and decreasing unemployment between 1990 and 2007. In

France, the current crisis has mainly impacted on industrial jobs located in former industrial regions. The Great Lyon region, which still has an important industrial sector, has been hardly hit by the crisis, with the closure of several plants. But, like other large French city-regions, the *Grand Lyon* area, with its variegated and tertiarized economic structure, has resisted better than other territories. The chapter analyses the complex system of governance ruling institutional interventions for urban competitiveness and housing affordability. It also shows in this case the strong preference of the urban government for neo-liberal tools to foster attractiveness – a preference sometimes even stronger than the national one.

Nicola Headlam's focus in Chapter 9 is on the system of governance ruling housing and the production of skills for competitiveness in Manchester. This is a city that has dramatically shifted from being a manufacturing city to the second financial capital of United Kingdom. However, this pattern of development has promoted a severe dualization of the labour market in an urban context already characterized by wide social and spatial divisions. The author argues that, more than the economic crisis, austerity programmes are the key to understanding how local governments are facing the economic and social challenges. Austerity, localism and cuts to public sector funding have resulted in a very limited range of policies with which to counter structural issues in the housing and labour markets.

The case of Milan is described by Rossana Torri in Chapter 10. In the Italian city the economic growth rate was high in the 1990s, but already negative or close to zero in the 2000s, demonstrating the recent decline in the city's competitiveness and attractiveness. Demographic trends were negative in the 1990s and positive but quite low in the past decade. The unemployment rate was diminishing until 2007, but housing prices increased hugely in the 2000s. The crisis has partially changed this scenario, with the unemployment rate increasing and the reduction of prices in the housing market countered by the deep crisis of the loan system, which makes housing affordability even harder. Milan was governed by centre–right coalitions uninterruptedly between 1993 and 2011, distinguishing it as one of the cities with the greatest continuity in terms of political rule in Italy. 2011 marked a major turning point, with the election victory of a centre–left alliance, in office until June 2016. The chapter analyses the dynamics of transformation that have contributed to changing the face of the city over the period under consideration – with a focus on the long cycle of property-led urban generation and on the city's tertiary transition – and policies promoted at the local level to support and steer these processes, which became all the more critical in light of the financial crisis that began in 2008.

Conversely, Munich is described by Alain Thierstein, Irina Auernhammer and Fabian Wenner in Chapter 11 as a city that has managed issues relative to social integration as assets for urban competitiveness. Munich is the only city not affected by the crisis. It achieved high growth in real GDP in the 1990s, and still positive growth in the 2000s, as well as an enlargement in the size of its resident population. Within the favourable context of Germany, Munich is a centre of excellence. One of the main reasons why Munich has remained resilient during the financial crisis is the diverse economic base of the region of Munich, which is referred to as the "Munich Mix". This means that Munich has several poles of economic development with strong positive effects on the diversity and flexibility of the local labour market. A wide range of sectors, including SMEs and global players, define the composition of the "Munich Mix". Medium-sized businesses have a strong and stable impact on the local labour market's development. The high employment level also of women has generated growing demand for childcare services outside the family, for financial support of single parents and appropriate housing solutions. The high level of rents on the privately financed housing market has also intensified the demand for social housing. However, socio-spatial segregation seems to be intensified by diverse price trends in the city's various districts and housing quarters. The economic success of the city has nevertheless created new social problems. Owing to the attractiveness of Munich and demographic changes, the demand for appropriate housing remains at a high level, accompanied by continuously rising rents and property prices. Munich's high attractiveness is exacerbating income disparities. A rise in renting prices increases the demand for social housing and the risk of social and spatial segregation in specific districts. Today, this challenge is one of the key issues for Munich's local strategy for urban development.

Finally, the third and final part of the book puts forward some final considerations.

Chapter 12 by Costanzo Ranci examines how the general interconnection between competitiveness and social integration is shaped in these six cities. It considers the increasing social inequalities within the cities in relation to the specificities of their local production regime; the trade-offs between local interests protection and an ability to attract global flows of financial and human resources (i.e. tensions in the relationship between space of places and space of flows); and the new social morphologies emerging in these cities as a consequence of their globalization (such as gentrification, or urban sprawl contributing to the formation of big city-regions). Overall, these facts show that, although the six cities examined are embedded in different welfare capitalism regimes, they are characterized by a common trend towards higher internal disorganization.

In the final chapter, Costanzo Ranci and Roberta Cucca discuss the importance of a policy agenda addressing competitiveness and social integration within a neo-liberal policy framework. They propose a typology of possible orientations of local government towards economic development and social integration: cities following the neo-liberal rhetoric of economic growth as the driver of social development; cities prioritizing interventions for economic development but trying to mitigate its possible negative effects on social and spatial inequalities; cities that have considered social integration as an important asset for the economic growth of the urban context. To sum up, governing the post-industrial city in Europe is no mere extension of the past, and the analysis of this transformation seems to be growing in importance, especially at this time of crisis. The reason being that, even if it is true that urban policies have contributed to sharpening social inequalities in these cities during the post-Fordist era in Europe, at the same time they have become even more crucial for preserving social integration in a time of welfare state austerity. It is through this paradoxical and contradictory dynamic that urban policies have gradually reduced their historical capacity to govern the economic and social trends taking place within their territory.

Note

1 The European Commission states that is both a relative and multidimensional concept: good jobs comprise equal opportunities, good and flexible work organization enabling the better reconciliation of working and personal life, lifelong learning, health and safety at work, employee involvement and diversity in working life. Kalleberg (2011: 9) considers also the economic dimension of job quality, such as wages, fringe benefits, regularity or intermittence, to define a good job as one that: (a) pays relatively high earnings and provides opportunities for increases in earnings over time; (b) provides adequate fringe benefits and social protections; (c) enables the worker to have opportunities for autonomy and control over work activities; (d) gives the worker some flexibility and control over scheduling and terms of employment; (e) provides the worker with some control over the termination of the job.

References

Ache, P., Andersen, H. T., Maloutas, T., Raco, M. and Tasan-Kok, T. (2008). *Cities between Competitiveness and Cohesion: Discourses, Realities and Implementation*. Dordrecht: Springer.

Andersen, H. T. and Winther, L. (2010). Crisis in the Resurgent City? The Rise of Copenhagen. *International Journal of Urban and Regional Research*, 34(3): 693–700.

Arbaci, S. and Malheiros, J. (2009). De-segregation, Peripheralisation and the Social Exclusion of Immigrants: Southern European Cities in the 1990s. *Journal of Ethnic and Migration Studies*, 36(2): 227–255.

Arbaci, S. and Rae, I. (2010). *Mixed Tenure Neighbourhoods in London: Policy Myth of Effective Device for Social Mobility*. Paper presented at the ISA Conference in Göteborg.

Bagnasco, A. and Le Galès, P. (eds) (2000). *Cities in Contemporary Europe*: Cambridge: Cambridge University Press.

Begg, I. (1999). City and Competitiveness. *Urban Studies*, 36(5/6): 795–809.

Bricocoli, M. and Cucca, R. (2016). Social Mix and Housing Policy: Local Effects of a Misleading Rhetoric: The Case of Milan. *Urban Studies*, 53(1): 77–91.

Bridge, G., Butler, T. and Lees, L. (eds) (2011). *Mixed Communities: Gentrification by Stealth?* Bristol: Policy Press Scholarship.

Buck, N. (2005). Social Cohesion in Cities. In: Buck, N., Gordon, I., Harding, A. and Turok, I. (eds). *Changing Cities: Rethinking Urban Competitiveness, Cohesion and Governance*, pp. 44–61. New York: Palgrave.

Buck, N., Gordon, I., Harding, A. and Turok, I. (eds) (2005). *Changing Cities: Rethinking Urban Competitiveness, Cohesion and Governance*. New York: Palgrave.

Cassiers, T. and Kesteloot, C. (2012). Socio-spatial Inequalities and Social Cohesion in European Cities. *Urban Studies*, 49(9): 1909–1924, July 2012.

Castells, M. (1996). *The Rise of the Network Society, the Information Age: Economy, Society and Culture, Vol. 1*. Cambridge, MA: Blackwell.

16   R. Cucca and C. Ranci

Cattacin, S. (2006). *Why Not "Ghettos"? The Governance of Migration in the Splintering City.* Willy Brandt Series of Working Papers in International Migration and Ethnic Relations 2/06, Malmo, Sweden: Malmo University.

Cheshire, P. (1999). Cities in Competition: Articulating the Gains from Integration. *Urban Studies*, 36: 843–864.

Cousin, B. and Chauvin, S. (2014). Globalizing Forms of Elite Sociability: Varieties of Cosmopolitanism in Paris Social Clubs. *Ethnic and Racial Studies*, 37(12): 2209–2225.

Cucca, R. (2011). *Unequal Development: Economic Competitiveness and Social Inequalities in Six European Cities.* Paper presented at 41a Conference Urban Affairs Associations, New Orleans, USA.

D'Ovidio, M. and Ranci, C. (2014), Social Cohesion and Global Competitiveness. Clustering Cities. In: Ranci, C., Brandsen, T. and Sabatinelli, S. (eds) (2014). *Social Vulnerability in European Cities: the Role of Local Welfare in Times of Crisis.* London: Palgrave Macmillan.

Emmenegger, P., Häusermann, S., Palier, B. and Seeleib-Kaiser, M. (2013). Structural Change and the Politics of Dualization. *Rassegna Italiana di Sociologia*, 14(2): 201–226.

European Commission, Directorate General for Regional Policy (2006). *Cities and the Lisbon Agenda: Assessing the Performance of Cities.* Brussels.

European Commission, Directorate General for Regional Policy (2011). *Cities of Tomorrow: Challenges, Visions, Ways Forward.* Brussels.

Fainstein, S. (2010). *The Just City.* Ithaca, NY and London: Cornell University Press.

Gallie, D. (2007). Production Regimes and the Quality of Employment in Europe. *Annual Review of Sociology*, 33: 85–104.

Gordon, I. and Turok, I. (2005). How Urban Labor Markets Matter. In: Buck, N., Gordon, I., Harding, A. and Turok, I. (eds) *Changing Cities: Rethinking Urban Competitiveness, Cohesion and Governance.* New York: Palgrave.

Hall, Peter A. and Soskice, David (eds) (2001). *Varieties of Capitalism: The Institutional Foundations of Comparative Advantage.* Oxford, UK: Oxford University Press.

Halpern, C., Lascoumes, P. and Le Galès, P. (2014). *L'Instrumentation de L'Action Publique: Controverses, Résistance, Effets.* Paris: Presses de Sciences Po, Académique.

Hamnett, C. (1994). Social Polarisation in Global Cities: Theory and Evidence. *Urban Studies*, 31(3): 401–424.

Hamnett, C. (2003). *Unequal City: London in the Global Arena.* London: Routledge.

Harvey, D. (2006). *Spaces of Global Capitalism.* London: Verso.

Harding, A. (1997). Urban Regimes in a Europe of the Cities? *European Urban and Regional Studies,* 4(4): 291–314.

Häussermann, H. and Haila, A. (2005). The European City: a Conceptual Framework and Normative Project. In: Kazepov, Y. (ed.). *Changing Contexts, Local Arrangements, and the Challenge to Urban Cohesion,* pp. 43–63. Malden, MA: Blackwell.

Häussermann, H. and Siebel, W. (2001). Integration und Segregation: Überlegungen zu einer alten Debatte. *Deutsch Zeitschrift für Kommunalwissenschaften,* 40: 68–79.

Harvey, D. (2006). *The Global and the Local: Spaces of Global Capitalism: Towards a Theory of Uneven Geographical Development.* London and New York: Verso.

Kalleberg, A. E. (2011). *Good Jobs, Bad Jobs: The Rise of Polarized and Precarious Employment Systems in the United States, 1970s to 2000s.* New York: Russell Sage Press.

Kazepov, Y. (ed.) (2005). *Cities of Europe: Changing Contexts, Local Arrangements, and the Challenge of Urban Cohesion.* Malden, MA: Blackwell.

Kutsar, D. and Kuronen, M. (eds) (2015). *Local Welfare Policy Making In European Cities*. New York: Springer.

Le Galès, P. (2002). *European Cities: Social Conflicts and Governance*. Oxford: Oxford University Press.

Le Galès, P. and Vitale, T. (2013), *Governing the Large Metropolis: A Research Agenda*. Working papers du Programme Cities are Back in Town 2013-06, Sciences Po.

Lopez, A., Mella-Marquez, J. and Steinberg, F. (2008). Competitiveness and Cohesion in the Spanish Provinces: A Territorial Approach. In: Ache, P., Andersen, H. T., Maloutas, T., Raco, M. and Tasan-Kok, T. (eds). *Cities between Competitiveness and Cohesion*, pp. 61–78. New York: Springer.

Maloutas, T. and Fujita, K. (2012). *Residential Segregation in Comparative Perspective: Making Sense of Contextual Diversity*. Farnham: Ashgate Publishing.

Massey, D. (1984). *Spatial Division of Labour: Social Structures and the Geography of Production*. London: Macmillan.

Massey, D. S. and Denton, N. A. (1992). *American Apartheid: Segregation and the Making of the Underclass*. Cambridge: Harvard University Press.

Molotch, H. (1976). The City as a Growth Machine: Toward a Political Economy of Place. *American Journal of Sociology*, 82(2): 309–332.

Musterd, S. (2005). Social and Ethnic Segregation in Europe: Levels, Causes and Effects. *Journal of Urban Affairs*, 27: 331–348.

Musterd, S. and Andersson, R. (2005). Housing Mix, Social Mix and Social Opportunities. *Urban Affairs Review*, 40(6): 1–30.

Musterd, S. and Murie, M. (eds) (2010). *Making Competitive Cities*. Oxford, UK: Wiley-Blackwell.

Panebianco, S. (2008). Are Entrepreneurial Cities More Successful? Empirical Evidence from 50 German Cities. In: Ache, P., Andersen, H. T., Maloutas, T., Raco, M. and Tasan-Kok, T. (eds). *Cities between Competitiveness and Cohesion*, pp. 41–60. New York: Springe.

Pratschke, J. and Morlicchio, E. (2012). Social Polarisation, the Labour Market and Economic Restructuring in Europe: An Urban Perspective. *Urban Studies*, 49(9): 1891–1907, July.

Préteceille, E. (2000). Segregation, Class and Politics in Large Cities. In: Bagnasco, A. and Le Galès, P. (eds). *Cities in Contemporary Europe*, pp. 74–97. Cambridge: Cambridge University Press.

Ranci, C. (2011). Competitiveness and Social Cohesion in Western European Cities. *Urban Studies*, 48(13): 2789–2804.

Ranci, C., Brandsen, T. and Sabatinelli, S. (eds) (2014). *Social Vulnerability in European Cities: The Role of Local Welfare in Times of Crisis*. London: Palgrave Macmillan.

Rheinisch-Westfälisches Institut für Wirtschaftsforschung (2010). *Second State of European Cities Report*. Research Project for the European Commission, DG Regional Policy.

Sassen, S. (1991). *The Global City*. Princeton, NJ: Princeton University Press.

Sassen, S. (2000). *Cities in a World Economy*. London: Pine Forge Press

Smith, N. (1979). Toward a Theory of Gentrification: A Back to the City Movement by Capital, not People. *Journal of the American Planning Association*, 45(4): 538–548.

Stone, C. (1993). Urban Regimes and the Capacity to Govern: A Political Economy Approach. *Journal of Urban Affairs*, 15: 1–28.

Stone, C. (2013). The Empowerment Puzzle: In Pursuit of a New Dimension in Governing the City. Paper, online, available at: http://papers.ssrn.com/sol3/papers.cfm?abstract_id=2300658.

Tammaru, T., Marcińczak S., van Ham, M. and Musterd, S. (2016). *Socio-economic Segregation in European Capital Cities: East meets West.* London and New York: Routledge, Taylor & Francis Group.

Taylor, P. J. (2003). *World City Network: A Global Urban Analysis.* London: Routledge.

Van Kempen, R., Dekker, K., Hall, S. and Tosics, I. (2005). *Restructuring Large Housing Estates in Europe.* Bristol: Policy Press.

Part I

Urban trends and social tensions

A comparative view

2 Varieties of post-Fordist transitions and labour market inequalities

Roberta Cucca and Lara Maestripieri

2.1 Introduction

This chapter focuses on the relations between economic specialisation, occupational structure and effects of these features on the socio-economic inequalities characterising middle-sized European cities. In particular, it focuses on the major transformations of the last two decades in order to understand how the post-industrial transition has affected the economic specialisation of these urban contexts and, more recently, what the impacts of the financial crisis on these cities' labour market have been.

As it is well known, recent and less recent trajectories of European cities, both in terms of administrative reforms (Jouve and Lefevre, 2002), urban planning (Newman and Thornley, 2005; Salet *et al.*, 2003), and economic specialisation and performance, have been heterogeneous since urban contexts are embedded in different production regimes and because they have responded differently to globalisation dynamics (Gallie, 2007; Hall and Soskice, 2001). Savitch and Kantor (2002) have in particular shown that cities in the same, as well as in different countries (the United States, Canada, the United Kingdom, France and Italy), have followed different development trajectories over the last 30 years, certainly in response to globalisation and Europeanisation but without evidence of convergence of urban development paths. Cities have exhibited different trends in their general transition from a Fordist economic structure to a service-based economy by attracting global capital and high-skilled workers through investments in infrastructures for connectivity, urban renewal programmes, cultural and housing schemes, and different kinds of urban projects oriented to foster specific economic sectors through differentiated policy tools (Brenner, 2004; van Der Heiden and Terhorst, 2007).

The spatial division of labour within firms' production processes (Massey, 1984) has reinforced the diverse occupational structures of cities, and this has also fostered dissimilar patterns of inequality in the labour market structure among urban contexts (Cucca, 2010; Pratschke and Morlicchio, 2012).

If a specialisation pattern oriented towards advanced business services and technological innovation has been estimated to be favourable for the economic growth of the region (as for example, the OECD innovation strategy launched in

2010[1]), academic arguments linking specialisation to metropolitan economic performance contain different, and sometimes conflicting, claims (Kemeny and Storper, 2012). It is especially difficult to come by hard evidence on how different levels and types of specialisation affect employment and socio-economic inequalities.

In North America, the shift to a service-based society has been mainly represented as a progressive trend of social polarisation between the populations at the extremes of the labour market structure (Sassen, 1991; Nannicini, 2005): on the one hand, a substantial increase of *high-skilled workers* in the fields of ICT and finance; on the other, a conspicuous growth of *low-skilled* workers employed in services with low specialisation tasks, badly paid and scarcely protected against unemployment risk.

As regards European contexts experiencing a huge shift towards the service sector, the main theoretical and empirical contributions on this topic have focused on the increase of income inequalities between social groups (Hamnett, 2003), rather than on the polarisation of the workforce (Fleming *et al.*, 2004; Sassen, 2008; Goos *et al.*, 2009; Oesch and Rodriguez Menes, 2010; Fernandez-Macias, 2012). The passage from an economy based on manual labour to a system based on services is supposed to have promoted a substantial increase in medium to highly qualified jobs and a significant decrease in the lesser qualified ones. Investigations carried out on creative economy in cities (Florida, 2004) have further strengthened this theory, focusing on the identification of a progressive process of *professionalisation* of the urban middle classes in the first decade of the new century (Hamnett, 2003). In the last decade, however, more complex configurations and effects of this post-industrial transition on the labour market in mid-sized cities have been estimated (Musterd and Murie, 2010).

In this chapter, we analyse the relations between the economic specialisation of cities and the transformations of the urban labour market during the past two decades, with a focus on how exogenous factors, such as the pre-crisis growth and the recession affecting most European countries since 2007, have been changing these patterns.

In the next section of the chapter, we analyse the main economic features of the local contexts in comparative view, with a focus on the changing structures of the occupational structure. In Section 2.3, we describe the main patterns of economic specialisation followed by the cities and the impacts on the structure of labour market inequalities before and after the crisis. Finally, we link our empirical evidences to the most general theoretical literature to open new paths of analysis.

2.2 The socio-economic structure of the six cities

As already mentioned in the introduction, in order to take into consideration the varieties of urban systems existing in Europe (Gallie, 2007; Hall and Soskice, 2001), this book deals with six mid-sized cities – Milan, Barcelona, Munich,

Copenhagen, Lyon and Manchester – comparable in terms of economic perform-ance, but different as regards their welfare regimes (Esping Andersen *et al.*, 2002).

It is worth starting by an analysis of their relative importance in the global economy: the urban economies included in the present research appear to be dif-ferently located in the worldwide economic geography. The six cities are all European mid-sized cities, very different from global cities (Bagnasco and Le Galés, 2000) such as London, New York and Tokyo (Sassen, 2000) both in terms of size and of hegemony in global dynamics. Nevertheless, they all represent one of the main economic poles in their national countries, if not their main pole with the exception of the United Kingdom and France, whose capital cities are the most important global cities of Europe (Bagnasco and Le Galés, 2000).

According to the GaWC ranking (GaWC, 2008), Milan especially plays a role of crucial importance in the European economy, being the place of the Italian Stock Exchange. Barcelona and Munich, the productive capital of Spain and the capital of Bavaria Lander, are lower in position when compared to the Italian city, but still very important globally; Manchester and Lyon, although important to their national economies, seem to "suffer" the central role of the capital cities in their respective countries. A different situation concerns Copenhagen, which is the administrative capital of Denmark: in this case, the role played by such a small country in the global network is limited, so that the Danish city suffers a more peripheral role compared to the entire country in globalisation dynamics.

As a second element of similarity, the six cities have been affected by the same economic trends during the 2000s, with a differentiation that emerged only after the financial crisis, determined more by the relatively different economical performances of their nation states and by the different composition of their local productive systems (Crouch *et al.*, 2001). During the first years of the last decade, in fact, all the cities experienced a GDP growth between 2000 and 2007 (Figure 2.1).

This similarity in the economic trend has been progressively disrupted by the financial crisis, with cities like Barcelona and Manchester suffering from the fin-ancial crisis more than others, although Manchester has been recovering in the most recent years. Copenhagen and Munich, rather, have continued their positive

Table 2.1 The six cities by inhabitants and global city ranking (2012)

City	Inhabitants	GaWC ranking
Copenhagen	549,050	Beta+
Munich	1,364,920	Alpha−
Barcelona	1,620,943	Alpha−
Lyon	1,321,495	Beta−
Milan	1,262,101	Alpha
Manchester	506,800	Beta

Source: Eurostat Urban Audit and GaWC network.[2]

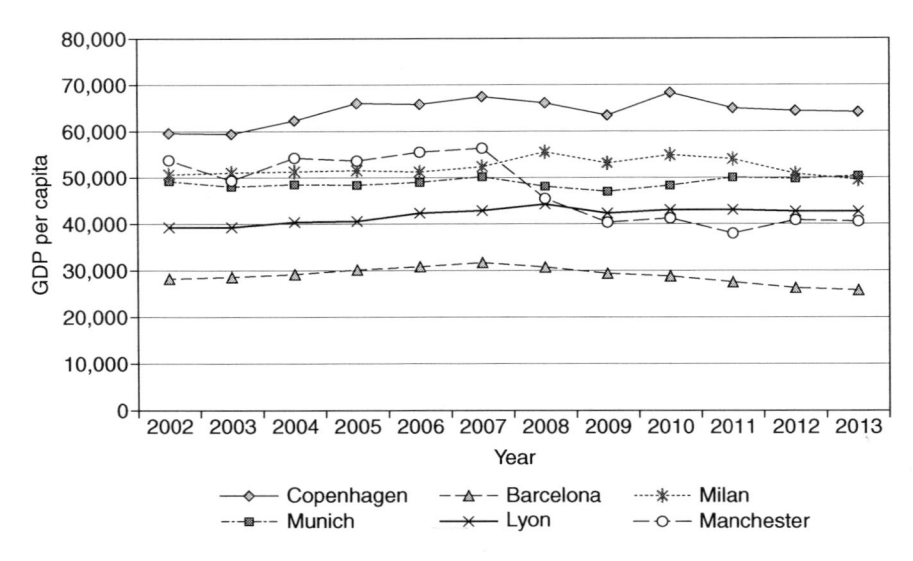

Figure 2.1 Time series of variations in the GDP per capita NUTS 3 level (2002–2013).

Source: authors' elaborations on Eurostat Urban Audit. Price at 2015.

trend in terms of GDP growth even during the financial crisis years, while Milan and Barcelona are still stuck in the crisis. According to this indicator, cities such as Copenhagen and Munich, while taking a weaker position in the globalisation process, have experienced strong economic growth, while other cities more relevant in the global economic geography, such as Milan, have registered a lower increase in economic wealth.

This crisis has also greatly affected the unemployment situation (Figure 2.2). Before the crisis, economic trends led to a general convergence in the increase of employment although the cities were starting from extremely different situations.

During the crisis, however, the situation changed significantly; Munich maintained steady growth in employment even after 2007, Lyon basically kept the same employment rate, and cities like Barcelona, Milan, Copenhagen and Manchester have been much more affected by unemployment (although Manchester and Barcelona seem to be recovering as of the most recent figures). To sum up, the crisis has affected most of the cities included in our investigation and has especially contributed towards increasing inequalities between cities from Northern and Southern Europe, also affecting competitive contexts such as Barcelona and Milan which, before the recession, had employment rates quite similar to the other urban contexts.

In terms of effects on the structure of inequalities inside the cities, however, the crisis has had a more similar effect. With the exception of the United

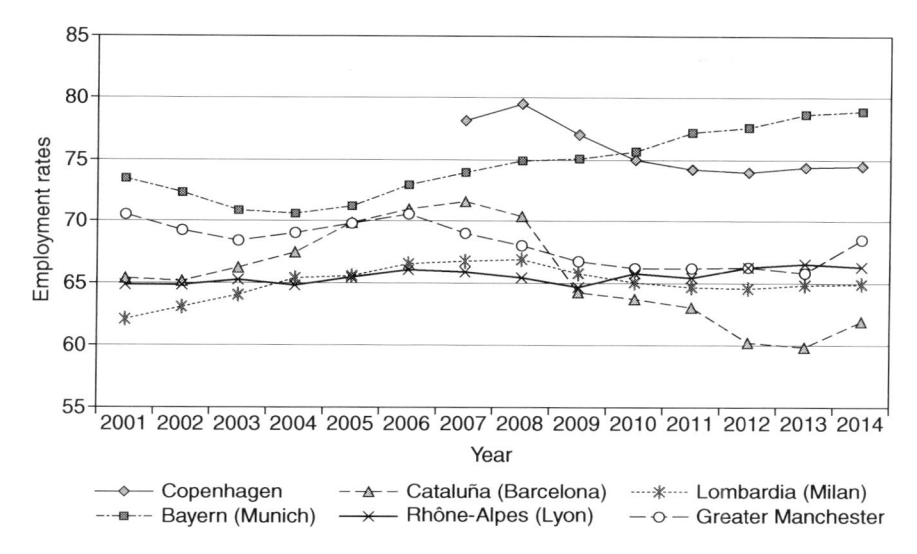

Figure 2.2 Time series of variations in total employment rates, NUTS 2 level (2001–2014).

Source: authors' elaboration on Eurostat Urban Audit.

Kingdom and France, in which the capitals, London and Paris, play a very important role in defining these trends, there has been a huge increase in the process of social polarisation in cities during the crisis. On the one hand, especially in the contexts more affected by the recession, there has been a strong concentration of wealthy inhabitants (Table 2.2); on the other, there has been an increase of households at risk of poverty (Table 2.3).

The trend in growing inequalities, established in Europe before the financial crisis, has been magnified by the concurrent negative economic trend (Piketty, 2014). There are several factors affecting this trend, but in this chapter we

Table 2.2 Percentage of households having an income over 160% of the median income in cities (definition Eurostat), (2008–2014)

	2008	2009	2010	2011	2012	2013	2014	2008–2014 (%)
Germany	18.2	18	18.4	18.3	16.7	17.7	18.3	+0.1
Denmark	13.1	12	12.9	15.6	13.7	13.2	14.2	+1.1
Spain	25.4	25.4	25.8	27.3	27.1	–	27.6	+2.2
France	18.5	19	18.1	19.4	18.8	19.4	17.6	−0.9
Italy	20.1	21	21.7	21	21.3	21.2	21.3	+1.2
United Kingdom	19	18.6	17.9	19.9	18.8	18.8	17.7	−2.3

Source: authors' elaboration on the Eurostat Dataset.

Table 2.3 At risk of poverty rates in cities (definition Eurostat) (2008–2014)

	2008	2009	2010	2011	2012	2013	2014	2008–2014 (%)
Germany	15.1	14.8	15.9	14.2	16.4	16.2	17	+1.9
Denmark	16	16.8	16.2	16.4	19.6	18.3	19.3	+3.3
Spain	16.9	16.7	16.9	16.2	18	16.6	19	+2.1
France	14.2	14.1	15.1	16.4	15.3	14.1	14.2	=
Italy	17.6	17	17.9	19.4	18.8	18.3	18.5	+0.9
United Kingdom	20	18.6	18.5	17.3	17.9	17.9	18.6	−1.4

Source: authors' elaboration on the Eurostat Dataset.

identify the changing economic specialisation of cities and the effects on the labour market as one important factor to take into consideration in order to understand how the structure of socio-inequalities has been changing in European cities.

2.3 Patterns of post-Fordist transitions

In the following paragraphs, we present different patterns of post-industrial transition that we consider quite exemplary in representing the shift towards an urban service-based society in Europe. These cities are located in areas (NUTS 2)[3] where the shift towards a service-based society has been mostly achieved, although at different levels and following different economic specialisations. In some areas, manufacturing still plays a relevant role: in the province of Milan, one-fifth of the workforce is still employed in manufacturing, while in Munich and Manchester this percentage is much lower. Huge differences also characterise the percentage of the workforce employed in public administration, education and care: again, the most important differences can be found by focusing on the case of Milan (16.3 per cent) and Munich (34.6 per cent) (Table 2.4).

Additionally, the economic structure of these cities has been oriented towards different specialisations identifying a variety of post-industrial transitions.

First, we focus on Manchester and Milan. These cities symbolise an urban transition to post-Fordism characterised by a shift from a context historically based on manufacture to a local economy oriented on the financial sector and the creativity industry. However, after the crisis, while Manchester is increasing its employment performance in the advanced business sector, Milan demonstrates the potential difficulty of a transition into post-industrial economy. In fact, although the city council has remarkably invested in sectors such as design or fashion, the local production system is still predominantly composed of traditional services, such as food and accommodation, care or transport and medium-advanced manufacturing. Those branches are in general characterised by a demand of low-skilled labour and poor job quality (seasonal or temporary contracts, with reduced working times or characterised by a strong turnover of the

Table 2.4 Employment structure, NUTS 2 level (2014) (%)

	Munich	Copenhagen	Barcelona	Lyon	Milan	Manchester
Industry	8.70	19.80	18.40	17.70	26.40	11.00
Construction	4.20	5.80	6.00	6.70	6.20	7.20
Traditional services	21.80	21.50	28.20	21.10	22.50	25.50
Advanced business services	23.40	23.10	17.70	16.10	19.50	19.60
Public administration, education and care	34.60	23.60	19.90	29.60	16.30	30.10
Other services	6.60	4.60	8.30	5.30	7.60	5.00
Total (thousands)	866.40	2,342.10	3,006.10	2,673.60	4,152.40	1,234.40

Source: authors' elaboration on Eurostat Regional Database.

workforce). The crisis has even magnified the trend as the only growing occupational sector is food and accommodation (Table 2.5).

Munich and Lyon present an urban economy particularly oriented towards research and innovation, thanks to a body of strong public policies supporting a mixed path of development. This is a pathway towards a service-based economy also characterised by a high level of coordination, with a huge role still played by the public sector in providing services for citizens and a stable situation of manufacturing also during the crisis (Table 2.5).

Barcelona and Copenhagen have developed strategies oriented towards urban renewal. However, while in Barcelona urban renewal has mostly gone with the development of tourism and construction before the crisis (sectors that are still strongly affected by the crisis), in Copenhagen this infrastructural development has been more oriented in supporting an advanced pattern of production. Through advanced production, we mean all those activities that need a highly skilled workforce to be put in place and which possesses knowledge as one of the main input factors in its production: this is valid for the service sectors, since advanced activities are consultancies or professional services, and for production, advanced activities are high-tech companies or R&D enterprises.

In the next paragraphs we describe how these patterns have been changing over the past decades and the main effects on the occupational structures of cities.

2.3.1 Cities of finance

2.3.1.1 Manchester

Manchester symbolises an urban transition to post-Fordism characterised by a clear shift from a productive context historically based on manufacture to a local economy focused on an advanced service sector and especially the financial sector.

During the nineteenth and twentieth centuries, Manchester was the symbol of the industrial and Fordist metropolis, while at the beginning of the twenty-first century it is a city where financing and support activities, such as banks, insurance companies, law firms, labour supply companies and accounting agencies are the main engines of economic growth (Manchester City Council, 2014). Professional and financial services are now considered key sectors: outside London, Greater Manchester is the United Kingdom's main centre for this sector, employing 324,000 people and generating £16.2 billion of GVA annually. Another important sector is the one represented by life sciences, in particular by biotechnology and health services provided for by the National Health Service. It employs 177,000 people generating an annual GVA of £4.2 billion. Another two specialised sectors are increasingly important: the ICT industry (hardware, software, IT management) and the world of creative industry (publicity, TV and cinema, architecture, electronic publishing), which together account for about 10 per cent of the local workforce, but they play a strategic role in defining the specificity of the urban economy (Manchester City Council, 2014).

Table 2.5 Employment growth rates, NUTS 2 level (comparison between 2008 and 2013) (%)

	Munich	Copenhagen	Barcelona	Lyon*	Milan	Manchester
Manufacturing	17.50	3.40	−28.00	−2.50	−15.00	−9.80
Construction	197.90	−10.10	−53.30	−3.50	−11.30**	−28.70
Wholesale and retail	22.40	−1.80	−11.40	−0.30	−4.30	−0.90
Transportation and storage	12.60	−5.20	−16.80	−2.10	−6.60	−5.30
Accommodation and food service activities	44.00	−20.90	−3.00	−7.40	9.00	−4.30
Information and communication	36.20	9.40	−10.50	−8.30	−4.60	−5.20
Real estate activities	12.80	−6.70	−26.00	21.90	−17.20	52.80
Professional activities	33.90	9.60	−10.80	9.70	−1.20	15.80
Administrative and support service activities	45.50	−11.70	−9.00	3.00	4.80	3.60

Source: Authors' elaboration on Eurostat Regional Database.

Notes
* value for 2010.
** value for 2011.

Together with the above-mentioned strategic sectors, Manchester still shows the traditional manufacturing legacy: the total of food, beverage, textile, engineering, car and chemical industries accounts for about 11 per cent of the global workforce (MIER, 2009). This figure is, however, constantly diminishing because of the reduction of the number of employed people due to both the introduction of massive and intensive labour technologies, and to the increasing foreign competition based on lower labour costs. The crisis has just dramatised this trend: between 2008 and 2013 (Figure 2.3), these sectors lost 10 per cent of the labour force in the region. This pattern, which is strongly oriented towards the financial and advanced sector, has led to a more polarised society, at least in terms of occupational structure. In the English city, around 30 per cent of employment is today considered as *highly skilled*, a percentage very similar to the presence of *low-skilled* workers, which composes, therefore, a picture of a particularly polarised labour market (MIER, 2009). During the last 20 years, in fact, Manchester has seen a 120 per cent increase of employment in this sector, and a vertiginous decrease of medium skilled workers employed in the manufacturing sector, gradually aligning the city labour market situation to other English contexts (MIER, 2009). Here, the process of financialisation has affected a larger sector of the labour force, while workers in the services sector and part of the manpower expelled from the industrial sector at the end of the 1980s, lie at the bottom of the social structure. The passage from the urban contexts in the past characterised by a strong industrial and productive system, gradually substituted by activities connected to the financial sector and to non-regulated services for the person, has promoted severe social cleavages. The path of Manchester seems rather emblematic: a large strata of the former industrial working class have not had a painless access to the new post-Fordist economy, being affected by low salaries and unemployment, while other social classes have gradually emerged into the financial and knowledge economy (Manchester City Council, 2014).

In comparison to other UK cities (Figure 2.3), Manchester shows a more polarised structure of the labour market: approximately 23 per cent employed as professionals in comparison to the 20 per cent at national level, but more workers employed in elementary occupation (13.4 per cent) compared to the English average (10.6 per cent). The data represent this urban context as a pattern oriented to polarisation in the occupational structure (Sassen, 2001).

2.3.1.2 Milan

Among the urban contexts analysed in this book, the Italian city of Milan is the context with the higher relevance in the manufacturing sector, although not having a knowledge-intensive orientation (Mutinelli *et al.*, 2007), and a service sector that is strongly oriented to finance.

For most of the twentieth century, Milan represented the engine driving the industrial development of the nation, showing a growth model based on big industries and on a specialisation mostly oriented on mechanics. From the end of

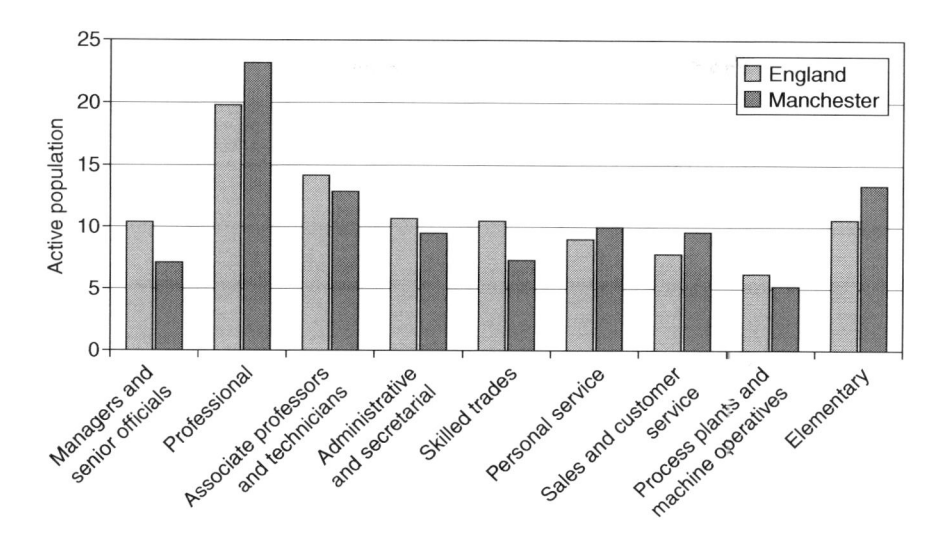

Figure 2.3 England and Manchester: active population (15–64) per socio-professional category (2013).

Source: authors' elaboration on ONS.

the last century, this model has largely disappeared and has been substituted by a different production pattern (Artoni, 2005): according to the national picture, an industrial sector mainly oriented towards medium technologically-advanced specialisations, a lower presence of big companies in the manufacturing sector, and a gradual expansion of advanced business services. More recently the main projects and investments for Milan have been focused on the organisation of the International Expo 2015, a project first characterised by scandals and contestations, but lately considered quite successful for the city in terms of international visibility and urban branding, although the final impacts on the urban economy have not been clearly estimated (Ambrosianeum, 2014).

Milan presents an economic structure that is highly fragmented in different sectors with low coordination: it is highly diversified, relatively non-specialised and service based, but also anchored to the manufacturing sector. However, a few strategic sectors symbolise the Milanese economy abroad: in particular, these activities are connected to fashion, design and publishing, but most of all to finance. It is the degree of financing of the local economy that mostly defines Milan as an important centre of global economy, being the place of the Italian Stock Exchange. More recently, there has been huge attention to the development of innovative forms of a sharing economy that has been the new strategic orientation of the economic policies of the new municipal administration (since 2011) and the assumption is that they can not only produce high-skilled employment, but also occupational inclusion for broad sections of the population.

However, it is too early to see the first concrete results of this strategy in terms of employment recovery and social inclusion.

The last available data on the occupational structure of the city show that, in comparison to Manchester, the driving financial and advanced services sector, as well the creative industry, does not seem to have had such a significant widespread impact on the urban employment structure from a point of view of professionalisation. While between 1971–1991 (Petsimeris and Rimoldi, 2015) the increase in entrepreneurs and professionals has been huge: this group only represented 3 per cent of the labour force in 1971, 11 per cent in 1991, and only increased by 2 per cent between 1991–2011, now weighting about 13 per cent of employed individuals. However, this group is the only one that has not been dramatically affected by the recent economic crisis: between 2001–2011, medium-high skilled workers such as managers, executives and white collar workers have showed a sharp decrease (−11 per cent), and the share of other dependent workers has dropped by 20 per cent (Petsimeris and Rimoldi, 2015). This was mainly due to the huge retrenchment of the labour force employed in the manufacturing and construction sectors, as regional data show (Table 2.4). The only sectors that experienced growth after the crisis are in the traditional service area, such as care, food and accommodation, perhaps due to the effect of the recent international Event Expo 2015.

To sum up, the pattern of Milan's economic development seems to follow a "lower road" (Trigilia and Burroni, 2009), mainly based on traditional services, in comparison to other European cities where the advanced service sector has been a key ingredient of economic growth. However, the crisis has just exasperated a trend already at work before 2008, due to the high relevance of sectors such as the construction sector and the not highly innovative manufacturing productions in the economy of the region and of the city. This pattern has been mainly characterised by the increase of inequalities in terms of income distribution. In fact, among OECD countries, Italy is the context where the difference between the middle class and the richest group has grown most quickly during recent decades (IRES, 2010; Fiorio, 2011) and before the crisis, Milan was in 2009 estimated as being the most unequal city in the country (D'Ovidio, 2009). To sum up, Milan represents a development pattern of increasing inequalities between the few high-income households and the remaining population affected by low salaries and unemployment, in a general national framework of increasing relative deprivation for the middle class (Ranci, 2010).

2.3.2 Cities of research and innovation

2.3.2.1 Lyon

The urban economy of Lyon is characterised by a production sector oriented towards research and innovation, promoted by a strong body of public policies (Musterd and Murie, 2010). In this city it is wrong to consider the survival of the manufacturing sector as marginal or as an element of backwardness, being the result of local development policies promoted especially by regional and/or national strategies. Among the most important clusters of production we can find medical industries profiting from synergies with an important system of hospitals and institutes for medical research; environmental industries specialised in non-polluting chemical activities; the car industry and the textile industry, still employing a relevant number of workers; sectors more connected to the creative economy such as video games, multimedia, cinema and the fashion industry, with more than 18,000 people employed (Observatoire Partenarial en Èconomie Lyon, 2016).

Public intervention has played a crucial role in this pattern of development, often reinforcing key sectors for local competitiveness, with particular reference to the so-called CP-Clusters for competitiveness introduced from 2004 onwards by the French government, which finances them together with local authorities (Observatoire Partenarial en Èconomie Lyon, 2016). Their aim is to embody an association of business partnerships, research centres and formation institutes having the purpose of creating high levels of innovation. As a result, there is a widespread presence of leading French firms in Lyon, also in sectors that are not particularly advanced (like the car sector or the cosmetic sector), which are mostly financed by the state, but they provide for the payment of local taxes for the establishment of these activities on the territory. The crisis has only partly affected this mixed pattern of development, with manufacturing losing only 2.5 per cent of the workforce after 2008 in the whole region (Table 2.5).

Although this context (Table 2.4) also shows a prevailing occupation in services, this tendency is definitely less marked compared to other urban realities analysed in the present research: in fact, more than a quarter of the workforce is employed in public administration, educational and social or sanitary services; approximately 16 per cent is employed in advanced business services and a fifth in the traditional services sector.

As far as the occupational structure is concerned (Figure 2.4), the situation of Lyon is still characterised by the presence of jobs requiring a medium level of specialisation that is coherent with the profile of a quite mixed urban economy where big industries still play an important role beside public employment. However, the situation of Lyon also appears substantially oriented towards a progressive professionalisation due to the increase of *medium* and *high-skilled* positions: at the same time, low-qualified workers are less present in the labour market since this is the group that is more affected by unemployment.

In terms of income distribution and consistently with the national picture, before the crisis Lyon used to be characterised by low inequalities in comparison to the other cities.[4] However the effects of the crisis have been relevant to the lowest income earners (Keeley, 2015): at national level, the top 10 per cent of real incomes in France increased by 2 per cent per year during the crisis, while the income of the bottom 10 per cent decreased by 1 per cent each year (compared to an average annual decrease of 2 per cent).To sum up, and also in this context, the crisis has accelerated a process of professionalisation fostering more inequality between high and low income earners (INSEE, 2015).

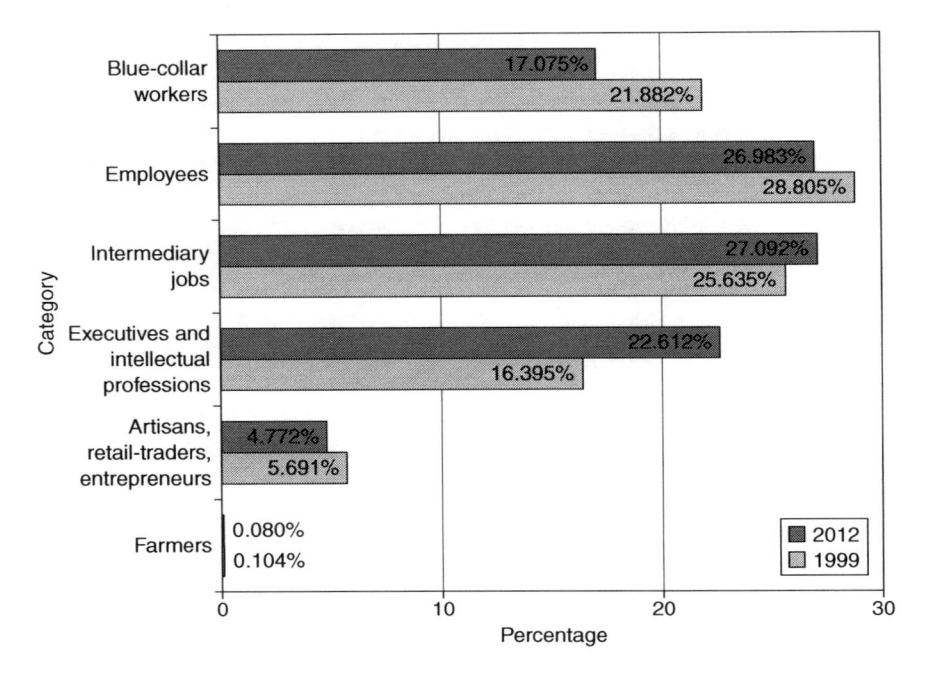

Figure 2.4 Lyon: active population (15–64) per socio-professional category (1999 and 2012).

Source: INSEE *Recensement de la population 1999 and 2012*, Données locales.

2.3.2.2 Munich

Transformations marking the recent economic transition in Munich are summarised in the concept of *Muenchner Mix*, an original combination of different production sectors and economic policy strategies, represented by clusters of entrepreneurial, research and training institutions with a rather homogeneous territorial diffusion into the whole urban area. Among the production clusters, there are many links between sectors apparently belonging to different phases of the economic history of the city. For example, the sector of advanced technology, instrumentation and control has "wedged into" the traditional car industry. Similarly, the historical industry of medical instrumentation and pharmacology has given birth to more advanced branches of biotechnology. For these reasons, Munich is not only a city of big multinational companies but it is also an urban context where small and large business firms meet and mingle together. In fact, the *Muenchner Mix* model also includes a specific protection plan for small business firms and handicraft, with the creation of the *Gewerbehoefe*, a sort of business park with a concentration of small and very small business firms. With respect to other urban realities focusing only on a closed number of production sectors, the strength of this city appears to be this diversification and mingling, because the crisis of a sector can be absorbed and balanced by the presence of other sectors (Mazzoleni and Pechmann, 2014).

These clusters of companies operating in the manufacturing sector as well as in cognitive, service and creative fields are characterised by a strong relationship between academic and scientific research. In fact, a particularly lively sector in Munich is represented by creative and knowledge industries, employing approximately one-third of the workforce. Funding for research and development (R&D expenses) has been increased considerably, not only in the city but also in the entire suburban area.

It is also important to highlight that at NUTS 2 level (Table 2.4), more than one-third of the workforce is employed in the public sector, in education, care services and especially in local administration. In Munich, public authorities have shown a good capability in defining the economic system's present characteristics. In particular, we refer to the so-called *Perspective Muenchen*, an urban development strategy adopted by the municipal government since 1998 onwards, and taking into consideration various elements of the town's development: in fact, it is not only focused on economic aspects, but it also deals with different priorities from time to time.

Very successful labour market figures keep Munich upfront in statistical comparisons of Germany's major cities. No other city with more than 500,000 inhabitants has a lower unemployment rate (EMM, 2015).

The service industry accounted for the largest share of employment growth in 2014, creating around 13,500 new jobs and thus expanding by 2.1 per cent in just one year. Demand was especially strong in MINT jobs (mathematics, information technology, natural and technical sciences), in retail, healthcare and in social services. However, and as a counter-tendency in respect to all the other cities studied in this research, very fast growth was also seen in the manufacturing sector (+7.2 per cent, adding about 6,500 new jobs).

In Munich, the *Muenchner Mix* of innovative and diversified clusters has generated the highest condensation of *high-skilled* workers (approximately one-third of the workforce) of any city in the whole of Germany, mainly employed in the sectors of creative industry, research and development and finance (Mazzoleni and Pechmann, 2014). This pattern has fostered a high concentration of highly-specialised workers, but at the same time it has coincided with an increase of high-skilled workers in the traditional service sector and in the construction sector. Furthermore, the labour market is more polarised in the Munich region than in Germany as a whole. Although this fact has negative effects in terms of income inequalities, it is partly compensated by a welfare system that tries to mitigate income inequalities (Mazzoleni and Pechmann, 2014). In terms of income distribution, the situation of Munich before the crisis was slightly higher than the one registered in Lyon. However, inequalities in Germany did not increase remarkably after 2008 (Keeley, 2015). This mixed pattern of development has been quite successful at creating employment conditions corresponding to both high-skilled workers employed as professionals and managers, and to a large group of technicians and employees. The dark side of this still positive picture is a progressive pattern of polarisation that has not developed in its negative features as in other cities investigated in the present research, due to the very good economic performance of the urban and regional context as a whole.

2.3.3 Cities investing in urban renewal

2.3.3.1 Barcelona

The stress on urban renewal is the urban development peculiarity which, in the last two decades, has characterised Barcelona. During the nineteenth and twentieth centuries, Barcelona grew like a classical Fordist urban context, very "dense and compact", profiting also from its position on the sea. From many aspects, although there was a strong shift to a service-based economy, the area of Barcelona has been the main engine of Spain's industrial development for a very long time. An indication of this feature is that Catalonia (and the metropolitan region of Barcelona, in the internal part of the region) is the biggest exporting area of all of Spain. The upswing of the Catalan economy before the huge crisis in 2007 has mostly been due to a combination of factors, such as Spain's entrance in the EEC (1986), the economic international cycle of the 1980s and the strong economic growth of Spain, whose GDP, until 2007, constantly expanded beyond the average of EU countries (Degen and Garcia, 2012).

However, a series of endogenous causes have converged on the contextual factor, among which: the existence of a lively local production, mainly represented by small and medium-sized business firms; strong local identities and a growing entrepreneurial culture; a particularly dynamic institutional environment open to the demands of the production system; and finally, the promotion of huge projects of urban development. In spite of the persistence of some "industrial" characteristics from the 1990s onwards, the shift to a service-based economy significantly changed the urban aspect, partly because of the delocalisation of manufacturing activities outside the *core* area of the city and also due to the forced introduction of a knowledge economy in the urban context (Pareja-Eastaway and Pradel, 2015).

However, the ability of local actors to identify and mobilise capitals and resources supporting dynamics for urban development has been particularly important, especially having a positive effect on the expansion of the touristic sector. This was mainly due to opportunities generated by the Olympic Games in 1992 which increased tourist flows. These flows are also the result of a significant increase in activities connected to art and culture, often as a result of urban requalification programmes and the strategic management of important events (in particular, the Olympic Games in 1992).

As previously outlined, especially in the core area of the town, a huge driver has been represented by the role undertaken by the building sector, which steadily increased from 1992 to 2007 thanks to the incentive created by important events (the Olympic Games and the Forum of Cultures in 2004) and then began to significantly suffer from the consequences of the financial crisis until becoming one of the most important causes of the recent economic collapse. In Spain, the main features of the financial crisis have been the speculative bubble in the real estate sector and the decrease of demand in all the other sectors. For the last ten years, the real estate sector was Spain's main economic sector, acting as a locomotive of the other economic sectors. The financial flexibility in obtaining credit from the banks reinforced the dynamism of the sector with increasing prices for housing. Whereas in some regions of Spain the real estate sector was by far the most relevant activity, in Barcelona the structure remained more diversified and with several economic activities. Nevertheless, the crisis has also affected the region with a decrease in the demand of goods and services and a decrease in tourism.

As far as the effects on the occupational structure of the city are concerned (Figure 2.5), the crisis has basically frozen the slow process of professionalisation characterising the city before 2007 (Pareja-Eastaway and Pradel, 2015), due to the entrance of Barcelona in the sector of the knowledge economy, whose cultural liveliness has progressively attracted not only tourism, but also competences and professionals from every part of Europe.

However, like Milan, Barcelona seems to be oriented towards developing an economic structure based on a "low road" to post-Fordism development (Trigilia and Burroni, 2009). The most recent data show quite clearly that most of the

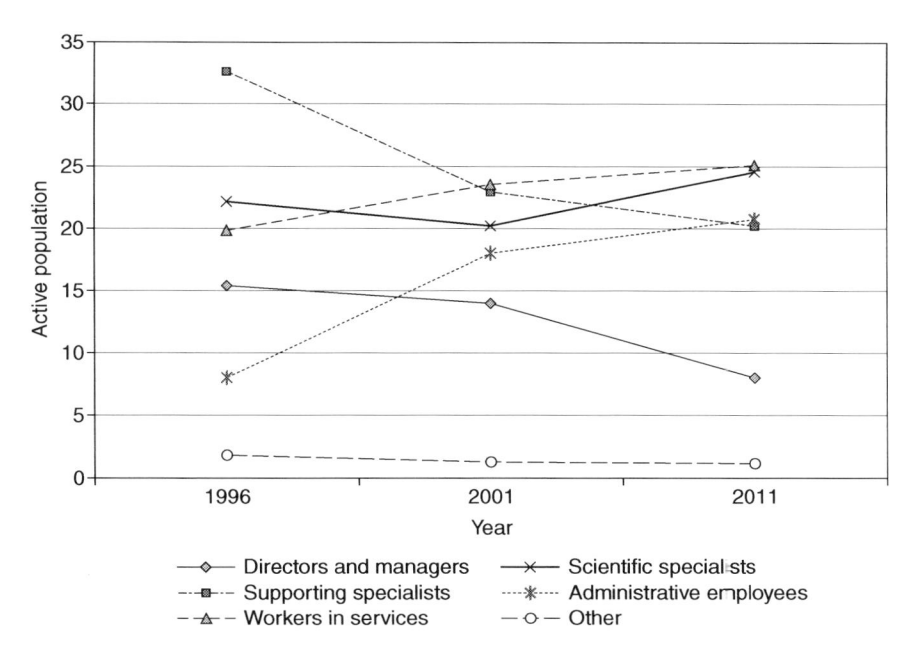

Figure 2.5 Barcelona: active population (15–64) per socio-professional category (1996–2011).

Source: authors' elaboration on Idescat.

38   R. Cucca and L. Maestripieri

recent slow recovery from the crisis has been focused on non-advanced services (Idescat, 2015).

2.3.3.2 Copenhagen

Copenhagen is the only capital among the urban contexts analysed in this research, and this element is an important aspect to be taken into consideration in order to grasp the characteristics of the economic profile of the Danish city. Although the transition from a Fordist to a post-Fordist urban context is a significant interpretation also in the case of Copenhagen, its administrative and political role has been crucial for the whole of the twentieth century, associating industrial aspects with the presence of a strong administrative sector. Moreover, during the twentieth century, the Danish welfare pattern has promoted the diffusion of an economy founded on a strong public sector of services. This historical heritage today matches a pronounced shift to a service-based economy, although less "high technology-oriented" in comparison to cities such as Munich or Manchester (OECD, 2009). However, Copenhagen's economy presents a solid export-oriented position in various economic sectors: transportation, logistics, business services, agricultural products, technological products, biopharmaceutical products and medical instruments.

This pattern of development has been fostered by huge infrastructural projects, the most important being Ørestad (Majoor, 2008). It has been part of a broader process of urban development in the Danish capital through the creation of the Transfrontier region (Denmark–Sweden) of Øresund, thanks to a bridge connecting Copenhagen to Malmö. The area extends to the south of Copenhagen and has been planned to host high-tech firms (60 per cent), research centres and universities (20 per cent), as well as middle-class houses (20 per cent). The whole Øresund region project, coupled with the expansion of flight routes, has transformed Copenhagen into the most important hub for North European countries (Majoor, 2008). However, it is also a project that has been affected by important re-orientation as a result of the crisis that has affected Copenhagen (Majoor, 2015), although more lightly than other contexts.

Urban development policies have also had a direct effect on the city's capacity to attract professionals. Between 1997 and 2013 the percentage of high-skilled workers (top managers, upper-level employees and professionals) has grown from 17 per cent of the labour force to 37 per cent, while at national level the increase has been 10 per cent less (our elaboration on Statistik Denmark, 2015), while the percentage of low-skilled people has gradually decreased (−11 per cent).

This has triggered off *gentrification* processes (Chapter 4 in this volume) that, on one hand, have gradually led to the partial replacement of the urban population (Bayliss, 2007), and on the other, have promoted Copenhagen's image at an international level as a beautiful, sustainable and liveable town, also enhancing its touristic potentialities. A far as the social impacts of the economic pattern in Copenhagen is concerned, the replacement of the population and the expulsion

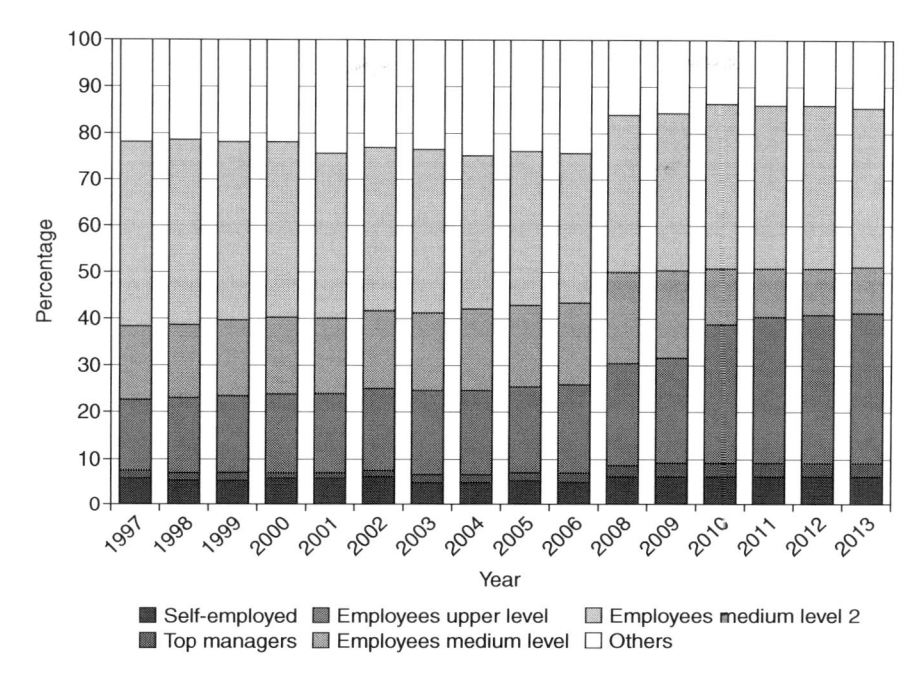

Figure 2.6 Copenhagen: active population (15–64) per socio-professional category (1997–2013).

Source: authors' elaboration on Statistics Denmark.

of the low–middle class represent the most important dimension of inequalities (Chapter 4 in this volume). This is the most important mechanism to understand the change in the Danish city's income distribution: in a few years, the number of high income taxpayers has doubled. It is a pattern consistent with the city's general upward social mobility that corresponds to the severe increase in the cost of living (UBS, 2009).

2.4 Concluding remarks

The socio-economic structure of European cities has dramatically changed over the past 20 years. The effects of transition, from Fordist economic and productive structures to economic realities differently shifted into the service-based economy and in global economic flows, have materialised in new social assets showing different tendencies.

The analysis of the main transformations experienced by the urban economies and labour markets confirms Hamnett's assumption (2003): European cities have answered, and are still answering, in a different way to the challenges presented by globalisation dynamics, by developing (or not developing) strategies to support diverse economic sectors, in most cases as results of the entanglement of multi-level governance structures. Huge differences exist and have been magnified by the recent crisis. These different trajectories greatly influence the recovery chances of the local economy and the labour market.

In general, we can state that the crisis has been a severe "stress test" for these cities. The economic trends were mainly positive in the last decade before the crisis, both in terms of GDP per capita and transformation of the labour market structure (decreasing unemployment and professionalisation). However, also before the crisis, it was clear that the post-industrial transition was characterised by the reproduction of strong inequalities, fostering a situation that has indeed been magnified by the concurrent negative economic trend (Piketty, 2014).

Already before the crisis, the trajectories of these cities were oriented, more or less consistently with the national picture, to different patterns of post-industrial transitions. The strategies the cities followed within their international economic activities can be explained by both the specific market conditions the city faces and the role of the national state within the specific form of urban capitalism (van Der Heiden and Terhorst 2007). Cities such as Munich and Lyon have been characterised by a "high road to post-industrial transition"; in these cities the economic system is particularly oriented towards research and innovation, thanks to a body of strong public policies supported by national, regional and local levels of governance reinforcing a mixed path of development. This is a pathway towards a service-based economy also characterised by a high level of coordination, with a huge role played by the public sector in providing services for citizens and good jobs. This pattern has been the most successful in terms of ability to answer to the crisis by maintaining or increasing local participation in the labour market, and to some extent containing inequalities in the labour market, although polarisation in Munich and distance between professional groups in Lyon have also been growing in these contexts.

Manchester and Milan symbolise an urban transition to post-Fordism characterised by a shift from a context historically based on manufacture to a local economy oriented towards the financial sector. Besides this important characteristic, however, these cities also present two important differences: while in Manchester the post-industrial shift has reached its peak, Milan is still anchored to less advanced sectors, both in manufacturing and in the service sector, while occupation in public administration is still very high in Manchester. In these two cities, the effects of the crisis on unemployment has been quite important, but while Manchester seems to be recovering recently, especially with a growth in advanced services, Milan is still stuck in a difficult situation and the recent growth of non-advanced services seems to be oriented to a "low road" of post-industrial transition. In these contexts, polarisation (in Manchester) and income inequalities between professional groups (in Milan) are sharply increasing.

Barcelona and Copenhagen have both developed strategies that are strongly oriented towards urban renewal and infrastructural projects before the crisis. The decline in the participation in the labour market has been huge in both cities, although they were in very different positions before. However, while in

Barcelona urban renewal has especially gone with the development of tourism and construction before the crisis (which are sectors that are still strongly affected by the crisis), in Copenhagen this infrastructural development has been more oriented in supporting a more advanced pattern of production. Also in this case, the South European context seems to suffer an orientation towards a lower road in its transition, while Copenhagen is recovering occupation in many strategic sectors.

To sum up, cities that have been able to invest and develop in a "high road" to post-industrial transition (Munich and Lyon) have been the contexts suffering a lower crisis impact in terms of occupational structure, while cities oriented to a "low-road" have more problems in coping with the effects of the recession.

As far as labour market inequalities are concerned, especially after the crisis, "trends" towards the professionalisation of the workforce are indeed the results of an expulsion process of groups that are not able to find room in a very tiny and selective labour market. This is the cost of professionalisation in Europe. In general, what is emerging is a general process of labour market dualisation: in some contexts, the orientation is towards a clear polarisation of the workforce; in other contexts, the social cost of professionalisation is the expulsion of a large part of the workforce. Only a few cities that have been able to develop and consolidate a "higher road" of post-Fordist transition (in most cases embedded in a supportive multi-level system of governance) are still, but only in part, close to the picture representing European cities as places where the middle class still has room for self-preservation.

Notes

1 For more information see the OECD website, online, available at: www.oecd.org/innovation/launchoftheoecdsinnovationstrategy.htm.
2 To access the GaWC ranking please consult Loughborough University's GaWC website, online, available at: www.lboro.ac.uk/gawc/world2012t.html.
3 NUTS 2 level data are the only data available in the Eurostat Database suitable for comparative analysis.
4 Again, the comparison with Milan is quite meaningful: in 2005 in Milan, the rate between the first decile and the tenth decile was more than 20 times higher, while in Lyon the rate between the ninth decile and the first was barely five times higher (Cucca, 2010).

References

Ambrosianeum Fondazione Culturale (2014) *Rapporto sulla citta' Milano 2014, Expo, Laboratorio Metropolitano, cantiere per un nuovo mondo*. Milan: Franco Angeli.

Artoni, R. (2005) Alcune considerazioni sull'economia milanese. *Impresa e Stato*, 71/2005, 43–52.

Bagnasco, A. and Le Galès, P. (eds) (2000) *Cities in Contemporary Europe*. Cambridge: Cambridge University Press.

Bayliss, D. (2007) The Rise of the Creative City: Culture and Creativity in Copenhagen. *European Planning Studies*, 15(7): 889–903.

Brenner, N. (2004) Urban Governance and the Production of New State Spaces in Western Europe, 1960–2000. *Review of International Political Economy*, 11(3): 447–488.

Crouch, C., Le Galès, P., Trigilia, C. and Voelzkow, H. (eds) (2001) *Local Production Systems in Europe: Rise or Demise?* Oxford: Oxford University Press.

Cucca, R. (2010) Crescita diseguale: Gli impatti sociali della transizione al post-fordismo nelle città europee. In: Ranci, C., *Città nella rete globale: Competitività e disuguaglianze in sei città europee*. Milan: Bruno Mondadori, pp. 79–115.

Degen, M. and García, M. (2012) The Transformation of the "Barcelona Model": An Analysis of Culture, Urban Regeneration and Governance. *International Journal of Urban and Regional Research*, 36(5): 1022–1038.

D'Ovidio, M. (2009) Milano, città duale? In: Ranci, C. (ed.). *I limiti sociali della crescita: Milano e le città d'Europa, tra competitività e disuguaglianze*. Milan: Maggioli, pp. 9–72.

EMM (Europäische Metropolregion) e.V. (2015) *Die Metropolregion München*. Online, available at: http://goo.gl/qntW9F.

Esping-Andersen, G., Gallie, D., Hemerijck, A. and Myles, J. (2002) *Why We Need a New Welfare State*. Oxford: Oxford University Press.

Fernandez-Macias, E. (2012) Job Polarization in Europe? Changes in the Employment Structure and Job Quality, 1995–2007. *Work and Occupations*, 39(2): 157–182.

Fiorio, C. (2011) Understanding Italian Inequality Trends. *Oxford Bulletin of Economics and Statistics*, 73: 255–275.

Fleming, P., Harley, B. and Sewell, G. (2004) A Little Knowledge is a Dangerous Thing: Getting below the Surface of the Growth of "Knowledge Work" in Australia. *Work, Employment and Society*, 18(4): 725–747.

Florida, R. (2004) *Cities and the Creative Class*. London: Routledge.

Gallie, D. (2007) Production Regimes and the Quality of Employment in Europe. *Annual Review of Sociology*, 33: 85–104.

GaWC (2008) Global City Network. Online, available at: www.lboro.ac.uk/gawc/.

Goos, M., Manning, A. and Salomons, A. (2009) Job Polarization in Europe. *American Economic Review*, 99(2): 58–63.

Hall, P. and Soskice, D. (2001) Introduction. In: Hall, P. and Soskice, D. (eds). *Varieties of Capitalism: the Institutional Foundations of Comparative Advantage*, Oxford: Oxford University Press, pp. 1–68.

Hamnett, Chris (2003) *Unequal City: London in the Global Arena*. London: Routledge.

Heiden, N. van der, and Terhorst, P. (2007) Varieties of Glocalisation: the International Economic Strategies of Amsterdam, Manchester, and Zurich Compared. *Environment and Planning C-Government and Policy*, 25(3): 341–356.

INSEE (2015) *Rhône-Alpes: une région riche mais des inégalités qui s'accentuent*. Insee Analyses Rhône-Alpes, 18, February.

INSEE-DGI (2015) *Revenus fiscaux des ménages*. Online, available at: www.insee.fr.

IRES (2010) La crisi dei salari – Crescita, occupazione e redditi perduti negli anni duemila, *Osservatorio Salari e Distribuzione del reddito*, 16/2010. Online, available at: www.ires.it.

Jouve, B. and Lefevre, C. (eds) (2002) *Local Power, Territory and Institutions in European Metropolitan Regions*. London: Frank Cass.

Keeley, B. (2015) *Income Inequality: the Gap between Rich and Poor*. Paris: OECD Publishing.

Kemeny, T. and Storper, M. (2012) The Sources of Urban Development: Wages,

Housing, and Amenity Gaps across American Cities. *Journal of Regional Science*, 52: 85–108.

Majoor, S. (2008) *Disconnected Innovation: New Urbanity in Large-Scale Development Projects: Zuidas Amsterdam, Orestad Copenhagen and Forum Barcelona*. Delft: Eburon.

Majoor, S. (2015) Urban Megaprojects in Crisis? Ørestad Copenhager. Revisited. *European Planning Studies*, 23(12): 2497–2515.

Manchester City Council (2014) *Manchester Economic Factsheet*. Online, available at: www.manchester.gov.uk.

Massey, D. B. (1984) *Spatial Divisions of Labour: Social Structures and the Geography of Production*. New York: Methuen.

Mazzoleni, C. and Pechmann, A. (2016) Geographies of Knowledge-Creating Services and Urban Policies in the Greater Munich. In: Cusinato, A. and Philippopoulos-Mihalopoulos, A. (eds). *Knowledge-Creating Milieus in Europe: Firms, Cities, Territories*, Heidelberg: Springer.

MIER-Manchester Independent Economic Review (2009) *Understanding Labour Markets, Skills and Talents*. Main Report. Online, available at: www.manchester-review.org.uk.

Musterd, S. and Murie, M. (2010) *Making Competitive Cities*. Oxford: Wiley-Blackwell.

Mutinelli, M., Mariotti, S. and Bannò, M. (2007) *L'internazionalizzazione produttiva in Milano Produttiva 2007*. Online, available at: www.mi.camcom.it.

Nannicini, T. (2005) L'analisi economica della flessibilità nel mercato del lavoro. In: Giovani, F. (ed.). *Lavoro flessibile: opportunità o vincolo?* Milan: Franco Angeli.

Newman, P. and Thornley, A. (2005) *Planning World Cities: Globalization and Urban Politics*, Basingstoke, Hampshire: Palgrave Macmillan.

Observatoire Partenarial en Economie Lyon (2016) *Regard sur l'Economie et les Entreprises Lyonnaises*. Online, available at: www.opale-lyon.com/AffichePDF/20150.

OECD (2009) *Territorial Reviews: Copenhagen, Denmark*. Online, available at: www.oecd.org.

Oesch, Daniel and Menes, J. Rodriguez (2010) Upgrading or Polarization? Occupational Change in Britain, Germany, Spain and Switzerland, 1990–2008. *Socio-Economic Review*, 9(3): 503–531.

OST – Observatoire des Sciences et Techniques (2006) *Report on R&D in Europe*. Online, available at: www.obs-ost.frand.

Pareja-Eastaway, M. and Pradel, M. (2015) Towards the Creative and Knowledge Economies: Analysing Diverse Pathways in Spanish Cities. *European Planning Studies*, 23(12): 2404–2422.

Petsimeris, P. and Rimoldi, S. (2015) Socio-Economic Divisions of Space in Milan in the Post-Fordist Era. In: Tammaru, T., Marcińczak, S., van Ham, M. and Musterd, S. (eds). *Socio-Economic Segregation in European Capital Cities: East meets West*. Abingdon, Oxford: Routledge, pp. 186–213.

Piketty, T. (2014) *Capital in the Twenty-First Century*. Cambridge: Harvard University Press.

Pratschke, J. and Morlicchio, E. (2012) Social Polarisation, the Labour Market and Economic Restructuring in Europe: An Urban Perspective. *Urban Studies*, 49(9): 1891–1907.

Ranci, C. (2010) Competitiveness and Social Cohesion in Western European Cities. *Urban Studies*, 48(13): 2789–2804.

Salet, W., Thornley, A. and Kreukels, A. (eds) (2003) *Metropolitan Governance and Spatial Planning*. London: Spon Press.

Sassen, S. (1991) *The Global City: New York, London, Tokyo.* Princeton: Princeton University Press.

Sassen, S. (2000) *Cities in a World Economy.* London: Pine Forge Press.

Sassen, S. (2008), Service Employment Regimes and the New Inequality. In: Mingione, E. (ed.). *Urban Poverty and the Underclass: A Reader.* Oxford: Blackwell Publishers Ltd.

Savitch, H. V. and Kantor, P. (2002) *Cities in the International Marketplace.* Princeton, NJ: Princeton University Press.

Trigilia, C. and Burroni, L. (2009) Italy: Rise, Decline and Restructuring of a Regionalized Capitalism, *Economy and Society,* 38 (4): 630–653.

UBS (2009) *Prezzi e stipendi.* Online, available at: www.ubs.com.

Websites

http://dati.comune.milano.it/statistiche.html
www.idescat.cat/
www.insee.fr/fr/
www.dst.dk/en
http://open.manchester.gov.uk/
www.muenchen.de/rathaus/Stadtinfos/Statistik.html
www.ons.gov.uk/

3 The forces of attraction

Cities between flows and places

Agostino Petrillo

3.1 Introduction

The notion of urban attractiveness has become increasingly relevant in recent years and now constitutes one of the central themes in the debate about the driving forces of cities. The growing importance of multinational firms in the global economy and the opening up of cities to increasingly mobile investment flows has contributed to raising awareness of a new form of competition among places for the reception of international investments. But, no clear understanding of the factors underlying a city's ability to attract new investment, visitors, young talent and innovative growth opportunities has yet emerged due to the number of variables contributing to it and to the diverse groups who are the objects of attraction (Atkinson *et al.* 2013). Since cities vary for economic, historical and morphological reasons, their attractiveness also differs. Moreover, foreign investment is potentially not only encouraged but also 'attracted' by specific local policies. Positive action is not only a matter of traditional economic competitiveness – offering advanced capabilities, services, infrastructures and logistics – but also of making the city attractive to the new elites that constitute an essential component of globalised cities (Marcuse and van Kempen 2000). Leisure opportunities, quality of life and artistic and cultural amenities matching the tastes of the new professional class have become extremely important.

To prioritise this set of factors and enable empirical verification to take place, a distinction was drawn between the 'hard' and 'soft' factors that contribute in various ways to urban attractiveness (OECD 2005). Much discussion has taken place on the various roles played by these hard and soft factors, although some recent research would seem to confirm the prevalence of 'concreteness' and suggest the prevalence of the hard factor par excellence: highly qualified workers seem, unsurprisingly, to prefer to go where the highest salaries are available (Moretti 2012; Buch *et al.* 2014).

Still unaddressed in this overall picture is the issue of the relationship between the demands of global attractiveness, on one hand, and satisfying the needs of the local populations on the other. (Graham and Marvin 2001). For example, infrastructure provision is not something that can be taken for granted and its provision and maintenance are closely linked to social inequalities in cities

(Müller and Sträter 2011). The questions addressed in the chapter relate to the extent to which the action necessary to sustain global challenges constitutes an advantage or a disadvantage as far as local interests expressed by the production system and the population are concerned; whether local government action is capable or not of influencing the overall trend of flows (Servillo *et al.* 2012). In the next section (3.2) I will examine the role played by Foreign Direct Investment; in Section 3.3 I will focus on the impact of the 2008 crisis; in Section 3.4 I will analyse the hard and soft factors that contribute to attractiveness. In Section 3.5 I will assess the ability of cities to attract skilled workers, and in my conclusion I will stress the importance of local government in managing this kind of process and the risks linked to attractiveness policies.

3.2 Foreign direct investment and internationalisation

Foreign direct investment (FDI) in cities constitutes a broad and controversial field of analysis because the importance of FDI is not solely economic: foreign investment brings not just capital but also knowledge, technologies and cultures. It is not simply *what* is produced that is important but also *how* it is produced (Matzenetter and Musil 2011). Moreover, FDI potentially competes with local firms in situations of labour shortage or when staff with specific skills are needed. Overall, however, FDI contributes to reinforcing the institutional system by prompting it to operate in a broader framework than the local context. It obliges local firms to measure themselves against the global technology frontier and also introduces elements of crisis and contradiction (Poelhekke and van der Ploegg 2009).

The analysis that follows was originally based on 2001–2007 period data. It has therefore been reconsidered in the light of the great economic crisis of 2008. Immediately before the crisis, on the basis of 2003–2006 surveys of the top 50 cities in the world ranked according to their ability to attract investments, four of the cities studied in this book are ranked.

Two cities show negative or modest global attractiveness trends in the year immediately before the crisis: Copenhagen and Milan (Table 3.1). Copenhagen, with −11 per cent growth over three years, shows a notable downturn in its investment attraction capability. It should be borne in mind that Copenhagen has

Table 3.1 FDI by city prior to the crisis (2003–2006)

City	Ranking	Direct investments 2003–2006 (in number of projects)	Growth during the 2003–2006 period (%)
Copenhagen	26	176	−11
Milan	31	162	+8
Munich	36	140	+18
Barcelona	38	138	+15

Source: author's elaboration on *Foreign Direct Investments Quarterly*, no. 5, summer 2007.

one of the lowest levels of manufacturing employment of the cities considered, whilst service sector employment is very high (OECD 2009). Of the explanations put forward for Copenhagen's foreign investment reduction, the most important would seem to be that the city has failed to re-orient its economy to strategic sectors, especially financial services. Scant specialisation in a sector where the capacity to acquire sophisticated skills and supply extremely diversified services, is increasingly crucial, would therefore seem to be the cause of Copenhagen's momentary decline (Taylor and Aranya 2007).

Milan's FDI grew by 8 per cent in the period 2003–2006, down from the 12 per cent increase registered in 2000–2002. However, this less positive trend has not significantly damaged the city's positive ranking, which is indicative of continuity in a stock of previously acquired internationalisation (Magatti *et al.* 2005). Some 52 per cent of total foreign shareholdings in Italy are concentrated in Lombardy (42 per cent in Milan). In particular, Milan and its hinterland is the preferred location for the headquarters of foreign tertiary sector multinationals. Milan province, moreover, continues to maintain a significant presence in manufacturing, especially in the medium technology-intensive sectors (OECD 2006). The main problem for the economic development of the city seems to be the modest attractiveness of the national economic system as a whole since Italy has continued to lose ground as a destination country for world FDI in recent years because of the increasing share in investments taken up by both emerging markets and other European countries (Onida *et al.* 2007).

All the other cities considered here have shown a progressive rise in investment attractiveness.

Munich has grown considerably (Table 3.1) succeeding in becoming the preferred investment destination over other 'regional' competitors, especially Vienna (OIIP 2009). It should be noted that many of the global players present in Munich are of German origin. Whilst this indicates a specific 'national vocation' in Munich's economic development, which originated in the second post-war period, it does not exclude the presence of a total of 800 foreign firm investments. More than 40 venture capital and private equity companies have headquarters in Munich, especially in communication and media technologies and medicine and biotechnologies (von Streit 2010). A further attraction is the city's strong and diversified service sector. Munich thus offers a wide range of investment opportunities, which are attracting the interest of the Oriental giants, India and China. More than 70 Indian companies are currently operating in Bavaria and, crisis notwithstanding, the volume of trade between India and Bavaria grew by 25 per cent in 2008/2009 and a further 21 per cent in 2010/2011 (IHK 2012).

This success can also be accounted for by a particularly aggressive technology upgrading policy: the High-Tech Offensive launched in 1999, which saw investments of almost €1.5 billion, was followed by a cluster-offensive, this, too, accompanied by lavish investment (Bayerisches Staatsministerium 2008). Three clusters are currently undergoing rapid development: TIMES (technology, information, media, entertainment and safety), which in 2006 comprised 27,386 firms, some of them absolutely top level, such as the cinema industry with its extraordinary capacity for technological renewal (Kaiser and Liecke 2007); an aerospace cluster, which has become the most important in Germany, specialising in satellite technology (involving 234 firms and seven research institutes with sales amounting to €4.7 billion and 15,000 employees; IHK 2007); and a life sciences industry cluster, which comprises more than 160 firms, some of which are world leaders in the field. Studies have identified numerous 'naturally grown' clusters which 'consist of an agglomeration of firms in their respective sectors' and comprise networks of SMEs and large enterprises, the numerous research and educational institutions in the Munich area, as well commercialisation protagonists.

Barcelona has continued with an internationalisation process that has been ongoing for some time, and linked it with an overall 're-invention' of the city's image centred on the new communication, design and knowledge sectors and its role as logistical hub for Southern Europe. Both European and American investors, interested mostly in real estate and construction sector development, are present in Barcelona. The country experienced a long boom, underpinned by a housing bubble financed by cheap loans to builders and homebuyers, until 2008. House prices rose 44 per cent from 2004 to 2008, at the tail end of the housing boom. Since the bubble burst in 2008 these have fallen by a third (Meliveo 2014). This has led to changes in the Great Events policy inaugurated in the 1990s and the city government's programme aiming to redress territorial imbalances and enhance the housing stock with an urban renewal policy (Degen and Garcia 2008).

If we look at the sectors that attract the largest amounts of foreign investment, we find manufacturing and services experiencing a constantly upward trend since 1995. Capital has been attracted by the businesses that have set up in Barcelona's new innovation district. In 2000, the city decided to regenerate the historic Poblenou industrial district and turn it into a centre for scientific research, innovation and technology. The new centre has been carefully marketed and under the '22@' aegis it has become a cluster of research organisations, university institutes, enterprise incubation and media technologies, biotechnologies and energy. The project will cover four million square metres of land of which 3.2 million will be used for productive activities and 800,000 for housing and services.

Manchester and Lyon do not appear in the top 50 ranking shown in Table 3.1. Nevertheless there were 53 FDI projects in Lyon in 2006 and 69 in 2007 which is indicative of substantial progress. There are around 375 firms with foreign capital in Lyon, employing 71,000 people. In this case, the basis of the city's revival after the deindustrialisation process has been decisive intervention by the state starting at the end of the 1990s (McDonald 2013). In 2004, France decided to create 'competitiveness clusters' in order to reinforce its industrial policies. Support by the state and local authorities for these clusters has taken the form of direct funding and tax exemption. The results have been positive: in Lyon today there are leading pharmaceutical product and medical diagnostics sector companies. Hence, intervention by the state and local government taking the form of encouraging and creating better connections between research centres and firms has contributed considerably to increasing foreign investment. The decision to locate the 'Biopole' in the Gerland-Lyon zone has proved well-judged in both logistics and transport terms, given the excellent transport links between the city centre and the zone's stations.

Manchester has recorded even more significant growth, from 24 FDI projects in 2004–2005 to 47 in 2007–2008. This a leap forward that signals the city's renewed international importance and which placed it for a while in second place only to London among English cities. In this case growth has been driven mainly by the banking and insurance sector: Manchester is the only English city apart from London to rank in the top 20 European business locations, mainly by virtue of its concentration of large business banks and financial institutions. Indeed, it was in Manchester that the Bank of India opened its first foreign branch. Another expanding sector that has attracted foreign investors is the life sciences industry sector, which has established close links with universities in which biology and chemistry are achieving high levels of excellence, and with internationally famous hospitals. High knowledge-intensive sectors account for 11.4 per cent of employment in Manchester's city and 12.6 per cent in its urban region. Two further sectors have played a part in the city's international relaunch, which employ around 10 per cent of the local labour force: the technologies and media and, still in the embryonic stage, the creative industries sector. The obstacle to Manchester's further development seems to be the relatively scant diversification of areas in which it is possible to invest. The city's industrial past still weighs heavily on it, its deindustrialisation and decline prevent the balanced growth of the various production sectors due to the survival of 'old' forms of production in many areas, and contribute to worsening its spatial inequalities (Oakey 2007). In particular, the legacy of a once highly-developed manufacturing sector has left traces both in the mentality of part of the city's population, and in its economic structure. Although manufacturing accounts for only 12 per cent of employment, percentages are considerably higher in some boroughs where a traditional working-class culture survives. Moreover, the sector's high labour-intensive productivity means that, notwithstanding its small number of workers, it accounts for almost one-fifth of overall output by the Manchester urban region (Manchester Partnership 2009a). Consequently, although investment projects have grown considerably, the majority seem to have been hampered both by the relative failure of the local economy to furnish a broader range of services, and by socio-spatial imbalances. In spite of considerable success in rebuilding its economy over the past 25 years, the city-region retains significant pockets of multiple deprivation, closely connected with the conurbation's uneven spatial development (Harding *et al.* 2010).

3.3 The impact of the crisis

During and after the crisis, in particular in the 2008–2012 period, some interesting variations took place. The great economic crisis that began in 2008 led to a substantial reduction in international investment and marked the definitive conclusion of the upward trend. Not only has the number of projects shown some remarkable shifts but there have also been important changes in city ranking (see Table 3.2).

Cities have reacted variously to the economic crisis. Some have experienced a true downturn, while others have been only partially affected by the crisis and have quickly recovered through economic or political restructuring.

Milan and Barcelona have been the worst affected by the crisis. While in 2008 Milan was still in fourth position, in the 2009–2012 period it dropped to eighth and thirteenth place (FDI Monitor 2014). Between 2011 and 2013, Milan recorded an average of 34 FDI projects per year compared with a 58 project per year average between 2006 and 2010 and a peak of 70 FDI projects in 2008. This has been prompted by substantial economic stagnation and reduced Italian investor affordability (Magatti and Sapelli 2012).

In the years after 2008, notwithstanding its deep real estate sector crisis, Barcelona maintained significant FDI levels and developed the 22@ district, which was 70 per cent complete, becoming the most vital part of the city. At the end of 2010 around 90,000 people were working in Poblenou. Including old and new sectors, around 1,500 companies, 15 per cent of which are foreign-owned, have located to the district (Ajuntament de Barcelona 2010). However, Barcelona's Great Events policy has been criticised (Borja 2010; Degen and Garcia 2012). Optimism about Barcelona's attractiveness as a trade fair, conference and large event capital would appear not be fully justified. More than 223 new events to 2021 have been confirmed, but the new city government has doubts about the sustainability of this event level.

By contrast, Manchester's growth model has been successful: after having outperformed most other British cities in the 2003–2006 period, local government policy decisions have brought substantial continuity in development. Within the United Kingdom, Manchester has secured more FDI than any other city outside London. Between 1991 and 2011 the city centre's population increased to over 17,000 and the overall population grew by one-fifth from 2001 to 2011. Industrial decline left empty spaces that have now been reclaimed by a

Table 3.2 FDI by city after the crisis (2008–2012)

	Number of projects					
	2008	*2009*	*2010*	*2011*	*2012*	*Total 2008–2012*
Barcelona	70	61	50	55	60	296
Munich	70	56	65	47	49	289
Milan	70	46	58	33	34	241
Copenhagen	34	18	22	18	13	105
Manchester	28	34	27	33	22	153
Lyon	38	23	21	8	14	94

Source: author's elaboration on *Financial Times* FDI Intelligence data.

new generation of entrepreneurs: the Sharp Project in northeast Manchester is home to more than 60 companies, working in a 100,000 m² space. Drawing on robust economic research, Manchester has focused on key sectors and international markets. The city is now 'an ideal location for a second office'. A global forecaster has predicted that the city will grow faster than the average for the rest of the country over the next ten years, with 110,000 new jobs being created by 2024, most of them (30 per cent) in finance and business (Oxford Economics 2015). However, in the first decade of the new millennium inequality in the city has sharply increased.

Even Munich survived the 2008 financial and economic crisis relatively unscathed due to close and intensive joint working between private partners, public institutions and universities/research institutions. Munich has more than one developmental centre and this played an especially important role during the economic downturn. Economic output diversity has strengthened the resilience of the city and made the region stronger. For this reason Munich has a lower unemployment rate than other German cities. In 2010, for example, unemployment rates in Berlin and Hamburg were 13.5 and 8.2 per cent respectively, whilst Munich's was only 4.7 per cent (Hoogerbrugge and Willems 2012).

Copenhagen's long term economic development strategy has also had positive effects. After a reduction in FDI in 2003/2006, the city has recovered importance and centrality due to smart urban design and the capacity to create new market links in key clusters. Nevertheless social problems related to high rents and limited social integration have remained unresolved.

Finally, Lyon maintained reasonably good FDI performance levels, with the exception of 2011 (a difficult year for the French economy), and reinforced its governmental structures: in 2012 the Metropolitan Polo was set up, which brings together four agglomerations of the city-region (Lyon, Saint Etienne, ViennAgglo and Porte de l'Isère) paving the way for further inter-municipal cooperation. After the opening of the new Metropolitan Polo there was a leap forward in the number of projects, from 56 in 2013 to 83 in 2014 (a 48 per cent increase; Ernst and Young 2015). The Lyon region's 1,500 decision centres make the urban area one of the largest economic centres in France. In 2012, €5.6 billion were invested in R&D in the region (12 per cent of the national total). This dynamism has also attracted international organisations such as Interpol, Euronews and the World Health Organisation, and helped spur the development of top-ranked clusters such as biotech, clean technologies and digital entertainment (World's Most Competitive Cities 2013). Moreover, an ambitious new urban development project has been planned in a central area, at the confluence of the Rhône and the Saône rivers. This plan will double the city centre area, regenerating 150 ha of industrial area. The population is expected to increase (from 7,000 to 17,000 inhabitants), respecting its socially mixed composition (33 per cent of the new housing is planned to be standard and mid-price rental and 23 per cent will be social housing). New economic activities will also be developed creating 14,000, perhaps even 27,000, new jobs.

A city's resilience to crisis depends on a range of factors. First, specific economic sectors attract the highest levels of international investment and are therefore decisive for the success of cities. Knowledge, creative and life sciences industries are the areas on which research efforts and expectations of economic returns are focused today. Second, the ability of local governments to orient flows and allocate attractive spaces for innovative businesses is also crucial. Decentralisation policies implemented in Munich and Lyon envisage the diffusion of new activities across a broad area and have been particularly effective in attracting investment. In Munich, the Martinsried and Garching districts have changed from semi-rural areas to a bio-tech industry centre and an advanced physics and applied science research centre, respectively (Hessler 2007). In Martinsried, local government has facilitated new economic activity, part of which has nothing to do with local traditions. In the space of just a few years, a close relation between the state, university, research companies and entrepreneurs has given rise to the Martinsried 'bio-valley', which today employs 5,000 scientists in a suburb whose population was no more than 10,000 just a few years ago. This case shows not solely significant innovation attraction ability but also high-quality space management: the area was deliberately selected for the creation of this new industrial cluster precisely because of the absence of a relevant economy (von Streit *et al.* 2010). A similar strategy of spatial and productive decentralisation has been adopted by the Lyon government, too, albeit on a smaller scale, with positive attractiveness and economic-territorial balance results.

Less effective spatial management capability in Manchester, by contrast, has created growing imbalances between the productive and innovative capacities of some areas compared with others, which may dampen growth processes. A response to these developments has been the deal struck between the British government and Greater Manchester to devolve significant powers and funding to the city-region. In exchange for Greater Manchester directly electing a mayor to work in partnership with the combined authority, a series of powers will be devolved including transport, planning, housing, policing and skills (Centre for Cities 2015, p. 4). In different ways cities like Milan and Barcelona have strengthened their international positions using their natural and cultural features, rather than their economic assets to attract mobility flows (ESPON and University Rovira i Virgili 2013).

3.4 Hard and soft factors

The greater or lesser attractiveness of a city may be determined by a wide range of factors. A general distinction can be drawn between hard and soft factors: the former are the conditions required by classic location theory: availability of capital and adequately skilled labour, suitable institutional contexts, infrastructure and accessibility. The latter comprise the amenities that may make a city attractive and encourage creative talents and high-skilled technical personnel to settle there (Musterd and Murie 2011). These factors have played different roles in each city.

In Barcelona, soft factors seem to have played a decisive role in the pattern of urban development. Quality of life and cultural diversity have been important factors in many knowledge workers' decisions to settle in the city. Barcelona's mild climate, its tradition of tolerance and its vibrant atmosphere, as well as a proliferation of creative talents in diverse fields, have further enhanced the city's positive image internationally. Moreover, relatively low real estate prices have contributed to Barcelona's overall attractiveness, especially as regards the cost of office space, as well as the cost of living, which is much lower than in other large European cities. But hard factors have played an important role as well: the availability of skilled human resources at relatively low cost and the size of the metropolitan area market (Pareja-Eastaway *et al.* 2008).

Copenhagen is one of the easiest places in the world to start up a firm as Denmark has very simple licence application procedures and an import–export business can be set up in just a few days. Start-up requires a week at most and does not entail particular costs. Business taxation is competitive from an international point of view. In terms of the cost of leasing an office, Copenhagen is one of the cheapest cities in Europe, costing a quarter of London prices (Cushman and Wakefield 2007) and it has one of the lowest empty office rates in Europe. However, income tax is still very high, which is certainly not an incentive for entrepreneurs (OECD 2009).

Economic diversification combined with a capacity to establish a wide range of international relations, also by virtue of the vivacity of its trade fair system, is a feature of Munich. Principal among its hard factors is certainly the Munich Mix, which has two main characteristics: on one hand, extreme production sector diversification; on the other, an economic policy that, whilst targeting tertiary and services sector development, has also protected more traditional industries so that new areas of business are tied to manufacturing with a close relationship between scientific research and production. For these reasons, Munich is not only a city of large multinational companies, but also a place where small- and large-scale entrepreneurship meet and mix. This diversification and mixture is a strength when compared to other cities. Moreover, in Munich there are strong bonds between public, private and third sector players that contribute to creating an 'institutional thickness' (Amin and Thrift 2001) that has produced a clear sense of common purpose, and in the long term, focused policy interventions. 'The key elements are strong institutions, high levels of interaction. At the time of the crisis Munich had all of these elements in place' (Colantonio *et al.* 2014, p. 136).

As regards the skilled labour force, Munich stands out from the other cities considered: in 2014 more than 28 per cent of those employed had a university qualification, and highly skilled workers made up almost 30 per cent of the city's labour force (City of Munich 2015). Not only are there advanced research centres, but the city provides support and facilities for creative economies in various other ways too, functioning as a cluster of clusters. Technological know-how, outstanding education provision and high levels of human capital have made it Germany's leading technology city, rated first in Europe for specialist knowledge. The metropolitan area alone produces 10–15 per cent of Germany's patents, and is home to 13 higher education establishments. As a result, its performance on innovation and human capital benchmarks is outstanding. In 2014, it ranked as the seventh best performing European city on A. T. Kearney's 'human capital' benchmark and seventh globally for innovation (Clark and Moonen 2015). But Munich is in need of more technicians: forecasts show a growing gap between highly skilled workforce supply and business demand, which will peak in 2030 (IHK *Fachkräftemonitor* 2013).

The city has also been able to promote soft factors: Munich is constantly presented as 'green, compact and sustainable'. Environmental aspects have been among the main focuses of local government action. In 2007 *Monocle* magazine ranked Munich as the most liveable city on the planet (Department of Labour 2007). And Munich has remained top ranking, winning first place in 2010 too (*Monocle* 2011). In 2013/2014/2015 Munich won fourth place in the global *Mercer's Quality of Living* index (Mercer 2015).

In Manchester the question of hard and soft factors is posed in different terms. Whilst strategically well positioned and extremely buoyant in banking and financial terms, Manchester has still to erase its traditional polluted image. The quality of life in Manchester is still rather poor today, with high levels of water and air pollution due both to the persistence of traditional industrial activities and to extreme traffic congestion. The city government has adopted strategies to remedy this situation and restore the urban environment to health under the aegis of the 'Manchester green city' slogan, targeting emission reductions, expansion of the city's underground railway network, waste recycling and green space creation.

The city also has skilled labour force shortcomings. On one hand, it has a relatively large number of skilled workers, given that around 47 per cent of the population have upper-secondary school diplomas or degrees, while on the other, a large percentage (around 20 per cent) of the population is low-skilled. Almost 18 per cent of firms, in fact, complain of a lack of skilled personnel, especially in engineering, life sciences and new technologies.

One of Lyon's principal 'hard' attractiveness factors is its spatial specialisation: businesses choose to locate to zones where other firms and research centres operating in the same sector are already present. The total amount of available space currently stands at around 950,000 m^2, an enormous surface area, with few equals in Europe. Prominent among its 'soft' factors is culture, which contributes notably to the city's attractiveness, with its numerous associations, a rich array of museums and a lively local culture tradition. In this field, too, Lyon has concentrated its efforts on encouraging specificity and originality, supporting initiatives that are not simply replicas of similar ones by more important cities but instead contributing to strengthening local identity. Another factor is the cost of living in Lyon, which is much lower than in other European cities. A drawback, however, is the city's environmental profile – air quality is poor and traffic is extremely congested. It is difficult to get into Lyon in the morning because its main access routes are almost entirely gridlocked. The intention is to tackle the city's traffic congestion with high-speed railway links. Finally, as far as Lyon's labour force is concerned, the number of skilled workers rose significantly between 1999 and 2006 and now accounts for more than 40 per cent of the population, with 25 per cent having degrees or equivalents and 15 per cent upper-secondary diplomas.

In Milan, the regional government has acted to support business competitiveness in seven spheres: innovation, internationalisation, urban and environmental improvement, governmental modernisation, artisan and micro-firm schemes, and Lombard market and infrastructure promotion. Overall, €295 million were pumped in between 2006 and 2009. The funds were also used to foster micro firm clustering, to simplify bureaucratic procedures and, especially, to develop artisan firm and micro firm networks of excellence. Moreover, the city is looking extremely 'stable' for potential investors and economically interesting in terms of objective indicators like labour productivity and GDP per capita. However, Milan suffers from a number of decidedly negative features that extend beyond its non-linear political-administrative system and a sometimes oppressive bureaucracy. Firms are also hampered by the real estate market's scant ability to offer suitable locations for new offices amid rather high prices per square metre. Owing to these two factors, Milan ranks twenty-third and twenty-fourth respectively in terms of the attractiveness of the city for new locations of business among 33 cities (Cushman and Wakefield 2007). As regards labour force skills, almost 45 per cent of Milan's population has a degree or an upper-secondary diploma and 28 per cent of the employed are graduates (ISTAT 2001). It is, however, in relation to soft factors, and an assessment of the city's overall liveability, that Milan has lost ground in recent years. It invariably ranks low for air quality and fifteenth of 25 areas analysed for liveability. Hence, despite Milan's business vocation it is still unable to construct and transmit a positive city image. Milan has been consistently outperforming the national economy since the crisis began. Despite the general Italian situation, financial and business services employment grew by 1.5 per cent per annum from 2010 to 2014. But office supply remains a problem with a general lack of flexible, modern spaces (Cushman and Wakefield 2015). Expo 2015 certainly attempted to launch a new international image of the city, and the current government has obtained some positive results in reducing urban traffic, but the need to activate policies providing the preconditions for increasing territorial attractiveness remains.

This analysis therefore makes it clear that soft factors perform an important role and are becoming a decisive component in city government attractiveness strategies. Consequently, cities boasting outstanding architecture, a vibrant cultural life, house-hunting services and environmental quality are working to improve these still further. Munich, Lyon and Barcelona have different combinations of these factors, with policymakers who are aware of them and striving to enhance them. One of the qualities that makes Copenhagen such a strong location for shared services centres, for example, is high German and English fluency rates. In 2012 the city ranked very high (first place) for worker motivation (IMD 2012). For the other cities – Milan and Manchester – that are particularly disadvantaged in this regard, this combination of factors is an example to emulate and a road to follow.

3.5 Highly skilled workers: presence and demand

Cities compete to attract highly skilled labour. Because the large metropolises absorb the bulk of such labour, competition among medium-sized cities is intensifying. But in order to be competitive, medium-sized cities must 'sell' themselves as effectively as they can. To this end, they develop marketing strategies aimed at promoting themselves as centres of innovation able to attract highly skilled labour by offering not only good pay prospects but also better life, work and research conditions. Cities can no longer take their qualities for granted, but must actively advertise their positive features, 'positioning themselves on the market' in such a way as to be recognised as such – or, indeed, in certain cases, partly 're-inventing themselves'. A further important factor is the presence of foreign students, which is significant not only because they may stay in the city when they have completed their studies, but also because they constitute an important predictor of future skilled migrant inflows.

City attractiveness is therefore closely bound up with the presence of skilled and highly-skilled staff. If we examine the cities considered here, it is evident that Lyon has the largest share of university graduates, followed closely by Munich. Lyon's good performance is boosted by the presence in its urban region of around 500 public laboratories employing almost 10,000 researchers. In the *Grand Lyon* area there are 126,000 students, of whom around 10 per cent come from foreign countries.

Copenhagen's university system does not seem to particularly attract students from abroad: 6 per cent of its university students are foreign as compared with an OECD average of 6.7 per cent. Nor is the percentage of foreign researchers high – 7 per cent as against an OECD average of 16.5 per cent – and growth is sluggish (OECD 2008). In general, Copenhagen's attractiveness to highly skilled workers is low: the majority of immigrants are refugees or people who have come to the city to join their families. The explanations put forward for this phenomenon include the city's small number of international firms, limited opportunities for career advancement and professional development, together with a certain cultural closedness. The Danish business system seems to be a 'small world' based on personal bonds and characterised by a limited number of internationally-oriented firms (Sinani *et al.* 2008).

The persistent problem of Milan's universities seems to be their scant capacity to attract foreign students. In effect, as far as foreign students and researchers are concerned, Milan is very different from other European cities except in the cutting-edge sectors of fashion and design, which are the only sectors in which the Milanese production and services system is of central importance globally. In some sectors, such as design and fashion, Milan is still quite attractive and, for professionals working in these sectors, moving to Milan is motivated by the city's international image and the availability of international graduate and postgraduate courses. The decision to stay on is then in part related to the great job opportunities available (ACRE Reports 2009). Finally, there are fewer foreign students in Milan than in the other cities considered. In order to attract foreign students, a more liveable city is one of Milan's local government, university and production system priorities.

Manchester finds it difficult to attract highly skilled workers too. On one hand, an excellent university system has furnished critical support for innovation in key sectors of the economy and research and attracts highly skilled workers, having transformed Manchester into an extremely vibrant city in terms of opportunities for training and professional development. It is young people from ethnic minority groups who have contributed to this dynamism and also given new demographic impetus to the city. On the other hand, however, a number of limitations, largely due to the difficulty of achieving homogeneous growth of the population's skill levels, does exist. These are especially low in the inner city where there are districts in which 37 per cent of the population have no qualifications and only 13 per cent have upper-secondary diplomas or degrees. It is as if Manchester's university and research system has remained an enclave that is struggling to exert any significant effect on the city as a whole.

Munich offers a wide variety of highly skilled and well-paid jobs as well as a good quality of life and ample leisure facilities. There are numerous foreign students in the city, amounting to around 10 per cent of its 90,000-strong university population, and there has been a constant inflow of highly skilled foreign workers into the city in recent years. This is also because Germany has long lacked adequate numbers of new technology professionals. To solve this problem, the government has decided to grant work permits to non-EU nationals through a green card programme. But doubts have been raised as to educational and professional qualifications, which are evaluated according to rather restrictive criteria. In short, on one hand Munich attracts, or would like to attract, highly skilled foreigners, on the other, it does not take adequate steps to stabilise their presence in the city. There is a large number of foreign students in Munich but they have great difficulties in finding accommodation because of the high rents charged.

Although Barcelona has a large highly skilled foreign worker population – the majority (80 per cent) concentrated in the city centre – it still has problems as regards the functioning of the university and its internationalisation (Pareja-Eastaway *et al.* 2008). Precise data on the presence of highly skilled workers in Barcelona is not available, but it is known for certain that in some sectors – particularly the creative, architecture and design sectors – these constitute a large and growing component of the workforce and that some firms complain about a relative shortage of them. Surprisingly, in the Poblenou 'technological' district, demand for high-skilled workers is at present less than was foreseen, which is perhaps indicative of the fact that 'old activities' are giving way to 'new ones' more slowly than was expected (Viladecans and Arauzo 2008).

To sum up, the main problem for the cities considered here is the ability to attract groups of highly skilled experts and young educated talents moving to cities offering a good balance of low entry barriers and opportunities for start-ups (for example Munich and Barcelona). They are mobilised by a wider range of factors than simply good employment or leisure amenities, 'encompassing intangibles such as social and cultural vibrancy, safety and tolerance and good public services' (Servillo *et al.* 2012). The high costs of housing and other premises may also have a particular impact on the creative sector, where the incomes generated are not high – and this represents in some sense a similar problem to those of Milan and Munich where rents are high.

3.6 Conclusions

Contrary to theories envisaging a 'global order' structured according to a specific urban hierarchy in which each city occupies the place assigned to it in a rigid international division of labour (Feagin and Smith 1998), what has emerged from this comparative analysis is a picture that very much resembles a global network of cities self-organised in a multifunctional manner in which roles are being constantly redefined (Taylor 2004).

In this general framework the role played by city administrations remains unclear: in some cases they seem to have scant capacity to intervene in a shifting context of this kind; in others they seem to act in a very effective and successful way. There is no doubt that urban policies are moving increasingly towards strategic action to position cities within a 'global market' and highlight their distinctiveness, but it is difficult to adjust entire social and territorial systems at the speed at which the demands of globalisation are changing. Whilst firms have no alternative but to react as rapidly as possible to the changed conditions of international competition, the constant reorganisation of production clusters and networks requires city governments to make mammoth efforts to muster the resources and powers necessary to keep pace with change. The mix of activities in cities is difficult to steer politically but cities are not powerless in the face of globalisation. Moreover, powers and resources vary from city to city, as we have seen in the cases of Lyon and Copenhagen and to a considerable extent also in Munich (and negatively in the case of Milan where the absence or inefficiency of the central state has limited the city's growth potential), and many of the bureaucratic-governmental skills and economic resources necessary to maintain attractiveness remain in the hands of the state.

What cities can undoubtedly do is to create conditions that are more conducive to future economic development by capitalising on their cultural and social assets so that they can respond promptly to changes and make the best of their opportunities. Crucially, basing the attractiveness of localities on clusters that are characterised by accumulated knowledge provides an alternative to seeking to attract FDI through cheap labour or other short-term incentives (Pitelis *et al.* 2006, p. 8). At the global level, cities have created favourable conditions for overall business development by lowering financial and macroeconomic risks, reducing start-up costs and improving the quality of human capital resources (see Munich and Lyon). At a regional level, they can strengthen local cluster competitivity by encouraging complementary players on the same territory to work to common objectives and specific projects (see Munich, Lyon, Manchester and Barcelona). At a local level, cities can ensure the best material and financial conditions for the realization of functional projects (infrastructures, offices, spaces, qualifying land supply), facilitate administrative procedures (tax cuts, support for labour training) or take advantage of specific characteristics. Moreover, growing partnerships have been encouraged with non-administrative stakeholders: companies, associations, universities, citizens and unions.

This research has also highlighted problematic aspects that do not directly relate to the capacity to attract large scale investment. In nearly all the cities considered, the increasing importance of the knowledge economy has altered the regional development and specialisation of spatial functions. Its impact has frequently outweighed the effects of official development policies and governance systems. If one considers the growth of the knowledge economies in terms of value production, it is evident that they follow a functional and spatial logic of connection that is not always easy to interpret. But this is a logic that, despite dispersion processes, is frequently still tied to specific centrality criteria. Munich and Barcelona, for example, exhibit accelerated concentration of advanced knowledge functions in the core city. In other cities, like Milan and Manchester, the dialectic between monocentrism and polycentrism appears more complex and the *Grand Lyon* agglomeration is a still more dispersed model.

In any case, all the case studies have shown the crucial role of strategic spatial planning. There is, in fact, relative consensus on the need for a level of government that reflects the de facto city rather than the *de jure* city. Strategic planning and the delivery of public policies on economic development, the labour market, mobility and transport, housing, education, water, energy, waste and immigration cannot be addressed at too local a level (European Commission 2011). This means that new governance systems must be introduced to address the problems of urban mega-regions whose proper functioning requires not only less centralised planning but also the granting of a greater voice to neighbouring cities, given that these belong to interrelated and increasingly complex economic and spatial systems – as is very well evidenced by the trend of flows to Barcelona, Munich, Copenhagen and, to some extent, Milan. A good example is Manchester, where ten local authorities have worked together to establish a new tier of statutory authority, the Greater Manchester Combined Authority (GMCA), which is an administrative city-region level structure and the first of its kind in the United Kingdom (ESPON TANGO 2013) and a similar transformation will soon take place in Lyon, with the formalisation of the pre-existing *Communauté Urbaine de Lyon* and the creation of 'La Métropole de Lyon' endowed with decisional powers and considerable fiscal autonomy.

In Munich, city government has been considerably assisted in its practical action by an innovative instrument – *Perspektive Muenchen* – which has become the model to imitate for numerous German cities. Introduced in 1998, this innovative concept of urban development is based on the participatory planning paradigm but changes its methodology and radically extends its horizons. As an extremely elastic and open form of strategic planning it does not furnish detailed recommendations on objectives, quantities or measures. The guidelines set out models, forecasts and scenarios as well as general principles. At a lower level, the guidelines consist in action programmes allocated budgets and set out in detail. Concepts and action programmes are drawn up with the close participation of various professional sectors, associations, firms, and of course the public, and then adopted after discussion by the city council (Reiss-Schmidt 2006). However, in Munich the governance of the mega-city-region is still an unresolved issue.

In Milan, a metropolis that has continued to extend its boundaries featuring

> a basic absence of control over urban development, the recently introduced *Città Metropolitane* law does not seem to introduce substantial changes to the way the area is organised, which is still based on a traditional municipal approach paving the way for strong conflicts between the core city and the centres located in the urban region.
>
> (Gibelli 2015)

The position of Barcelona is original in many respects, given that the city government has invested in a 'colloquial' system whereby Barcelona's leading players meet to evaluate the city's strengths and weaknesses in a debate with the representatives of its surrounding areas. In 2010 AMB (*Area Metropolitana Barcelona*) was created to improve public service provision in the Barcelona metropolitan area through citizen involvement and participation and by means of dialogue with economic and social players. The metropolitan government also supports the management of the town councils that make it up. This participatory process facilitates the coordination of various interventions and is characterised by a high level of consensus, and it is of great importance for the city, which economically depends on its urban region (Degan and Garcia 2012).

Copenhagen is certainly the case study with the most complex governance problems, which are crucial to its internationalisation and attractiveness represented by the cross-border area of Øresund. Within this cross-border metropolitan region, Copenhagen and Malmoe could potentially cooperate on issues such as transport and regional planning, economic development, tourism, culture, research, education and employment. In the future Copenhagen and Malmoe should interact more, exchange experiences and learn from each other, forming a sort of twin-system. The Øresund Region is a technology hub with excellent innovation potential, world-class scientific infrastructure and a positive environment for start-ups. But this innovative and ambitious project continues to present real barriers to effective integration: bureaucracy, tax and policy obstacles continue to impede cross-border mobility (Nauwelaers *et al.* 2013). In 2007, the institutional structure of the bi-lateral Øresund Committee (Danish–Swedish) was strengthened, in parallel with an increased focus on policy formulation. This resulted in a strategic vision for Øresund in 2008 that will lead on to a common development strategy in the coming years (OECD 2009). In this case, too, the building of a new institutional capital evidently requires time for vertical and horizontal relationships (mutual trust, institutional settings), to develop, as well as the involvement of citizens and the private sector.

Common aspects have emerged from the analysis of city governments as have considerable differences in policies and forms of intervention resulting in different path-dependent developmental 'logics'. The various attractiveness strategies have some elements in common: strong service and infrastructure components, pleasant environments, high skill levels, real public policy efficacy. Beyond these aspects Munich stands out as a good example of successful versatility. The 'Munich Model', in fact, is a winning formula with its combination of local and global, large and small firms and an extremely close and functional relationship between manufacturing and services. In Munich, there are deep bonds between public, private and third sector players, an 'institutional thickness' (Amin and Thrift 2001) which has produced a clear sense of common purpose and long term, focused policy interventions. Lyon has also sought to reconcile internationalisation with local identity. There is no trace of Barcelona's gigantism here but rather, in cultural terms, a careful search for local characteristics, which are evident, for example, in the Confluence project. Lyon today is a strong 'provincial' city-region with high productive base diversification. These various features are linked to a decentralisation policy, which has fostered a more general territorial equilibrium preventing the creation of marginalised zones in a way that recalls Munich's localisation policies, albeit on a smaller scale. It is a choice that has yielded positive results in terms both of attractiveness and economic-territorial balances.

Effective urban management capability is crucial for the emergence of new projects, as is shown, in particular, by Munich and Lyon. But the growth of attractiveness requires progressive adaptation efforts, long-term strategies and citizen involvement in the transformation of the institutional framework. The importance of the time factor should also be stressed. Munich and Lyon's attractiveness strategies were launched in the mid-1980s and showed some tangible results in the late 1990s and especially in the 2000s. There is inevitably a time-lag between action and results, and this requires a long term perspective. In both cases past industrial history has played an important role: in Lyon several contemporary specialisations are closely linked to its precocious industrialisation (Pinson *et al.* 2010). In Munich, the aerospace sector was built on the basis of the expertise of the pre-existing Bayerische Motoren Werke (BMW) and Siemens, and the biotechnologies sector grew out of the experience of the Bayer Konzern. History counts, and not only in a positive way, as the case of Manchester shows: a heritage of obsolete forms of production can represent an obstacle, conditioning whole areas or requiring radical and expensive intervention as in Barcelona's historic Poblenou industrial district.

Sometimes the attractiveness process can be problematic right from the outset, as in the case of Manchester, where the process suffered initial difficulties and developed perhaps too quickly and in a non-homogeneous way. Despite its local government's outstanding ability to project the city's image internationally – as evidenced by a high level of connectivity – Manchester has undergone a certain physical concentration of its most important activities. This is due, on one hand, to development outstripping spatial planning, and, on the other, to international banks and insurance companies locating in the central zones of the city and its residential districts. It is worth recalling that the city's revival was due in large part to a small association formed by corporate chief executives whose primary purpose was to link leaders of the business community and government officials without having to go through electoral politics or legislative review. These executives autonomously designed a strategy involving recruiting transnational firms to Manchester (Hodos quoted in Abrahamson 2004). Many problems have been solved thanks to the Greater Manchester City Region's ability to maintain a governance stratum at city-region level and this is perhaps the strongest indication of the capacity of a city to adapt and innovate in the face of changing circumstances – locally, nationally and internationally. As has been noted: 'At the heart of Manchester's most recent moves towards more robust and autonomous city-regional governance has been a process of internal capacity development, reform of governance arrangements, and ongoing negotiation with central Government' (Harding and Rees 2013, p. 34).

Copenhagen, where the city's past public policies have been strongly conditioned by an attempt to act as the 'locomotive' of the national economy, is a very different matter (Bayliss 2007). In many respects, economic growth has become the main goal of urban policies and this explains the proliferation of infrastructural projects. The government believes that these projects will act as global landmarks effectively signalling Copenhagen's presence on the new global economic map and thereby reducing the disadvantages arising from the city's rather unfortunate geographical location (Desfor and Jorgensen 2004).

Milan is still waiting to discover new attractiveness. There are evident shortcomings in the Milan city government's management of flows and transport, liveability, and attractiveness to foreign students and highly skilled workers. Despite the efforts made, the past decade has seen a deceleration of Milan's internationalisation at various levels due to loss of competitivity by some manufacturing sectors, a failure to keep pace with technological change and the preference given to the demand for low skilled labour. The interweaving of administrative levels makes identifying responsibilities complex. Whilst in some spheres the city could objectively do more – for example, by upgrading the airport and improving connections with it – there are others that depend on other administrative levels and the central state. From this point of view, Expo 2015 was an opportunity for the city to reacquire overall competitivity, renew its infrastructure, improve the quality of life and the environment and recover international prestige.

In all the cities considered, there are possible dangers tied to the politics of attractiveness, a sort of 'heterogenesis of ends' in the Weberian sense. Some territories that were extremely attractive in the period up to 2007 (such as Barcelona) have become 'fragile' in the current crisis – it appears that they may have been overexposed and that their attractiveness was based on flows that were not embedded in the local context (ESPON and University Rovira i Virgili 2013).

In the case of Barcelona, the danger is that the city will fall back on one of its points of excellence – principally good quality of life – to the detriment of closer metropolitan scale integration (Degen and Garcia 2012). This is also because Barcelona – which is very compact and surrounded by mountains – has no further space for expansion, and one of the city's problems is its capacity to absorb the large inflows, due precisely to its increased international attractiveness, smoothly. There has perhaps been excessive exposure to the outside, an insistence on internationalisation at all costs without adequate assessment of its social impact (Delgado 2007). Another of Barcelona's unsolved problems at present seems to be its future capacity to transform the 'knowledge city' paradigm into something more than a branding campaign, however effective. Even in Munich, the successful city 'model', there is a flip side of the coin: Munich is 'just too good' (Van den Berg and Russo 2004). The city's enormous attractiveness has generated a situation in which lower-income groups cannot afford to pay its high rent and real estate prices (Thierstein *et al.*, this volume). But the *Clusterinitiativepolitik* season also seems to have reached 'a turning point'. In part this reflects a genuine desire to shift the focus onto helping maturing clusters to develop further; it also reflects the fact that funds from share sales have been exhausted, necessitating a shift towards lower-key project support, dialogue and mobilising private resources (von Streit *et al.* 2010).

For Copenhagen the problem seems not simply to be governance of the Øresund cross border area but also efforts to portray the city as a post-industrial, knowledge-based economy. Despite such efforts and the capital invested in them, results to date have been modest owing to a lack of true business culture in the city and a certain closedness, which is typical of a capital with marked provincial features (Andersen and Ploger 2009).

In Lyon, the ambitious urban *La Confluence* project has been criticised for its rising costs, the presence of Archistars and aspects of real estate speculation, but the main problem seems to be its real impact on job opportunities and the city's economic life (Canol 2015). Expo 2015 in Milan presented similar problems. Although the Expo concluded positively from the point of view of visitor numbers and international appeal, the main challenge remains how to assure attractiveness now that it is over and its local economic impact.

More generally speaking, it can be noted that the difficult task faced by city governments is combining a series of factors to ensure that cities are attractive locations for investors without social aspects being neglected. While a more attractive urban environment can more easily capture the attention of several groups of investors and consumers, it has turned out to be equally true that an increase in attractiveness can, at times, have unexpected social and economic consequences. To counter such phenomena the strategies and action taken to achieve attractiveness advantages should be developed from the starting point of the geographical, cultural, economic and social structures of a given territory (ESPON and University Rovira i Virgili 2013).

References and further reading

Abrahamson, M. (2004). *Global Cities*. New York: Oxford University Press.

ACI (Airport Councils International) (2013). *Airport World Development News*. Montréal: ACI Aero.

ACI (Airport Councils International) (2015). *2014 World Airport Traffic Report*. Montréal: ACI Aero.

ACRE Reports (2009). *International Milan? A Global City in a Country Lagging Behind: the View of Transnational Migrants*. Amsterdam: University of Amsterdam.

Aéroport Saint-Exupéry de Lyon (2014). *Statistiques de traffic*. Lyon.

Agentur für Arbeit (2007). *Arbeitsmarktreport*. Berichtsmonat Oktober, München.

Agenzia per la Mobilità e l'Ambiente Comune di Milano (2009). *Monitoraggio Ecopass Gennaio-Dicembre 2008*. Milan.

Ajuntament de Barcelona/22@bcn (2010). *22@Barcelona: 10 anys de creixement econòmic*, Ajuntament de Barcelona, Barcelona.

Amin, A. and Thrift, N. (2001). *Living In the Global: Globalization, Institutions, and Regional Development in Europe*. Oxford: Oxford University Press.

Andersen, J. and Ploger, J. (2009). *The Janus Face of Urban Governance in Denmark*. Paper Crises. Online, available at: www.crises.uqam.ca.

Andersson, A., Andersson, D. and Holmberg, I. (2010). *Öresunds-Regionens framtid: En ungdomsgenerations värderingar*. Malmoe: Sydsvenska Industri- och Handelskammaren.

Atkinson, R., Russo, A. and Servillo, L. (2013). Attractiveness in the EU Policy Debate and a Research Field for Territorial Cohesion. In: *The Attractiveness of European Regions and Cities for Residents and Visitors*. ESPON Reports, pp. 1–16.

Balducci, A., Fedeli, V. and Pasqui, G. (2011). *Strategic Planning for Urban Regions: City of Cities: a Project for Milan*. London: Ashgate.

Barcelona City Council – Municipal Council of Environment and Sustainability (2013). *Indicators 21*. Barcelona, December 2013.

Bayerisches Staatsministerium für Wirtschaft, Infrastruktur, Verkehr und Technologie (2008). *Cluster-Offensive Bayern: Im Netzwerk zum Erfolg*. Muenchen.

Bayliss, D. (2007). The Rise of the Creative City: Culture and Creativity in Copenhagen. *European Planning Studies*, 15(7).

Borja, J. (2010). *Luces y sombras del urbanismo de Barcelona*. Barcelona: Editorial de la Universitat Oberta de Catalunya (UOC).

Buch, T., Hamann, S., Niebuhr, A. and Rossen, A. (2014). *How to Woo the Smart Ones? Evaluating the Determinants that Particularly Attract Highly Qualified People to Cities*. HWWI Research Papers, Hamburg Institute of International Economics.

CANOL (2015). *Dossier Musée des Confluences*. Online, available at: www.canol.fr/le-musee-des-confluences.html.

Centre for Cities (2015). *Cities Outlook 2015*. London: Centre for Cities.

City of Munich, Department of Labour and Economic Development (2015). *Munich as a Business Location: Facts and Figures 2015*. Muenchen.

Clark, G. and Moonen, T. (2014). *Munich: A Globally Fluent Metropolitan Economy: A Case Study for the Global Cities Initiative*. Joint Project of Brookings and J. P. Morgan Chase.

Colantonio, A., Burdett, R. and Rode, P. (2014). *Transforming Urban Economies: Policy Lessons from European and Asian Cities*. London: Routledge.

COMET (Competitive Metropolises Economic Transformation) (2007). *Barcelona Region: Spain's Gateway to Europe*. Vienna.

Cushman and Wakefield (2007). *European Cities Monitor 2007*. London.

Cushman and Wakefield (2015). *European Cities Monitor 2015*. London.

Degen, M. and Garcia, M. (eds) (2008). *La Metaciudad: Barcelona: Transformacion de una Metropolis*. Barcelona: Anthropos.

Degen, M. and Garcia, M. (2012). The Transformation of the Barcelona Model? An Analysis of Culture, Urban Regeneration and Governance. *International Journal of Urban and Regional Research*, 36(5): 1022–1038.

Delgado, M. (2007). *La ciudad mentirosa: Fraude y miseria del 'Modelo Barcelona'*. Barcelona: Los Libros de la Catarata.

Department of Labour and Economic Development, City of Munich (2006). *Munich Because*. Munich.

Desfor, G. and Jørgensen, J. (2004). Flexible Urban Governance: the Case of Copenhagen's Recent Waterfront Development. *European Planning Studies*, 12(4), 479–476.

Ernst and Young (2015). *Europe Attractiveness Survey*. London: Ernst & Young Publications.

ESPON and University Rovira i Virgili (2013). *ATTREG – The Attractiveness of Regions and Cities for Residents and Visitors: Final Report*. Luxembourg.

ESPON TANGO (Territorial Approaches for New Governance Applied Research) (2013). Annex 7: *Reinventing Regional Territorial Governance Greater Manchester Combined Authority*, June, Prepared by Paul Cowie, Simin Davoudi, Ali Madanipour and Geoff Vigar. Newcastle upon Tyne: Newcastle University.

European Commission (2011). *Cities of Tomorrow: Challenges, Visions, Ways Forward*, Directorate-General for Regional Policy, Luxembourg: Publications Office of the European Union.

European Union Regional Policy (2011). *Cities of Tomorrow: Challenges, Visions, Ways Forward*. Brussels.

Eurispes (2014). *Libro bianco sulla mobilità e i trasporti*. Rome: Eurispes.

FDI Monitor (2014). *Invest in Lombardy, Key Trends in Italy in 2013*. Milan: Chamber of Commerce.

Feagin, J. and Smith, M. P. (1998). Cities and the New International Division of Labour. In: Feagin, J. (ed.). *The New Urban Paradigm, Critical Perspectives on the City*, Lanham/Oxford: Rowman & Littlefield.

Flughafen Muenchen Statistik (2015). *Daten zum Luftverkehr*. Online, available at: www.munich-airport.de/de/company/facts/verkehr/index.jsp.

FOCI (Future Orientations for Cities) (2013). *Final Scientific Report: Version 15/12/2010*, Luxembourg: ESPON.

Gibelli, M. C. (2015). Urban Crisis or Urban Decay? Italian Cities Facing the Effects of a Long Wave towards Privatization of Urban Policies and Planning. In: Eckardt, F. and Sanchez, J. V. (eds). *City of Crisis: the Multiple Contestation of Southern European Cities*. Bielefeld: Transcript Verlag.

Graham, S. and Marvin, S. (2001). *Splintering Urbanism: Networked Infrastructures, Technological Mobilities and the Urban Condition*. London: Routledge.

Harding, A. and Rees, J. (2013). *Manchester Case Study*. CAEE the Case for Agglomeration Economies in Europe. Luxembourg: ESPON.

Harding, A., Harloe, M. and Rees, J. (2010). Manchester's Bust Regime. *International Journal of Urban and Regional Research*, 34(4), 981–991.

Hessler, M. (2007). *Die Kreative Stadt: Zur Neuerfindung eines Topos*. Bielefeld: Transcript Verlag.

Hodos, J. I. (2010). *Second Cities: Globalization and Local Politics in Manchester and Philadelphia*. Philadelphia: Temple University Press.

Hoogerbrugge, M. and Willems, K. (2012). *Economic Vitality of Munich*. The Hague: European Metropolitan Network Institute.

IHK (Industrie und Handelskammer fuer Muenchen und Oberbayern) (2012). *Der Aussenhandel Bayerns*. Landeshauptstadt Muenchen.

IHK (Industrie und Handelskammer fuer Muenchen und Oberbayern) (2013). *Fachkraefte Monitor*. Landeshauptstadt Muenchen.

Institute for Management Development (IMD) World Competitiveness Center (2012). *World Talent Report*. Lausanne, Switzerland.

ISTAT (2001). *Censimento 2001. L'Istruzione della popolazione*. Rome.

Kaiser, R. and Liecke, M. (2007). The Munich Feature Film Cluster: The Degree of Global Integration and Explanations for its Relative Success. *Industry and Innovation*, 14(4): 385–399.

Landeshauptstadt Muenchen Statistisches Amt (2015). *Open Data Flughafen Muenchen*. ZIMAS – Datenbank: Zentrales Informationsmanagement- und Analyse- system der Stadtverwaltung München.

McDonald, S. M. (2013). *Lyon 1990: A Historical Study of Urban Internationalization*. Saarbrucken: Scholars Press.

Magatti, M. (ed.) (2005). *Milano nodo della rete globale*. Milan: Bruno Mondadori.

Magatti, M. and Sapelli, G. (eds) (2012). *Progetto Milano: Idee e proposte per la città di domani*. Milan: Bruno Mondadori.

Manchester City Council (2008a). *A Profile of Manchester's Special Migrations Statistics*. Manchester.

Manchester City Council (2008b). *Manchester Economic Factsheet*. Manchester.

Manchester Partnership (2009a). *Manchester's State of the City: Report 2008/9*. Manchester: Manchester City Council.

Manchester Partnership (2009b). *Manchester's State of the Wards: Report 2008/9*. Manchester: Manchester City Council.

Marcuse, P. and van Kempen, R. (2000). *Globalising Cities: A New Spatial Order?* London: Blackwell.

Matznetter, R. and Musil, R. (eds) (2011). *Europa: Metropolen im Wandel*, pp. 274–294. Wien: Mandelbaum-Verlag.

Meliveo, J. (2014). *Tax Incentives and the Housing Bubble: The Spanish Case*. Madrid: Universidad Complutense de Madrid.

Mercer (2015). *Best Cities in the World*. Mercer Reports.

Monocle (2011). Online, available at: https://monocle.com/magazine/issues/45/the-liveable-cities-index-2011/.

Moretti, E. (2012). *The New Geography of Jobs*. Houghton Mifflin Harcourt.

Müller, W. and Sträter, D. (2011). Wer lenkt die Stadt? Wie die Neoliberalisierung der Stadt die kommunale Selbstverwaltung aushebelt. In: Belina, B., Gestring, N., Müller, W. and Sträter, D. (eds). *Urbane Differenzen: Disparitäten innerhalb und zwischen Städten*. pp. 132–162. Münster: Westfälisches Dampfboot.

Musterd, S. and Murie, A. (eds) (2011). *Making Competitive Cities*. London: Wiley-Blackwell.

Nauwelaers, C., Maguire, K. and Ajmone Marsan, G. (2013). *The Case of Oresund (Denmark-Sweden) – Regions and Innovation: Collaborating Across Borders*. OECD Regional Development Working Papers, 2013/21. Paris: OECD Publishing.

Oakey, R. (2007). *Problems with Regional Development Planning: the Case of Clustering*. Manchester: Manchester Business School.

OECD (2005). International Symposium 'Enhancing City Attractiveness for the Future', 2–3 June. Japan: Nagoya Congress Centre.

OECD (2006). *Milan, Italy*. OECD Territorial Reviews. Paris: OECD Publishing.

OECD (2009). *Copenhagen, Denmark*. OECD Territorial Reviews. Paris: OECD Publishing.

OIIP (2009). *Konkurrierende Metropolen*. Wien: Oesterreichisches Institut fuer Internationale Politik.

Onida F. (ed.) (2007). *Le Multinazionali Estere in Lombardia e in Italia: Opportunità, tendenze e prospettive*. Milan: Egea.

OTI, Osservatorio territoriale infrastrutture Nord-Ovest (2015). *Rapporto 2014*, Milan.

Oxford Economics (2015). *Greater Manchester Forecasting Model*, Manchester: Manchester City Council.

Pareja-Eastaway, M., Turmo Garuz, J., García Ferrando, L., Pradel, M., Miquel, I. and Simó Solsona, M. (eds) (2008). *Why in Barcelona? Understanding the Attractiveness of the Region for Creative Knowledge Workers*. ACRE Report WP5.2. Amsterdam: ACRE.

Perspektive Muenchen (2006). *Verkehrsentwicklungsplan*. Landeshauptstadt Muenchen.

Pinson, G., Maitrallet, L. and Morel-Journel, C. (2010). *Lyon Case Study*, ESPON CAEE. Luxembourg: Manchester Seminar Reports.

Pitelis, C., Sugden, R. and Wilson, J. R. (2006). *Clusters and Globalisation: the Development of Urban and Regional Economies*. Northampton, MA: Elgar.

Poelhekke, S. and van der Ploegg, F. (2009). Foreign Direct Investments and Urban Concentration: Unbundling Spatial Lags. *Journal of Regional Science*, 49(4): 749–775.

Referat für Arbeit und Wirtschaft (2008a). *IuK und Medienstandort Muenchen 2007*. Landeshauptstadt München.

Referat für Arbeit und Wirtschaft (2008b). *Wirtschaftsbericht München 2007–8*. Landeshauptstadt München.

Referat für Arbeit und Wirtschaft (2009). *Der Wirtschaftsstandort München*. Landeshauptstadt München.

Reiss-Schmidt, S. (2006). Urban Development Management as a Quality Assurance Tool. *Deutsche Zeitschrift fuer Kommunalwissenschaften*, 45(1).

Reiss-Schmidt, S. (2007). Wachstum nach Innen – das Beispiel München. In: *Stadtgespräche*, pp. 45–54. Zürich: Institut für Raum und Landschaftsentwicklung, ETH.

Servillo, L., Atkinson, R. and Russo, A. (2012). Territorial Attractiveness in EU Urban and Spatial Policy: a Critical Review and Future Research Agenda. *European Urban and Regional Studies*, 19(4): 349–365.

Sinani, E., Thomsen, S., Stafsudd, A., Edling, C. and Randøy, T. (2008). Corporate Governance in Scandinavia: Comparing Networks and Formal Institutions. *European Management Review*, 5(1): 27–40.

Sytral-Grand Lyon (2007). *Enquête ménages déplacements*. Lyon: CERTU.

Taylor, P. J. (2004). *World City Network: A Global Urban Analysis*. London: Routledge.

Taylor, P. J. and Aranya, R. (2007). A Global 'Urban Roller Coaster'? Connectivity Changes in the World City Network, 2000–04. *Regional Studies*, 42: 1–16.

Taylor, P. J., Evans, D. M., Hoyler, M., Derudder, B. and Pain, K. (2009). The UK Space Economy by Advanced Producer Service Firms: Identifying Two Distinctive Polycentric City-Regional Processes in Contemporary Britain. *International Journal of Urban and Regional Research*, 33(3), September: 700–718.

Van den Berg, L. and Russo, A. (2004). *The Student City: Strategic Planning for Student Communities in EU Cities*. Aldershot: Ashgate.

Von Streit, A., Rode, P., Nathan, M., Schwinger, P. and Kippenberg, G. (2010). *Munich Metropolitan Region: Staying Ahead on Innovation*. Paper presented at London School of Economics and Political Science.

Viladecans, E. and Arauzo, J. M. (2008). *Knowledge Spillovers and Firm Location: An Analysis of Barcelona's 22@ District*. Draft in publication.

Waiting for the Sun (2012). Numero speciale di *Infrastrutture e Trasporti*, 1(April).

World Association of Investment Promotion Agencies (WAIPA) (2009). *Annual Report 2008*. Online, available at: www.waipa.org.

World's Most Competitive Cities (2013). *A Global Investor's Perspective on True City Competitiveness.* New York: IBM Global Business Service.

Zeller, C. and Oßenbrügge, J. (2000). *The Biotech Region of Munich and the Spatial Organisation of its Innovation Networks: Technological Change and Regional Development in Europe.* L. Schätzl. Heidelberg: Springer Verlag.

4 The new social division of the urban space
Gentrification in times of economic crisis

Yvonne Franz and Rossana Torri

4.1 Introduction: moving beyond the crisis in the gentrification debate

Over the last 20 years there has been a lively discussion about the presence of major spatial organisation processes in many European cities. The debate has focused on forms of new social and spatial polarisations related to globalisation, deindustrialisation and the increasing inequalities caused by those processes. The leitmotif in many studies carried out about Europe is the identification of factors that have a "regulating" or "limiting" effect on the results of such changes in comparison to American cities (Musterd and Ostendorf 1998; Musterd 2005; Van Kempen and Murie 2009), such as the role of the states that traditionally support interventions (Burgers and Musterd 2002), and a number of distinctive features of the cities themselves (Le Galès 2002; Kazepov 2005). However, unravelling the effects of these factors has become increasingly complex as globalisation and localisation coexist (McCann 2008).

Taking the interplay between the two levels of global and local transformation processes into consideration, this chapter aims to detect the impact of these transformations on local neighbourhood changes by using the concept of gentrification as a key notion. In the current gentrification discourse, there is a common understanding of post-industrial transition as a driving force for transformations, having an impact both on the labour market and on the real estate market (Ley 1994; Hamnett 2003; Lees 2003; Butler and Lees 2006; Bridge 2007). Consequently, gentrification can no longer be considered an isolated process, but rather remains an effect based on interdependencies between macro-scale transitions (such as post-industrialisation or economic crises) and micro-scale changes (Franz 2015). In times of economic crisis and ongoing austerity, questions arise about how far cities still "act as a drag on the economy" (European Union 2013 in Dijkstra *et al.* 2015) and in what ways gentrification has been recently spurred on or impeded in European cities.

Since Ruth Glass (1964) invented the term "gentrification' the scientific debate has been long characterised by a sharp divide between "supply-siders" and "demand-siders" (Smith 1979; Zukin 1982; Hamnett and Randolph 1984, 1988; Lees 2003; Butler 2007). However, those two mechanisms do not contradict each other, and the processes analysed in this chapter show an entanglement of factors that are partly to be attributed to the demand and partly to the supply side (Redfern 2003). While academics continued operationalising the negative effects of gentrification, policymakers in different European contexts began to implement governed gentrification interventions to create socially mixed neighbourhoods. The so-called *state-led gentrification* aims to increase social mix in the segregated – mainly single class – urban districts (Larsen and Hansen 2008; Lees 2008; Watt 2009; Bricocoli and Cucca 2016). The question on local administrations and their power arises with regards to either the encouragement or discouragement of real estate investments by using their control over building permits, or by applying mechanisms in order to control rents or to protect the occupants at risk of being "pushed out" of their houses.

Following the need to overcome the limits of solely supply or demand-side explanation models and to actually deconstruct the complexities of gentrification processes (Ward 2010; McCann and Ward 2012; Lagendijk *et al.* 2014), this chapter responds to the need for more relational approaches in the context of urban research, and multi-layered approaches in gentrification analysis (Phillips 2004). There is a clear need for actor-centred approaches considering the relational connectivity and the emergence of spaces in transition that occur at overlaps between divergent lines of development, the so-called "trajectories" (Massey 2005; Healey 2007). This chapter is organised in three further sections. The first describes the conceptual categories applied to analyse the gentrification processes characterising the six European cities used as examples. The second focuses on the analysis of the cities' patterns. Finally, we present final considerations, emphasising the role of housing policies and the role of the public sector.

4.2 Setting up the framework

Beginning with considerable changes in the real estate sector, all cities included in this analysis have experienced remarkable increases in house prices over the last 25 years.[1] However, some important changes have occurred following the financial crisis. While in most cities real estate prices have continued to grow, Manchester and Barcelona (Table 4.1) show different patterns in the time period between 2004 and 2015. In order to explain such variations, Van der Heijden *et al.* (2011: 301) attempted to combine the economic crisis with the economics of Western European housing markets and showed that "the crisis had varying impacts on house prices and sales", for instance, in the Netherlands, Germany or United Kingdom. They apply the notion of dynamic and static housing systems to explain the differing effects and impact of the economic crisis. Dynamic housing systems, such as the Dutch and UK systems, add owner-occupied housing units built by commercial market players to the stock. Whereas in static housing systems, such as in Germany, private individuals are the primary builders of new residential properties (Van der Heijden *et al.* 2011). Although the link to gentrification has not been made in their analysis, the authors indicate a higher vulnerability of dynamic housing systems that depend on large transaction numbers and

Table 4.1 Average price (€/m²) dwellings on sale in cities (1991–2015)

	Munich	Copenhagen	Barcelona*	Manchester	Lyon	Milan**
1991	2,400		1,289			1,936
1996	2,200	848	1,291			1,715
2001	2,114	1,661	2,388	2,175	1,200	2,241
2004	2,500	2,770	3,672	3,137		2,715
2015***[2]	4,975	3,020	2,355	2,162	2,760	3,197

Source: Eurostat-Urban Audit, * Fiscal Studies Department – Municipality of Barcelona, ** OSMI-Real Estate Exchange, *** Numbeo.com.

continuous purchasing activity by first-time buyers. Static housing systems are less dependent on speculative development, but more on construction costs such as building and land costs. As a result, housing markets such as in the United Kingdom were more heavily impacted by the economic crisis than in Germany, where dwelling adaptations are favoured to new property purchases. This interpretation may help us to understand the most recent trajectories of the housing market in these cities.

In the framework of these changing housing markets, gentrification processes[3] have played an important role, although the local processes follow different mechanisms. In particular, we will highlight in the case study examples the various diverging mechanisms behind the obvious processes of real estate dynamics. The focus lies on three specific drivers fostering gentrification processes and a general decrease in affordable housing options:

1   The effects of urban renewal strategies on the housing market led by public authorities. Here, the area-based initiatives in Copenhagen (Agger 2015) or the soft urban renewal programme and the tax incentive system for real estate investment in Germany (Franz 2015) serve as examples.
2   The effects of the retrenchment of municipal/social housing stock starting with privatisation in United Kingdom in the 1980s and continuing for instance in Germany and the Netherlands in the early 1990s (Albers and Holm 2008; Kadi and Musterd 2014).
3   The effects of the most recent economic transitions on the socio-demographic profile of the population (see the outmigration processes of the unemployed younger generations in Italy or Spain). This includes restructuring processes due to (de-)localisation strategies and related changes in the local labour market (Rehfeld 2013; Vivant 2013).

We argue that the drivers are interrelated and played an important role in framing gentrification patterns in the cities we analyse. However, some predominant mechanisms are recognisable in each city. For instance, the active role of public authorities and policymakers to either support (see the reform of the cooperative housing in Copenhagen) or inhibit gentrification (see the Munich case with its socially equitable land-use approach), or, a decrease in social housing through various changes in the supply system. Finally, the transition of the economy, which – depending on the local context – had a huge positive (see Munich) or negative impact (see Barcelona) on the labour market.

4.3 Patterns of gentrification in European cities

4.3.1 Munich: professionalisation as driver of gentrification

Munich is well known for its socially equitable land-use approach on its way to becoming a knowledge-based and highly competitive polycentric city (Chapters 2 and 3 in this book; Evans and Karecha 2013; Mazzoleni and Pechmann 2016). At the same time, Munich has also gained unintentional popularity for its tight housing market in central locations enhancing gentrification processes through increasingly unaffordable housing options (Bayer *et al.* 2014), which have become even more apparent during economic crisis.

The economic transition is characterised by the relocation of many firms from the city centre of Munich to the first metropolitan belt. This has contributed to the development of rural districts (including for instance Dachau, Freising, Ebersberg, or Starnberg) based on a tax benefit for companies. Nevertheless, Munich has recently offered the highest concentration of highly qualified and prestigious jobs for the new service economy, and this has attracted both commuter flows and new residents, contributing to the population growth. The intensification of relationships between the city, the urban region and the rest of Bavaria, is mirrored by the increasing number of commuters to and from Munich. In 2011, 325,000 employees commuted to and 135,000 from Munich (München – Statistisches Amt 2012), utilising the very efficient modes of transport, especially the public transport system.

Munich is now presenting a "second demographic transition". The number of families has increased from 653,000 in 1987 to 742,000 in 2007, with 50 per cent of this population consisting of singles or new forms of cohabitation. In addition, Munich has one of the highest percentages of immigrant population in Germany, with a well-established Turkish community in Ludwigsvorstadt and the diverse neighbourhood of Sendling (Mazzoleni and Pechmann 2016). These demographic shifts stimulate new and diversified needs due to different lifestyles or specific stages of personal life, and have had a remarkable effect on housing demand. As a consequence of a strong increase in housing costs, many families with children and modest incomes have had to move out of the city centre. Although Munich has been traditionally a rental city (the share of owned houses is only 24 per cent) and real estate ownership in the inner city is still underdeveloped, private real estate investors have more recently been able to increase the number of high-end apartments on sale, catering to an economically well-off urban clientele. Therefore, a transformation process acknowledged as "revanchist city", "colonisation" or "super-gentrification" (Smith 1996; Butler and Robson 2003; Lees 2003) has taken place, carried out by professionals in the fields of communication, knowledge and new technologies. Examples in Munich refer to

Isarvorstadt/Ludwigsvorstadt, or Maxvorstadt, where rent prices have increased from 5.11 €/m² in 1987, to 12.60 €/m² in 2008 (Landeshauptstadt München 2009), urging families with children to move to areas outside the city centre. As a consequence, Munich ranks highest in terms of rent prices in Germany in 2015 (Statista no date).

In order to limit this trend, Munich began in 1994 already with a socially equitable land-use approach – "Sozialgerechte Bodennutzung"– aimed at sharing the costs of new housing developments with the investor (Landeshauptstadt München 2009). Joint property cooperatives are supported by the "München Modell", whereby one-third of the building plot is assigned to free market interventions, another third to cooperatives and the remaining third to rental social housing interventions. Cooperatives are also in charge of the sale of property being resold on the housing market, avoiding price increases with speculative roots, and thus contributing to a reduction in private housing prices. This planning instrument resulted in approximately 40,000 new housing units, including 10,000 subsidised units by 2014.[4]

To summarise, Munich's housing market has become polarised between prestigious and expensive housing choices (particularly for rent) and the persistence of rental houses (for instance in the northern parts of Munich such as Feldmoching-Hasenbergl) that are neither attractive nor renovated, but meet the strategies of immigrants as well as of the low-income population (Mazzoleni and Pechmann 2016). In a saturated spatial context such as Munich, the creation of new housing becomes increasingly difficult due to the limited availability of building plots and rising construction costs. As a result, the successful "competitiveness" of Munich's urban region and growing attractiveness might be challenged by growing socio-spatial inequalities. The gentrification processes taking place in Munich are likely to be regarded as one of the many effects of the professionalised middle class becoming a well-funded actor on the real estate market.

4.3.2 Barcelona: between professionalisation and touristification

Gentrification literature on Barcelona largely refers to notions of de-industrialisation, the creative class and *touristification* (Cóccla Gant 2013; Navarro Yáñez 2013) related to global events such as the Olympic Games in 1992. Over the last 20 years, the metropolitan region of Barcelona has attracted a diversified range of economic activities, partly resulting from production being relocated to more decentralised areas. This trend has been accompanied by major infrastructural improvements, allowing Barcelona to develop into a polycentric metropolitan area (Miralles-Guasch 2000; Mazzucato 2008) and build a strong international brand, including a high level of living quality (Parkinson 2013). Starting in the 1990s, jobs have been distributed in over 30 smaller urban centres, some of them neighbouring the city of Barcelona with others scattered outside the metropolitan area, and sometimes specialised in a specific economic sector. This phenomenon has also been the result of the real estate market trend affecting the city centre since the Olympics until the most recent real estate activities related to the 2004 Culture Forum, offering expensive newly built houses. Due to affordability constraints, many families have moved to the suburbs where house prices are lower or where they have converted their second properties into their principal residence.

Within this framework, gentrification has been mainly driven by two key processes. On the one side, the urban transformations triggered by the big events in 1992 and 2004, on the other side the increasing internationalisation of capital and people flows attracted over the same period. Both processes had a significant impact on Barcelona's real estate market, which turned to be strongly appreciated after the renewal and the building of new houses. Real estate property in Barcelona became internationalised through many Europeans purchasing their first and second houses in Barcelona, mainly in the refurbished buildings of the historic centre. Additionally, the specialised real estate activities in rentals of apartments for short periods showed quick and strong growth.

The selling price per square metre of new or refurbished houses in the district of Ciutat Vella – the historic centre – increased from $1,075 €/m^2$ in 1992 to $6,864 €/m^2$ in 2007, according to statistics supplied by the municipality. The appreciation of real estate assets, both for rent and for sale, was also the direct consequence of an urban policy aimed at enhancing the historic centre through the establishment of new top functions for tourism and cultural attractiveness.

The visible result is a hybrid situation. The central areas are still densely populated by the lower class groups (Spanish inhabitants and non-European Union immigrants), but are visited daily by high flows of tourists and "city users" (Martinotti 1993). Here, an overlap of different real estate segments can be found. On the one hand, processes of displacement of the traditional inhabitants by high-income persons can be identified. On the other hand, the creation of "islands" (individual apartment buildings, building blocks) can be seen, mainly amongst immigrants. They apply collective property strategies, overcrowding, indebtedness and subletting, and inhabit the less attractive housing stock in order to remain living in the city centre (Moser and Horn 2015; Palomera 2014 for the suburban area). On the other hand, another privatisation phenomenon is taking place: many central areas have been completely redesigned by the widespread presence of global commercial brands, historic buildings have been refurbished and turned into first class hotels or fashionable clubs, creating in this way a repetitive space meant for the consumption of such forms of entertainment. Such a process is defined as *urban branding* (Muñoz 2008). Some scholars have described the gentrification of Barcelona as "random" or "at a slow rhythm".[5] Perhaps others would define the case of Barcelona's historical centre as super-gentrification (Lees 2003; Butler and Lees 2006), emphasising that both tourists and Europeans renting or purchasing houses in this area are nowadays second-generation gentrifiers.

In contrast to all the other cities analysed in this chapter, Barcelona – as in the rest of Spain – has a tiny sector of social housing for rent.[6] In Spain, the definition of social housing indicates different forms of public economic support aiming at encouraging access to property for a consistent percentage of the population (Pareja-Eastaway and San Martin 1999). This could be the supporting factor for the negative impact of the transformation described so far, although still moderate or small scale. Among them, there is first of all the risk that, through the filter of the real estate market, the social mixture and the low segregation level still characterising the city in its more central areas leave room to a configuration of space that is more polarised between the city of flow and the city of places (Chapter 3 in this volume). This will create a number of sustainability problems for those mechanisms contributing to the global growth and positioning of Barcelona, by depositing at the same time, meaningful resources and opportunities for the residents. Moreover, through the transmission belt of the real estate market, even Barcelona risks being too difficult to reside in for those people greatly affected by the unstable labour market, the majority of whom are young people. In fact, the Province of Barcelona has experienced an increase in unemployment between 2007 and 2009 from 5.7 per cent to 17.2 per cent, peaking at 23.7 per cent in 2013 and dropping to 17.6 per cent in 2015 (Idescat 2016). The risk of unaffordable housing costs became even more probable due to the lack of public housing provision.

4.3.3 Milan: qualified economies, large-scale urban renewal projects beside real estate dynamics

In Milan, gentrification was mainly driven by trends in the housing market combined with large scale requalification projects in central areas of the city (Diappi and Bolchi 2013; Manzo 2012). In the last decades, Milan has been able to consolidate a strategic position in Europe, particularly in the sector of finance, marketing, product design and fashion (Chapter 2 in this volume). This high level of economic competitiveness has produced higher employment rates in the past than the country average. However, due to economic crisis and ongoing transition in the manufacturing sector, the unemployment rate has grown remarkably during the last decade, hitting low qualified workers hardest and accompanied by an alarming increase of youth unemployment (Carnevali *et al.* 2011; Fellini *et al.* 2011).

Between 1999 and 2008, the municipality of Milan lost 66,000 residents, who mainly moved to other municipalities in the province; new inhabitants mainly came from foreign countries. A double process was therefore in place: the city attracted new residents from distant areas (from 1999 to 2008 there were 150,000 new foreign residents who represented 16.4 per cent of the municipal population in 2010), especially due to employment opportunities; at the same time, the city lost part of its original population, particularly because of the difficult housing market conditions.

In contrast to Munich, Milan shows real estate property percentages that are remarkably high. Since 2000, housing shortages were faced by new housing construction, which catered mainly to a prestigious, high-end clientele instead of groups searching for affordable housing options (Bricocoli and Cucca 2016).

Activities in the rental and social housing market remained low in supporting Milan's position as the third most expensive housing market in Italy (after Rome and Venice) (Mugnano and Palvarini 2011).

Over the years, public interventions have, however, positively impacted the real estate sector through a number of interventions: redemption of state-owned real estate, contributions in the form of free grants for house purchasing purposes, tax relief and an amendment to the law on private rent (L. 431/98) that cancelled the "rent control" and liberalised rental fees. As a result, housing prices have continued to increase, in particular in the densely populated urban areas. The expansion cycle for the real estate market in Milan started at the end of the 1990s, after a decreasing cycle dating from 1993 to 1997. Such appreciation involved, on different levels, all city areas, from the centre to the outskirts. In some of them, prices increased by more than 20 per cent in a six-month period. Also, the crisis has not affected increasing housing costs in Milan in a significant way (Table 4.1). As a direct consequence of the amendment to the law, the property rental sector has also recorded a fast and pronounced price growth.

At the same time, Milan has undergone many large urban renewal projects, particularly aimed at converting former industrial areas and railway yards. These have been the PRUs (*Programmi di riqualificazione urbana*, i.e. urban renewal programmes), the large projects in "Garibaldi-Repubblica", the conversion of Porta Vittoria railway yard, the new residential districts in Santa Giulia, Citylife, the new fairground in Rho-Pero. The real estate markets in the surroundings of these converted areas have been influenced significantly, as the increase in property value in these projects was higher than the city average (OSMI 2007).

As consequence of such trends, Milan has been characterised by the spread of a soft gentrification process. This process has been concentrated in the intermediate areas where urbanisation started at the beginning of the twentieth century as a consequence of industrial growth: a "spreading process from the centre" that is selectively activated only in districts with specific morphologic features, such as easy accessibility, protection from urban flows, the presence of prestigious houses to be refurbished (Diappi 2009). Isola is one of the most investigated cases. Starting back in the early 1990s, this traditional working class district has become one of the most attractive areas in the city for fashion operators, designers, artists and show-business professionals. There was a quick flourishing of new activities linked to music entertainment, catering, cultural consumption or the art market, which perfectly integrated into the pre-existing economic fabric, characterised by a tight network of small businesses, traditional handicraft activities and the traditional Milan headquarters of some left-wing parties. Its attractiveness was also linked to the large availability of historic buildings with its "casa di ringhiera", an apartment block featuring a shared balcony for all apartments on the same storey.

The current processes can be understood as a widening of the gentrification action that started in Milan in the 1960s, following a double process. First, the erosion of the lower class residential functions due to the pressure of an emerging tertiary sector in search for central positions. Second, the appreciation of historic housing in order to satisfy upper class demand.[7] Currently, the propagating forces of the gentrification process are represented by the exponential growth of real estate values and by the professional development of the advanced tertiary sector, following a spill-over effect of the housing demand from neighbouring areas, as described by Hamnett (2003) for London.

4.3.4 Manchester: between professionalisation, large scale redevelopment and the retrenchment of public housing provision

The large-scale redevelopment processes transforming the formerly industrial Manchester into a knowledge-based city have affected the demographic composition of the city considerably. The notions of re-invention and neighbourhood change can be found in gentrification literature relating to Manchester (see Ravetz and Warhurst 2012; Hincks 2015). The city of Manchester is characterised by a concentration of businesses with high added value (finance, advanced services to firms) and innovative sectors, such as life science, IT and digital communication industry (Chapter 2 in this volume). Those businesses are mainly situated in the city area, while some of them are located in Salford, where new BBC buildings were built in the MediaCityUK site.[8]

Manchester's transition from an important industrial hub into an established service sector centre has partially caused social inequalities, exacerbated by a low level of connectivity in the territory. More than the 60 per cent of people employed in Manchester comprise of commuters mainly living in the Southern area of Greater Manchester. Furthermore, the urban area of Manchester was characterised by a low number of transport connections among the various districts of the city. The outdated and undersized public transport network (the lack of an underground network) is considered to have caused territorial imbalances, affecting both job opportunities and living conditions. In particular, the northern area of Greater Manchester is isolated from more economically developed areas. This phenomenon is also emphasised by a low level of commuter flows to the principal town. Moreover, the lack of transport connections negatively affects the possibility of setting up new businesses in those areas.

This double inequality axis – city centre–outskirts and north–south – has to be interpreted in the light of the different natures of the development trends that have characterised the territory. While historically the north represented the most industrialised area, the south has a long trade tradition, which over the years has moderated the powerful effects of industrial dismantling and which today allows the area to benefit from economic growth connected to new businesses in the city of Manchester.

Trends in the housing market seem to exacerbate these territorial inequalities. In 2001, the housing market in Manchester included mainly privately owned houses (42 per cent), social housing (39.5 per cent), and a lower number of rented houses (19 per cent) on the private market (Eurostat, Urban Audit database). Although there are no chronologically set data available, official statistics show a growth trend in the number of privately owned houses[9] (reaching 46 per cent in 2009), together with a considerable decrease in social housing (35 per cent) and, more moderately, in private rent (18 per cent) (Manchester City Council 2009). The sell-off of public housing and the erosion of private rented houses have exposed middle and lower middle class households to situations of greater vulnerability, despite rent control and economic support measures to pay high rental costs. At the same time, Manchester experienced a strong appreciation of real estate profits (especially since the late 1990s). Between 2001 and 2004 apartment prices per square metre went up by 60 per cent, while the cost of a house almost doubled. From 2002 to 2006, affordable housing for sale dropped from 50 per cent to 23 per cent. As a consequence of the parallel sale of a high proportion of public property and the development of new residences promoted by public–private partnerships aiming at higher income households, central working class districts (such as Hulme, for example) have become mixed areas. On the one hand, the effects of this trend are an increased diversity in populations residing within the same districts and new lines of demarcation between owners and rental occupants. On the other hand, a progressive decrease in housing designed for low-income groups has led to longer waiting lists for council accommodation.

Implicitly, the property-supporting strategies fostered by the Manchester administration are in line with these trends. These measures aim to create new residential possibilities for social groups and are integrated into the most competitive sectors of economy. We identify a risk of division, not only at a spatial level, but also in terms of new lines of inequality between the part of the city of Manchester travelling rapidly along the tracks of new economies of knowledge, and another still linked to its traditional industrial structure. In the long term, such processes may have a considerable impact on new generations, with economic disadvantages, poor opportunities for education and employment, and also highly limited social mobility possibilities.

4.3.5 Copenhagen and the "gentle gentrification" induced by urban renewal and housing policies

The Danish tradition of social movements and cooperative housing forms is represented as a constant element within the discourse about gentrification in Denmark. When it comes to gentrification processes in Copenhagen, references to gentle methods of redevelopment as well as social engineering can be identified (see Larsen and Hansen 2008; Thörn 2012). Nevertheless, it is important to remember Copenhagen's phases of neighbourhood decay and loss in social cohesion in the 1960s and 1970s resulting in notions of both well-off and more deprived neighbourhoods that have even been called "ghettos" (Agger 2015).

Copenhagen's real estate market path has to be seen through the lens of the changes to the law that occurred in the 1990s. These laws induced the "privatisation" of the management of large state-owned property – mainly concentrated in Copenhagen[10] – and a transformation of the cooperative housing sector, which had allowed low-income groups to purchase housing at a controlled price. This cooperative sector increased moderately until 1995 when, following a strong economic crisis in the municipal administration, around 20,000 houses owned by the municipality were sold and transformed into cooperatives, with a significant increase in the number of families on the waiting list for a social house – with a wait, according to the latest figures, of up to 20 years. Beside the cooperative system, a moderate percentage of private rental houses, sometimes without own bathroom or central heating, represented an alternative solution for the poorer residents until the mid-1990s.

Afterwards, the urban renewal programmes, which involved different city areas contributed to a significant increase in rental prices, also due to the less stringently used rent control measures after 1990. Since then private rentals have continually and considerably decreased. At the same time, there was an increase in properties and subsidised housing, although moderate. The most consistent increase has been seen in cooperative housing, while social housing – directly managed by public bodies – has decreased markedly for the reasons already mentioned. Although in Copenhagen the house prices have for a long time been lower than the Danish average and many other cities and provinces, since the late 1990s the trend has gradually been inverted. Rental costs constantly increased up to 2009, without relevant differences among the available housing typologies.

The transformation of a considerable part of public housing assets into cooperatives, and the subsequent regulation that allowed the selling of such houses at a market price are the basis of the mechanism that created an increase in house prices in Copenhagen, with the consequent social turnover in some central districts of the city. As a direct consequence of the government provision, the price differential between the private market and the cooperative system reduced drastically; this latter showed a six-fold increase between 2000 and 2008, according to the municipal statistics. In the short term, there was no outflow of Copenhagen inhabitants from their residential districts, but rather an enrichment related to the strong appreciation of the apartments originally bought at reduced prices. These profits allowed many families to buy higher-quality house solutions. Since many of them belonged to the poorer segment of the housing demand, the reform of the cooperative system resulted in a soft, though effective, mechanism for social turnover, with the migration of the original inhabitants toward the outskirts, consequently leaving the space for new segments of demand with a higher level of purchasing power.

A second mechanism is linked to urban renewal policies endorsed by the administration since the 1980s. The areas involved in such programmes are mainly mid-central districts, neighbouring in the north (Nørrebro) and west (Vesterbro) of the Copenhagen historic centre, with the exception of Amager Vest, located in the most peripheral area of Orestad. Today, the most relevant proportion of new housing are concentrated there. In Nørrebro, 13.2 per cent of the overall housing stock is made up of buildings built after 1980; in Vesterbro 10.3 per cent and in Amager Vest 24.4 per cent (Copenhagen municipal statistics

2009). From such figures, it is possible to conclude that these were also the areas that mostly suffered the impact of the increase in housing costs.[11]

By applying these urban renewal policies, Copenhagen's administration played a significant role in supporting the social turnover processes from low and middle class to upper class neighbourhood composition. As a matter of fact, Copenhagen had for a long time welcomed disadvantaged populations, who otherwise would have been pushed out toward the city margins due to their difficulties in affording the housing costs. Nowadays, this prerogative is challenged by the strong increase in the housing costs, not only following the many renewal programmes in some central and mid central areas of the city, but also as a direct consequence of the variations introduced by the current national regulation on the housing cooperatives.

4.3.6 Lyon: the ambiguous effects of policies fostering urban renewal and social mix

Social inequality and exclusion through urban regeneration are the predominant narratives within the limited available gentrification literature on Lyon (Stouten and Rosenboom 2013; Rousseau 2015; Souche *et al.* 2015). Over the last decades, Lyon's economic development involved its entire metropolitan territory through the diffusion of multi-national high-tech industries (OPALE 2009). The city centre has a relatively high number of businesses operating in the most prestigious and innovative economic sectors; and is characterised by a good level of integration and wider economic dynamism.

With a rather high spread of businesses, a remarkable outward residential mobility (particularly of households with children) can be seen, due to a rather low level of one-family housing provision in the town centre. Here, the real estate market is mainly characterised by temporary apartments, some of them dating back to the first decades of the twentieth century, and therefore needing renovation.

Despite the overall positive economic and demographic trends regarding the entire urban area of the city of Lyon, there are still territorial differences to be registered, mainly on its east–west axis. In particular, the western suburbs of *Grand Lyon*, where commuting levels are low – and especially the Nord Ouest and Val de Saône areas, – are characterised by considerably higher income inhabitants, mainly in management or highly professional positions (INSEE 2006). On the contrary, the east side is the most deprived part of the *Grand Lyon* area, where the education level is 5 per cent lower than the average level (INSEE 2006). Moreover, the east–west axis division is also marked by the real estate market, placing north west towns on the same levels of the city centre (2,900€/m^2), with the highest prices registered in particularly wealthy towns such as Limonest (3,300€/m^2).

Compared to the other cities analysed in this chapter, Lyon's changes in the housing market have been less significant. Between 1999 and 2006, there was a considerable growth in private ownership houses, from 44.2 per cent to 46.5 per cent, and at the same time a slight growth in the absolute value of houses for rent, also in social housing, with an increase of around 3,000 units (INSEE 2006). On the contrary, the purchase price of new houses has significantly increased in the last decade. The average sale price of a newly built apartment is 3,200 €/m² (with an increase of 82 per cent between 1998 and 2008) and 2,600 €/m² for a resale apartment (+166 per cent) (OTIF 2012).

In this context, gentrification has been a process to some extent controlled by specific local public policies, aimed at promoting an urban social mix. The case of the district of St Georges, one of the historic parts of the city of Lyon, is a good example of such dynamics. Having been significantly hit by urban and housing decay in the 1960s, the district of St Georges was the target of an urban regeneration programme promoted by the municipal administration in 1982, which triggered some significant changes in its social composition. The urban renewal was therefore supported through the allocation of a huge amount of public investments (€18 million between 1995 and 1998). The high housing appreciation following this urban renewal has strengthened the presence of upper/upper middle class families in the area. New local micro-differentiations within the area emerged as a consequence not only of the urban renewal, but also of combinations among rotation processes, mobility and family stabilisation. At least 20 years after its renewal, the St Georges district is today a fragmented area, consisting of highly diversified and partially segregated social micro-areas.

Therefore, we can claim that the mechanism of urban regeneration, characterising some of the cities studied in this research work, has partly triggered social turnover processes that have been emphasised in the districts of the city of Lyon. The above-mentioned urban requalification policy appears to have fostered renewal processes within those districts under a strong public control, thus contributing to somehow "protect" them from exogenous exploitation interests. On the other hand, state-led gentrification aimed at increasing the social mix in specific urban areas has mainly resulted into spatial fragmentation and "segregation" of different populations (Lelévrier 2013).

4.4 Final considerations

As we show in this chapter, there are numerous divergent mechanisms behind the obvious processes of real estate dynamics. According to our initial argument of interrelated processes at the macro level and micro level, the analysis highlights in most cases how the combination of the demand and supply side practices forms the basis of the observed gentrification processes.

At the supply level, there is the sector of urban regeneration policies explicitly aimed at the transformation of substantial parts of the city under the administration's control. Such control can be more or less strong, more or less able to "govern" the transformations by producing common goods as an added value. In addition, there are operations of intervention in the cities promoted by developers and private investors with the main purpose of benefiting from the gap between the current and potential income of a degraded real estate stock. In this case, the role of the public administration as a proactive "designer" of the investment process is relevant, too. However, experience shows that there is no automatic result in an added value for society by those operations.

At demand level, there are new jobs and professions resulting in new demand patterns for residency, including cultural and lifestyle values by a new middle class attracted to the centrally located city areas. Housing policies focusing on affordability and social mix are a powerful specific factor that is able to trigger social change processes in the districts. As policies are able to have a remarkable impact on the demand and supply dynamics of housing market, they act as a powerful mechanism of social inclusion and exclusion. In general, housing policies are still practices of intervention orientation by the central states and the local administrations. These may vary a lot, independently from their different welfare regimes (Arbaci 2007). Although these mechanisms work in all the cities analysed in this chapter, we may identify three main patterns.

Munich is a representative for a *professionalisation-led gentrification*. Here the focus is on the importance of employment in the advanced sector located in the central part of the cities. We described the important role of the post-industrial economic transition, the changes on the labour market and on the housing demand of the affluent classes as know from theoretical debate (Hamnett 2003; Bayer *et al.* 2014; Mazzoleni and Pechmann 2016).

Manchester and Copenhagen are characterised by a *housing policy-led gentrification process*. We refer to Manchester with its major support of homeownership (*Right to Buy Scheme*) and partially to Copenhagen with its transition from cooperative housing to free market housing system as examples. There is a significant shift from rental to ownership logics in both cities. However, the transition process cannot be analysed without considering public urban renewal interventions.

Barcelona, Milan and Lyon are characterised by *urban renewal policy-led gentrification*. Urban renewal policies in central and inner-city districts may have dramatic effects on economically weaker households. Both, renovation operations and the construction of residences have proven a double-edged sword. As illustrated in this chapter, prices have increased and part of the rental stock was removed from the rent control mechanism that in many cities, is no longer applicable to more recent buildings. With regard to gentrification in the strictest sense and its essential component of displacement, Barcelona represents the most typical case. Recovery interventions and urban regeneration, as clearly shown by the Olympic Village, impact severely on the socioeconomic structure in inner-city neighbourhoods, attracting a sort of European professional class, particularly in the fields of architecture and culture. Moreover, the great gentrification engine in the historical districts of the city is represented by the remarkable development of tourism with the subsequent expansion of the temporary rent sector. Milan experiences an exaggerated increase of real estate prices that caters to a predominantly prestigious, high-end clientele. On the other hand, the Lyon case is able to show what the governance of gentrification can look like. Here, the public administration's role in the regeneration and valorisation processes of districts has had a remarkable effects on such transformations. The

French OPAH[12] – aimed at the requalification of existing housing and the coordination between private and public actors – partly softened expulsion phenomena through careful control by the local administration. As a result, this contributed to a sort of social heterogeneity in districts that have become more attractive both for the upper classes and tourists.

In general, an important result of this comparison is the important role of urban policies (both urban renewal programmes and the retrenchment of housing policies) in framing different patterns of gentrification and loss of housing affordability in the central areas of the cities in Europe – especially in comparison with the US context (Maloutas 2011; Kadi and Musterd 2014; Franz 2015). Concluding with our interest in the impact of gentrification in times of economic crisis, the body of literature is still underdeveloped, especially in relation to gentrification research. As a result, the analysis remains weak, too, due to a lack of appropriate parameters that can be applied to measure the links between economic constraints and real-estate activities. As Dijkstra *et al.* (2015: 948) point out, "much of the crisis has been transmitted by real estate-related financial linkages which have subsequently spread beyond the real estate arena and into the balance sheet positions of the real economy". While this field of analysis remains under-researched, the interlinkages between different lines of development become clear and support the argument presented in this chapter for more relational research approaches in the gentrification debate.

Notes

1 The preferred source for data to perform a comparison in terms of house selling prices is the Urban Audit database (Eurostat). Since for some cities there is no historical data available, the information was integrated by using local administration sources; it was not always possible to compare the same type of houses (whether new-build or not, and how recently houses were built). It should also be noted that the comparison is partly influenced by the different nature of the sources.

2 The 2015 figures have been included to illustrate the status quo and the development pattern of rising property costs. These numbers derive from the online database numbeo.com and include housing sale prices outside of the city centre.

3 The notion of gentrification as it is understood in this chapter refers to changing demographic profiles of neighbourhoods because of increasing housing prices and decreasing housing options.

4 The highest share in cost takeover by investors can be found with approximately €220 million in the provision of public transport areas (e.g. streets) and with approximately €170 million in shared costs for social infrastructure. For details see the official website for the city of Munich, online, available at: www.muenchen.de/rathaus/Stadtverwaltung/Kommunalreferat/immobilien/sobon.html.

5 Referring to the definition by Marisol García, speaking at a seminar promoted by the Social Policy Laboratory at the Polytechnic University in Milan, October 2009.

6 Social housing seen as a public production of housing to be rented to the low-income population, ended with the fall of Franco. The last social housing districts, so-called "polygons" date back to 1965–1975 and were not presented again, due to the problems that they highlighted over time.

7 While a segment of the high-level demand was focused on new great dimension interventions in the municipalities of the first metropolitan belt (such as Milano 2), due to

the lack of creation of high-level residences in the city expansion areas during the 1970s and the 1980s, another segment consolidated its presence in the central areas of the city, with the subsequent expulsion of the weaker classes (Diappi 2009). A good example is shown by the fights, during the 1960s, among evicted tenants in Corso Garibaldi and in the Navigli area, which were to become elite districts of the Milan bourgeoisie (Daolio 1974; Della Pergola 1974).

8 See MediaCityUK website, online, available at: www.mediacityuk.co.uk/occupiers/ bbc.

9 The pronounced increase in ownership can be explained by the scheme drawn by the central government, which, since 1980, has allowed the occupants of council housing to purchase such houses at reduced prices, thus strengthening a line of action already pursued with different tools by the local administration.

10 Since 1990, the management has been entrusted to non-profit associations. To calculate the overall consistence of the public stock for rent after such change, the social housing with public direct management must be added to the subsided housing, managed by non-profit bodies.

11 It must be remembered that there is a dispensation for the application of the rent-control mechanism for stock built after 1990.

12 Programmed operation of improvement of housing (Opération Programmée d'Amélioration de l'Habitat – OPAH).

References

Agger, A. (2015). "Wonderful Copenhagen": Coping with Segregation and Ghettoization. In: Björkdahl, A. and Strömbom, L. (eds). *Divided Cities: Governing Diversity*. Lund, Sweden: Nordic Academic Press, pp. 87–106.

Albers, M. B. and Holm, A. (2008). Privatising Social Housing in Europe: the Cases of Amsterdam and Berlin. In: Adelhof, K., Glock, B., Lossau, J. and Schulz, M. (eds). *Urban trends in Berlin and Amsterdam*. Berlin: Geographisches Institut der Humboldt-Universität zu Berlin.

Andersen, J. and Pløger, J. (2007). The Dualism of Urban Governance in Denmark. *European Planning Studies*, 15(10), 1349–1367.

Arbaci, S. (2007). Ethnic Segregation, Housing Systems and Welfare Regimes in Europe. *European Journal of Housing Policy*, 7(4), 401–433.

Bayer, N., Holm, A. and Lebhuhn, H. (2014). Städtische Diskurse um Migration im Wandel. Integration, Diversity und Soziale Bewegungen in München und Berlin. *Sub-urban*, 2(3), 81–92.

Bricocoli, M. and Cucca, R. (2016). Social Mix and Housing Policy: Local Effects of a Misleading Rhetoric: The Case of Milan. *Urban Studies*, 53(1), 77–91.

Bridge, G. (2007). A Global Gentrifier Class? *Environment and Planning*, 39, 32–46.

Burgers, J. and Musterd, S. (2002). Understanding Urban Inequality: A Model Based on Existing Theories and an Empirical Illustration. *International Journal of Urban and Regional Research*, 26(2), 403–413.

Butler, T. (2007). For Gentrification? *Environment and Planning A*, 39, 162–181.

Butler, T. and Lees, L. (2006). Super-gentrification in Barnsbury, London: Globalization and Gentrifying Global Elites at the Neighbourhood Level. *Transactions of the Institute of British Geographers*, 31, 467–487.

Butler, T. and Robson, G. (2001). Social Capital, Gentrification and Neighbourhood Change in London: A Comparison of Three South London Neighbourhoods. *Urban Studies*, 38(12), 2145–2162.

Carnevali, R., Signorelli, A., Tajani, C. and Vaia, R. (2011). *Il lavoro a Milano*, 5, January.

Cócola Gant, A. (2013). The Invention of the Barcelona Gothic Quarter. *Journal of Heritage Tourism*, 9(1), 18–34.

Daolio, A. (1974). *Le lotte per la casa in Italia: Milano, Torino, Roma, Napoli*. Milan: Feltrinelli.

Della Pergola, G. (1974). *Diritto alla città e lotte urbane: saggi di sociologia critica*. Milan: Feltrinelli,

Diappi, L. (ed.) (2009). *Rigenerazione urbana e ricambio sociale: Gentrification in atto nei quartieri storici italiani*. Milan: Franco Angeli.

Diappi, L. and Bolchi, P. (2013). Redevelopments and Gentrification: A MAS Model of the Urban Housing Market in Milan. In: Diappi, L. (ed.). *Emergent Phenomena in Housing Markets*. Berlin: Springer, pp. 85–99.

Dijkstra, L., Garcilazo, E. and McCann, P. (2015). The Effects of the Global Financial Crisis on European Regions and Cities. *Journal of Economic Geography*, 15, 935–949.

Evans, R. and Karecha, J. (2013). Staying on Top: Why is Munich so Resilient and Successful? *European Planning Studies*, 22(6), 1259–1279.

Fellini, I., Negrelli, S. and Rossi, P. (2011). *Il rilevatore dei "Segnali Deboli" del mercato del lavoro di Milano*. Rapporto Finale, Comune di Milano, Settore Lavoro e Occupazione.

Franz, Y. (2015). *Gentrification in Neighbourhood Development: Case Studies from New York City, Berlin and Vienna*. Vienna: V&R Unipress Vienna University Press.

Glass, R. (ed.) (1964). Introduction: Aspects of Change. In: *Centre for Urban Studies, London: Aspects of Change*, London: MacGibbon and Kee, pp. xiii–xlii.

Hamnett, C. (2003). Gentrification and the Middle-class Remaking of Inner London, 1961–2001. *Urban Studies*, 40(12), 2401–2426.

Hamnett, C. and Randolph, W. (1984). The Role of Landlord Disinvestment in Housing Market Transformation: An Analysis of the Flat Break-up Market in Central London. *Transactions of the Institute of British Geographers: New Series*, 9(3). 259–279.

Hamnett, C. and Randolph, W. (1988). Labour and Housing Market Change in London: A Longitudinal Analysis, 1971–1981. *Urban Studies*, 25(5), 380–398.

Healey, P. (2007). *Urban Complexity and Spatial Strategies towards a Relational Planning for Our Times*. London: Routledge.

Hincks, S. (2015). Neighbourhood Change and Deprivation in the Greater Manchester City-Region. *Environment and Planning A*, 47(2), 430–449.

Idescat, Official Statistics Website of Catalonia. Online, available at: www.idescat.cat/pub/?id=aec&n=318&lang=en.

INSEE National Institute of Statistics and Economic Studies (1990–1999–2006). Online, available at: www.recensement.insee.fr.

ISTAT (1991, 2001). Censimento della Popolazione e delle Abitazioni.

Kadi, J. and Musterd, S. (2014). Housing for the Poor in a Neo-liberal Just City: Still Affordable, but Increasingly Inaccessible. *Tijdschriftvoor Economischeen Sociale Geografie* DOI:10.1111/tesg.12101, 1–17.

Kazepov, Y. (ed.) (2005). *Cities of Europe: Changing Contexts, Local Arrangements, and the Challenge of Urban Cohesion*. Cambridge, MA: Blackwell.

Lagendijk, A., Van Melik, R., De Haan, F., Ernste, H., Ploegmakers, H. and Kayasu, S. (2014). Comparative Approaches to Gentrification: A Research Framework. *Tijdschrift voor economische en sociale geografie*, 105(3), 358–365.

Landeshauptstadt München (2009). *Die Sozialgerechte Bodennutzung: Der Münchner Weg*.

Larsen, H. G. and Hansen, A. L. (2008). Gentrification – Gentle or Traumatic? Urban

Renewal Policies and Socioeconomic Transformations in Copenhagen. *Urban Studies*, 45(12), 2429–2448.

Le Galès, P. (2002). *European Cities: Social Conflicts and Governance*. New York: Oxford University Press, Oxford.

Lees, L. (2003). Super-gentrification: The Case of Brooklyn Heights, New York City. *Urban Studies*, 40, 2487–2509.

Lees, L. (2008). Gentrification and Social Mixing: Towards an Inclusive Urban Renaissance? *Urban Studies*, 45(12), 2449–2470.

Lelévrier, C. (2013). Social Mix Neighbourhood Policies and Social Interaction: the Experience of Newcomers in Three New Renewal Developments in France. *Cities*, 35, 409–416.

Ley, D. (1994). Gentrification and the Politics of the New Middle-class. *Environment and Planning D*, 12, 53–74.

McCann, E. and Ward, K. (2012). Super-gentrification: The Case of Brooklyn Heights, New York City. *Environment and Planning A*, 44, 42–51.

McCann, P. (2008). Globalization and Economic Geography: The World is Curved not Flat. *Cambridge Journal of Regions, Economy and Society*, 1(3), 351–370.

Maloutas, T. (2011). Contextual Diversity in Gentrification Research. *Critical Sociology*, 38(1), 33–48.

Manchester Economic Factsheet, City Council File (2008).

Manchester Economic Factsheet, City Council File (2009).

Manzo, L. (2012). On People in Changing Neighborhoods: Gentrification and Social Mix: Boundaries and Resistance: a Comparative Ethnography of Two Historic Neighborhoods in Milan (Italy) and Brooklyn (New York, USA). *CIDADES, Comunidades e Territórios: Lisboa*, 24, 1–29.

Martinotti, G. (1993). *Metropoli: La nuova morfologia sociale della città*. Bologna: Il Mulino.

Massey, D. (2005). *For Space*. London: Sage.

Mazzoleni, C. and Pechmann, A. (2016). Geographies of Knowledge-creating Services and Urban Policies in the Greater Munich. In: Cusinato, A. and Philippopoulos-Mihalopoulos, A. (eds). *Knowledge-creating Milieus in Europe*. Berlin: Springer, pp. 171–214.

Mazzucato, V. (2008). *Le città metropolitane nella prospettiva europea: Milano e Barcellona: due metropoli a confronto*. Padua: Università degli Studi di Padova, tesi di Laurea.

Miralles-Guasch, C. (2000). La regione metropolitana di Barcellona: tra policentrismo e centralità. In: "*Economia Pubblica*", 3.

Moser, C. O. N. and Horn, P. (2015). Does Economic Crisis Always Harm International Migrants? Longitudinal Evidence from Ecuadorians in Barcelona. *International Migration*, 53(2), 274–290.

Mugnano, S. and Palvarini, P. (2011). *How Milan Housing Market is Responding to the Financial Crisis?* Paper presented at Enhr Conference 2011, 5–8 July, Toulouse.

München – Statistisches Amt. Online, available at: www.muenchen.de/Rathaus/dir/statistik/.

Muñoz, F. (2008). Brandcelona: de la reconstrucción urbana al urban sprawl. In: Degen, M. and García, M. (eds). *La metaciudad: Barcelona: Transformación de una metropolis*, Barcelona: Anthropos, Rubí.

Musterd, S. (2005). Social and Ethnic Segregation in Europe: Levels, Causes, and Effects. *Journal of Urban Affairs*, 27(3), 331–348.

Musterd, S. and Ostendorf, W. (eds) (1998). *Urban Segregation and the Welfare State: Inequality and Exclusion in Western Cities*, London and New York: Routledge.

Navarro Yáñez, C. J. (2013). Do "Creative Cities" Have a Dark Side? Cultural Scenes and Socioeconomic Status in Barcelona and Madrid (1991–2001), *Cities*, 35, 213–220.

OPAH – Opération Programmée d'Amélioration de l'Habitat.

OPALE – Observatoire Partenarial Lyonnais en Economie (2009). Les Territoires de l'Economie Lyonnaise. Online, available at: www.opale-lyon.com.

OSMI-Borsa Immobiliare, *Il mercato immobiliare milanese e il circolo virtuoso della riqualificazione urbana*, 2007.

OTIF (Observatoire des transactions immobilières et foncières à la Réunion) of *Grand Lyon*, Foncier et immobilier du *Grand Lyon*: étude des charges foncières des logements neufs à Lyon et Villeurbanne de 2005 à 2010, Etudes foncières, revue bimestrielle, 156, March to April 2012.

Palomera, J. (2014). How Did Finance Capital Infiltrate the World of the Urban Poor? Homeownership and Social Fragmentation in a Spanish Neighborhood. *Urban and Regional Research*, 38(1), 218–235.

Pareja-Eastaway, M. and San Martin, I. (1999). General Trends in Financing Social Housing in Spain. *Urban Studies*, 36(4), 699–714.

Parkinson, M. (2013). *Barcelona*. ESPON 2013 Programme.

Phillips, M. (2004). Other Geographies of Gentrification. *Progress in Human Geography*, 28, 5–30.

Ravetz, J. and Warhurst, P. (2013). Manchester: Re-Inventing the Local–Global in the Peri-Urban City-Region. In: Nilsson, K., Pauleit, S., Bell, S., Aalbers, C. and Sick Nielson, T. A. (eds) (2013). *Peri-urban Futures: Scenarios and Models for Land Use Change in Europe*. Berlin: Springer, pp. 169–207.

Redfern, P. A. (2003). What Makes Gentrification "Gentrification"? *Urban Studies*, 40(12), 2351–2366.

Rehfeld, D. (2013). Clusterpolitik, intelligente Spezialisierung, soziale Innovationen – neue Impulse in der Innovationspolitik, *Forschung Aktuell*, Institut Arbeit und Technik (IAT), Gelsenkirchen, 04/2013. Online, available at: http://nbn-resolving.de/urn:nbn:de:0176-201304012.

Rousseau, M. (2015). "Many Rivers to Cross": Suburban Densification and the Social Status Quo in Greater Lyon. *International Journal of Urban and Regional Research*, 39(3), 622–632.

Sassen, S. (1991). *The Global City*. Princeton: Princeton University Press.

Scott, A. J. (ed.) (2001). *Global City-Regions: Trends, Theory, Policy*. Oxford: Oxford University Press.

Smith, N. (1979). Towards a Theory of Gentrification: A Back to the City Movement by Capital, not People. *Journal of the American Planning Association*, 45, 538–549.

Smith, N. (1996). *The New Urban Frontier: Gentrification and the Revanchist City*. London: Routledge.

Souche, S., Mercier, A. and Ovtracht, N. (2015). The Impacts of Urban Pricing on Social and Spatial Inequalities: the Case Study of Lyon (France). *Urban Studies*, published online before print.

Statista (no date). Online, available at: http://de.statista.com/statistik/daten/studie/1885/umfrage/mietpreise-in-den-groessten-staedten-deutschlands/ (accessed 24 August 2015).

Stouten, P. and Rosenboom, H. (2013). Urban Regeneration in Lyon. Connectivity and Social Exclusion. *European Spatial Research and Policy*, 20(1), 97–117.

Thörn, H. (2012). In Between Social Engineering and Gentrification: Urban Restructuring, Social Movements, and the Place Politics of Open Space. *Journal of Urban Affairs*, 34, 153–168.

Van der Heijden, H., Dol, K. and Oxley, M. (2011). Western European Housing Systems and the Impact of the International Financial Crisis. *Journal for Housing and the Built Environment*, 26, 295–313.

Van Kempen, R. and Murie, A. (2009). The New Divided City: Changing Patterns in European Cities, *Tijdschrift voor Economischeen Sociale Geografie*, 100(4), 377–398.

Vivant, E. (2013). Creatives in the City: Urban Contradictions of the Creative City. *City, Culture and Society*, 4(2), 57–63.

Ward, K. (2010). Towards a Relational Comparative Approach to the Study of Cities. *Progress in Human Geography*, 34(4), 471–487.

Watt, P. (2009). Housing Stock Transfers, Regeneration and State-Led Gentrification in London. *Urban Policy and Research*, 27(3), 229–242.

Zukin, S. (1982). *Loft Living: Culture and Capital in Urban Change*. Baltimore and London: Johns Hopkins University Press.

5 Immigrants and ethnic minorities

The right workers for the wrong jobs?

Nathalie Kakpo and Roberta Cucca

5.1 Introduction

In the last two decades, most large European cities have experienced major economic transformations while also affected by the arrival of new immigrants and the presence of long-settled ethnic minorities. Immigrant groups have drastically transformed the urban demographic landscape, which has become more ethnically diverse. Although studies on integration processes and policies at the lower levels of cities and municipalities are more recent than national studies, they are already consistent. The main focus of these city and municipality level studies comprises the political aspect of integration and in policies encouraging civic and political participation (Garbaye 2005). Other studies analyse specific aspects of local policies, such as housing and segregation patterns in cities (Tammaru *et al.* 2016; Musterd 2005; Arbaci 2007). Studies on multi-ethnic cities have focused on the significant changes occurred in the urban context affected by growing religious and cultural diversities and an increase in ethnic businesses (Senik and Verdier 2010; Alietti 2001). More recently, there have also been attempts to compare local integration policies (Caponio and Borkert 2001). Moreover, many studies have analysed immigration and its effects on urban and regional economies focusing on productivity and labour markets (Kemeny 2012).

However, despite their interesting contents, many studies tend to overlook how economic changes and their impact on urban structures and processes affect immigrants' integration and their everyday interactions with the native people. Indeed, economy plays a key role in shaping the opportunities that immigrants may or may not access, and strongly affects their relationships with other ethnic groups (Reyneri and Fullin 2011). Therefore, exploring immigrant groups' trajectories within the city requires taking into account the local economy and its transformations.

This chapter will focus on how immigrant groups integrate in the changing labour markets of the six cities considered in this book. We will test theories stemming from previous studies. The first theory argues that the transformation of industrial cities into places of advanced service economy has meant a progressive exclusion of low-skilled immigrants and ethnic minorities that had previously been employed for manufacturing jobs (Rosholm *et al.* 2006; Kogan

2005). Another important theory argues the possibility of a growing polarization: the disappearance of the middle class labour market and an increasing polarization in the economy structure (Sassen 1991); more and more jobs concentrated in sectors requiring high skills or in the lowest levels such as services, retailing or in the remnants of manufacturing, with the involvement of immigrants and ethnic minorities mainly in these low sectors. These theories have been strongly challenged by Hammett, Randolph and Waldinger in their researches on London and New York. In London, there has been a dispersion in the original job segments, an upward social mobility and a growing divergence between Asians and West Indians (Hammett and Randolph 1988). In New York, Waldinger showed that minorities made significant improvements in the period studied, with an increasing share of employment in services and white collar jobs, but also a surfacing of a pattern of ethnic niches (Waldinger 1988).

Some 25 years after the publication of Waldinger's and Hammett's significant studies, where do immigrants and ethnic minority groups (EMGs) stand in the labour market of Milan, Manchester, Munich, Lyon, Copenhagen and Barcelona? The key question is: does a knowledge-based economy imply an exclusion of immigrants from the labour market and their massive concentration in the low employment sectors, or rather are we witnessing complex processes involving different groups' trajectories? How do factors such as ethnicity and social classes affect the ways immigrants and EMGs settle in the local labour markets?

A second question is related to the dynamics of the post-industrial transformations taking place in the six cities here considered. In a major study, Wilson called attention to the structure of the local economy and how it influences ethnic minorities' working opportunities and conditions: the problems of the poor black people are also related to "the availability of jobs that pay decent wages and that provide opportunities for advancement … self-respect and feeling of self worth" (Wilson 1978: 166). Although the cities investigated are mostly post-industrial, we expect to find differences between those cities in which the manufacturing and public sectors are still important, providing more stable working conditions, and cities in which these sectors are much less significant (Chapter 2 in this volume). As we will argue, these differences have an impact on integration processes for immigrants and EMGs in the labour market and the entanglement with other contextual factors (such as, laws regulating immigration flows, the labour market, housing affordability, education, timing of arrival, etc.), thus fostering different patterns of urban integration in Europe.

This chapter is divided into two parts. The first will analyse immigrants in the labour market of Milan, Barcelona and Copenhagen: these three cities were considered together because they share a similar evolution; in fact, their massive immigration experience is a rather recent and fast process (Figure 5.1), and therefore workers are mainly members of the first generation. The second will consider immigrants and EMGs in Manchester, Lyon and Munich, where the first waves of immigrants arrived in the 1950s and 1960s (Figure 5.1); in these cities workers are not only immigrants, but also members of second generations, and this aspect has a strong impact on the final outcomes of integration in the labour market.

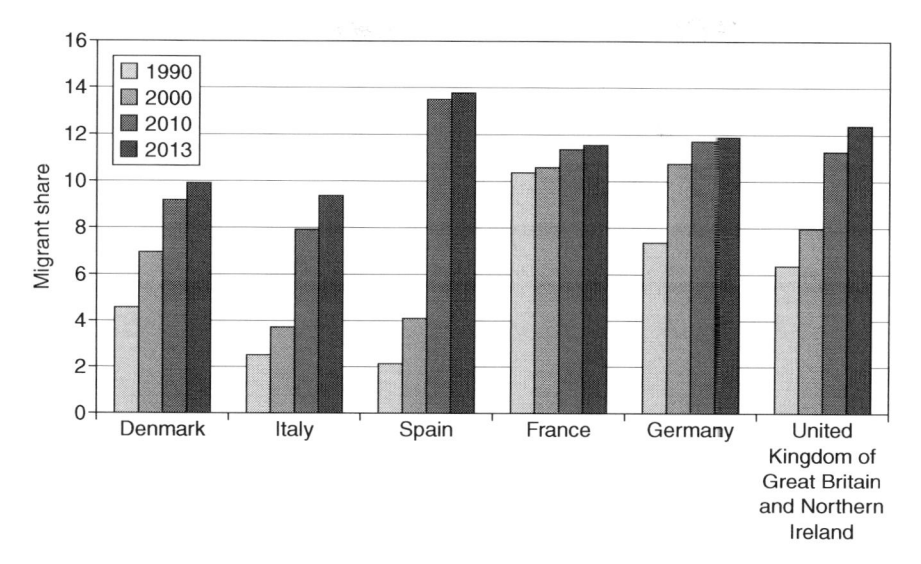

Figure 5.1 Share of international migrants at national level (1990–2013).

Source: authors' elaboration on The United Nations (2013).

5.2 Immigrants and their children in Barcelona, Copenhagen and Milan

5.2.1 An ethnically segmented labour market?

Milan, Barcelona and Copenhagen show differences in their welfare and employment patterns, but at the same time they have shared a highly significant migration phenomena since the 1990s: immigrants now represent approximately one-fifth of the total population in each of the cities mentioned (Figure 5.2).

In January 2000, only 3.5 per cent of Barcelona's population comprised of foreigners, while in 2013 immigrants represented 17.5 per cent of the total population, although the number of new arrivals since the beginning of the violent economic crisis and austerity measures in Spain have decreased (−25 per cent in 2013 compared to 2008) (Municipal Statistics Barcelona 2014). The largest groups come from South America (especially Bolivia, Ecuador, Peru), but there is also a significant amount of Pakistani, Moroccan, Chinese and Italian populations. Migrants coming from Southern and Central America amount to approximately 50 per cent of the migrants registered in Barcelona and, in line with Italian migrants, are the fastest growing group (Municipal Statistics Barcelona 2015).

Populations from South America are also significantly present in Milan, with an increasing number of people coming from Peru and Ecuador. However, in this city, migrants from Egypt and the Philippines are the most numerous, with

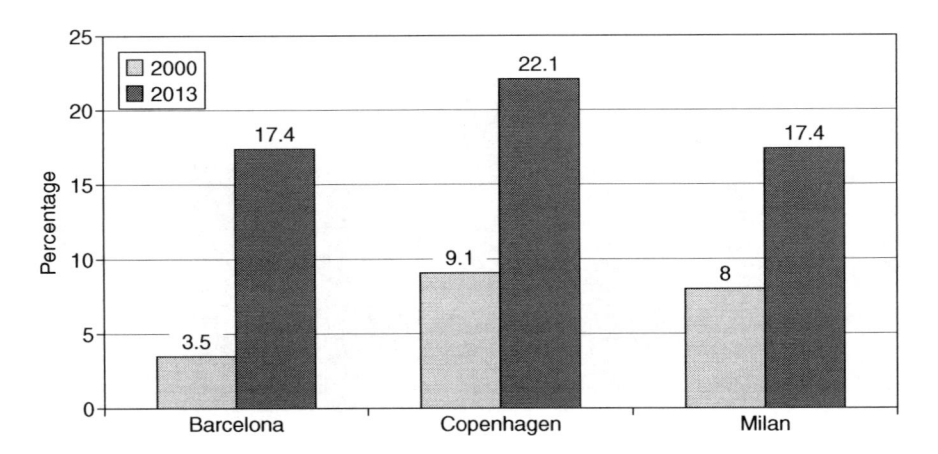

Figure 5.2 The immigrant population out of the total population in Barcelona, Milan and Copenhagen (2000–2013).

Source: authors' elaboration on Municipal Statistics: Barcelona, Copenhagen, Milan.

the Chinese ranking third. Immigrants in 2013 represented 17 per cent of the Milanese population, while the figure was only 8 per cent ten years before (Municipal Statistics Milan 2015).

Finally, Denmark and Copenhagen received the first waves of immigrants – coming from Chile and Vietnam – two decades ago, only representing 9 per cent of the population in 1990. Significant numbers of immigrants arrived in the 1990s from Bosnia, Iran, Iraq, Somalia, Afghanistan and Lebanon. Immigrants (and second generations) in 2013 represented almost 22 per cent of the city's total population. The most important groups are the Pakistani, Turkish, Iraqi and to a lesser extent the Polish (Municipal Statistics Copenhagen 2014).

To sum up, these cities – especially Barcelona – have undergone a major shift in the profile of their populations in the last two decades. It is certainly important to mention that Denmark, Italy and Spain did not undertake colonization to the same extent as France and England. Permanent interactions between natives and non-European immigrants do not belong to the national genealogy.

In Barcelona, Milan and Copenhagen there is a peculiar pattern of immigrant employment, which marks a contrast with that of the native population, in terms of: (a) unemployment; (b) horizontal segregation and (c) vertical segregation.

With reference to the first aspect (unemployment), in all the cities mentioned, immigrants experience a much higher exposure to unemployment, with a very extreme situation in Catalonia due to the severe impact of the economic crisis in Spain. In fact, in this city 40 per cent of the immigrant population is unemployed, while for the native population the percentage is around 20 per cent.

With reference to the horizontal segregation (Table 5.1), at regional and city levels, immigrants in Barcelona are much more represented in domestic services

Table 5.1 Immigrant workers and native workers (%) per economic sector in Barcelona (2013)

Sector	Natives	Immigrants	Total
Agriculture	0.5	0.3	1.4
Manufacturing	9.4	10.5	4.7
Construction	9.4	8.2	15
Services	77	78.1	72
Other	3.7	3	6.9

Source: authors' elaboration on Municipal Statistics Barcelona.

(elderly and children care) than the native population, and show a higher concentration in the construction sector (+7 per cent compared to natives), in tourism and trade (Municipality of Barcelona 2014), and a lower concentration in manufacturing (−6 per cent).

In Milan, men are more concentrated in construction, industry, domestic services, hospitality and cleaning (Marcaletti 2015). In Copenhagen, the characteristics of immigrants in the labour market are significantly peculiar. In fact, the first generation shows a dual pattern: it is more concentrated in the traditional service sector; in addition, there is a good presence in advanced service sectors such as consultancy, finance and insurance, telecommunications, real estate activities, education. Although the level of horizontal segregation in Copenhagen is less relevant, a large proportion of non-Western immigrants in Copenhagen is heavily concentrated at the bottom of the ladder in the labour market, showing a high level of vertical segregation. Only 21 per cent of the immigrant workers in Copenhagen have a medium-high job compared to 45 per cent of the native population (Municipal Statistics Copenhagen 2013). However, the presence of immigrants in intermediate and good jobs (frequently provided in the public sector) is higher in Copenhagen than in Milan and Barcelona.

In Lombardy (Table 5.2), only 3.1 per cent of immigrants are classified in intellectual jobs, 1.7 per cent in medicine and paramedical, and 3.3 per cent have an intermediate job (Marcaletti 2014). Specifically in Milan (Table 5.2) a large proportion of the immigrants are concentrated in cleaning, construction (men), manufacturing (men) and care services.

It is interesting to notice that women are significantly present in the majority of the intermediate jobs (employees or social workers) suggesting perhaps the beginning of a gender gap at least in intermediate skills. The data also show that immigrants in Spain are heavily concentrated in low skilled jobs.[1]

This first overview suggests strong points in common regarding immigrants in Milan, Barcelona and Copenhagen (in all three cities immigrants are affected more than natives by unemployment and segregation), but there are also some differences. Proportionally, immigrants are more numerous in the manufacturing and construction sectors in Milan compared to Copenhagen, for instance. A possible explanation is the more important weight of these industries in the Italian economy, which marks a contrast with the Danish city. Differences in the

Table 5.2 Professions of immigrants in Milan (2012), per gender (%)

Professions	Men	Women	Total
Household services	17.4	46.7	30.4
Manual workers in manufacture and construction	26.9	0.4	15.3
Manual workers in tertiary services	14.1	10.1	12.3
Employee	2.9	6.7	4.6
Social workers	1.3	7.1	3.8
Cook	4.4	0.8	2.8
Peddler (illegal)	4.8	0.4	2.8
Other	28.2	27.8	28.0
Total	100.0	100.0	100.0

Source: authors' elaboration on Orim (2014).

employment sectors suggest different working conditions and raise several questions about immigrants' future in the labour market. Foreign workers in Milan and Barcelona are concentrated in intensive labour activities requiring a high level of physical effort. This employment pattern does not only increase health problems among workers, but it also means job insecurity for the oldest and the youngest (due to the large presence of undocumented and temporary jobs) as a result of the strong impact of the crisis in the construction sector both in Milan and Barcelona.

Explaining this employment pattern leads to the exploration of the time dimension in immigrants' integration processes. The creation of broad and diverse networks, the knowledge of the local labour market and the language are all key advantages concerning the time necessary for integration. Time also impacts the administrative status that directly affects working opportunities and access to services. Time can mean strengthening the administrative status, but this aspect should be qualified, as the economic crisis has highlighted the very precarious situation of migrants without a permanent residence permit: welcomed for many years and then suddenly, in a fragile situation, asked to go back to their country of origin due to the changing economic situation. In cities such as Barcelona and Milan – strongly affected by the economic crisis and austerity measures – time is playing a more residual role in defining the situation of the first and second generations of immigrants in the local labour market.

5.2.2 Diversity among the ways of integrating in the labour market

Common opinions on recent migrations often suggest the presence of a homogeneous under-class without resources coming to Europe in search of a better life. This representation is even stronger for non-Western immigrants. Some academic studies tend to reinforce this representation by focusing only on domination processes or ethnic prejudice in the labour market and in society, or by defending the idea of a concentration only in low employment sectors.

What these sectors have in common is their embeddedness in the global, post-Fordist economy, and their essentially pre-Fordist labour relations.... This location in the economy reproduces that Otherness from within, as immigrants' status as an underclass of workers with substandard wages and working conditions impedes their full membership in the national community.

(Calavita 2005: 173)

Our investigation leads to adopt a less fatalist perspective about immigrants in countries experiencing new waves of migrations: concentration in low employment sectors, bad jobs, precarious residence status, hard living/working conditions and a significant vulnerability in front of economic changes should not hide other processes at work. In this case, the key words are heterogeneity of the groups, ways of settling in the host society and changing working conditions.

First of all, the data challenge the representation of a homogeneous low or non-educated migrant population: in Barcelona, Milan and Copenhagen, some groups of immigrants contribute to maintain and even raise the qualification level of the local population. In Barcelona almost 32.5 per cent of migrants have an academic degree (2012). Especially immigrants from South America have a higher educational level, while Ecuadorians, North African, sub-Saharan and Centre-Asiatic groups present lower educational levels. Only 8 per cent of sub-Saharan Africans have a higher education degree, which marks a huge contrast with immigrants from Central America. Data concerning Milan show that the idea that immigrants are a heavily non-educated population is not relevant; only 0.6 per cent of immigrants do not have a secondary school qualification, while 18 per cent have a university degree (Colombo 2014). Only in Copenhagen do foreigners have a lower level of education than natives, due to the higher level of education of native people in Denmark; however, 64 per cent of foreigners have an intermediate or a university degree.

The integration of migrants in the labour market in Milan, Barcelona and Copenhagen highlights the key issue of many immigrants being employed at a much lower level than their degree could equip them for. This situation is linked to the fact that for recent immigrants to find a good job requires time and integration in society and, at the same time, the urban economies here considered need fewer high-skilled workers than theories related to the Creative Economy announced (Florida 2005). At the same time, data related to the level of education of migrant people raise the issue of the lack of recognition of degrees obtained overseas, especially those coming from non-European countries. Therefore, are immigrants allowed to compete with natives for good jobs or is there a kind of glass ceiling preventing them from moving up? Sociologists have shown that ethnicity is mainly an interaction in which some groups attribute certain characteristics to other groups according to criteria such as the colour of skin or religion (Elias and Scotson 1997). This gap between employment and the level of education may create a distortion and a frustration for immigrants who do not find a way to have their skills recognized. At the same time, it may also mean a strong involvement in their children's school experience. Several sociological studies have shown that the first generation immigrants that were not able to access good jobs despite their intermediate and higher degrees tend to have not only higher school expectations for their children but also an everyday engagement in the achievement of this (Kakpo 2007). To sum up, the analysis of the educational level of migrants shows outcomes far from the picture of migrants as a non-educated labour force and solely as a source of problems for a city and its future.

Another line of cleavage amongst immigrants concerns their residence statuses and types of contracts. In Milan, only 26 per cent of Chinese and 43 per cent of Moroccans are regular workers, while this percentage is much higher among Filipinos (76 per cent) and Ecuadorians (71 per cent). Amongst regular workers, Filipinos and Ecuadorians are also the most important groups, with long-term and full-time contracts (43 per cent), which marks a significant contrast with the Chinese, of whom only 14 per cent have these types of contracts. Differences are also observable among irregular workers (Egyptians and Romanians have the highest rate): almost 15 per cent of the Chinese and only 6.5 per cent of Moroccans have a stable job (Marcaletti 2014). Different types of contracts and administrative statuses shape different living and working conditions as well as diverse contributions to the city's economic development.

Moreover, different studies show that the mentioned migration countries present a diffuse pattern of immigrants and descendants in a more diverse range of employment sectors over time (Peach 2005). Even though migrants are heavily concentrated in low employment sectors and low positions, there has been a slight dispersion of the initial employment sectors. In Barcelona, the presence of foreigners in domestic services greatly decreased in 2006 as a consequence of their regularization: many of the people with jobs in domestic services, who regularized their status in 2005, moved to other jobs. However, we can still find a huge representation of immigrant workers in the building sector, which has suffered important consequences due to the recent crisis and has worsened the labour market situation of many immigrants in the city. While in 2010 in Barcelona, 27.2 per cent of the contracts were signed by an immigrant, in 2014 this percentage decreased to 20.4 per cent (Municipal Statistics Barcelona 2014).

In Milan, it is possible to witness a similar shift from domestic services to industrial and commercial activities. It seems that the longer immigrants have been living in the host city, the greater the diffusion in the different employment sectors.

Finally, the presence of second generation workers in Copenhagen allows to explore the intergenerational social mobility (Table 5.3). Proportionally and surprisingly, if we compare the rate of immigrants of first and second generations with the total employed population, it is evident that in higher jobs there is a lower representation of the second generation (17 per cent) compared to the first generation (25 per cent).

Table 5.3 Socio-economic status (profession) by origin (%) in Copenhagen (2013)

	Danish	*Immigrants*	*Descendants*
Professional/entrepreneur	6.0	8.5	5.0
Manager	3.3	1.5	1.4
High-skilled employee	33.9	22.9	16.3
Medium-skilled employee	10.9	6.4	8.4
Low-skilled employee	36.1	29.5	52.0
Low-skilled worker	9.8	31.1	16.9

Source: authors' elaboration of Copenhagen Municipal Statistics (2013).

However, they are also more present in intermediate jobs compared to their parents. A significant line of cleavage may be linked to the fact that only very few children of immigrants are entrepreneurs, which marks a huge contrast with their parents. Ethnic entrepreneurship appears indeed as a way for intra-generational social mobility for some immigrants in Copenhagen.

Actually, different models of entrepreneurship are evident in Milan, Barcelona and Copenhagen. By analysing them it is possible to understand why certain businesses created by immigrants are successful whereas others are not. There are mainly three theories explaining ethnic entrepreneurship. The first is the "disadvantage thesis", which explains the setting up of businesses as a reaction to the barriers that immigrants face in the labour market (Rath and Kloosterman 2001), The second is a "favourable opportunity structure" (the existence of consumers with unsatisfied demand, unexploited markets with little competition or forms of regulations), which can encourage business creation (Aldrich and Waldinger 2001). The third approach emphasizes the features of immigrant groups: in their country of origin they developed self-employment and they are likely to carry on with this path in the host society. In this chapter, we will not explore entrepreneurs' motivations; rather, we will explore profiles of ethnic businesses found in Copenhagen and Barcelona, emphasizing the different types of contributions to the cities' economies.

Small companies created by immigrants in Copenhagen are very numerous in hotels, restaurants and food activities, wholesale and retail trade and transportation (1613 companies as a whole), but there are also small firms in advanced service sectors such as publishing, information services, consultancy, advertising, health activities and finance/real estate. A survey carried out in 2006 with 730 people (Stoumann 2006) showed that 30 per cent of immigrant entrepreneurs had a master's degree.

Ethnic businesses in Barcelona are quite different. Business services represent only a little more than 100 firms, which is a quite low number at city level. Firms are heavily concentrated in hotels and restaurants, construction that is sectors employing mostly migrants and that have been affected the most by the recent crisis. Ethnic entrepreneurship can mean different living and working conditions compared to those experienced by employees, but this pattern of entrepreneurship does not enable immigrants to access the highest employment sectors in the city.

However, Spanish studies show that these businesses significantly contribute to the regeneration of depressed areas, which become more dynamic owing to ethnic firms (Fundacion La Caixa 2007: 153–161).

Another line of cleavage separating Barcelona's pattern from the Danish one is the labour force working in firms. More than 90 per cent of immigrant entrepreneurs in Copenhagen employ one or more natives (Stoumann 2006). Employing Danish workers gives the ethnic entrepreneurs an enhanced possibility to extend their Danish networks. Moreover, native workers can supply the company with special skills and knowledge about cultural and commercial matters that non-native entrepreneurs may not have at the same level. With reference to Copenhagen, ethnic businesses are often a way to acquire a better social integration. This marks a very significant contrast with the Spanish city, where immigrant entrepreneurs mainly work with people of the same family or share a similar ethnic origin.

To sum up, the analysis of immigrant employment patterns in the three cities shows important commonalities. Massive immigrant waves are recent, and non-natives are heavily concentrated in employment sectors with low wages and hard employment conditions. Not only does time matter in the integration process, but also with reference to the cities and their features. Although Milan, Barcelona and Copenhagen are post-industrial cities, they show highly significant differences regarding employment distribution (Chapter 2 in this volume). These cities do not offer similar jobs to immigrants, which are more likely to work in the manufacturing and construction sectors in the Southern cities in comparison to the Danish capital. In the current crisis, immigrants are affected by a particular vulnerability, not only in terms of their employment status, but also in terms of the legal entitlement to live in the country after possibly losing their job. One important characteristic of Copenhagen, on the other hand, is the relevance of employment in the public sector, which marks a huge contrast with the Italian and Spanish cities. The American case highlights that employment in the public sector has played an important role in shaping the black middle class. Immigrants are under-represented in the Danish public sector compared to the native population, but this percentage is higher than in other OECD countries, and measures have been implemented to increase the number of immigrants (OECD 2009). The public sector provides more secure jobs than the private sector, and also working conditions are better as a whole. This feature of Copenhagen's may have a significant impact on the future employment patterns of descendants of migrants, while austerity measures are decreasing new hiring (and wages) in Milan and Barcelona, limiting the positive effects of this mechanism in terms of social mobility, both for immigrants and natives.

5.3 The rise of a middle-class ethnic minority in Lyon, Manchester and Munich

5.3.1 First generations, descendants and new immigrants

France, the United Kingdom and to a lesser extent Germany are old immigration countries. In Lyon, first significant waves of migrants arrived in the late 1950s and in the 1960s, mainly from North Africa and especially from Algeria. Lyon has a specific status: the first migrants to arrive were Algerians, after the First World War in the 1920s. They were not numerous, but most of them settled in the city, creating a famous multi-ethnic neighbourhood known as "La place du Pont" with a long history of immigration. The first North African "cafés" and prayer rooms were built in the 1930s and they became places for conflicts between immigrants and local authorities. These past events highlight that Lyon as a multi-ethnic city hosting non-European migrants is not a recent process. Much more than in many big French cities, the different stages of Lyon's economic evolution throughout the last century proceeded hand in hand with immigration waves. Italians, Spanish, Portuguese along with Algerians and Moroccans represent 60 per cent of the total immigrant population in the Rhône-Alpes area. The Turkish populations who arrived in the mid-1970s are also part of Lyon's immigration landscape. Immigrants in 2012 represented 12 per cent of Lyon's population, but it is also necessary to take into account descendants, which in most cases are French. There are also new immigrants; besides newcomers from Algeria, the region now has immigrants from the former federal republic of Yugoslavia, Switzerland, Cameroon, Madagascar and Senegal.

Manchester is one of the most multicultural cities in the United Kingdom (Figure 5.3). The first waves of migrants arrived in the 1950s and 1960s. Residents born outside the United Kingdom in 2011 amounted to 22.1 per cent of the local population, the main groups being Pakistani, Afro Caribbean, Black and White Caribbean (mixed race). There are also significant numbers of Indians, Chinese and Black Africans. Once again, colonization contributed in building

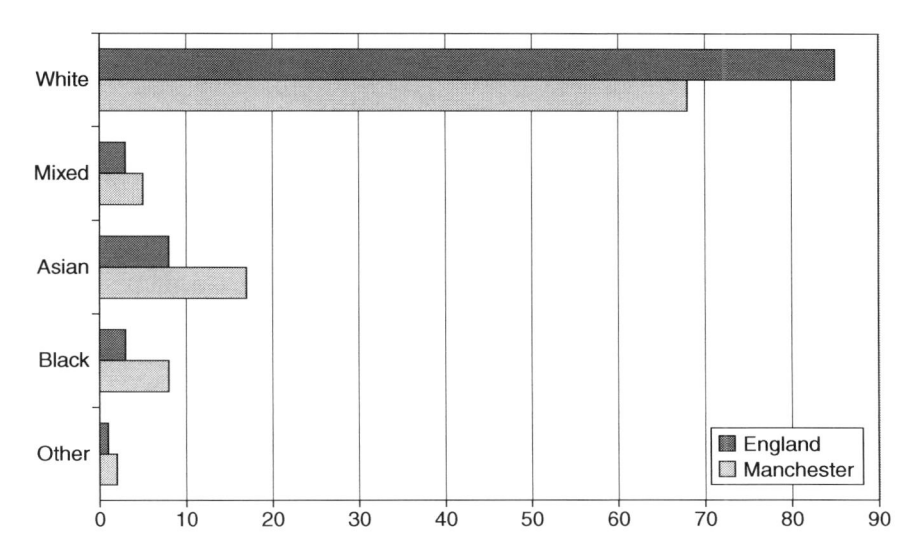

Figure 5.3 EMG City of Manchester and England (2011).

Source: authors' elaboration on UK Census 2011.

strong and often conflictual relationships between White British and non-White groups. However, a large part of the EMGs (33 per cent of the total population) is composed of citizens born in the United Kingdom: this datum marks a huge contrast with the first city pattern in which immigrant populations were massively born abroad and especially in non-European countries.

Munich experienced its first waves of immigrants at the end of the 1950s with Italian, Greek and Turkish populations who, after the Second World War, contributed to Munich's shift from a city focused on commercial activities to a manufacturing city. On the basis of the German law, immigrants were recognized as "invited workers". The 1973 economic crisis caused a stop in the arrival of immigrant workers and the beginning of family reunification. The 1990s witnessed new and significant waves of immigrants coming from the former federal republic of Yugoslavia but also from Ukraine, Bulgaria and Russia. In 2013 immigrants represented 24 per cent of the total population, the highest percentage in our six cities. The Turkish population is the most important group, followed by Croatians and Serbians, but there are also significant populations from Greece, Italy and Bosnia. One-third of the foreign population in Munich comes from EU countries (Municipality of Munich 2013).

A clear contribution of immigrants and their children to the city's development is related to demography and age structure. In Munich, in 2014, immigrants and people with a non-German background represented 40.1 per cent of the population and 56.8 per cent were under 18 years of age. Lyon's[2] data show that immigrant households are larger than the others (3.1 people versus 2.4) and this

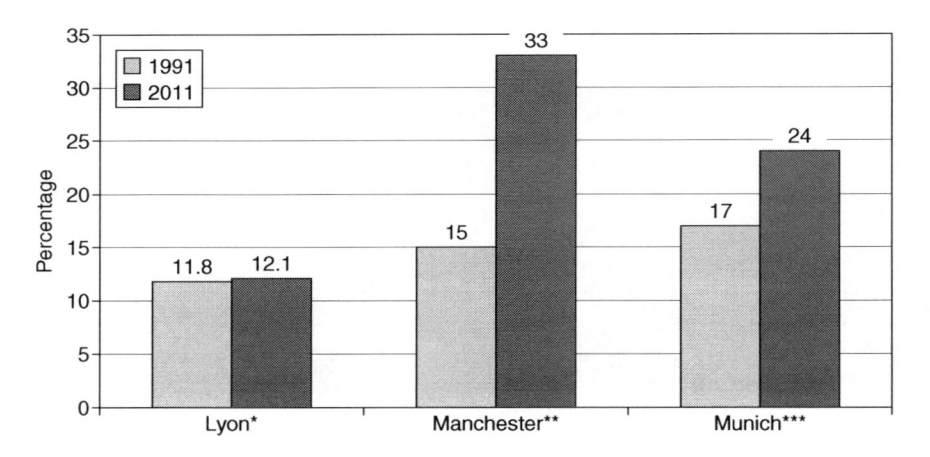

Figure 5.4 The immigrant population out of the total population in Lyon, Manchester and Munich (1991–2011).

Source: Municipal Statistics.

Notes
*   Residents in France but without French Citizenship.
**   Non-white EMGs.
*** Born outside of Germany.

is especially true for African families (3.7) and Asian ones (3.6). Some 19.8 per cent of African families comprise six people or more, and the percentage is 15.5 per cent for Asian families. The average regional percentage for all households is 8.8 per cent. Data strongly suggest that immigrants contribute to demographic growth at regional level; insofar as Lyon is the city where it is possible to find the highest number of immigrants in the region, we assume that this research finding at regional level is relevant also for the city (INSEE database 2014).

Between 1990 and 1999, Manchester's local population decreased, not very significantly but regularly each year (Manchester Municipality 2007). In 2000 the trend reversed, reaching 458,000 residents in 2007. The high number of births does not seem to be a significant factor to explain the increase of the population. Between 1995 and 2003, births decreased. Since 2003, this trend has reversed but not in a highly significant way. However, ethnic minorities contribute to this (precarious) demographic growth in a significant way: they are substantially younger than the white population. The 0–15 age bracket in 2011 represented one-third of EMG populations against one-fifth of the white population (Manchester City Council 2014).

To sum up, in all three cities the demographic contribution is relevant, but recently especially so in Munich and Manchester; while in Lyon, during the last decade, the percentage of immigrant population out of the total population has remained stable.

5.3.2 The making of the ethnic disadvantage

Data concerning Manchester, Lyon and Munich show that there is a specific pattern of ethnic minorities' integration in the labour market. In Manchester, the level of economic activity, the type of contracts and the unemployment rate display significant differences between natives and EMGs (Figure 5.5). EMGs have higher unemployment levels than British born populations, with the exception of Other whites, Indians and Chinese. Conversely to other groups, between 2001 and 2011 such EMGs did not witness an unemployment increase. The types of contracts also show EMGs to be disadvantaged. The quick growth of part-time employment has been one of the most significant features of employment change in Britain in recent decades. A higher proportion of employees from all EMGs (28.4 per cent) were part-time workers compared to 20 per cent of white groups (Manchester City Council 2014).

A similar ethnic disadvantage is also observable in Munich, where temporary employment is increasingly significant: between 2003 and 2007, it increased by 119 per cent for native populations and by 130 per cent for immigrant workers. Temporary immigrant workers are mainly concentrated in the sectors of construction, food activities and manufacturing. Furthermore, in 2013, 5.6 per cent of immigrants were unemployed, which is a significant rate with respect to their weight in the native population (3.6 per cent), but still very low and not affected by the crisis.

Finally, the immigrant population in the Rhône-Alpes region has a much higher unemployment rate than that of the native population. In 1999, the unemployment

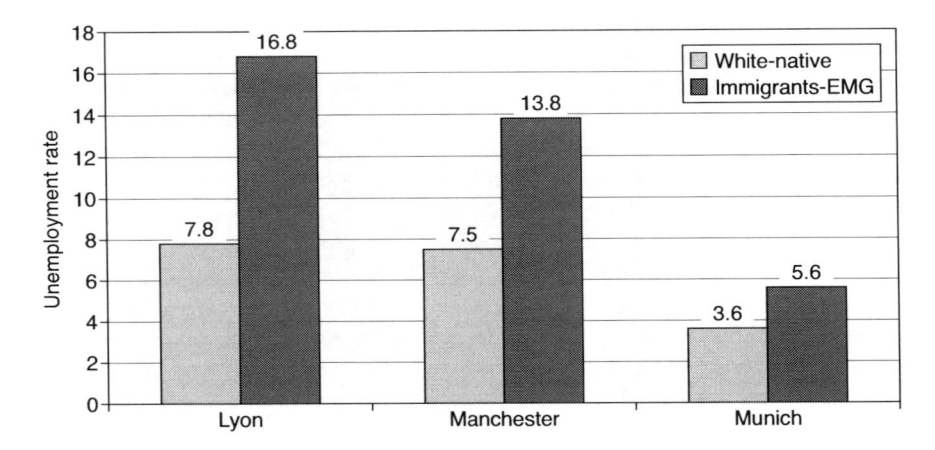

Figure 5.5 Unemployment rates (immigrants-EMG, white-native) in Lyon, Manchester and Munich (2011).

Source: authors' elaboration of Municipal Statistics.

rate was 19.8 per cent, whereas the figure for the natives was 11 per cent. Data for 2012 show that at a national level (INSEE database 2014) the unemployment rate of the native working population was 7.8 per cent, while for foreigners the number was 16.8 per cent. This figure is even worse for foreigners born outside of the 27 EU member countries (22 per cent). Nevertheless, immigrants in the Rhône-Alpes region are not concentrated in part-time and short-term jobs. This may be linked to the fact that many immigrants work in the manufacturing sector at the city scale. However, immigrants have a slightly more significant rate of temporary jobs, and citizens with a foreign nationality are not allowed to enter the public administration, which provides permanent jobs in France. As a whole, since the 1950s/1960s ethnic minorities have continued to suffer from an ethnic disadvantage that hampers their involvement in the labour market.

However, once again, context matters: there is a significant contrast between Lyon and Manchester regarding the types of contracts. The large increase of part-time and short-term contracts is a feature that characterizes Manchester and, more widely, England. This is less the case in Lyon, which provides more secure jobs as a whole. The first generation takes advantage of this context, which is likely to supply more stable working conditions for families than in England, with different impacts upon children's education and school attainment.

5.3.3 The rise of a middle and upper middle-class ethnic minority in the advanced services sectors

Regarding occupation and employment sectors, the ethnic minorities in Germany, France and England experience significantly different situations.

In Manchester, EMGs are much less present than native populations in the manufacturing sector (8.3 per cent EMGs; 14.5 per cent White British), but they are more numerous in constructions and traditional services. With reference to this key sector of Manchester's economy regarding employment and GDP, the difference between the level of involvement of EMGs and that of the natives is not high: 18.7 per cent of the White groups are employed in financial/business activities compared to 17.3 per cent of EMGs. Some groups contribute very significantly to this dimension of the city's development: Chinese and Bangladeshi in hotels and restaurants, as well as Indians and Pakistanis in the wholesale and retail trade are numerous. EMGs contribute to the economic development of the city in different ways. Specificities of EMGs in employment sectors are much less significant than in Barcelona, Copenhagen and Milan. There are, however, significant differences among groups; differences in banking and real estate activities, public administration, health and education are not significantly high, while they are more significant in other sectors. Pakistani immigrants comprise the most important group in manufacturing, whereas Chinese, African, Indian and White/Asian are the most represented in the finance and banking sector. Regarding professional, managerial and intermediate jobs, Indians have good and intermediate jobs, this rate being much higher than that of White British, Chinese do well also. Looking at low and non-skilled jobs, the highest rate is that of Pakistanis. There are not highly significant differences between white groups and EMGs when taking into consideration the occupational structure of employed people, which suggests that the problem is less about the social stratification of working people than about the major cleavage between those who work and those who do not. This line of division is between the white and the non-white, but also amongst ethnic minorities.

In Lyon, the pattern of immigrants and their children in employment sectors is quite different. Concerning immigrants, they mostly work in services such as social care, domestic services, education and health, but at a significantly less important level than the native population. This is because many immigrants, and especially men, work in the manufacturing and construction sectors and are over-represented in this sector. This fact is linked to France's immigration history, but also to the structure of the city's economy, for which manufacturing is important. This figure concerning immigrants in employment sectors contrasts with that of EMGs in Manchester, where they are under-represented in the manufacturing sector. French sociologists have provided many and fine analyses of the integration of the second generations in the labour market (Beauchemin *et al.* 2010, 2016). The occupational structure at a national level shows that 41 per cent of the male descendants of immigrants work in the manufacturing sector (against 34 per cent of the male native population) but, unlike their parents, many are qualified workers; men are also employees and medium-skilled workers in the service sector. A great majority of the female descendants are employees or have an intermediate job. Regarding employment sectors, differences are evident between young adults whose parents were born in Southern Europe on the one hand, and those born in North Africa on the other hand

(Meurs and Pailhé 2008). Young men of a Portuguese background are more likely to work in manufacturing, construction and food activities than their counterparts with a North African background, who are more present in transport, tourism and social care as youth workers. There are only a few in the banking sector, real estate activities and administration. As a whole, there has been upward social mobility, since immigrants' children have higher wages, better jobs and more opportunities than their parents, who mainly work in the manufacturing sector.

However, this pattern of social mobility needs to be qualified. First of all, access to highly-skilled and executive jobs remains challenging: 12 per cent of EMG males have these types of jobs against 17 per cent of the French-born male population. The figure is significantly lower for children of Algerian and Portuguese immigrants who are less represented in high skilled professions than other groups. More importantly perhaps, some children of immigrants thought that having a university degree would enable them to be senior managers, lawyers, doctors or engineers; they never considered that getting a skilled job in the manufacturing sector was a path to social mobility. The discrepancy between social expectations and real opportunities has been shaping a significant resentment among the youth living in the most disadvantaged and ethnically segregated neighbourhoods.

The occupational structure of immigrants and second generations shows different patterns in Lyon from those in Manchester. In the French city, old immigrants are heavily concentrated in non-skilled and low skilled jobs. The upward social mobility of immigrants' children faces many challenges and it is at the core of many academic and public debates: young people from North Africa are less likely to access a qualified job than native populations, even when they have an intermediate university degree. Once they have a non-qualified job, it is also difficult to access a qualified job. A lower level of educational attainment affects

Table 5.4 Percentage of high–medium-skilled workers by country of origin among EMGs in Lyon (2012)

Country of origin	High-skilled	Medium-skilled
Portugal	7.2	6.4
Italy	15.3	8.8
Spain	13.2	13.2
Other 27 EU	21.7	18.1
Other EU	10.6	11.0
Algeria	4.2	6.9
Morocco	9.4	13.2
Tunisia	5.0	8.3
Other countries in Africa	8.5	10.1
Turkey	10.0	7.9
Other	15.8	125
Total	10.4	10.5

Source: authors' elaboration of INSEE Data (2012).

this disadvantage, but once again even with a degree, they face more difficulties than the others. Sharp debates in France are focused on factors influencing these more important difficulties faced by graduates: social class background, lack of wide and diversified networks, university of origin. Ethnic prejudice has been silenced for a long time in French public debates, but in these last few years, with recent anti-discrimination policies, the perspective has changed. Despite strong challenges, some North African graduates manage to find intermediate and even good jobs: there is a slow rise of a lower and middle class within the North African population in Lyon (Santelli 2001).

This is also the case in Munich, although this trend is very limited. In 2010, more than half of the immigrant working population was employed in traditional services (Table 5.5). Most immigrants and their children have low qualified jobs. However, they are more and more represented in sectors in which higher qualifications are demanded. For instance, only 9 per cent of employees in the banking and insurance sectors have an ethnic minority origin (Municipality of Munchen 2013). Moreover, immigrants and their children are also present in journalism, research and education. However, once again, this trend is limited. It is partly explained by the significant educational level of natives and EMGs. In 2010, only 9 per cent of the foreign workforce had a university degree, whereas the rate for the native labour force was 20 per cent. A low education is likely to be even more problematic in Germany than in other countries: indeed, the level of education of Germans is higher than the average of the OECD countries, as more than half of the population has an upper secondary or a post-secondary level (ISCED 3 A/B, 4A). Therefore, EMGs in Munich face challenges for accessing intermediate and good jobs.

The analysis of the sectors in which minorities are employed shows peculiarities among the cities. The manufacturing sector employs more people in Lyon than in Manchester and Munich; in the French city, immigrants and their children are overrepresented in this sector with respect to the total working population. This contrasts with Manchester and Munich where ethnic minorities are

Table 5.5 Service sector in Munich and immigration background (2013) (%)

Area	Immigrants	Natives with migration background	Natives with German background	Total
Finance and administration	2.5	6.1	91.4	100
ICT	4.7	8.3	89.0	100
Social work	7.2	8.5	84.3	100
Education (school and university)	2.3	5.8	84.3	100
Education (kindergarten and creches)	9.2	9.0	81.7	100
Other	23.0	10.7	66.2	100

Source: authors' elaboration on Munich Statistics.

more likely to work in low service activities such as cleaning, restaurants and hotels. The rise of a middle-class is a commonality shared by cities. However, this trend is significantly higher in the British city than in Lyon or Munich, and the EMGs matter. British ethnic minorities access the highest employment positions: with reference to managerial and senior official positions, British Indians definitely outperform their White counterparts.

5.4 Conclusions

The aim of this chapter was to try and understand the role occupied by immigrants and EMGs in the labour markets of Milan, Manchester, Munich, Lyon, Copenhagen and Barcelona. In particular, the attempt was to understand if a knowledge-based economy implies an exclusion of immigrants from the labour market and their massive concentration in the low employment sectors, or rather complex processes including different group's trajectories. Our research findings basically agree with Roger Waldinger's statement according to which: "what is needed is a closer look at … the complex process by which groups are sorted among jobs and labour markets" rather than "emphasizing a mismatch between employers and urban, non white people" (Waldinger 1988). Barcelona, Milan and Copenhagen are cities in which significant migrations are recent and an ethnically segmented labour market is present as immigrants are more concentrated in the traditional service sector, construction, manufacturing. They are also more often employed in low positions with hard working conditions; however, cleavages are also evident among immigrants regarding levels of education, residence statuses and types of contracts, meaning that the so-called "under-class coming from the third world" is actually more diverse than what many think.

Commonalities among immigrant employment patterns in the three cities should not hide significant differences, which are likely to widen in future different types of integration in the host societies. Immigrants in Barcelona and Milan have settled in cities characterized by a great proportion of small companies, a high share of informal economy and in which the impact of the crisis, especially in the sectors that over-represent immigrants, has been more severe. Meanwhile, profound social changes have increased the level of education with a growing aversion towards low-skilled and ill-paid jobs, while female participation in the labour market has increased the demand for domestic workers. This Southern European development pattern means a demand for immigrant workers but, at the same time, they are likely to suffer from strong subordinate relationships in the working place. Domestic jobs and positions in small firms lacking trade unions can mean employments not protected by labour laws and a dependence of immigrant workers with respect to their employers. The crisis has deeply worsened this pattern of horizontal and vertical segregation for immigrants in these cities.

The case of Copenhagen is quite different: domestic services are not as widespread as in Milan and Barcelona due to the relevance of the welfare state in providing services for care. Moreover, immigrants are not under-represented in large companies. However, the second generation still seems in a situation of disadvantage, segregated in medium-low skilled jobs, and with less attitude to self-employment due to a more uncertain economic situation. Copenhagen's local authorities work in order to integrate more immigrants into the public sector, playing an important role in the local labour market in which the protection of workers by labour laws is higher than in private and small firms. This measure may contribute, among other factors, to the rise of a middle-class in the next two decades, whereas this trend appears, at the moment, much more uncertain in Milan and Barcelona. In Spain, immigrants who arrived before the 2007 recession had little trouble finding work immediately, but those who arrived after 2007 struggled to find work as Spanish unemployment rates skyrocketed. Immigrants' individual characteristics had a limited effect on their employment trajectories. Although many immigrants who arrived in Spain between 2000 and 2007 were able to find work and eventually move out of the low skilled positions, the nature of their jobs meant that they were not protected from the recession, and many became unemployed as the economy shed low- and middle-skilled jobs in sectors dominated by immigrants. The paradox is that, in the long term, Spain will likely need immigrants to cover labour shortages because of its aging population and the emigration of native-born workers to other countries (Rodríguez-Planas and Nollenberger, 2014).

The ethnic disadvantage of EMGs is at work in Lyon, Manchester and Munich as well. As a whole, unemployment and job insecurity are of greater concern for EMGs than the native populations. However, the main characteristic of these multi-ethnic cities is the great diversity of employment patterns of EMGs, meaning that groups contribute to the city's economic growth in different ways, not only regarding employment sectors but also with respect to occupations. The rise of a middle-class ethnic minority is also a characteristic of the second pattern, which marks a significant contrast with the first one. In Munich, conversely to Copenhagen, the situation of the second generation in terms of labour market integration is much better than that of the first generation. Surprisingly, this middle class is overlooked by sociologists. As Ruber Gowricharn, who studied the elite formation of EMGs in European countries, writes: "The dominant focus on ethnic minorities has been in terms of underclass with low educational levels, unemployment, poverty, and so forth as outstanding features; yet the upward social mobility of ethnic minorities has been noticed by some researchers" (Gowricharn 2001: 155). With respect to economic growth, these middle class groups matter: not only they are good consumers but also some of them are likely to contribute to forge links with countries. The London Change Institute conducted research into the business relationships between the United Kingdom and India, emphasizing how "cultural matters" challenge the British managers' ability to build ties with their Indian counterparts (London Change Institute 2007). Not surprisingly, the labour market integration of Indian and Chinese EMGs is much better in Manchester in comparison with other EMGs.

A key question about this second pattern is: do post-industrial cities with a growing advanced service sector place greater emphasis on the educational level in shaping employment patterns, or are we witnessing a persistent impact of ethnicity and ethnic discriminations on labour market outcomes? This research suggests that the answer may not be straightforward. We are likely to find different patterns according to the cities. In Manchester, ethnic penalty seems to work as a barrier to employment for EMGs with low qualifications, leading to refer once again to Wilson, who writes that the "vulnerability of poor blacks is beyond racial considerations: inferior educational opportunities reinforce their low position in the labour market and contribute to the widening gulf in economic resources between the have and the have-not in the Black community" (Wilson 1978: 171–172). An overview of EMG groups in Manchester also shows this division between those with the lowest abilities and those at the top of the social ladder who are no less represented than the Whites in the highest positions. There is an exclusion of certain groups from the labour market and a *long lasting* presence in the low wage employment sectors with bad jobs. Along with certain forms of ethnically and socially-based segregation, this employment pattern is likely to be challenging for this city. We may hypothesize that employment patterns of EMGs in the British city have commonalities with Wilson's outcomes. Our research suggests that the case of Lyon is different: the French data suggest that ethnicity not only matters for the lowest educated but also for graduates. Not only they are less likely to work in advanced service sectors, but they may face a glass ceiling at the early stage of their integration in the labour market with a long lasting impact on their opportunities in life.

These research findings question the factors shaping the differences among cities. One dimension is related to the wider institutional context in the countries and how states tackle racism and discrimination. British policymakers made race and ethnicity a valid category of analysis. In fact, the 1968 Act tackled *access racism* providing safeguards against discrimination in employment and housing, and definitely marked the birth of race as an autonomous policy sphere (Bleich 2003: 83–113). Most French policymakers and intellectuals refuse racial and ethnic categorization, arguing that those are socially divisive. Moreover, over the last few decades, human rights groups (and especially the MRAP) were charged with shaping the anti-racism French legislation; "rather than responding to concerns about discrimination against post-colonial immigrant minority groups, the MRAP (The Movement Against Racism and for Friendship among Peoples) leadership focused on expressive racism and especially anti-Semitism" (Bleich 2003: 173). From the beginning of this century, we have observed an increasing awareness of racial discriminations strongly due to the EU anti-racism policies (Calvès 2002). Moreover, new measures were implemented almost four decades after the first British Acts. In the past decades a common debate on non-European immigrants in France argued that time would have favoured the upward social mobility of the second and third generations, but final outcomes are not so convincing. The French pattern is an example to be taken into consideration in Copenhagen, Milan and Barcelona, where some people may legitimately think that "time will do the job".

Notes

1 However, the lack of precision in city and regional data prevent from making a distinction between European immigrants (from France and Italy) and non-European immigrants.
2 When exploring Lyon's demographic growth it is necessary to take into account immigrants' children who are mostly French. In France, we only have data on second and third generations *if they live with their parents*. If they are French and do not live with their parents, it is not possible to locate them. Therefore we can show data about households in which the father/mother was born overseas at regional level and not at city level.

References

Aldrich, H. and Waldinger, R. (1990). Ethnicity and Entrepreneurship. *Annual Review of Sociology*, 16, 111–135.

Alietti, A. (2001). "Il mio vicino é nero", Analisi della relazioni di coabitazione in un quartiere popolare. *Critica sociologica*, 137, 57–67.

Arbaci, S. (2007). Ethnic Segregation, Housing Systems and Welfare Regimes in Europe. *European Journal of Housing Policy*, 7(4), 401–433.

Beauchemin, C., Hamel, C. and Simon, P. (2010). *Trajectoires et origines, enquête sur la diversité des populations en France.* Premiers résultats. Paris: INED.

Beauchemin, C., Hamel, C. and Simon, P. (2016). *Trajectoires et origines, enquête sur la diversité des populations en France.* Paris: INED.

Bleich, E. (2003). *Race Politics in Britain and France: Ideas and Policymaking since the 1960s.* Cambridge: Cambridge University Press.

Calavita, K. (2005). *Law, Race and Exclusion in Southern Europe.* Cambridge: Cambridge University Press.

Calves, G. (2002). Il n'y Pas de Race Ici: Le Modèle Français à l'Epreuve de l'Intégration européenne. *Critique Internationale*, 17.

Caponio, T. and Borkert, M. (eds) (2010). *The Local Dimension of Migration Policymaking.* Amsterdam: Amsterdam University Press.

Change Institute (2007). *Global Business Leadership: UK/India Business: What's Getting in the Way?* London: Change Institute.

Colombo, M., Cordini, M. and Barabanti, P. (2014). Stranieri nel Sistema scolastico e formativo Lombardo in Lombardia, *Gli immigrati in Lombardia*, Osservatorio Regionale per l'integrazione e la multietnicità, Eupolis Lombardia, Regione Lombardia, Fondazione Ismu, pp. 33–76.

Elias, N. and Scotson, J. (1997). *Les logiques de l'exlusion.* Paris: Fayard.

Florida, R. (2005). *Cities and the Creative Class.* London and New York: Routledge.

Fundacion La Caixa (2007). Programas intergeneracionales Hacia una sociedad para todas las edades, *Colección Estudios Sociales* 23, online, available at: www.laCaixa.es/ObraSocial.

Garbaye, R. (2005). *Getting Into Local Power: The Politics of Ethnic Minorities in British and French Cities.* Oxford: Blackwell.

Gowricharn, G. (2001). Ethnic Minorities and Elite Formation. *Journal of International Migration and Integration*, 2(2), 155–167.

Hamnett, C. and Randolph, B. (1988). EMG in the London Labour Market: A Longitudinal Study. *Communities*, xiv, 3: 333–346.

INSEE (2000). *Atlas des populations immigrées en Rhone Alpes.* Lyon.

Kakpo, N. (2007). *L'islam, un recours pour les jeunes.* Paris: Presses de Sciences Po.

Kemeny, Thomas (2012). Cultural Diversity, Institutions, and Urban Economic Performance. *Environment and Planning A*, 44(9): 2134–2152.

Kemeny, Thomas (2013). *Immigrant Diversity and Economic Development in Cities: A Critical Review*. SERC Discussion Papers, SERCDP0149. Spatial Economics Research Centre (SERC), London School of Economics and Political Science, London, UK.

Kogan, I. (2005). Last Hired, First Fired? The Unemployment Dynamics of Male Immigrants in Germany. *European Sociological Review*, 20(5), 445–461.

London Change Institute (2007). *Global Business Leadership. UK/India Business – What's Getting in the Way?* Online, available at: www.changeinstitute.co.uk.

Manchester City Council (2014). *Community of Interest 2014*. State of the City Report.

Mercaletti, F. (2014). I segnali contrastanti della partecipazione ai mercati del lavoro, *Gli immigrati in Lombardia*, Osservatorio Regionale per l'integrazione e la multietnicità, Eupolis Lombardia, Regione Lombardia, Fondazione Ismu, pp. 127–155.

Meurs, D. and Pailhé, A. (2008). Descendantes d'immigrés en France: une double vulnérabilité sur le marché du travail?, *Travail, genre et sociétés*, 2008/2, (20), 87–107.

Municipality of Manchester (2007). *Manchester's Population from 1086*. Online, available at: www.manchester.gov.uk/info/200088/statistics_and_census/438/public_intelligence/3.

Municipality of Munchen (2013). *Interkultureller Integrationsbericht München lebt Vielfalt*. Online, available at: www.muenchen.de/interkult.

Musterd, S. (2005). Social and Ethnic Segregation in Europe: Levels, Causes and Effects. *Journal of Urban Affairs*, 27(3): 331–348.

OECD (2009). *Territorial Reviews: Copenhagen, Denmark*. Paris: OECD.

Peach, C. (2005). The Ghetto and the Ethnic Enclave. In: D. P. Varady (ed.). *Desegregating the City: Ghettos, Enclaves and Inequalities*. Albany, NY: SUNY Press, pp: 31–48.

Rath, J. and Kloosterman, R. (2001). Immigrant Entrepreneurs in Advanced Economies: Mixed Embeddedness Further Explored. *Journal of Ethnic and Migration Studies*, 27(2), 189–202.

Reyneri, E. and Fullin, G. (2011). Labour Market Penalties of New Immigrants in New and Old Receiving West European Countries. *International Migration* 49(1), 31–57.

Rodríguez-Planas, N. and Nollenberger, N. (2014). *Labor Market Integration of New Immigrants in Spain*. IZA Policy Paper No. 93.

Rosholm, M., Scott, K. and Husted, L. (2006). The Times They Are a-Changin: Declining Immigrant Employment Opportunities in Scandinavia. *International Migration Review*, 40(2), 318–347.

Santelli, E. (2001). *La mobilité sociale dans l'immigration, Itinéraires de réussite des enfants d'origine algérienne*. Toulouse: Presses Universitaires du Mirail.

Sassen, S. (1991). *The Global City: New York, London and Tokyo*. Princeton: Princeton University Press.

Senik, C. and Verdier, T. (2011). Segregation, Entrepreneurship and Work Values: The Case of France. *Journal of Population Economics*, 24, 1207–1234.

Stoumann, J. (2006). *Moving Out of the Shadow Economy: Tools and Methods for an Inclusive Entrepreneurship Approach*. Denmark: EVU's Knowledge Centre for Ethnic Entrepreneurship.

Tammaru, T., Marcińczak, S., Ham, M. van and Musterd, S. (eds) (2016). *Socio-economic Segregation in European Capital Cities: East meets West*. London and New York: Routledge.

United Nations (2013). *Trends in International Migrant Stock: The 2013 Revision*. United

Nations database, POP/DB/MIG/Stock/Rev.2013, Department of Economic and Social Affairs.

Waldinger, R. (1988). The Ethnic Division of Labour Transformed: Native Minorities and New Immigrants in Post Industrial NY. *Communities*, xiv, (3), 318–332.

Wilson, W. J. (1978). *The Declining Significance of Race, Blacks and the Changing American Institutions*. Chicago, IL: Chicago Press.

Part II

Urban policies for affordable housing and good quality employment

Six case studies

6 Barcelona

Policies for social cohesion in the context of urban competitiveness

Ana Belén Cano Hila, Marc Pradel Miquel and Marisol Garcia

6.1 Introduction[1]

The growth and decline of cities has been a constant theme in urban literature and policymaking (Kantor and Turok, 2012). The 2008 financial and economic crisis has accentuated this concern in European cities, where historically a compromise had been reached between particular economic interests and social responsibility (Häussermann and Haila, 2005: 53). While urban governing elites of all major cities are enthralled by the idea of city marketing and claim competitive advantage to attract important events such as Olympic Games, festivals and the like (Martinotti, 2005: 91) there is a need for more nuanced analysis of the institutional choices required to maintain a balance between the capacity to compete in the global economy and to maintain social cohesion (Ranci, 2013). Although national regulatory structures (with the exception of financial markets) play a strong role in European cities (Le Galès, 2002, 2005; Kazepov, 2005; García and Judd, 2012), local actors can exhibit relative autonomy in their policy choices in order to achieve social cohesion through welfare policy instruments (Andreotti *et al.*, 2012). Two policy fields in governance decision-making that impact directly on the population: employment, and housing and neighbourhood cohesion.

This chapter[2] analyses the development of policies for economic development and social cohesion in Barcelona during the period 2003–2014. We focus on the changes in these two policy fields. First we examine housing policies in Barcelona in the context of the expanding – and then bursting – Spanish housing bubble. We look at the regenerated section of the East-side nineteenth-century industrial neighbourhood of *Poblenou*, where the knowledge-economy district of 22@ was planned and developed from the late 1990s. Second, we will examine active employment-policy changes in relation to the creation of good quality jobs. Since the 2008 economic crisis, policies targeting the quality of jobs have been increasingly substituted by policies to mitigate increased unemployment in a context where housing affordability and accessibility have become an acute problem for those who cannot afford paying their mortgage or their rent. The concept of social cohesion is articulated at different levels of government, from national to neighbourhood (Eizaguirre *et al.*, 2012). In this chapter we take the national level as the regulatory background whose employment and housing laws have influenced local policies while we focus on the territorial scales of city and neighbourhood.

The Barcelona story is particularly telling because of the city's important economic diversification in the post-industrial urban regeneration over many years and of the policy readjustments before and during the economic crisis both in employment and housing and moreover because of a political change in the governing majority. Barcelona was governed by left-wing coalitions for 32 years, from 1979 to 2011, and by a conservative minority from 2011 to 2015. This change accounts for the transformation of a model of governance developed during the first period, and for different policies for social cohesion and economic development.

Historically, Barcelona's modern development since 1979 occurred in a context of consolidation of democracy and of a redistribution of power over three levels of government in Spanish administration: central, autonomic (regional) and local (provincial[3] and city). The local level saw its competences increased, although financial resources were transferred mainly from central government to regional administrations, limiting the possibilities for developing policies at the local level. A process of regional recentralization concurrent with the devolution from central government of financial resources prompted local authorities to create mechanisms for coordination with regional and central governments. This governance structure has conditioned the implementation of local policies in Barcelona since the required financial support was controlled by the regional government.

Politically, Barcelona's left-wing coalition government, led by the Catalan Socialist Party, often had to confront the conservative Catalan regional government (CiU) that ruled from 1980 until 2015 with the exception of a seven-year period between 2003 and 2010, when the left-wing coalition also governed at the regional, Catalan level. This seven-year period of aggregated power was instrumental for the implementation of housing and neighbourhood policies, as we will explain later on. The long period of political hegemony by a socialist-led coalition at the local level explains the consolidation of the governance model of the city, based on public leadership with participation from civil society and consensus-building with private and civil society actors (Blackeley, 2005; García, 2003, 2008; Degen and García, 2012). As Michael Parkinson (OECD, 2005) has pointed out, *place shaping* was actually first introduced in Barcelona, where the local government developed a governance model based on strong links with civil society, especially neighbourhood associations and trade unions, but also with the Chamber of Commerce and the institutions behind the Barcelona trade shows (Ferias). This model made possible the necessary consensus to implement a programme of redistribution of urban resources based on the consolidation of civic, social and political rights.

Social cohesion as a main policy objective was introduced by the progressive coalition fronted by the charismatic mayor Pasqual Maragall in the early 1980s. This good negotiator coordinated a flow of resources from many levels – the EU, and national and regional funds – to the city to implement policies in education, social services and many other fields (Truño, 2000: 65). He also improved the public realm through the engagement of citizens in urban regeneration. However, Barcelona's governing coalition initiated an internal transformation with the successful bid for hosting the Olympic Games of 1992. The nomination for the games in 1986 brought the creation of public-led partnerships with private actors to develop urban projects, and the reorganization of the local administration in order to improve efficiency. Private actors were further stimulated by the entrance of Spain into the European Community in 1986, which yielded a new pool of resources for policies linked to economic development and exports to European markets. As a result Barcelona experienced an urban and economic transformation with an increase of 64.4 per cent in per-capita GDP between 1986 and 1999 (Pareja-Eastaway *et al.*, 2007).

The celebration of the Olympic Games consolidated a model of local governance based on public–private partnerships and strategic planning (Degen and García, 2012: 3). The so-called "Barcelona model" has shaped policies for economic growth since then. After the games, strategic planning was extended to different policy areas such as transport, tourism or culture, with an increasing emphasis on competitiveness in attracting businesses and tourists. While innovation and foreign investments were gaining priority in local government with an economic agenda for growth, the quality of life of the population and social cohesion still figured on the policy agenda.

Successive city mayors emphasized economics by reinforcing the strategy for economic growth based on knowledge-intensive activities and culture linked to urban regeneration. In 2000 the city council started the urban renewal of the eastside of the city (*Littoral front and 22@ district*), a former industrial area destined to become a knowledge-based district. This intervention generated concerns regarding the over-emphasis on business and the neglect of social housing, and weakened the consensus with neighbourhood associations, which actively challenged the new turn in the development of the city. These concerns grew with the organization of the mega project *Forum de les Cultures* in 2004, seen as a project that served only particular interests rather than the whole city (García-Ramon *et al.*, 2000; Miles, 2008). The forum, a four-month macro event, functioned as a catalyst to develop the Diagonal-Mar neighbourhood, with exclusive new housing designed for high-income consumers promoted entirely by private developers worldwide. Seen as the demise of the "Barcelona model" (Borja, 2010; Miles, 2008) this private intervention and the strong opposition it generated was yet another incentive for the Catalan parliamentary debate in the same year and the consequent passing of the Neighbourhood Act. We will come back to the importance of this Act in our analysis of housing policies.

In sum, Barcelona's intense economic transformation brought a weakening of the governance model of the city, which was based on combining growth and social cohesion via social consensus. In 2011 a new conservative leadership took office and ruled the city until 2015.[4] This new government brought important changes in policies and in the debates on the model for the development of

Barcelona and of the metropolitan area. We concentrate here on the changes in approaches to housing and to employment policies in Barcelona with the outbreak of the crisis and the change of political colour in the city council. We focus on policies during 2003–2014 and on the effects of the beginning of financial crisis in 2007.

6.2 Measures to foster housing affordability

6.2.1 The policy arena: actors' coalitions and the policy agenda

One of the main features of the housing market in Spain is the weakness of the rental sector compared to ownership. This pattern started in the 1960s and accelerated after the return of democracy. This trend was the result of legislative changes that discouraged owners from renting out their properties and that also changed demand patterns. During the Franco regime, populist laws enforced low rent and automatic rent contract renewals for households, disadvantaging owners. With the economic boom of the 1960s, new real-estate investors opted to build houses destined for ownership due to the strict regulation of the rental market. In addition, existing rental housing stock was not maintained as the result of a lack of investment by owners. As a result, the rental sector shrank while the rental stock deteriorated. The arrival of democracy brought new perspectives and the new socialist government tried to promote a total liberalization of the rental sector (1985), without rules on the duration of contracts and their renewal, in an attempt to stimulate the rental sector. Nevertheless, the reform did not manage to shift the trend and a new law was adopted prescribing a minimum of five years rental contract. On the other hand, housing policies were basically directed to foster ownership by subsidizing private housing production. The main tool of housing policies in Spain has been the "Officially Protected Housing" (Viviendas de Protección Official (VPO)) that can be built by private or public actors while regulated by the government with regard to surface area and price. This tool has been used extensively at regional and local levels in the case of Barcelona.

As in many other policy areas, in the 1980s the competences for housing policies were transferred to Autonomous Communities, but without a corresponding resource endowment. The result was less involvement of public administration in the provision of housing. The complexity of managing the public housing stock, the lack of experience of regional governments and their ideological positions induced regional and local governments to privatize their public housing, following the pattern of the United Kingdom (Pareja-Eastaway and Varo, 2002). Thus, public housing in Barcelona is framed by central government legislation on land use and building, and by the regional and local governments with formal competences for housing policies. Housing policy in Catalonia and Barcelona city responds to a dual model of the housing system according to Kemeny's classification (1995). This is characterized by a significant shortage of public housing for rent and a low PIB expenditure on public and subsidized housing

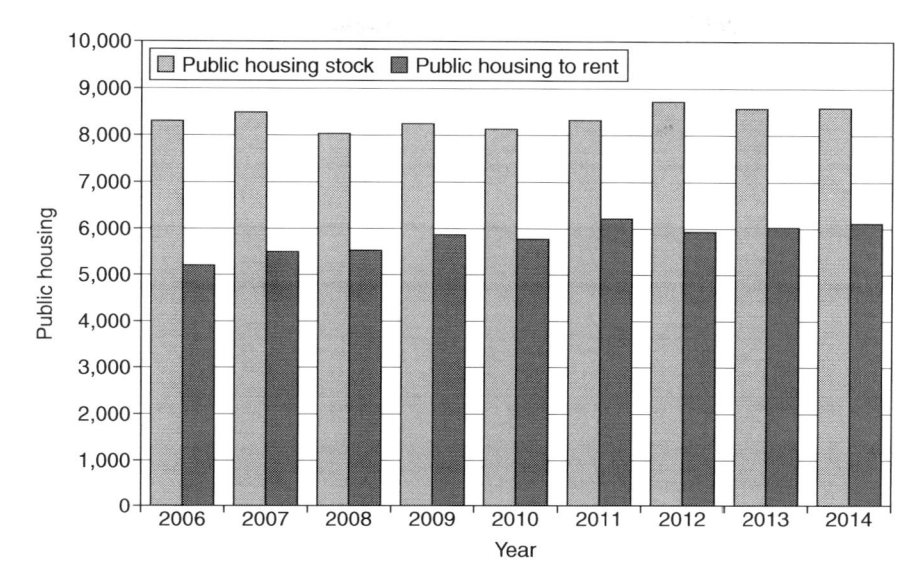

Figure 6.1 Evolution of public housing stock and public housing for rent in Barcelona (2006–2014).

Source: authors' elaboration on Patronat Municipal de l'Habitatge (online, available at: www.pmhb.org).

(see Figure 6.1). According to the Ministry of Planning and Sustainability, the Catalan Housing Agency and Municipal Housing, Catalonia had, in 2013, 14,000 rental houses; while Barcelona had 11,000. Other municipal public promoters built 3,000 public housing units for rent in the last decade. Overall, the public housing stock for rent in Catalonia (including Barcelona) is approximately 30,000 dwellings, which represents around 2 per cent of the total housing stock (about 2.8 million first-residence dwellings). These figures show a significant shortage of social housing for rent to cover social needs, in both a regional and local context[5] (Taula d'Entitats del Tercer Sector Social de Catalunya, 2013).

This duality is explained by the residual nature of public housing (Bosch, 2011: 89). The outcome of this model of housing policy is a significant social housing shortage and an imbalance between affordable housing supply and demand. In fact, this imbalance was intensified in the boom period, when the price per square meter increased exponentially; it declined after the onset of the crisis (see Figure 6.2).

At the national level, the debate has been around two main issues: legislation on land use, and measures to foster renting instead of ownership. The frame of these debates was the economic crisis and the bursting of the speculative housing bubble (1998–2007). In 1998 the central government adopted a new Land Use law, allowing greater liberalization of land. The objective, as declared by government, was twofold: first to generate economic growth through the real-estate

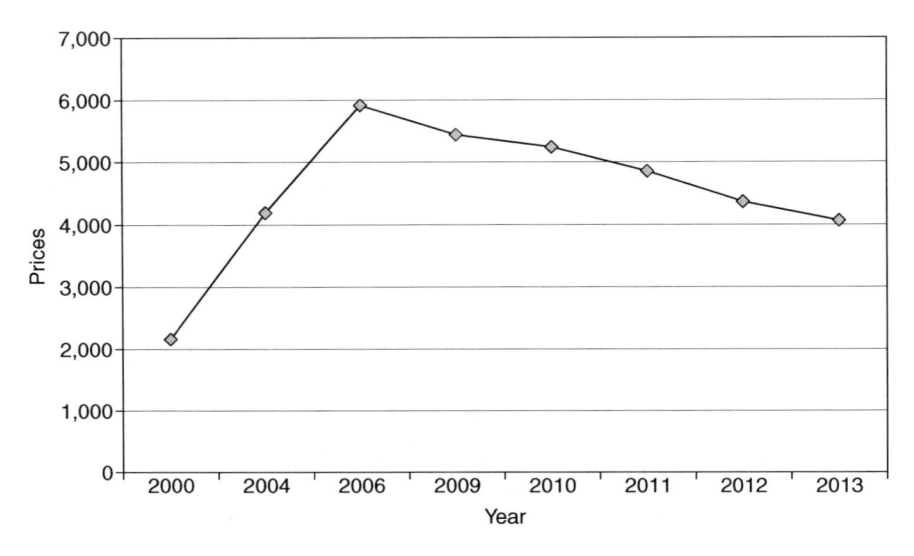

Figure 6.2 Evolution of housing prices in Barcelona €/m² (2000–2013).

Source: authors' elaboration on Ajuntament de Barcelona.

sector and second to generate more supply and reduce the rising price of housing. However, the real impact of land liberalization was still higher prices. Between 1998 and 2007 housing prices skyrocketed in Spain, especially in large cities where demand was higher and where the small rental sector supply and the rising house prices brought problems in housing accessibility, especially for young people. As a result, between 2006 and 2008 a wave of mobilizations started in Barcelona, Bilbao and Madrid, demanding policies for affordable housing, a real focus on the rental sector and the involvement of national, regional and local governments in housing policies. This wave of protests occurred alongside national and regional parliamentary debates and the adoption of new laws and plans to provide access to housing (Camargo Correa, 2009).

In Barcelona the left-wing coalition that governed Catalonia brought new approaches and debates on housing and urban policies. First, the new government promoted a decentralization of resources for urban renewal and the active involvement of citizens and local authorities through the Neighbourhood Act (2/2004), which enforced a programme for urban renewal in collaboration with city councils. Second, the Catalan government drafted legislation to avoid the negative effects of the speculative bubble, trying to create some regulations concerning the housing market.

However, the bursting of the housing bubble and the financial crisis brought considerable changes in the debates and policies, as well as new social problems. One of these is the emerging crisis created by housing evictions as the result of unemployment and mortgage arrears, since Spanish legislation does not stipulate that repossession of a property by banks cancels the debt of the former owner. As a result, not only are families evicted from their houses but remain in debt. Since 2009 the PAH (Platform for Mortgage Victims) movement has urged legislation for structural changes in housing policies. Catalonia is the Spanish region with the most evictions in the years 2007–2013 (79,043) compared to 44,616 in Madrid (PAH, 15/06/2015).[6] A new motion was prepared in this region in 2014, based on the Catalan legislation on Right to Housing, providing legal grounds to municipalities and Autonomous Community governments to fine financial institutions for vacant housing property (De Weerdt and García, 2015).

6.2.2 *Policy contents*

Returning to legislative and policy changes, in 2004 the national government, under the Spanish Socialist Party, created a new Ministry of Housing with the aim of improving accessibility to housing. This ministry launched several initiatives, such as a programme to help young people to get access to rental housing (grants of €210 per month with a rent contract). In 2008 it introduced the State Plan for Housing and Rehabilitation 2009–2012, with the aim of re-orientating housing policies to the rental sector, with 40 per cent of social housing based on rents instead of ownership, and subsidizing those private investors developing this social housing. In 2012, the conservative party (*Partido Popular*) approved the State Plan for Housing and Rehabilitation 2013–2016. That plan suppressed the previous one but also focussed on subsidizing loans and promoting housing rehabilitation.

The Catalan government developed the Neighbourhood Act (*Llei de Barris 2/2004*), which foresaw important public investment[7] in selected neighbourhoods in order to change the dynamics of the land and housing market, and to generate urban regeneration and social cohesion. The Neighbourhood Act inspired by the EU URBAN programme aimed to improve the quality of life in these disadvantaged neighbourhoods. The functioning of this programme represents an innovation in: (a) *multi-scale governance*, with municipalities and regional bodies sharing financing and responsibility (Martí-Costa and Parés, 2009; Nel. Io, 2010); (b) *multidimensionality and comprehensiveness*: the law presents a comprehensive intervention plan divided into different areas: economic, social, physical and environment; and (c) *citizen participation:* the participation of residents in the improvement of neighbourhoods is considered an essential element of this law. Some critics argue, however, that the Neighbourhood Act 2/2004 only includes citizen participation in the revision process, but not in the definition and implementation stage (Martí-Costa and Parés, 2009).[8] With the newly elected conservative government this programme was frozen in 2012 and all projects in the course of implementation were aborted. Despite criticisms concerning limited citizen participation, the neighbourhood programme was a success in many ways. Public spaces and road and mobility infrastructures were upgraded and welfare-service locations were refurbished. Between 2004 and 2007 the programme invested €792 million in 70 projects carried out in different neighbourhoods throughout Catalonia. In Barcelona the investment in redevelopment of six neighbourhoods amounted to €91 million (Nel. lo, 2008)

Complementing these efforts, in 2007, the Catalan government passed the Law on the Right to Housing (*Llei del dret a l'habitatge 2007*) as well as the National Pact for Housing (*Pacte Nacional per l'habitatge 2007–2016*). This pact was signed by the Catalan government – the driving force behind that agreement – by the city council of Barcelona and other local administrations as well as by social actors[9] and by the building sector (Bosch, 2011: 88). The National Pact for Housing constitutes a political and social commitment, whose main goal is to resolve the unmet needs of the Catalan population concerning access to decent housing before 2016. The agreement has four main goals: (a) improving access to housing, especially among young people; (b) improving the housing stock; (c) increasing the amount of rental housing, aiming to prevent social exclusion; (d) ensuring decent housing for all families (Generalitat de Catalunya, 2007). The measures proposed by the Catalan government are specified in a local housing plan to promote a proactive municipal housing policy. The local actors have to coordinate with the Catalan government in order to specify local housing policies and to create consortiums.

At the local level of Barcelona this governance arrangement has been concretized in three examples: the *Plan de Vivienda de Barcelona 2008–2016* (Barcelona Housing Plan 2008–2016), the *Pla Estratègic Metropolità* 2010–2020 (Strategic Plan 2010–2020) and the *Pla territorial metropolità de Barcelona* 2010–2026 (PTMB) (Barcelona Metropolitan Territorial Plan 2010–2026). All these plans and governance arrangements[10] intend to encourage mixed-housing neighbourhoods and a more socially cohesive city, but so far have had no visible results in terms of the creation of public housing or reducing housing demand through other means. In fact, the plans do not include a specific budget for housing development; financial resources depend on the context and possibilities of each government over the period of the plan (Esteban, 2012). On the whole it is too early to provide a sound assessment on the impact of these plans.

6.2.3 Housing policies and urban regeneration in Barcelona: the 22@ district

After the Olympic Games, most of the traditional industrial activity of *Poblenou* had moved to the rest of the metropolitan region, leaving hectares of derelict industrial premises. The neighbourhood suffered from a lack of investment and infrastructure and the housing stock was in a bad state. From 1996 the city council promoted the development of an urban plan for regeneration through the creation of a new district for innovation and knowledge-intensive companies. To this end, the Metropolitan General Plan changed the land-use objectives. The key element of the plan was to transform land use from industrial (22 in the planning code) to knowledge-intensive (the so-called 22@ activities). This change aimed at establishing attractive conditions for private investment in the area as well as directing this investment towards knowledge-based activities. The intervention affected 4,000,000 m² of constructed land, 3,200,000 for productive activities and 800,000 for other uses such as housing and collective services (Pareja-Eastaway *et al.*, 2007).

The 22@ urban renewal increased both housing stock and population and also brought a rise of housing prices. Figure 6.3 shows how, since 2001, the district of Sant Martí, where the 22@ project is located, reversed the trend towards losing population. Although this trend was general in Barcelona, if we compare Sant Martí with the two other east-side districts of Barcelona, Sant Andreu and Nou Barris (both traditional working class districts with decreasing or stagnant populations), we see a population increase along with the 22@ urban regeneration project.

The urban regeneration of the district brought considerable debate and strong opposition from neighbourhood associations, who felt that a major transformation of the neighbourhood was taking place without their being consulted. Organized citizens demanded facilities and public intervention in the neighbourhood and opposed a new project that meant a breakdown of the local traditional landscape and social life. Among the demands were the preservation of industrial heritage, the creation of public facilities and public and protected housing. There was also an identity issue: the 22@ project was proposing a new name for the district without taking into consideration the historical past of the neighbourhood and its

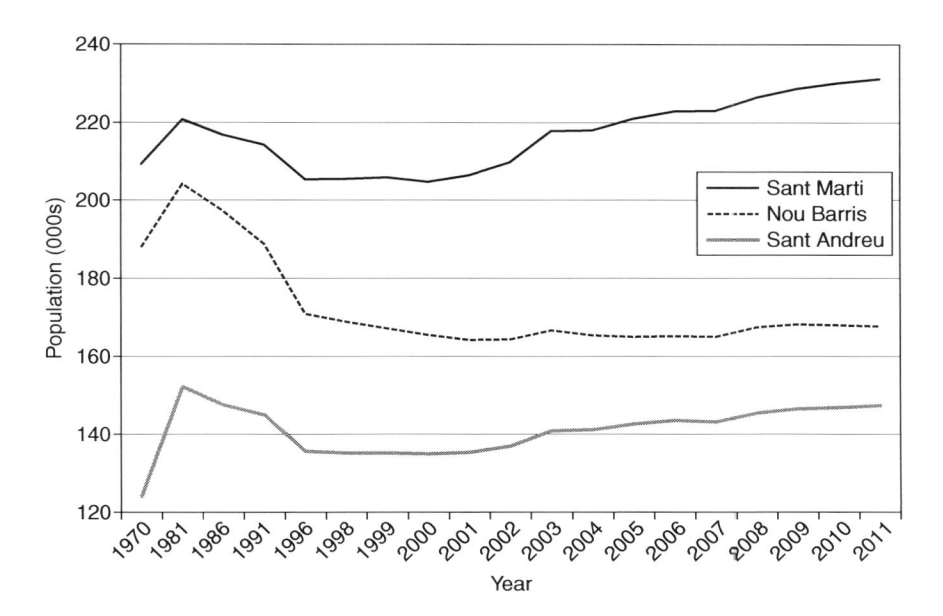

Figure 6.3 Evolution of population in the east side of the city (districts of Sant Martí, Nou Barris and Sant Andreu, Barcelona) (1970–2014).

Source: authors' elaboration on Municipal Data 2015.

existing economic and social activity. The project has been criticized for its lack of connectivity with already existing social life in the area, while the creators of a new industrial district considered the area as a "tabula rasa" (Martí-Costa and Bonet, 2008). The pressure of the inhabitants and further negotiations resulted in various improvements of the plan, including less density for private building in the area, the creation of public facilities to provide services to the whole new population attracted to the neighbourhood and the construction of protected housing.

As the 22@ plan represents urban planning without participative or social dimensions, the inhabitants included housing demands in their appeal to the city council. Foreseeing that the increase in population would bring gentrification with increasing housing prices, neighbourhood associations wanted to ensure that part of this protected housing would be reserved for the residents of *Poblenou*. "We want to continue living in *Poblenou*" was their motto in the mobilization of neighbours and one of the stronger demands. The plan that was agreed upon included the creation of 4,000 new protected dwellings in the neighbourhood mainly for the family members of existing residents, especially young ones, to be constructed over 15 years by public, private and civil society actors. However, development of protected housing in the district has been slow: after 12 years only 1,300 of the 4,000 anticipated dwellings have been constructed, and 500 more are under construction.[11]

The case of 22@ shows that despite the new approaches to housing and urban policies at the local level, developed from 2003 onwards and with decentralization of resources, and with active involvement of citizens and local authorities in the development of programmes for the improvement of neighbourhoods in favour of social cohesion, the real impacts have significant weak points. Although the plan included the idea of protected housing to foster a social mix, the district's renewal was not conceived as such and the emphasis on protected housing only came after the demand of the inhabitants of *Poblenou*. This conception of renewal has private actors as main protagonists, who assumed the costs of urbanization and expropriation in exchange for greater profit from the land redevelopment. In this framework the development of protected housing has been slower than the development of private stock. Moreover, this conception of renewal has prevented maintaining or improving the already existing housing stock, with private developers preferring expropriation and creation of new buildings. In fact, the development of the 22@ district must be contextualized in a period of economic growth with a strong building sector, which has brought intense private activity to the district. The amount of protected housing planned has not covered the demand. Also, the number of companies that decided to settle in the 22@ district and their activity are considered to fall short of the original targets, while the incentives for attracting more companies to the 22@ district and consolidating their business were drastically reduced in the years of austerity. Nonetheless, according to one of the presidents[12] of 22@ district part of the responsibility for the relative failure (over 1,000 small companies were located in the district) is due to the total lack of support from the regional government and the declining interest of the last socialist major to develop a competitive district.[13] For all these reasons, the 22@ district in Barcelona is considered an uncompleted project not only because of the impact the economic crisis has had but also because of difficulties to attract high-tech companies to the city and because of limited political will (Dot Jutgla *et al.*, 2010a, 2010b).

Besides, urban renewal has not meant an innovative approach to housing policies; only already existing instruments were deployed, which only made available more land in a system in which public or non-profit housing is marginal. We have to consider here the weak role that the local level plays in the provision of housing and the general context of absence of such policies. The economic crisis forced the city council to find new formulas and instruments aimed at maintaining public property of land and housing and at protecting the tenants of public housing from the operations of foreign vulture funds active in the depressed Spanish housing market.

6.3 Strategies of promotion of good quality jobs

6.3.1 Policy arena: actors, coalitions and the policy agenda

The city of Barcelona has a solid, dynamic and diversified economic structure generating 32 per cent of jobs in Catalonia. In the local economy service-sector employment accounts for 84 per cent of the working population, with construction at 10 per cent and industry at 6 per cent. The diversification of the city economy, the importance of tourism and the growth of the added-value activities and of activities of the third sector explain the lower unemployment rate in the city compared to the rest of Catalonia and Spain (see Figure 6.4).

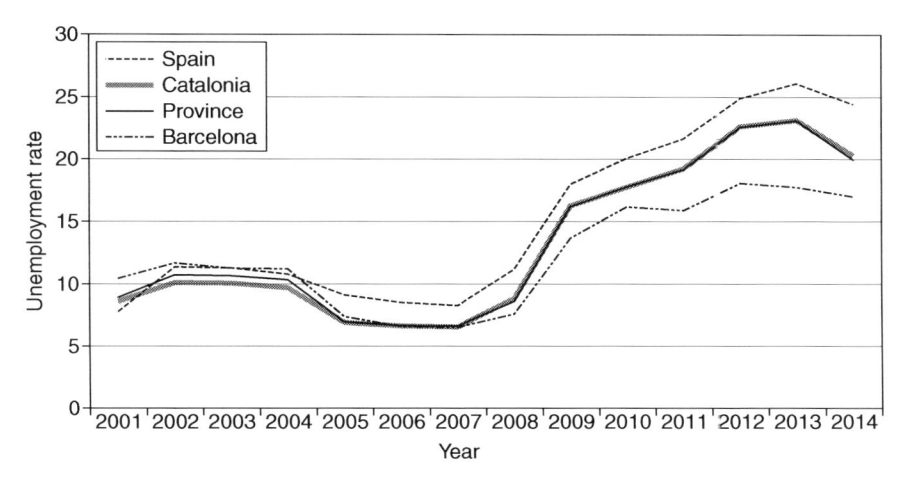

Figure 6.4 Evolution of unemployment rate in Spain, Catalonia, Province and Barcelona (2001–2014).

Source: authors' elaboration on Idescat data.

Between 2007 and 2010, the unemployment rate in Barcelona increased from 6.5 per cent to 16.5 per cent, reaching 18.1 per cent in 2012 and decreasing to 17 per cent in 2014 (data from the statistical office of Barcelona city council). This unemployment level is strongly related to the slump of the real-estate sector, which has been shrinking. The social groups most affected by the crisis are workers in the construction sector, people over 45 years, people who have a low educational level (those who leave the education system without completing the compulsory schooling, those who failed to get the certificate of compulsory secondary education, etc.), and especially young people[14] (16–24 years old) (see Figure 6.5).

The unemployment rate among young people, aged 16–29 years, is 32 per cent as against the 17.4 per cent for people aged 30 years and over (Interview with labour union representative UGT). According to the latest indicators presented by Eurostat, the youth unemployment rate was 22.2 per cent in the UE28 in June 2015. Among the member states, the highest youth unemployment rates were observed in Spain (53.2 per cent) and Greece (52.4 per cent). Data show the extent to which young people have been increasingly affected by the economic crisis. The risk of youth vulnerability is intensified by academic (non)performance. In Catalonia, during the last quarter of 2014, the youth unemployment rate rose to 45.7 per cent among those young people who have only compulsory schooling or have dropped out of the education system, whereas the unemployment rate was 24.5 per cent among those who had entered post-compulsory education (Catalan Observatory of Youth).[15]

These patterns of unemployment during the crisis have influenced the transformation of earlier employment and economic development policies of Barcelona,

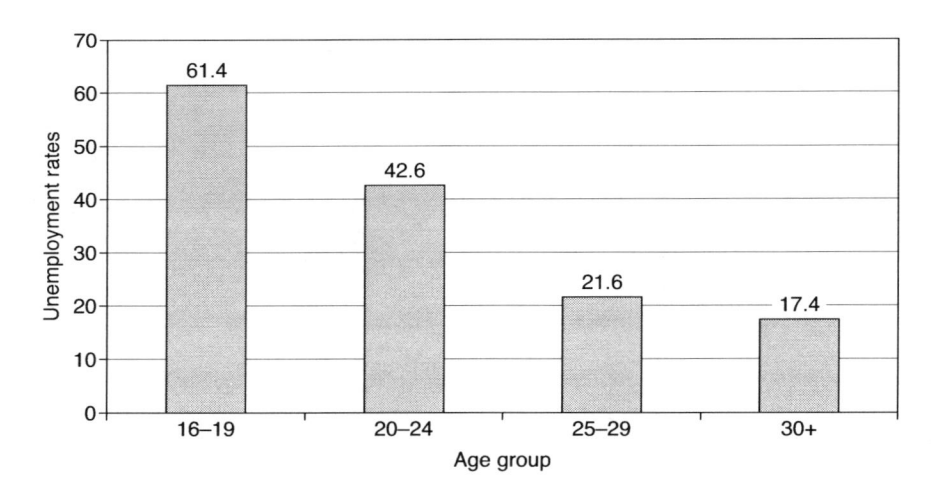

Figure 6.5 Unemployment rate: young people (16–29 years) and adult population, Catalonia, (last quarter, 2014).

Source: authors' elaboration on Catalan Observatory of Youth.

and the overall "Barcelona model" of urban regeneration in which active employment policies (for good quality jobs and for unemployed people) to foster human capital were important. Active employment policies have been part of a wider view of economic development that included large-scale projects such as the development of the 22@ district and that consists in fostering the knowledge economy in Barcelona. Nevertheless, these efforts must be contextualized in the complex framework of multi-level governance in which the local level has few competences and even fewer resources for employment and economic development policies.

Whereas passive employment policies (the management of unemployment benefits) remain under the control of the national government, active employment policies were transferred to the Catalan government in 1998. In the late 1990s the Catalan conservative government developed a centralized model of provision of policies consisting in a network of private and third-sector centres providing activation policies (Alós Moner, 1999). This model, strongly criticized by the left-wing parties, was completed by the actions of local governments, which received funds from the other levels of government.[16] In this framework municipalities of the metropolitan area have developed actions for economic development including entrepreneurship and training policies. These efforts have been undertaken against a background of scarcity of resources at the local level, and the need to find funds from other levels of government, especially the EU.

The city council of Barcelona sought to promote human capital to serve companies in key strategic sectors. Led by the consecutive socialist governments, trade unions and associations of entrepreneurs played a key role in the decision-making and implementation of employment policies, following the formal structure of decision-making at other governance levels. It is important to remember that social dialogue between trade unions and employer associations is a central element in the multi-level governance framework of employment policies in Spain. At the national level, employer associations and trade unions are represented in the board of the State Public Service of Employment (*Servicio Público de Empleo Estatal*). Resources for professional training at the national level are also managed by a partnership formed by employer associations, trade unions and public administration (*Fundación tripartita*). At the Catalan level there exists the Employment Service of Catalonia (*Servei d'Ocupació de Catalunya, SOC*), where trade unions and employer associations are also represented. However, these social agents have seen their decision-making capacity undermined by the strong influence of political party lines

Although decision-making in employment questions is the city council's responsibility through the Economic Promotion and Employment department, the implementation of policies falls to the agency for local economic development *Barcelona Activa*[17] located in *the* San Martin district. This agency, a public limited company with public capital, had from the start in the late 1980s the explicit aim of implementing activation policies for economic promotion and of improving employment in numbers and quality, as well as to offer know-how for the creation and consolidation of new small and medium-sized enterprises. Its board of directors consists of representatives of all the political municipal groups, employer associations, trade unions and university representatives. The activities of *Barcelona Activa* also include fundraising. From the very beginning the agency has adopted the European Union employment guidelines and the actions it develops focus on the central prescriptions of the European Employment Strategy: (a) improving the skills of unemployed and employed workers, (b) fostering entrepreneurship and, (c) developing specific programmes for women to further equal opportunities in the labour market. Until 2011, the left-wing city governing coalition and trade unions emphasized policies to develop employees' skills to fit the new service economy of the city. This orientation complemented the policy to attract new companies and to create of new clusters of activity (in the 22@ district) through active employment policies that included improving workers' qualifications.

After 2011 this consolidated model changed due to the restrictions imposed by austerity programmes and by the arrival of the Catalan conservative party into power in the city council. In fact, conservative parties and employer associations preferred to promote policies focused on companies' competitiveness as a way to create employment rather than on employees' skills. Furthermore, the new approach gave less relevance to social dialogue between trade unions and employer associations in favour of a more diverse participation of actors in the definition of policies for competitiveness (Interview with Labour Union Representative, UGT). From 2011 the city council promoted the forum Barcelona Growth (*Barcelona Creixement*), which tried to involve local and foreign actors (including not only the local Chamber of Commerce but also foreign chambers of commerce and other representatives of business interests abroad) in an overall strategy for economic growth.

Due to austerity measures at different levels, *Barcelona Activa* saw its budget decrease, which had relied heavily on external funds. In 2012, the budget of the agency was cut by 57 per cent, affecting particularly the strategies for employment[18] (training, professional orientation) (Interview with person responsible for Economic Growth and Resources, Barcelona City Council). The new conservative government took the new situation as an opportunity in favour of the reformulation of the model of development of active employment policies. The new formulation was based on putting companies at the centre of strategies for employment, and thus, reorganizing the whole agency towards bringing services to companies rather than services to citizens (Interview with Labour Union Representative, UGT). From 2012 the re-orientation of the employment development model was based on: (a) competitiveness, leaving social cohesion aside; and, (b) a sharper focus on the creation of employment regardless of its quality. With this new focus, the new local authorities emphasized the role of the private sector in the generation of employment and competitiveness for the city.

6.3.2 *Policy contents*

Until 2010 the strategic planning of employment policies was organized through employment pacts between the city council of Barcelona, the two largest trade unions of the city (and Spain) and the two main employer associations. The objective of the pacts was to create a consensus around employment-policy measures required in the city. After 2004 the pact was specifically focused on "quality of employment", with a collection of initiatives oriented towards the improvement of skills and the attraction and improvement of certain sectors. This pact was renewed in 2008 with a plan for the period 2008–2011 with the participation of the regional Catalan government.

The pact for quality in employment was explicitly aligned with the Lisbon Agenda (2000–2020) and the European Employment Strategy (2010–2020) as well as the National Action Plan and the objectives of the Catalan Strategy for Employment 2012–2020.[19] In line with the overall strategy of the city, this pact foresaw actions directed towards the creation of new companies and the internationalization of existing ones, as well as the reduction of unemployment – especially among young people – through improving skills, avoiding academic failure and the inclusion of more people, especially women, in the labour market. The pact included mechanisms for the analysis of results and of the evolution of the initiatives carried out by a commission in which all actors involved were represented. The measures to combat unemployment were: (a) attracting creative and innovative talent to the city; (b) designing a high-impact action plan for inclusion through the work of youths who drop out of the education system without even minimum qualifications; (c) designing a mechanism of orientation, training and professional insertion, tailor-made for people affected by reconversion of sectors in difficulties, such as construction or certain business activities; and (d) elaborating and developing a strategy of labour inclusion of groups suffering from high vulnerability in the labour market by means of new active policies that included training programmes and itineraries of personalized insertion closely coordinated and optimizing the overall resources and existing entities in the city. The pact included an explicit reference to the improvement of employment in service sectors linked to tourism. Despite the emphasis on added-value activities as the cornerstone of the future Barcelona economy, the growth of tourism had brought low-quality jobs. This triggered a debate on the "quality of tourism". As a result, the pact foresaw measures to attract tourism with greater purchasing power.

The agreements in the pact were transformed into specific policies through *Barcelona Activa*, which developed two main lines of action: the first directed at economic promotion and the second at employment services (Gentile, 2011). Economic promotion includes programmes linked to the creation of start-ups and programmes aimed at improving the competitiveness of existing companies. The line oriented towards employment is labelled "professional opportunities" and includes programmes for professional development, training for the unemployed, programmes on professional orientation and job search, and resources for improving capabilities linked with new technologies. Both lines were oriented towards the creation/maintenance of good quality jobs. To foster jobs of good quality *Barcelona Activa* seeks the qualification of workers and the creation of new start-ups providing added value and higher productivity, ready to create those good-quality jobs. However, there are no explicit measures to improve working conditions in companies.[20] Amongst the existing programmes, those related to human capital are based on professional development and life-long learning. This line explicitly aims at improving the working conditions of workers already employed through new skills.

The promotion of quality jobs was one of the main objectives of *Barcelona Activa*. In 2007, 78 per cent of the budget of the agency was dedicated to quality employment and only 18 per cent to business creation and growth and 4 per cent to innovation (Gentile, 2011). Moreover, the philosophy of the city concerning "*social dialogue*" – that is, fostering a consensus between representatives of workers and entrepreneurs at the local level, complementing social dialogue at national and regional levels – had an impact on debates and approaches concerning employment policies beyond the action of *Barcelona Activa*. With the 2008 economic crisis *Barcelona Activa* increased its services towards employment while the services towards entrepreneurship diminished. As a result, as Table 6.1 shows, the number of users of employment services increased between 2005 and 2011, whereas users of entrepreneurship services were fewer. But since 2011, the new approach of *Barcelona Activa* has reinforced entrepreneurship services in preference to employment services.

After its budget was cut by the conservative city government *Barcelona Activa* reoriented the provision of services from 2011. Since then, the six measures to enhance the competitiveness of Barcelona are: (a) to create a company counselling office; (b) to facilitate payment to suppliers in 30 days; (c) to promote the Barcelona Brand; (d) to develop a metropolitan programme for acceleration of growth; (e) to create a duty-free zone for entrepreneurs in Barcelona; and (f) to expand the Barcelona Growth network internationally.[21] These measures were selected by the city council from a list of 30 measures proposed by the Barcelona Growth forum, with a large list of participants. The main lines of work of the new *Barcelona Activa* are now more focused on companies. This new approach supplemented more urgent measures to mitigate unemployment rates in the context of national level debates on labour-market reforms.[22] Huge levels of unemployment, especially among young people, has brought more interest in creating employment and less concern about the quality of the jobs created. One salient measure has been a programme oriented to integrate young

Table 6.1 Distribution of users of *Barcelona Activa* according to services offered (%) (2005–2013)

	2005	2008	2011	2013
Entrepreneurship	27.7	13.4	14.7	18.9
Employment	37.1	51.4	58.5	45.5
Cibernarium	35.2	35.2	26.8	35.6
TOTAL	100.0	100.0	100.0	100.0

Source: our calculations from data of Barcelona Activa.

skilled workers in the labour market through subsidizing 70 per cent of the cost to companies for hiring young people. The policy aim is to create the opportunity for the young to work in the hiring company and hopefully to remain employed after the subsidy ends after a year.[23] According to an official of economic development policies at the city council, this approach gives the opportunity to both the company and the young to continue the contract after the end of the programme. Between 2010–2012, this programme promoted 559 labour contracts; 1,619 young people were given job orientation and 763 people received professional training courses.

This approach is not new in Catalonia, where similar programmes aiming to hire young unemployed qualified workers for a short-term period (six months) with the intention of updating their knowledge and providing them with new skills have been implemented for some time. However, the outcome was that this policy instrument did not mean better opportunities for those in the programme to find a job once the six months were over.[24] In a similar move, the city council launched the "commitment with employment" plan, which subsidizes companies that hire long-term unemployed workers over 40 years of age. In sum, the combination of austerity and the conservative leadership in the city caused a change in *Barcelona Activa*'s policy aims and instruments with a strong emphasis on competitiveness.

6.4 Conclusions

The first conclusion to draw from the foregoing analysis is that local policies to foster social cohesion and competitiveness are strongly conditioned by the multi-level governance framework, particularly by the strong role that regional governments play in the provision of housing and employment policies in Spain. The city council of Barcelona and other local actors, while being creative in developing specific social-policy models, have been constrained by depending on regional finances and cooperation. This multi-level governance pattern requires coordination and negotiation and gives prominence to regulation, politics and political alliances. We have seen that when party colours coincided in city and regional governments it was easier to implement policies for social cohesion with the support of regional institutions. Especially so when the party in power was committed to economic distribution, as in the case of the coalitions led by the Catalan Socialists' Party. We may conclude, then, that the complexities of multi-level governance are more likely to be addressed in a positive way in the absence of political confrontation. Therefore politics are a prominent factor in the Barcelona case.

Second, the economic crisis and the structural reforms introduced at the national and European level have influenced the capacity to implement policies at the city level. But not all impediments can be exclusively attributed to the 2008 financial and economic crisis. There are also structural factors, e.g. the characteristics of the dual labour market (divided into insiders and outsiders) that condition the effectiveness of policies in Barcelona (and in Spain). Other such factors are: the persistent low investment in social housing and the no less persistent high levels of youth unemployment. In other words, social problems like youth unemployment and the lack of social housing are not new in the city but they have been intensified by the economic crisis.

Concerning urban regeneration and housing *Poblenou* and the 22@ district exemplify the difficulties of changing the general framework of the housing market given the preponderance of ownership and the poor social-housing provision in Spain in general and in Barcelona in particular. With young people particularly affected by difficulties in access to housing, many of them organized in Barcelona (and in Madrid and Bilbao), but with poor results. Rent grants to support housing access were introduced in Barcelona without solving the issue of housing affordability. In the 22@ district, the creation of new public facilities and protected housing has fallen short of the expectations created by the project. Paradoxically, with the housing crisis that developed after the collapse of the housing bubble in 2008 there are thousands of empty housing units repossessed by the banks. This housing market mismatch has become central in the debate on housing in Barcelona as well as in the rest of Spain while housing renewal as a strategy for social cohesion has lost priority in the political agenda at the national, regional and local level.

Two policy innovations were implemented in Barcelona despite the unfavourable national framework. One has been the implementation of housing and neighbourhood regeneration that followed the Neighbourhood Act 2/2004. We have presented this policy as a good example of cooperation between governments to improve social cohesion. The other has come from civil society groups: For example, the Platform for Mortgage Victims (PAH) has challenged existing legislation through political actions contributing to innovative policy implemented by administrations to support the victims of housing repossessions. In May 2015 the leader of this platform was elected mayor of Barcelona after defeating the conservative previous mayor, with a programme that aims to institutionalize these innovative approaches to the housing problem. This positive institutionalization of innovations in housing and neighbourhood governance involves a revival of the distributive model that Barcelona developed during the 1980s and early 1990s. It also means that bottom-up social action again has access to institutional governance, balancing the tendency in more recent times to prioritize top-down competitive strategies.

A third conclusion to be drawn from this chapter's analysis concerns the combination of policy instruments with political ideas. In the policy field of housing and neighbourhood regeneration the Catalan conservative governments decided to stop a highly successful programme – the Neighbourhoods Act. We have not been able to find a rational justification for this decision other than austerity that has to be enforced. As we know from economic debates and empirical data the emphasis on austerity forms part of an ideology that may be adopted by policymakers in different degrees. In the case of the Catalan regional government, savings were needed to extricate an over-indebted administration. This was not the case of the city government. Therefore we see the lack of concern for housing of the conservative city administration, between 2011 and 2014, as a consciously chosen policy option. This is a clear indication that politics matters and that the Barcelona case shows the importance of political orientations in the design and implementation of policies.

Concerning employment and the quality of jobs, we have seen that the conservative regional Catalan government opted for a centralized model of provision of policies, consisting in a network of partnerships between the private and the third sector. This emphasis on supporting companies and not employees continued after 2008. To give an example, the Catalan government since 2010, with unemployment rising dramatically, spent six times more in economic incentives for companies than in occupational training (Catalan Service of Occupation) or employment policies (Interview with Labour Union Representative, UGT). Barcelona's city council, on the other hand, had for many years a model that combined a competitive strategy attracting companies with a programme of employment creation and job quality enhancement. We have seen this policy case as an example of a double objective (competitiveness + social cohesion) in action. The agency *Barcelona Activa* has been recognized internationally as innovative. However, this trend towards reinforcing social cohesion in the era of competitiveness changed with the arrival in the city administration of the conservative mayor in 2011. The new governing bodies implemented a liberal-oriented strategy focused on competitiveness, the creation of employment (without the criterion of job quality as a priority) and the attraction of foreign investors without signalling an interest in social cohesion. Moreover, whereas the number of the unemployed has continued to rise at the national, regional and local level, the investment in employment policies, especially those directly oriented towards improving the employability of the unemployed has been cut drastically. These cuts are particularly affecting the strategies of promotion of occupation, especially in the policies directed at youth employment and occupational training programmes.

A final reflection bring us back to our initial argument that local actors and institutions have relative autonomy to implement policies that can contribute to social cohesion while faced with global competition. The analysis presented in this chapter shows that there is room for effective local action in the policy fields of housing and employment. We see a more unyielding path dependency in the field of housing, with small scope for innovation given the limited social-housing production in Spain, and potentially more flexibility in employment policies. In the field of employment strategies, with Europe on the one hand, and party politics and social agents on the other, there is more room for variegated policies.

Notes

1 The authors want to thank Michiel Tegelaars for the English editing of this chapter.
2 This chapter is based on the analysis of policy documents and interviews with key planners involved in Barcelona's urban and cultural development; with the persons responsible for the economic growth and resources of the Barcelona city council and with a labour union representative (UGT).

3 Provinces and provincial governments continue to exist despite the organization of the state in Autonomous Communities. Since the coming into existence of Autonomous Communities, provincial authorities – the *Diputaciones* – are focused on providing funds and immaterial resources to municipalities, especially the smaller ones, to develop their own policies. The "*Diputació de Barcelona*" develops programmes in different fields such as economic development, tourism, housing or employment policies.

4 In May 2015, a new political coalition reached power in the city council with the promise of bringing more decision-making power to citizens. Nevertheless, there is considerable political fragmentation in the city council and no clear majorities.

5 This low percentage stands in marked contrast to the figure of 18 per cent in other European countries.

6 PAH document, online, available at: http://afectadosporlahipoteca.com/wp-content/uploads/2013/02/retrospectiva-sobre-desahucios-y-ejecuciones-hipotecarias-en-espa%c3%91a-colaualemany1.pdf (accessed 15 June 2015).

7 In the subsequent six years, comprehensive interventions took place in 117 neighbourhoods inhabited by over 900,000 people (12 per cent of the Catalan population) with an investment amounting to €1.2 billion, funded equally by both the regional government and the respective municipalities (Nel·lo, 2010: 686).

8 The programme was implemented in different municipalities of Catalonia, most of the projects being concentrated in the metropolitan area of Barcelona. Research has shown that the implementation of such projects brought positive outcomes in terms of the health of residents, improving public space and creation of cultural infrastructures and health centres (Martí-Costa and Parés, 2009; Mehdipanah *et al.*, 2014).

9 More than 30 actors participate in the agreement, including: Federation of Municipalities of Catalonia, labour unions (Comissions Obreres de Catalunya and Unió General de Treballadors de Catalunya).

10 For instance, the Consortium of Housing of Barcelona is made up not only of the Generalitat of Catalonia and Barcelona City Council, but also of a series of direct management agencies: (a) INCASOL (Catalan Land Institute); (b) ADIGSA (Administration and Development Management AS); (c) PMHB (Municipal Board of Housing of Barcelona); (d) BAGURSA (Barcelona Urban Management AS); (e) IMPUVQ (Municipal Institute of Urban Landscape and Quality of Life). Source: Generalitat de Catalunya website, online, available at: www.bcn.cat/consorcihabitatge/es/home.html (accessed 15 June 2015).

11 22@ website, accessed 29 August 2014.

12 Interview with Miquel Barceló in "Del éxito a la deriba" by C. Coll in *El Periodico*, online, available at: www.elperiodico.com/es/noticias/barcelona/del-exito-deriva-4591505 (accessed 16 October 2015).

13 *El Periodico*, 16 October 2015. Online, available at: www.elperiodico.com/es/noticias/barcelona/del-exito-deriva-4591505 (accessed 20 October 2015).

14 The youth unemployment rate has continued to increase and in 2011 was 37.1 per cent for young people between 16 and 19 years, and 44.5 per cent for those between 20 and 24 years. These youth unemployment figures are more than double those of the registered unemployment rate for other age groups, for example, for ages 25 and 54 (15.7 per cent), and people over 55 years (5.4 per cent).

15 Catalan Observatory of Youth. Data online, available at: http://treballiaferssocials.gencat.cat (accessed 1 October 2015).

16 The Catalan government created lines of funding to be developed by local authorities. The central government provides funds through the *Diputació de Barcelona*. Part of these funds are obtained from the ESF (Alós Moner, 1999).

17 *Barcelona Activa* website, online, available at: www.barcelonactiva.cat/barcelonactiva/cat/ (accessed 10 September 2012).

18 In 2013 the budget increased a little but without reaching the numbers of 2011.

19 See Generalitat of Catalonia website, online, available at: www.oficinadetreball. cat/socweb/export/sites/default/socweb_es/web_institucional/_fitxers/PDPO_def.pdf (accessed 24 July 2012).
20 Nevertheless, in the metropolitan region there have been pilot programmes to foster quality in employment, such as a task force developed in the county of Vallès Occidental between 1998 and 1999 with the participation of employer associations and trade unions. The objective was to work at company level to improve working conditions and productivity in tandem. Even though, as Lope and Gibert have stated, the experience could not reach its objective given that the general context of Spain (with low productivity patterns and specific cultures of industrial activity) did not allow to tackle quality of jobs and productivity only at company level (Lope *et al.*, 2001).
21 See http://ajuntament.barcelona.cat/premsa/2013/11/28/les-30-mesures-de-la-taula-barcelona-creixement-en-un-grau-avancat-dacompliment-dos-anys-despres-de-la-seva-creacio/ (accessed 20 July 2016).
22 In fact, since 2010 there have been two labour reforms in Spain. Both reforms generated strong opposition from trade unions, which organized two general strikes against them. Whereas employer associations defend the need for greater flexibility to allow innovation and competitiveness of companies, trade unions defend the need for greater quality of jobs in terms of better working conditions, better salaries and security for workers (I4, 9 July 2012). To this date the two labour reforms have had limited impact in terms of job creation, with 80 per cent of new jobs being short-term.
23 The programme has been complemented with similar programmes to help companies to hire long-term unemployed people. See *Barcelona Activa* website, online, available at: www.barcelonactiva.cat/barcelonactiva/images/cat/memoria_activitats_%202012_cat_tcm83–99182.pdf (accessed 21 September 2015).
24 The labour insertion rate after these programmes decreased over the last few years; from 62 per cent in 2009 to 30 per cent in 2014. See *Barcelona Activa* website, online, available at: www.barcelonactiva.cat/barcelonactiva/cat/que-es-barcelona-activa/estudis-i-publicacions (accessed 21 September 2015).

References

Alós-Moner, R. (1999). Las políticas de desarrollo local en Cataluña. *Papers Revista de Sociología*, 58, 75–93.

Andreotti, A., E. Mingione and E. Polizzi (2012). Local Welfare Systems: A Challenge for Social Cohesion. *Urban Studies*, 49(9), 1925–1940.

Blackeley, G. (2005). Local Governance and Local Democracy: The Barcelona Model. *Local Government Studies*, 31(2), 149–165.

Borja, J. (2010). *Urbanisme de Barcelona: llums i ombres* [*Urban Planning in Barcelona: Lights and Shadows*]. Barcelona: Edicions 62-Empúries.

Bosch, J. (2011). *Les polítiques metropolitans d'habitatge a Europa: Elscasos de Londres, París, Brussels i Barcelona*. Barcelona: Diputació de Barcelona.

Camargo Correa, S. (2009). *Movimiento surbanos: Intensidad y oleadas de protestaen Barcelona, Madrid y Bilbao*. Barcelona: Universitat de Barcelona.

Coll, C. (2015). Del éxito a la deriba, *El Periodico*. Online, available at: www.elperiodico.com/es/noticias/barcelona/del-exito-deriva-4591505 (accessed 16 October 2015).

De Weerdt, J. and M. García, (2015). Housing Crisis: The Platform of Mortgage Victims (PAH) Movement in Barcelona and Innovations in Governance. *Journal of Housing and the Built Environment*, 1–23. Online, available at: DOI:10.1007/s10901-015-9465-2.

Degen, M. and M. García (2012). The Transformation of the "Barcelona model": an Analysis of Culture, Urban Regeneration and Governance. *International Journal of Urban and Regional Research*, 36(5), 1022–1038.

Dot Jutgla, E., A. Casellas and M. Pallares-Barbera (2010a). Gentrificación productive en Barcelona: efectos del Nuevo espacio económico. *IV Jornadas de Geografía Económica*, 1–13.

Dot Jutgla, E., A. Casellas and M. Pallares-Barbera (2010b). The Fuzziness of Knowledge Intensive Production: the New Economic Space of Poblenou. *L'ambigüitat de La Producció Intensiva en Coneixement: El Nou Espai Econòmic Del Poblenou*, 56, 389–408.

Eizaguirre, S., M. Pradel, A. Terrones, X. Martinez-Celorrio and M. García (2012). Multilevel Governance and Social Cohesion: Bringing Back Conflict in Citizenship Practices. *Urban Studies*, 49(9), 1999–2016.

Esteban, J. (2012). El pla territorial metropolità de Barcelona en el planejament territorial de Catalunya. *Papers de l'IERMB*, 55, 20–31.

García, M. (2003). The Case of Barcelona. In: A. Kreukels, W. Salet and A. Thornley (eds). *Metropolitan Governance and Spatial Planning*. London: Taylor and Francis, pp. 337–358.

García M. (2008). Barcelona: ciudadanos y visitantes. In: Degen, M. and M. García (eds). *La Metaciudad: Barcelona, transformación de una metrópolis*. Barcelona: Anthropos, pp. 97–113.

García, M. and D. Judd (2012). The Competitive City. In: K. Mossberger, P. John and S. Clarke (eds). *The (Oxford) Handbook of Urban Politics*. Oxford: Oxford University Press, pp. 486–500.

García-Ramon, M. and A. Abet (2000). Commentary. Pre-Olympic and Post-Olympic Barcelona, a "Model" for Urban Regeneration Today? *Environment and Planning A*, 32, 1331–4.

Generalitat de Catalunya (2007). Pacte nacional per al'habitatge 2007–2016. Online, available at: http://territori.gencat.cat/web/.content/home/01_departament/actuacions_i_obres/actuacions_d_habitatge_i_millora_urbana/pacte_nacional_per_a_lhabitatge_2007–2016/docs/pacte_catala.pdf.

Gentile, A. (2011). Urban Governance of Employment Activation: The Case of Barcelona Activa (Spain). *Urbe: Revista Brasileira de Gestão Urbana*, 1, 41–54.

Häussermann, H. and A. Haila (2005). The European City: a Conceptual Framework and Normative Project. In: Y. Kazepov (ed.). *Cities of Europe: Changing Context, Local Arrangements and the Challenge to Urban Cohesion*. Oxford: Blackwell, pp. 43–64.

Kantor, P. and I. Turok (2012). The Politics of Urban Growth and Decline. In: K. Mossberger, P. John and S. Clarke (eds). *The (Oxford) Handbook of Urban Politics*, Oxford: Oxford University Press, pp. 468–485.

Kazepov, Y. (2005). *Cities of Europe: Changing Context, Local Arrangements and the Challenge to Urban Cohesion*. Oxford: Blackwell.

Kemeny, J. (1995). *From Public Housing to the Social Market: Rent Policy Strategies in Comparative Perspective*. London: Routledge.

Le Galès, P. (2002). *European Cities: Social Conflicts and Governance*. Oxford: Oxford University Press.

Le Galès, P. (2005). Elusive Urban Policies in Europe. In: Y. Kazepov (ed.). *Cities of Europe: Changing Context, Local Arrangements and the Challenge to Urban Cohesion*. Oxford: Blackwell, pp. 235–255.

Lope, A., F. Gibert and D. Ortiz de Vallacian (2001). *La regulación local de las nuevas formas de empleo y de trabajo: El caso de Catalunya*. Barcelona: QUIT-UAB.

Martí, M. and J. Bonet. (2009). Planning from Below: Heritage, Citizenship and Innovation in Barcelona. In: K. Shaw and L. Porter (eds). *Whose Urban Renaissance? An International Comparison*. London: Routledge, pp. 118–128.

Martí-Costa, M. and M. Parés (2009). *Llei de barris: cap a una política de regeneració urbana participa dai integral?* Barcelona: Escola d'Administració Pública de Catalunya. Generalitat de Catalunya.

Martinotti, G. (2005). Social Morphology and Governance in the New Metropolis. In: Y. Kazepov (ed.). *Cities of Europe: Changing Context, Local Arrangements and the Challenge to Urban Cohesion.* Oxford: Blackwell, pp. 90–108.

Mehdipanah, R., M. Rodríguez-Sanz, D. Malmusi, C. Muntaner, E. Diez, X. Bartoll and and C. Borrell (2014). The Effects of an Urban Renewal Project on Health and Health Inequalities: a Quasi-Experimental Study in Barcelona. *Journal of Epidemiology and Community Health*, 68(9), 811–817.

Miles, M. (2008). Una olimpiada cultural: el Forum Universal de las Culturas 2004 [A Cultural Olympiad: The Universal Forum of Culture, 2004]. In: M. García and M. Degen (eds). *La metaciudad: Barcelona – transformación de una metropolis [The Metacity: Barcelona: Transformation of a Metropolis].* Barcelona: Anthropos, pp. 65–82.

Nel·lo, O. (2008). Contra la segregació urbana i per la cohesió social: la Llei de barris de Catalunya. In: *Ciutats en (re)construcció: necessitats socials, transformació i millora de barris*, Barcelona: Diputació de Barcelona, pp. 227–246.

Nel·lo, O. (2010). The Challenges of Urban Renewal. Ten Lessons from the Catalan Experience. *Análise Social*, xlv(197), 685–715.

Pareja-Eastaway, M. and I. S. M. Varo (2002). The Tenure Imbalance in Spain: the Need for Social Housing Policy. *Urban Studies*, 39(2), 283–295.

Pareja-Eastaway, M., J. Garuz, M. Miquel, L. Ferrando and M. Solsona (2007). *The City of Marvels? Multiple Endeavours towards Competitiveness in Barcelona.* Amsterdam: Amidst.

Ranci, C. (2013). Le développement local et la cohesion sociale dans les métropoles européennes. In: C. Lefèvre, N. Roseau and T. Vitale (eds). *De La Ville À La Métropole: Les défis de la gouvernance.* Paris. L'Oeil d'Or, pp. 253–268.

Taula d'Entitats del Tercer Sector Social de Catalunya (2013). Un parque de vivienda de alquiler social: Una asignatura pendienteen Cataluña. *Dossier del Tercer Sector* (24), 2–17.

Truño, E. (2000). Un objectiu: la cohesió social. *Model Barcelona: Quaderns de gestió.* Barcelona: Aula Barcelona.

7 Copenhagen
The social costs of urban renewal

Hans Thor Andersen

7.1 Introduction

Copenhagen's destiny has since long been closely related to its status as national capital. Over the last 500 years or more, various governments have intervened in the development of the city. Warfare in the seventeenth and nineteenth centuries, in particular, further concentrated national resources in Copenhagen in order to make it a national powerhouse in both economic, cultural and military terms. Industrialization from the mid-nineteenth century onwards further fuelled the city's economy and was backed up by major investment in rail lines, harbour facilities, new fortifications (1880s) and various state functions. The result was a fast growing city, based economically on the manufacturing industry, trade, transport and public services as well as many private organizations. The manufacturing industry's solid position gave rise to the formation of labour unions and a political party, the Social Democratic Party. In around 1900 the working class succeeding in gaining political control of the city of Copenhagen – a control that was challenged, but never lost. One important outcome was the formation of a non-profit housing sector, which managed to produce a large number of affordable modern standard dwellings. The city developed the country's first municipal planning policy just as it initiated attempts to refurbish older, substandard housing.

Copenhagen's position in 1950 was a strong one as the nation's only international city with booming industry and high concentration of national functions. A number of welfare institutions also emerged and improved living conditions for ordinary citizens. However shortly afterwards suburbanization took place and large numbers of young families moved to the new, modern suburban housing areas. The city attempted to attract more people by improving existing housing stock and, in particular, developing new residential areas such as 'Urbanplanen', the first phase of a huge development on the island of Amager. Despite all these efforts, the population continued to decline through the 1960s and the decades that followed, together with a good deal of employment in the manufacturing industry, workshops and warehousing. The next decades saw a still more problematic situation emerging, with rising social demands, a declining tax base and an inability to break out of a deadlocked political situation in which rivalry between left and right wing parties blocked new initiatives. In the meantime, the city's fiscal situation worsened and led to a round of budget cuts. First of all the tax base decreased and social costs grew with rising numbers of people on public benefits and a range of support to elderly people. Politically Copenhagen suffered from a predominant decentralization policy at both national and regional level with central government taking very few initiatives to ease the situation for Copenhagen city during the 1970s and 1980s. Manufacturing industry closures produced a huge number of unemployed workers as well as a rising need for social benefits during the 1980s.

National economies are increasingly open to international conditions, conditions that have gradually made it more difficult to maintain the existing social model as the preconditions for it have been eroded. Industrial change – i.e. roughly speaking from an economy dominated by manufacturing to one dominated by advanced services – and the social changes accompanying it have excluded a growing number of adults from the labour market and thus undermined the Danish welfare model and set in motion a movement towards less generous welfare support. Much of this transformation is often considered the outcome of turmoil following globalization and continued economic liberalization including the European Single Market. During recent decades, a rising number of papers have discussed the trade-off between welfare and competitiveness (Ache *et al.*, 2008; Hermann and Mahnkopft, 2010; Engelstoft and Jørgensen, 1997).

Moreover, responsibility for a number of central government obligations have been transferred to local level. This includes labour market policy (although central government dictates the rules but leaves it to local governments to implement them), as well as housing policies. Taken together, they are changes aimed at trimming the public sector in which local governments are encouraged to identify their competitive edge and use this for specialization in order to increase their competitiveness.

The state's withdrawal from several key welfare policy roles is part of a wider shift towards greater market and less public involvement. However, what is taking place is not a simple transfer from the public to the private sector of key policy areas. Rather it has been the public sector that has been transformed into a more market-oriented version, cf. introducing market principles into the welfare sector (new public management, see Gross and Hambleton, 2007; Brenner and Theodore, 2002).

The trade-off between welfare and competitiveness has found its specific Copenhagen incarnation in structural conditions and local political relations. The huge impact of state policies has left very little room for local governments to develop and implement locally based policies in key areas such as taxation, spending, welfare services, research and education or labour market policies. Copenhagen city's tight budgeting is not decided locally but rather dictated by central government. Yet, two strategic fields have long since taken control – i.e. in the sense that both fields leave considerable room for local decision-makers – of local governments: housing and planning policies.

Copenhagen has developed along the lines described above since the post-war boom petered out around 1970, and has furthermore experienced accelerating job loss from that moment on. Moreover, the oil crisis and the period of stagflation, i.e. inflation and economic stagnation, that followed in combination with a still tighter budget made it clear that it was impossible to continue with the previous model. However, political disagreement and the administrative structure of Greater Copenhagen blocked a broad and lasting solution for years while problems increased in number and intensity. By the early 1980s, the city of Copenhagen was facing a constant and growing budget deficit, which in turn reduced its chances of covering the rising need for public benefits, modernization of its housing stock and key institutions such as hospitals and schools. A few years later the city was technically bankrupt but survived thanks to special grants and ad hoc solutions financed by the state.

The causes of this deeply problematic situation are of course manifold and complex, but at least five key factors caused Copenhagen's urban crisis in the 1970s and 1980s (Andersen and Winther, 2010). First and foremost, the 1973–1974 oil-crisis marked a strong divide in industrial development as a deep crisis led to an almost complete deindustrialization of the city centre. The period that followed produced constant business closures and rising unemployment. Although some growth took place in the service industry it was unable to compensate for this job loss. A second factor enhanced the effects of deindustrialization – suburbanization. In less than 40 years, the city of Copenhagen lost more than a third of its population. This third included young, well-educated families who fled the city centre in favour of the much better housing conditions in suburbia. Third, a great deal of the new service economy was in suburban districts where undeveloped land was available. In the beginning mostly relocating back-office functions and suburban service activities, but later also company headquarters, changed location from older city offices to new, spacious areas equipped with easy car access and sufficient parking space. This included finance and banking but also a considerable share of business services (Winther, 2007; Hansen and Winther, 2006).

A fourth factor that eroded Copenhagen's position was the housing and property market. This market was characterized by three main features; on the one hand a relatively large stock of old, small dwellings lacking modern facilities, a marked dominance of rental housing (private, municipal or non-profit housing) and third, a strict rental regulation scheme introduced at the outbreak of the Second World War in order to prevent rents from rising sharply due to housing shortages. The effect of this was, on one hand, frozen rents, which in turn stopped owners implementing major housing stock improvements and, on the other hand, a significant incentive to middle class people to leave the city and its poor housing quality (Andersen *et al.*, 2000). Finally, Copenhagen's local government system has caused major problems for its development; the dominant position of Copenhagen in the Danish urban system led the 1970-municipal reform decision-makers to propose a metropolitan council as a solution to Greater Copenhagen's coordination and partnership needs. However, the council proved unable to cope with the substantial challenges that faced it in the years to come, which called for local and regional cooperation (Harding, 1997; Andersen, 2008). Despite several attempts, combined resistance at both local and national level blocked metropolitan government reform. In the end, the government shifted to a solution involving a number of single-purpose quangos (quasi-autonomous non-governmental organizations) and public–private partnerships as vehicles for the most urgent policy fields. Hospital services, public transport, restructuring of the harbour area, the development of the new city annex (called Ørestad) and the construction of a new metro system to serve the central parts of the city.

General planning policy in Denmark is strongly articulated as country-wide decentralization and equal development. Partly due to the extensive growth in Greater Copenhagen in the 1950s and 1960s, parliament decided to compensate the provinces with massive public investment in infrastructure and various institutions such as new universities and secondary schools. The same decentralization strategy, labelled 'spatial Keynesianism' (Brenner, 2004), was adopted on the regional scale, where attention was focused on the suburban districts and outer urban areas. Both strongly undermined the city's economy.

A window of opportunity came as the overall situation of the city worsened in the 1980s. At the end of that decade a growth coalition consisting of a Conservative government, a Social Democratic opposition and the new lord mayor of Copenhagen together managed to launch a city renewal strategy that pushed all resistance aside (Andersen *et al.*, 2002; Hansen *et al.*, 2001; Andersen and Matthiessen, 1995). This coalition succeeded in transforming a longstanding tradition of welfare policy into a policy promoting economic competitiveness.

The worsening employment situation and a growing demand for welfare benefits caused still more financial difficulties, and by the end of the 1980s central government had reacted (Statsministeriet, 1989). Parliamentary debate on Copenhagen and its situation in March 1990 marked the turning point. The previously existing welfare regime in Copenhagen was challenged by the negative status quo and forced to change tack. Central government offered assistance but demanded a radical shift in policy from the city government. Despite strongly articulated resistance, city and central governments agreed to cooperate for a stronger and more financially competitive urban policy. The government declared its will to invest directly in a renewal of the central city and improve its overall position. However the city had to take a positive part in the modernization of its internal structures and organization, just as policies had to be reoriented to match the demands of the market.

Although the planned changes have taken several decades to bring to fruition, the transformation of Copenhagen has been thoroughgoing and large scale. The former head of urban planning in the city of Copenhagen, Holger Bisgaard, has claimed that city renewal could rightfully be considered the third great phase in the city's history, the other two being its foundation and Renaissance expansion in the sixteenth and seventeenth centuries. (Bisgaard, 2010). The key to this remarkable recovery has been a shift to a more business-oriented line at local level and a greater concern with capital by national government.

There is deeper meaning running through local urban policy in Copenhagen as the overall position of the city of Copenhagen worsened since the Second World War. In order to regain momentum, the ruling Social Democratic–Conservative coalition attempted to invent a game-changer, City Plan Vest (1968). A major reconstruction of the inner city district demanded major infra-structure improvements: a metro line and a motorway crossing below the office blocks. Yet, the plan met severe resistance at both local and national levels, par-ticularly in relation to the high costs and environmental effects of cutting two motorways through population dense areas. The abolition of the plan marked the start of a period of decline and political blockade of major initiatives as the left wing parties managed to safeguard public interest in the face of proposals launched by various investors.

The main hypothesis of this chapter is that these welfare-oriented policies were overwhelmed by growing economic, industrial and social problems and gave way to an adaption of market orientation in line with 'mainstream' pol-itics at a national level. This transformation involved a major change in most city policy fields. However, urban planning and housing policy, which offers the most strategic room for manoeuvre to Danish local governments, became the main arenas for the new business-friendly policy regime. Thanks to major support from national government, the Copenhagen Municipality managed successfully to shift policy within a relatively short time frame. However, there was a price to be paid. On one hand the stock of affordable, municipally owned dwellings was privatized and new housing has predominantly been owner occupied housing. On the other hand, the intensified refurbishment of the existing housing stock has substantially reduced the number of affordable dwellings. Finally, successful economic recovery has not been to the benefit of low-income groups, with the result that segregation has increased and to some degree forced a segment of low-earners to leave the city in their search for affordable housing.

It was property investors who felt the 2008 crisis most, as a great deal of building activities ceased for a couple of years leading to substantial losses in property values (up to a third). This cut in housing costs allowed more people to settle in central Copenhagen and lowered the need for affordable housing considerably. However, since 2013 economic activity has grown and the prop-erty market has recovered to an extent that has forced national government to modify housing. Thus rising housing costs and a constant migration of especially younger people to Copenhagen has tightened the housing market and in par-ticular it has become very difficult to find accommodation at a moderate cost. This continues to push low income groups out of the inner cities and transformed central Copenhagen into a middle/upper middle class city as new housing is mostly built for private ownership. Thus the policy shift in the early 1990s has had a long-standing effect on the social composition of the population, segrega-tion and general living conditions.

This chapter aims to set out Copenhagen's overall framework, i.e. the overall social, economic and political relations that form the specific conditions for urban policymaking in the city. A central theme, the shift from welfare management to business promotion, would seem to have been a painful transformation, the local political repercussions of which are still being felt. However the successful renewal of the city during the 1990s is closely related to the shift in housing and planning policy.

The first section of this chapter has given a brief overview of Copenhagen's most recent developments: its renewal from the mid-1990s onwards after nearly two decades of stagnation and decline. It is a change that has included a remarkable shift from traditional Social Democratic, Keynesian welfare policies to market-oriented, proactive business policy promotion. The second section will study the implementation of the policy of business promotion with a focus on urban planning and housing policies in greater depth. Its impact on housing, the labour market and social segregation as well as urban change is presented and discussed. The third section discusses the limits of local policy formulation. The last section summarizes current changes in relation to the city's ability to control transformation.

7.2 Implementing a proactive policy for business promotion

This section proposes a brief historical overview of the renewal of the city of Copenhagen from the mid-1990s after nearly two decades of stagnation and decline. As argued below, this change has encompassed a remarkable shift from traditional social democratic, Keynesian welfare policies to a market-oriented, proactive business policy in dealing with urban policies and interventions.

During the 1990s certain specific circumstances generated a deadlocked administrative-political situation and prevented in-depth solutions and the situation worsened to a degree that called for major government intervention. First and foremost was municipal autonomy. Local governments jealously guard their rights and struggle intensively against all central government attempts to dictate specific policies. Second, the national framework with its spatial polarization between the large capital region and the smaller provincial cities has effectively blocked earlier solutions. Only the city's deep crisis, and perhaps especially the fear of the costs of this for the country as a whole, established a window of opportunity. This window allowed both state intervention in municipal affairs and agreement to provide special funds to get Copenhagen back on track. Moreover, by letting the state take over land and other assets from the city as a way of co-financing huge infrastructure projects, central government managed to by-pass much opposition. Finally, industrial change towards a more service-oriented economy and the start of the Single Market shifted large cities from a burden to a national asset at the European level.

After losing political and economic momentum in the 1960s and beyond, the city did not manage to reform its internal government system. From the nineteenth century, the city was governed by the 'magistrat-system', a government system that gave most of the political parties represented in the city parliament access to political decision-making power. The system was expected to promote practical cooperation between the political parties and at the same time guarantee minority parties direct influence in daily political activities. It worked relatively smoothly for many decades, as the dominant party, the Social Democrats, could always get their policies accepted as they worked jointly with the Conservative Party in a stable coalition.

Cracks began to appear in Copenhagen's political landscape in the late 1960s when left wing parties were elected to parliament. Previous multi-party consensus on most policy issues melted away and over the next two decades a strong and bitter fight between the 'new left' and the Social Democratic Party came to the fore. This blocked a strategic plan when it was most needed, namely after huge loss of employment, particularly in the manufacturing sector. Instead, the modernization of an old and run down housing sector became a battlefield between right and left. The left wing advocated welfare as the 'leit motif' of its local policies, which in turn prevented major modernization of the infrastructure (roads, public transport) and city centre on the one hand, but on the other hand also blocked attempts at speeding up improvement of older housing estates.

For Bisgaard (2010), the main explanation for this was the complete change in local political objectives and performance, which shifted from a reactive, welfare oriented policy to a more proactive, business oriented policy in around 1990. This welfare policy ran into serious problems due to financial austerity at a time when the state was reducing its willingness to back up weaker cities and regions partly due to pressure from national government, partly as the Social Democratic regime was weakened during the 1980s (see Harding, 1997). Copenhagen's difficulties throughout the 1970s and 1980s not only led to economic collapse around 1990 but also marked the breakdown of the long term historical alliance between the Social Democratic Party, the labour unions and the business elite, which had delivered both rising welfare and living standards to the working class and at the same time, assured constant growth in productivity. Over the next few decades the Social Democratic regime more or less disintegrated. Housing associations, labour unions, various cultural associations and corporate businesses began to search for a broader political basis in order to ensure their long term interests.

During the 1980s and subsequently, Social Democratic hegemony vanished although the party managed to keep key positions in city government. Urban planning changed from primarily a subject of democratic negotiation into a guiding instrument for investors. The city planning department started actively to promote development opportunities and help investors identify construction sites. Furthermore, to accelerate the transformation of run down industrial space to residential areas the city established a development company to plan and implement larger projects in the harbour area.

The combined effects of this shift in urban policy are difficult to underestimate. In the space of a few years Copenhagen became one of the most successful cities in northern Europe in terms of progress and development. The many government investments triggered a major round of private capital flow into the built environment and a series of visible, rapid transformations of the city followed.

As construction activity increased so did general employment, and during the 1990s Copenhagen's unusually high level of unemployment fell from nearly 17 per cent to 6 per cent (Figure 7.1). Moreover, Copenhagen experienced a population increase for the first time since 1950. Some authors even claim that this period marks the city's rebirth (Bisgaard, 2010). Unfortunately it also led to marked growth in land as well as housing prices.

In fact, when Copenhagen city experienced severe financial problems, support was provided on the usual conditions: creditors were to dictate terms and conditions (Hansen *et al.*, 2001). The city had to sell a great deal of its land and other property including parts of the harbour and the western part of the island of Amager. The state also played a leading role in several joint Copenhagen–central government organizations, such as the new quango operating hospital services and the metro company. Thus, although it appeared a defeat for the city, this agreement between central and local government was the basis for the recovery of the years to come. Agreement brought a broad variety of central government investments to Copenhagen including massive upgrading of existing infrastructure such as a new train system, a new city annex called 'Ørestad' combined with a new metro (Andersen, 2008; Major, 2008), modernization and expansion of the main cultural institutions and museums as well as the universities, refinancing of the city's debt to ease the burden on the budget and furthermore shifting major costs away from the city (e.g. the health sector, which was transferred to a new central government company) and finally the construction of a new rail

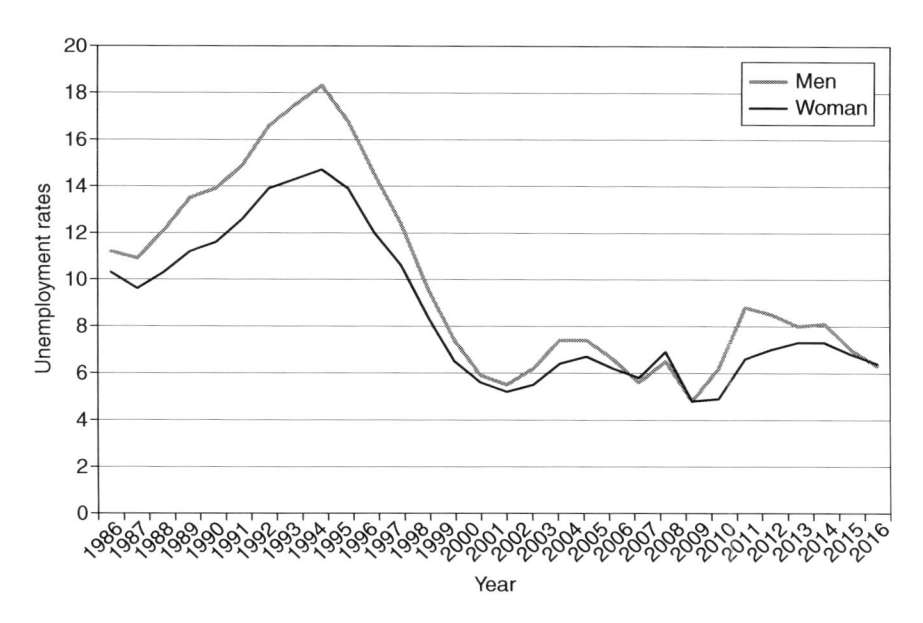

Figure 7.1 Unemployment rates (percentages) for men and women in Copenhagen (1986–2016).

Source: authors' elaboration on Statistikbanken.

and motorway link (tunnel/bridge) between Malmö in south Sweden to Copenhagen airport and Copenhagen central station. In return, the city had to transfer a proportion of its land to the state including small parts of Copenhagen harbour and land outside the city borders and sell off municipal housing stock (about 20,000). These latter were the cheapest and most outdated of the entire housing stock but they were an important stock of affordable housing.

The new regime did not abolish all its welfare policies, which continued to be an important part of urban politics but subordinated it to its overall objective of generating a competitive economy to make space for an independent urban policy. Traces of this surviving welfare policy are to be found in the long term struggle with central government over the need for affordable housing in order to maintain a socially balanced city and the newer policy of promoting diversity in Copenhagen (Andersen *et al.*, 2014).

However, for the first time the city systematically examined potential ways of bringing its overall financial improvement objectives to fruition. Moreover, it strove to reorganize its internal governance structure in order to ensure stronger leadership for the governing coalition. Yet despite this new partnership with central government the city proved unable to convince a majority of both local and national assemblies to support major changes in local government structure. However, strategic and business oriented policies were strengthened and much power was concentrated in the hands of the lord mayor of Copenhagen.

It was 2009/2010 before the effects of the fiscal crisis made themselves felt in Copenhagen. Initially the crisis was felt in worsening property market malaise while unemployment remained low (5–6 per cent). However, from 2010 labour shortage gave way to surplus. The elderly unemployed, in particular, had significant problems returning to the labour market, and youngsters with little or no work experience had similar problems. Moreover, many unskilled men and newly educated people with a university background in humanities and social sciences had problems gaining employment. Overall unemployment has risen since then.

In 2015 unemployment in Copenhagen is still higher than pre-crisis levels but it has been reducing for both genders since 2010. In recent years both private and public employment has increased in Copenhagen especially in trade, hotels and restaurants, business services, the financial sector as well as cultural activities. However, overall economic growth and hence job formation is slower than in neighbouring capitals and million cities such as Hamburg, Oslo, Stockholm, Amsterdam or Helsinki.

Recently Copenhagen has launched industrial policy goals, which include the creation of 20,000 new jobs over the next few years, which should be supported by a stronger infrastructure, in particular in Internet capacity, public transport and logistics. The city aims to promote the creative industries by generating greater education, business services, retail, hotel and restaurant and other knowledge related business activity variety. Moreover becoming CO_2-neutral in 2015 and a 'green city' are signals to visitors, business leaders and private firms, as well as to already established businesses that Copenhagen expects to develop a future inter-city competition edge. The city is also striving to make itself an attractive shopping and cruise tourism destination (it is one of the world's largest cruise destinations already), and of course to attract more conferences, business events and culture activities to intensify economic activity as a whole. Finally, the city is working closely together with its 'sister city' Malmö (a south Swedish city only 20 km from Copenhagen) and trying to implement a strategy to the benefit of both cities/regions on the Öresund (Sound).

A new instrument for local economic development has been the creation of 'creative zones' offering access to cheap and flexible accommodation in proximity to the city centre and often providing a vibrant ('creative') business environment. Copenhagen has designated ten such creative zones with a contemporary feel.

Only modest changes have been made to national policy to cope with the effects of the financial crisis. As mentioned above, labour market agreements are usually a non-political issue and salaries, social contributions etc. are not usually on the political agenda. Political attempts to direct labour market development towards greater flexibility and efficiency provide optimal conditions for business activities. Research and education have become matters of political concern over recent decades, just as cultural and leisure activities are nowadays believed to bring economic development and hence growth to vibrant localities.

In practice the lion's share of industrial policy is handed over to single purpose agencies formed by central government, the city and sometimes the wider region. Their mutual relationship and cooperation is difficult to estimate but they do at least divide up the work between them.

7.3 Housing policy

This section will study the implementation of the business promotion policy in greater depth, with a focus on urban planning and housing policies. As mentioned above, in around 1980 the Copenhagen housing market was still dominated by a high number of private rental dwellings, a large stock of municipal owned dwellings and a small corporate sector. The rental sector was, and still is, strictly regulated, which keeps rents at modest levels. One result of this was a steady decline in the private rental sector, due to both a reduction of rental dwellings through conversion into condominiums and corporate housing and a new building shortage. The city still owned about 20,000 dwellings until 1995, but these were sold off as part of the agreement with the government. They functioned as social housing and were traditionally used for urgent housing needs. Since they have been sold off, social housing obligations can only be met by the non-profit sector.

During the years of decline (1970s and 1980s) an urban redevelopment programme attempted to replace outdated and substandard housing with modern housing. Unfortunately however, the private sector refused to invest in new housing in renewal areas and non-profit organizations undertook redevelopment of the cleared land in former slum areas instead. This provided a stock of modern rental housing but also a concentration of relatively poor households as well as many third world immigrants.

Copenhagen selected planning and housing as the most promising fields of strategic interest with the potential to reinvent the city. As we have seen, the precondition for this was a radical shift in overall policy aims, namely a retreat from welfare policies in favour of a more demand led development policy. In practice, this shift included several components, such as a block on the building of additional non-profit (i.e. social) housing in order to reduce the inflow of low income groups, a block on the building of smaller sized dwellings and a check on available land for redevelopment for residential purposes. In addition the city succeeded in joining forces with central government to increase the speed of housing renewal programmes. These programmes made only slow progress up to the late 1980s and in most cases the new housing units replacing those demolished were non-profit. This kept the average income level low in the newest and most expensive housing too. However, the new Copenhagen city government made housing policy the cornerstone in its policy for economic and social recovery after the 1970s and 1980s downturn. The administration saw the housing sector as key to its efforts to provide a healthy, long term financial balance for the city. A strategic plan recommended increased homeownership in order to ensure private investment in the housing sector and keep middle class households within municipal borders. In 1995 the city government banned non-profit housing and only housing units of more than $90\,m^2$ were accepted. These decisions were taken in order to incentivize new middle class families to stay in the city centre instead of settling in suburbia.

This strategy demanded available space for house building and the city administration declared the Vesterbro area a new priority housing improvement area. Yet, it also searched for available space in former manufacturing sites, on railway land, abandoned harbour land and thought of creating a kind of city annex on reclaimed land in western Amager between the airport and the city. This shift in urban policy was strongly criticized, especially by left wing politicians who considered it a betrayal of social-democratic principles, yet it survived for some time and 15 years later non-profit housing was again supported by the city administration, now as a means of providing affordable housing.

The result of the new housing policy, combined with a proactive planning style, has been a sharp increase in private investment (Figure 7.2) as well as a remarkable change in the social composition of the population. From an ageing population the city is the now the nation's youngest (with many students) and income levels will shortly catch up with the rest of the region. This has further shifted the city's economic situation. Instead of constant budget problems, the city now has a booming economy and can lower taxation year by year. Partly due to rising income taxes, partly due to reduced need (as youngsters seldom need health services, etc.) the city's financial situation has improved considerably. This has allowed the city to further develop its potential as a liveable and creative city.

Today the social landscape of Copenhagen has changed considerably. The inner cities are attractive as never before and manage to attract large numbers of young people – students, the employed and young couples. The increase in

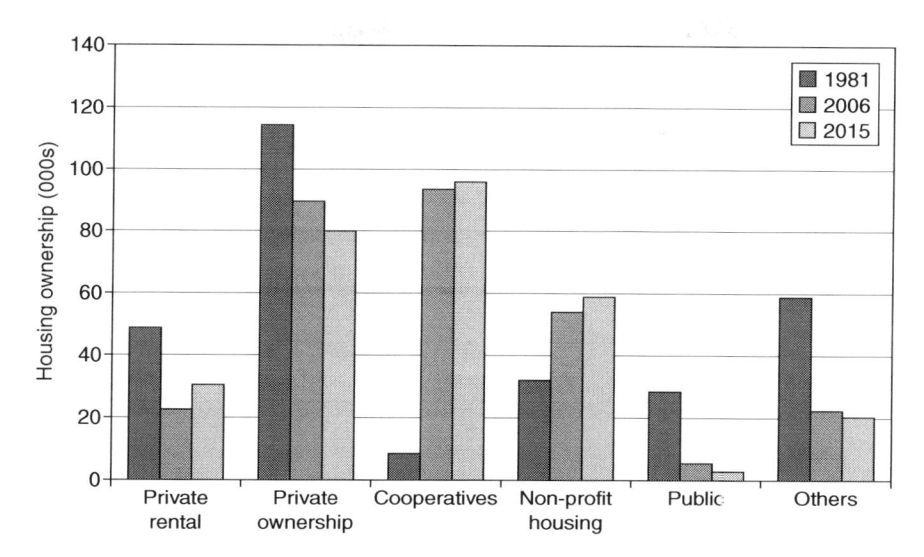

Figure 7.2 Copenhagen multistorey housing ownership structure (1981–2015).
Source: authors' elaboration on Statistikbanken.

young families has been remarkable and the city has needed to set up new kindergartens and schools to meet the demand. At the same time transformations in housing tenure in inner city Copenhagen have reduced income segregation and also made access to housing more difficult for young people, singles and others. Yet, the negative outcome of the 1995–2008 boom period has been sharpened polarization between homeowners and renters. In particular, those living in non-profit housing ('social housing') remain low income, under-employed and sometimes in ill health, too. The newer non-profit housing estates have formed pockets of poverty in an increasingly wealthy city. A growing share of tenants is marginalized, i.e. those retiring early, long term unemployed, low income, divorced, with health problems and so on. The income profile of detached housing owners is moving in the opposite direction. These processes are very important factors in relation to both local and national politics. They have, moreover, proved that segregation is more than just an academic debate. The 2008 crisis brought it to a temporary halt since recovery, in 2013, the housing market has tightened up once again, and once again excludes low-income groups and fuels segregation.

Figure 7.2 shows forms of multistorey housing ownership in Copenhagen, a category that encompasses more than 85 per cent of housing. A first observation is the sharp decline in privately owned housing units and a similar decline in public (municipal) owned housing. By contrast, cooperative housing expanded substantially during the 1980s and 1990s and today accounts for more than a third of housing stock. A smaller expansion of non-profit housing is also worthy of note although rising land prices make it difficult to build non-profit housing in central Copenhagen. In addition corporate and foundation owned housing is growing. Post 1993 rental housing is free of rent control and thus more profitable for investors as compared to older rental properties.

Copenhagen's successful renewal during the 1990s and later has significantly increased house prices from the mid-1990s to just before the crisis hit in 2008, see Figure 7.3 below. In particular, new loans from 2005 increased prices in one year by a huge 26 per cent!

An important reaction to this situation, i.e. growing difficulties in finding affordable housing for many people, has been demand for a new housing policy in Copenhagen city. While cheap but also outdated housing was available in sufficient quantities, the debate on housing issues mainly revolved around decent quality and a willingness to invest in maintenance. Yet, with an improving economic situation, housing prices have also gone up and both private and public efforts to modernize the housing stock have further fuelled prices. Moreover, as a part of an agreement with national government the city sold off its cheap municipal housing stock in the 1990s. Together with a policy of promoting private ownership, the number of affordable units has thus diminished rapidly. The effect of rising housing costs was, among others, a growing tendency to move out of the city centre in the late 1990s, and in 2005 net migration was negative as young families left central Copenhagen for the outer suburban areas. This was the opposite of what was expected and intended and, in turn, triggered a debate on the need to provide affordable housing.

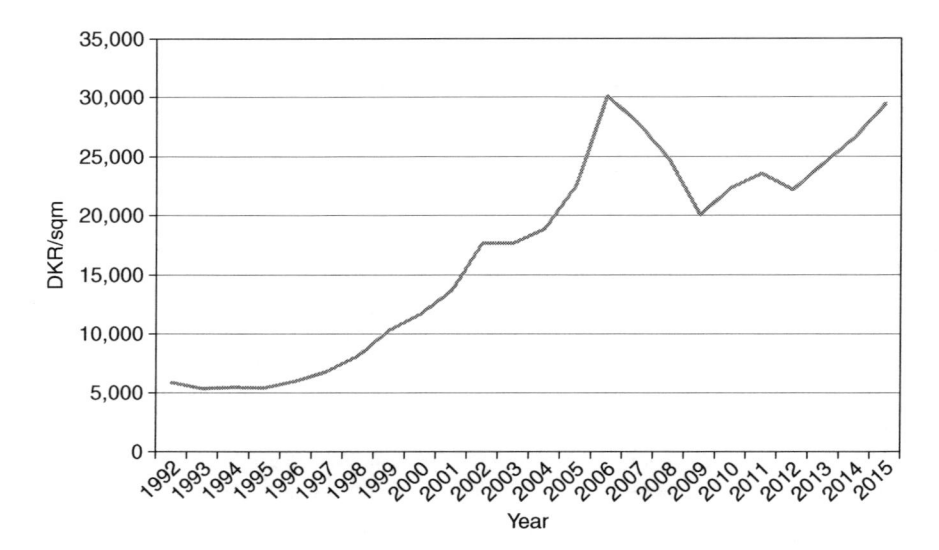

Figure 7.3 Sales prices for condominiums in Copenhagen city (1992–2015).
Source: authors' elaboration on Realkreditrådet.

The current lord mayor launched the idea of providing 5,000 new 95 m² housing units at a price of 5,000 DKR per month (about €700) – a policy soon known as '5 × 5'. Houses were to have been located on publicly owned land to reduce total costs, however the government ultimately decided that under-market-price sale of publicly owned properties would be illegal. The affordable housing policy thus failed and the lord mayor decided not to run for a second term. In the meantime, the crisis reduced housing costs by around a third and thus provided if not affordable at least cheaper housing than in previous years. Yet, the affordable housing debate resurfaced at the end of the crisis in 2013, now disguised as non-profit housing with the aim of preventing segregation in the city.

The third major initiative launched by Copenhagen was a territorial review by the OECD in 2009. The review recognized the city's major strengths but also pinpointed critical factors such as the housing market, high taxes and the governance system. The report compared Greater Copenhagen with other North European capitals and million cities and concluded that Copenhagen did not do particularly well in any key area. General economic growth was below average, the strategic position was less impressive than most Danes believed it to be and chances to benefit from the huge infrastructure investments made during the 1990s and beyond were limited by a problematic governmental system. No fewer than 35 municipalities and two regions existed in metropolitan Copenhagen and, if the eastern part of the Øresund is included, we have also to include the southern part of a different country (Sweden) with 20 different municipalities. Moreover, central government introduced a number of single-purpose quangos to compensate for absent metropolitan cooperation and coordination.

Since the Greater Copenhagen Council was abolished on 1 January 1990 no solution capable of providing an answer to calls for coordination and cooperation has been able to garner political support. The 1990s central government invested considerable energy into following up on the agreement between Copenhagen and the state but failed. The later Metropolitan development council (2001–2007) only delayed the challenge for a short period. Thus, the government reform, which could have given the metropolitan region a better chance of developing a long term strategy and improving its performance, was blocked politically at national as well as local level. Consequently, an important part of the stronger capital strategy failed.

7.4 Conclusions: the crisis and beyond – facing new growth?

The present population prognosis made by Statistics Denmark expects Copenhagen city's population to grow from today's 580,000 inhabitants to 688,000 in 2025 and 766,000 in 2040, an increase of about 32 per cent. Despite the uncertainty, this forecast shows that Copenhagen city can expect a prosperous future for the foreseeable future. The population development introduces a lasting trend of growth for Copenhagen.

The crisis has had a strong impact on the Danish economy in general. About a fifth of all jobs in the manufacturing industry were lost. As much of the boom period (mid-1990s to 2008) was financed by debts and private spending, the effect on housing markets was considerable. In parts of the country up to a third of property values disappeared. The housing market stood still for several years and it was difficult to sell houses outside the largest cities. Job loss and stagnating housing markets accelerated a process of migration from rural areas and small towns to the larger ones, especially Copenhagen and Århus. However, Copenhagen emerged from the crisis stronger. While employment fell by 5 per cent in the country as a whole, it increased by nearly 6 per cent in Copenhagen.

The housing market was severely hit by the crisis with a general loss of nearly a third of property values. Over the last two years, however, housing prices have recovered and have now almost returned to pre-crisis levels. Consequently, the affordable housing debate of ten years ago has reappeared, this time as an attempt to maintain levels of at least 20 per cent non-profit housing in all newer development schemes. The challenge is high land prices, which demand special financial support from municipal sources, which are unpopular with right wing parties.

Copenhagen has not been untouched by the crisis, although it appears to have passed through the difficult years more easily than most other parts of the country. Employment decreased only slightly in the first years of the crisis and is back to pre-crisis levels once again. However, the labour market has changed. There are fewer stable and relatively well-paid jobs, in particular for the unskilled. The gap between those belonging to the 'core group of the labour market', i.e. those who rarely face unemployment, and marginal labour market groups is increasing. The latter, sometimes labelled the 'precariat', suffer short term contracts, have fewer rights such as pensions and sickness and parenthood benefits and also include a rising number of people on part time contracts. Although the precariat and excluded groups form a minority they have consequences for urban development. First of all, there are clear signs of rising inequalities in the urban landscape. Formerly working class areas have been invaded by the creative, well-educated middle classes, which are slowly edging out former inhabitants. This in turn fuels urban renewal and thereby gentrification, a process promoted by existing housing legislation and Copenhagen city's local housing policy.

The third area of strategic actions has not been a success; local and national objections prevented a reform of Copenhagen's government system at both metropolitan and inner city levels. This has left Copenhagen with an unnecessarily weak capacity to develop and implement strategic visions for its own future and leaves the city needing support from national government as it did in the early 1990s. The abolition of a metropolitan authority has removed a coordinating organization and also a central political player in Greater Copenhagen.

Despite important efforts to change the city's structural framework it can thus be concluded that key areas such as economic, labour market, industrial or welfare policies are fields that are beyond the direct influence of the city. The outcome of newer rescaling of state power (Brenner, 2004) has been a changed division of labour between state and municipalities in which the latter have become service deliverers controlled by a regime of quality checks and budget limitations. Similarly labour market and industrial development have been fields of limited municipal influence with strict rules dictated by central government. Yet, in planning and housing policies local governments still have considerable influence, partly as they still have to finance investments. Both policy fields have the potential to influence the framework of the city in a long-term perspective. It should be remembered, however, that the state, via quangos, has given itself a solid and direct influence on Copenhagen's urban development. For better or worse – the city is not in control of its own destiny.

References

Ache, P., Andersen, H. T., Maloutas, T., Raco, M. and Tasan-Kok, T. (2008). *Cities between Competitiveness and Cohesion: Discourses, Realities and Implementation.* Dordrecht: Springer.

Andersen, H. T. (2008). The Emerging Danish Government Reform – Centralised Decentralisation. *Urban Research and Practice*, 1(1): 3–17.

Andersen, H. T. and Matthiessen, C. W. (1995). Metropolitan Marketing and Strategic Planning: A Copenhagen Perspective. *Geografisk Tidsskrift*, 71–82.

Andersen, H. T. and Winther, L. (2010). Crisis in the Resurgent City? The Rise of Copenhagen. *International Journal of Urban and Regional Geography*. 34(3): 693–700.

Andersen, H. S., Andersen, H. T. and Ærø, T. (2000). Social Polarisation in a Segmented Housing Market: Social Segregation in Greater Copenhagen. *Geografisk Tidsskrift*, 100: 71–83.

Andersen, H. T., Hansen, F. and Jørgensen, J. (2002). The Fall and Rise of Metropolitan Government in Copenhagen. *Geojournal*, 58: 43–52.

Andersen, H. T., Beckman, A. W., Blach, V. and Nielsen, R. S. (2014). Assessment of Diversity in Copenhagen, Denmark. *Report to Divercities*. Online, available at: www. urbandivercities.eu/wp-content/uploads/2013/05/Urban-Policies-on-Diversity-in-Copenhagen.pdf.

Bisgaard, H. (2010). *Københavns genrejsning 1990–2010*. København: Bogværket.

Brenner, N. (2004). *New State Spaces: Urban Governance and the Rescaling of Statehood.* Oxford: Oxford University Press.

Brenner, N. and Theodore, N. (2002). *Spaces of Neoliberalism: Urban Restructuring in North America and Western Europe*. London: Blackwell.

Engelstoft, S. and Jørgensen, J. (1997). Copenhagen: Redistributive City? In: Jensen-Butler, C., Shachar, A. and van Weesep, J. (eds). *European Cities in Competition.* Aldershot: Avebury.

Gross, J. S. and Hambleton, R. (2007). Global Trends, Diversity and Local Democracy. In: Gross, J. S. and Hambleton, R. (eds). *Governing Cities in a Global Era: Urban Innovation, Competition and Democratic Reform*, Basingstoke: Palgrave.

Hansen, A. L., Andersen, H. H. and Clark, E. (2001). Creative Copenhagen: Globalization, Urban Governance and Social Change. *European Planning Studies*, 9(7): 851–869.

Hansen, H. K. and Winther, L. (2006). The Economic Geographies of the Outer City – Industrial Dynamics and Imaginary Spaces of Location in Copenhagen. *European Planning Studies*, 14(10), 1387–1406.

Harding, A. (1997). Urban Regimes in a Europe of the Cities? *European Urban and Regional Studies*, 4: 291–314.

Hermann, C. and Mahnkopft, B. (2010). The Past and Future of the European Social Model. WP 5/2010. *Hochschule für Wirtschaft und Recht*, Berlin.

Major, S. (2008). *Disconnected Innovations: New Urbanity in Large-Scale Development Projects: Zuidas Amsterdam, Ørestad Copenhagen and Forum Barcelona.* Delft: Eburon.

OECD (2009). *Territorial Reviews: Copenhagen, Denmark.* Paris: OECD.

Statsministeriet (1989). *Hovedstaden: Hvadvilvi med den? [The capital – what to do with it?].* Copenhagen.

Winther, L. (2007). Location Dynamics of Business Services in the Urban Landscape of Copenhagen: Imaginary Spaces of Location. *Belgeo*, (1): 51–72.

8 Lyon

Unbreakable boundaries between economic development and social integration policies

Deborah Galimberti, Rémi Dormois and Gilles Pinson

8.1 Introduction

In France, since the decentralization laws of the early 1980s, local authorities and in particular regional councils and the inter-municipal cooperation authorities of large cities have developed increasingly large portfolios of measures in domains such as economic development, planning and social housing, and social integration. But are regional and local authorities still eager (and able) to pursue policies assuring both economic and social cohesion objectives? Following the explosion of social plans in retail services and traditional industries, social cohesion has regained centrality in the French national public debate. The unemployment figures released by INSEE in August 2012 exceeded the symbolic threshold of 3,000,000 (the highest since 1999). That said, the economic decline did not affect all territories indiscriminately: during this harsh employment crisis (2008–2013), city-regions – such as Toulouse, Lyon, Nantes and Bordeaux – performed actually quite well, with a net job creation in the high-tech sectors (Davezies, 2015). This situation makes the role of large cities in times of global economic crisis and austerity enigmatic. On the one hand, France's largest cities seem more likely to absorb some of the effects of the economic and social crisis. Indeed, urbanity, which goes along with agglomeration economies, density of skills and knowledge, is the best protection against the crisis. On the other hand, social cohesion and traditional redistribution mechanisms are threatened by global economic trends and austerity measures with which local governments must deal.

During the past 20 years, Lyon's inter-municipal cooperation authority, commonly named *Grand Lyon*, pursued a pro-active economic development strategy, which allowed to reinvigorate the economy by promoting high-tech and innovation sectors. However, despite the creation of new job opportunities, social inequalities continue to increase. As we will show, the articulation of social cohesion and economic development objectives implies political and institutional changes both for regional and local governments, challenging urban agendas and institutionalized modes of governance. In this regard, new policy tools and partnerships have been recently introduced to face the social effects of the crisis, which has strongly affected historically deprived municipalities in the Lyon area. Despite these initiatives, a "palliative" conception of policies tackling social integration at a metropolitan scale dominates the metropolitan agenda. Specific measures have been promoted to alleviate social exclusion, but they are far from including disadvantaged groups in the post-industrial turn of Lyon's metropolitan region. Indeed, a dualization process characterizes both housing and local economic development policies. Public interventions seem to go with neo-liberal economic trends, rather than struggling to fix them by promoting measures securing middle qualified jobs or opening up high-tech sectors to new social groups. This situation can be explained on the basis of political and institutional reasons. On the one hand, *Grand Lyon*'s political leaders chose to invest in the most profitable sectors in order to secure development, by leaving aside industrial sectors that international markets consider to be "dysfunctional". On the other hand, the organization of local administrations, which tend to reproduce a typical compartmentalization of French bureaucracy, represents an endogenous barrier for the implementation of policies articulating economic competitiveness and social cohesion. In this chapter we provide an account of Lyon's socio-economic and political institutional features, insisting in particular on how the economic crises of 2008 and 2011 affected the metropolitan agenda. This is followed by the analysis of the main actors, policy-tools and governing arrangements characterizing employment and housing policies. As we will see, despite the establishment of new partnerships and policy initiatives, economic development and social cohesion objectives at the metropolitan scale continue to be largely disconnected. This situation raises ultimately the issue of the risk of a dualization process affecting Lyon's urban society, which is already visible in the progressive substitution of traditional working-class groups with new emerging middle and high-qualified residents.

8.2 An aspiring competitive city-region facing increasing social inequalities

The metropolitan city[1] of Lyon counts 59 municipalities for 1,281,971 inhabitants (2014), and a quite high population density (2,484.6 inh/m^2). The population has been stable in the last 20 years, after a slight decrease during the 1980s. Lyon is a rich metropolitan area, with a value of median disposable income by consumption unit of €20,602 in 2012, against a national average of €19,786 (INSEE). Lyon's city-region is historically characterized by a diversified economic base, which is mainly tertiary, with a resilient industrial base that has been affected in the last ten years by the crisis, with the exception of more specialized and innovative sectors. Individual activities and PMEs represent the backbone of Lyon's economy: out of a total amount of 108,607 enterprises in 2009, 91.5 per cent had less than nine employees, and 60 per cent were individual enterprises. However, despite their limited number (2 per cent), medium and big companies (>50 employees) count for about 60 per cent of the total jobs, with bigger companies (>100 employees) counting for almost

Table 8.1 Employment per economic sector in Lyon 2013 (%)

	City-region – Lyon	Rhône-Alpes	France
Agriculture, forestry and fishing	0.06	0.59	1.13
Mining and quarrying, energy and water supply, waste management	1.86	1.93	1.74
Food, drink and tobacco production	0.83	2.06	2.47
Coke and refined petroleum manufacturing	0.16	0.05	0.04
Industrial equipment manufacturing	9.55	13.95	10.00
Construction	5.35	6.83	6.38
Wholesale and retail trade; repair of motor vehicles, motorcycles and personal and household goods	12.68	13.49	13.54
Transport and storage	5.83	6.00	6.03
Hotels and restaurants	4.20	4.61	4.15
Information and communication	5.20	2.57	3.08
Financial intermediation	4.37	3.03	3.74
Real estate	1.34	1.09	1.04
Technical and scientific activities, administrative and expertise services	15.26	10.51	10.85
Public administration, education, health and social work	29.70	29.95	32.13
Other service activities	3.58	3.32	3.68
	100.00	100.00	100.00

Source: authors' elaboration from INSEE, CLAP (connaissance locale de l'appareil productif). Last update: 1 December 2015.

one-half of the total jobs of the city-region (48.5 per cent) (INSEE, CLAP, 2011).

As for the institutional structure, Lyon's metropolitan area has been governed since the end of the 1960s by an inter-municipal authority, the *Grand Lyon*, nowadays named *Métropole de Lyon*.[2] The *Grand Lyon* intervenes in different policy domains, such as urban planning, social housing, collective transports, waste and water management, and economic development. *Grand Lyon*'s annual budget reached €1,932.5 million in 2013, which is mainly dedicated to urban planning, transports and road maintenance (about 40 per cent of the budget). Financial resources devoted to social housing are also particularly conspicuous, with about €70 million per year. As for economic development, the *Grand Lyon* intervenes only marginally with direct investments and cannot distribute financial subsides to companies. However, it does intervene extensively through urban planning tools, by enhancing the coordination among actors, both public and private, and by providing specific assistance to companies that want to redevelop or set up in the metropolitan area.

As for the political strategy, despite partisan turnover, *Grand Lyon*'s policies are characterized by a continuity of action. Gérard Collomb, socialist senator and mayor of Lyon, has been the president of *Grand Lyon* since 2001; his orientation is largely in the wake of his right-centre predecessors, former Prime Minister R. Barre (1995–2001) and M. Noir (1989–1994). Starting in the late 1970s, *Grand Lyon* brought forward a strong political agenda focused on strategic planning and economic development. During the 1980s, the metropolitan strategy mainly focused on the transition from a Fordist to a post-Fordist economy. If the issue of attractiveness and competitiveness was already central, this was combined with a clear orientation towards spatial equalization, in particular with reference to the Western/Eastern fracture (see Torri and Franz in this volume). In the last 20 years, the paradigm of interurban competition has become dominant, largely influencing the metropolitan action in different policy domains. The *Grand Lyon* has indeed strongly reinforced its policies aiming at enhancing the attractiveness of the city-region and at promoting the territory internationally (Galimberti *et al.*, 2015). *Grand Lyon* is nowadays the pivot of a policy network in economic development including institutional actors, in particular the local Chamber of Commerce, business groups and big companies. Despite the existence of institutional arenas (consultative assemblies) for citizen participation – i.e. the *Conseil de Développement* – the involvement of the civil society and in particular of employers' associations in the public decision-making is marginal. To this regard, some authors recently underlined the deployment of a neo-liberal and post-political turn in urban policies, characterizing Lyon's government model, stressing the consensus on territorial competitiveness (Jouve, 2009).

This strategy has successfully supported economic conversion and growth in the last two decades. Despite the crisis, Lyon's metropolitan area saw its disposable income grow between 2007 and 2011 (+2 per cent) (INSEE, 2015). However, a rather important dispersion of wealth among the population exists. Indeed, the indexes of spatial inequalities in the Lyon urban area have risen constantly during the last ten years (Galimberti and Pinson, 2012; INSEE, 2015). As for the spatial socio-economic differentiation, the city-region is characterized by a historical fracture between the wealthy western part and the working class neighbourhoods of the eastern part (INSEE, 2010). The eastern part of the city-region hosts many tertiary and industrial activities, thanks to its excellent connections to infrastructures (airport and highway) and to the presence of affordable land (following the dismantling of Fordist industrial companies in the 1980s). But it also historically concentrates the poorest municipalities of the Lyon metropolitan region in terms of household revenues. The changing economic structure of recent years (see Figure 8.1) has caused evident repercussions on the population's social structure. The working class has been "squeezed", whereas executives and intellectual professions along with intermediary jobs have increased remarkably (Cucca and Maestripieri in this volume). The population living in the southeastern part of the city-region marginally have benefited from this post-industrial and metropolization turn: indeed, these municipalities still register high poverty rates (around 30 per cent) against a metropolitan average of 14.8 per cent. Moreover, they are also experiencing a rapid increase of unemployment, with rates peaking above 20 per cent in the years following the economic crisis (INSEE, 2013).

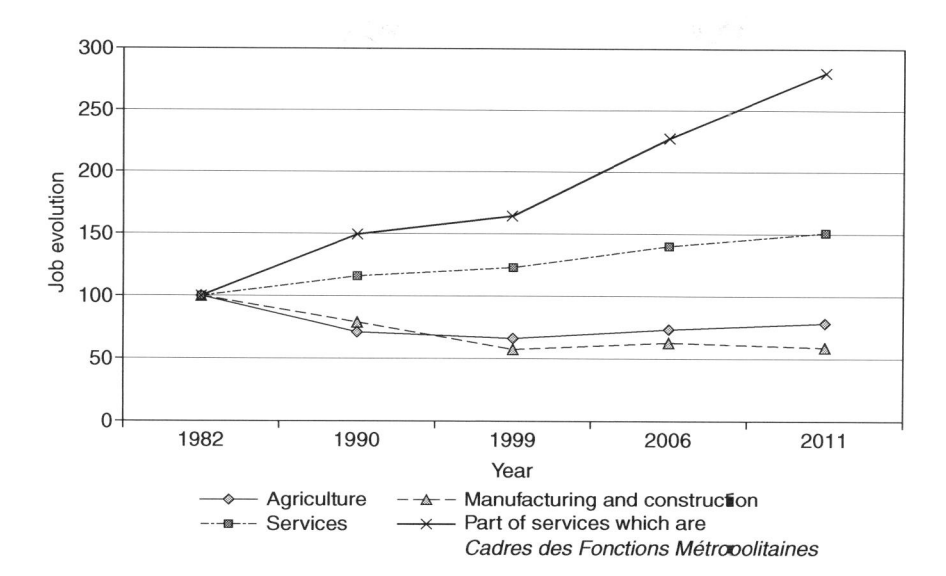

Figure 8.1 Job evolution per sector in Grand Lyon (1982–2011).

Source: authors' elaboration on *Analyse fonctionnelle des emplois*, INSEE 2014.

If we look at the data on unemployment in the Lyon metropolitan area, it is easy to notice that the social cohesion issue did not fall within *Grand Lyon*'s economic strategy. Indeed, the level of unemployment in Lyon is currently very close to the national average (10.2 per cent in 2012, INSEE).[3] Therefore, the effects of the crisis on the urban agenda have been very limited. No significant shift in the political debate around competitiveness and social cohesion has occurred in recent years. This is partially due to the fact that the unemployment rate has increased slowly, even if more brutally in some municipalities, historically concentrating marginalized social groups. *Grand Lyon*'s development strategy has remained primarily concentrated towards companies' needs (in particular high-tech), lacking of an explicit and proactive strategy for fostering and protecting employment, especially in more traditional industries. Therefore, the economic development strategy is mainly framed around increasing competitiveness through the promotion of specific leading industries. To this regard, the national *pôles de competitivité* policy (clusters) has contributed to the institutionalization of this orientation. Seizing the opportunity, the *Grand Lyon* has strongly contributed to the creation of clusters, and progressively reoriented its economic action towards the territory's high added-valued industries. The emphasis on high-tech industries has been progressively articulated, with a pro-active tertiary strategy in urban development, focused on several major urban projects: among others, the Part-Dieu project – the second French business district after La Défense in Paris – is the flagship project of Lyon's tertiary ambition.

Nevertheless, a progressive and discrete refinement of *Grand Lyon*'s development strategy has occurred during recent years. Since 2008 and the beginning of G. Collomb's second term, the *Grand Lyon* has started to pay more attention to middle-size companies, the so-called ETI (*Entreprises de taille intermediaires*), by providing specific assistance towards their development. These companies are usually family run, very diversified in terms of industries covered and more importantly, they appear to be those performing better despite the economic crisis. Since they are in a growing cycle, they manifest HR needs, mostly junior executives in IT, commercial and export activities. But, again this action is targeting primarily the so-called *professions intermédiaires* (middle management staff) and only marginally concerns production activities and therefore qualified blue collars.

Following the economic crisis, a concern for traditional industries progressively emerged, as the result of an internal debate within the *Grand Lyon* services brought about by technical circles and some vice-presidents. However, it is more a matter of sporadic and ad hoc interventions, not supported by a common and shared roadmap for the management and stabilization of the employment in the territory. An emblematic example is that of the reconversion of a Bosch plant producing car components (injection pump) located in Venissieux (a municipality in the Eastern Lyon metropolitan area). After the announcement in 2009 of the imminent shutting down of the production plant (850 employees), a coalition led by unions, employees, local councillors, *Grand Lyon* services and agencies (in particular *Aderly*, the local development agency) succeeded in advocating a reconversion of the industrial site to photovoltaic production. *Le Monde* newspaper spoke of a "lesson of reindustrialization".[4] However, after only two years, Bosch decided to stop the production of photovoltaic modules in Vénissieux, because of conspicuous losses of the production line worldwide. This example actually shows the constraints faced by local governments, whose scope of action is limited.

Moreover, since 2012 there have been some weak signs of a "smooth shift" in the urban agenda towards social issues related to economic development and city competitiveness. The lobbying of the mayors of *Grand Lyon*'s "poorest" municipalities gave way to a renewed interest for the social implications of development policies.[5] A recent initiative has been the organization of a public conference on local employment and training (*1ère Conférence Locale Emploi Formation*, 19 September 2012), jointly promoted by *Maison de l'emploi et de la formation* (MDEF, see below) an organization assembling different actors belonging to employment and social insertion (among others also *Grand Lyon*) and the regional council. This initiative could be interpreted as a first sign of a new local political interest in social cohesion. The smooth shift actually produced effects in terms of new partnerships and pilot initiatives, aiming at articulating competitiveness and social cohesion objectives. These measures are notable both on financial and qualitative terms. However, when examining them closely, it stands out that they are mainly oriented towards low-qualified people, with a clear focus on deprived neighbourhoods. Moreover, they tend to elude a global strategy, both in housing and employment, towards social cohesion, targeting also middle class households. In addition, there are coordination problems among different actors as well as conflicting interests among disadvantaged areas at the metropolitan scale.

8.3 Fostering and protecting local employment: in search of inclusive development policies

As mentioned above, in the last 20 years the *Grand Lyon* has pursued a proactive strategy fostering economic competitiveness mainly focused on high-tech sectors. This strategy does not integrate explicitly the "employment cause", which is taken in charge by the regional council or other actors, both national and local, working in the social integration field. The regional council struggles to promote the organization of territorial based employment strategies, with very limited results. Indeed, its action consists mainly in specific aids to companies (in particular SMEs) and sector animation policies. The different actors working in the social integration field intervene fore and foremost to help people that have been already dropped out from the employment market. Moreover, they interact rarely with *Grand Lyon*'s civil servants, assisting companies in their development and setting up in the metropolitan area. Some changes are on the way, but their impacts appear to be still very limited due to the lack of strong political backing.

In terms of institutional context, we can identify a multitude of policy tools and actors ready to support employment, which are, however, rarely coordinated, notably at the metropolitan scale. Employment has always been and still is mainly a national prerogative in France. *Pôle Emploi*, the main agency responsible for unemployment benefits, tutoring and orientation, is indeed nationally managed. The social and labour market programmes have been historically oriented to compensate marginalized social groups, the "victims" of economic liberalization, through generous monetary aids and transfers, in particular for unemployed people. These compensatory policies had the effect to structurally leave disadvantaged groups far from a full integration in the economic market (Levy, 2008). Starting in the mid-1990s, an incremental and back and forth process of *territorialization* was initiated, concerning in particular active employment policies (Berthet, 2010).[6] However, only since 2000 have local authorities been entitled to intervene in the employment field, mainly in the framework of negotiations and partnerships with the central state. This process brought about some innovations, allowing to better respond to employment needs on a local basis. Despite these initiatives supporting job seekers in developing specific competences and an autonomous professional project, employment policies at an urban scale are still framed around a "palliative" conception of economic and social integration.

Besides, it should be noticed that the current scenario of local employment policies is characterized by a high degree of fragmentation, an actual entanglement of different interventions: national measures coexist with local interventions, and the local autonomy to intervene in this field is highly dependent on local, political and institutional contexts (Balmary *et al.* 2004). The decentralization of national competences to local governments concerns specifically the *départements* and the regions, and to a lesser extent the municipalities. Whereas, metropolitan governments do not have mandatory competences in employment, even if they do intervene in economic development. *Départements* are entrusted with the management of the minimum wage, whereas the regions are responsible for professional training and the promotion of social dialogue. Regional governments have gradually enlarged their scope of action, emerging as employment policy coordinators in particular for the negotiation with unions and professional business organizations. However, the national state is still in charge of deciding guidelines and major programmes. Municipalities are historically statutory members of different organizations assisting specific segments of jobseekers, such as the *Missions Locales* (ML) and *Plan local pour l'insertion et l'emploi* (PLIE) (see below). Finally, metropolitan governments intervene in economic development and job creation, mainly through indirect actions sustaining innovation and entrepreneurship. They also develop specific policies for social integration, mainly focused on disadvantaged neighbourhoods (ZUS, *zones urbaines sensibles*) which are historically the target of *Politique de la Ville*. In the following, we will sketch out the different measures aiming at protecting and fostering occupation. The employment field is characterized by a multitude of actors that intervene at different scales (inter-municipal, municipal, and (rarely) metropolitan) through a mixture of different approaches (territorial, industry or individual based), and rely on different financial resources (European, national and regional). To summarize the different measures, we identified three main domains of intervention: employment stabilization and professional training; employment creation (innovation and entrepreneurship); activation policies specifically targeting low-qualified people and youngsters experiencing long-term unemployment.

8.3.1 Employment stabilization and professional training

The regional council is the most relevant actor in employment security (*"sécurisation de l'emploi"*), promoting measures whose final goal is to preserve, stabilize and guarantee employment. Within the regional administration, a specific service is in charge of implementing interventions and more generally of raising awareness in the regional staff engaged in economic and industrial policies concerning the importance of "employability", as a frame of regional action. The idea of "employability", which corresponds to the European guidelines on employment[7] is operationalized around two main dimensions: the preservation and stabilization of employment over time, and the improvement of general working conditions, as stated by a regional civil servant:

> The central idea is to match business performance and professional career stabilization: that is to say no rupture, continuity and job quality with respect to the type of contract (full-time, if it corresponds to the employee's option)

and fixed contract, with a regular access to training. The key for maintaining employment is to have access to training and always be employable. Therefore, the central idea is to develop employability by mixing the concept of sustainability and quality of jobs.

(Int. n. 3)

Employment stabilization is pursued through a strong articulation with professional training, which inter alia is a regional prerogative, following the policy idea of "*former plutôt que chômer!*" ("Training rather than being on the dole!").[8] Since 2008, no particular policy innovation has been introduced. Indeed, most of the current measures were already in place before the crisis.[9] Roughly speaking, the regional council combines a triple approach in employment: place based, industry based and firm/employee oriented. The territorial action is carried out through CTEF – *Contrats territoriaux emploi et formation* (Local contracts for employment and training), whose main objective is to coordinate active employment and training policies implemented at the inter-municipal scale by defining a common pluriannual strategy. In Lyon's city-region there are three CTEFs (Lyon Centre and North, South-East and Rhone South and West). As we will show, this administrative organization is not without consequence for the consistency of economic and social insertion policies at the metropolitan scale (see below). As for industry support, the regional council tries to promote stable and good employment by engaging in activities that enhance social dialogue among socio-economic partners, unions and companies (in particular for subcontractors). To this regard, the COEF – *Contrat d'Objectif Emploi Formation* (Contract for Employment and Training) is the main instrument for assuring shared objectives and coordinated actions for initial and continuing education and training.[10] Moreover, the regional council intervenes in partnership with central state field services in charge of employment and social affairs through special tools designed for people experiencing recruiting difficulties because of the lack of qualifications or discrimination. These interventions are also addressed to companies (mainly SMEs) to tackle HR management and to help them better adapt to market changes by both securing local employment and the company's competiveness. Despite the variety of measures, regional council efforts in the employment domain lack a substantial articulation with economic development policies, in particular those implemented by the *Grand Lyon*. In fact, the CTEFs turn out to be a sort of "administrative scene", bringing to the table only the actors that intervene in the social integration domain, with very little strategic impact on economic development policies (Int. n. 9).

8.3.2 *Entrepreneurship and innovation*

Job assuring measures are carried out without any implications of the metropolitan authority, which is on the contrary strongly engaged in pro-employment policies fostering innovation and entrepreneurship. High-tech innovation policies consist in financing clusters and incubators. The cluster policy is often perceived as "a policy designed by engineers for other engineers" (Int. n. 9), "disconnected with the social environment" (Int. n. 8), due to its impact on local SMEs and their connection with the local job market demand. If cluster policies are mainly oriented to high-skilled workers in high-tech sectors, the *Grand Lyon* also promotes a specific initiative to foster the "spirit of entrepreneurship" in different sectors, through a network called LVE – *Lyon Ville de l'entreprenariat* (Lyon City of Entrepreneurship), launched in 2002. Currently, the LVE network includes more than 50 associated partners, operating in consulting and coaching, seed capital and financing, incubation, and more classical services of the municipal economic department and of territorial branches of the local Chamber of Commerce. Since the launch of the initiative, specific associations for female entrepreneurship have been promoted. *Grand Lyon* (78 per cent of the total budget) and the region finance the programme for an amount equal to about €1 million per year, whereas the Chamber of Commerce provides staff and personnel. LVE's aim is to spread the culture of entrepreneurship and assure high quality services on the basis of common procedures and standards. The results of LVE are very positive: about 10,000 people have applied to one of the network's organizations, 40 per cent of these contacts led to the creation of a new business, 30 per cent are in a test phase, 60 per cent of the people supported by the LVE network were previously unemployed.[11] However, it should be noted that most of the people accessing LVE services are quite experienced. Efforts are being made in order to open up these services to new social groups, mostly youngsters (with a specific service for students) and inexperienced people (in the field of entrepreneurship) that want to try this career path (see below).

8.3.3 Social activation policies

The abovementioned measures in innovation and entrepreneurship mainly concern policymakers operating in local economic and industrial policies. They appear to be rather disconnected from interventions promoting social integration through employment, despite the effort of the regional council to bind them together. Indeed, social integration policies were initially conceived in the framework of regeneration policies and of the so-called *Politique de la Ville*, the place-based policy created in the early 1980s to address the specific problems of high-rise social housing estates. As we will show, this legacy is nowadays still relevant in order to analyse how social integration policies are territorially organized. First of all, it is possible to notice that the central state still plays an active role in regulating these measures. Besides monetary aids and assistance delivered by *Pole Emploi* agencies, the central state intervenes directly in local contexts through its field services (DIRRECTE), which are in charge of promoting social integration through economic activities.[12] It also intervenes indirectly by financing a large part of local organizations in charge of social and economic insertion (associations managing PLIE, *ML*, *Maisons de l'emploi et de la formation*, MDEF), which we will present herein briefly.

ML de l'Emploi: specifically targeting young people (15–25). ML are located in deprived neighbourhoods (in particular ZUS) and work through the proximity formula (providing proximity assistance to young people through their physical presence in the neighbourhoods, usually close to other public serv ces, cultural and commercial amenities).[13] They use national (mainly), European, regional and local resources to fulfil their missions and they provide global assistance to unemployed young people. Their assistance is not limited to the employment sphere, but aims at tackling different problems that could be an obstacle to work, such as housing, handicap and legal difficulties. They also develop specific col aborations with "big" public job suppliers, targeting young people (SNCF, La Poste, etc.). There are ten ML in the *Grand Lyon* city-region, including three in the city of Lyon. A recent agreement with *Grand Lyon* was signed, in order to develop "the youngsters' insertion" in diverse domains of intervention of *Grand Lyon*, in particular housing but also economic action. However, at the moment *Grand Lyon* mainly acts as a direct employer by recruiting young people from ML, or facilitating negotiations with big companies located in the city-region.

PLIE – Plan locaux d'insertion par l'économique (Local plans for Employment and Inclusion):[14] PLIE are inter-municipal platforms act ve in reducing social exclusion through labour market integration, by promoting stable and long-term employment. They provide support to job seekers (12 months), offering individual and personalized assistance to very marginalized populations. In the Lyon city-region, two associations, Uni-Est for the Southeast Lyon metropolitan area (15 municipalities) and Alliés for Lyon's municipality, are the principal associations managing PLIE. The two associations saw their scope of action gradually enlarge, until becoming the key actors for the coordination and management of EU (ESF), national and regional measures for economic and social integration in Lyon's city-region. They also host the ML. They are a particularly interesting and successful case of local activism, which unfortunately encounters problems of adaptation in the local job market, which exceeds the geographical scope of action of the two associations, and embraces the whole city-region. This mismatch would justify the fusion of the two PLIE (as is the case in other city-regions in France, where the PLIE is intended at the metropolitan level), or a coordination of their actions with economic development policies carried out by the *Grand Lyon*.

Maison de l'emploi et de la formation (MDEF): in 2005 the national government introduced the MDEF, which is a territorial organization aimed at coordinating interventions among different actors in the field of economic and social insertion. The MDEF for Lyon's city centre was created in 2008. The MDEF's budget is mainly funded by the central state, whose contribution for 2011 stands at €1 million (decreased since 2010, when it was 50 per cent higher), and partially by ESF. MDEF are a national programme, their intervention and requirements are quite similar in all territories, and involve developing a common territorial strategy and a market observatory; anticipating job market restructuring and assisting companies (SMEs) in case of HR concerns; intervening in the development of "local jobs" (by organizing forums and job-market days and promoting "social clauses"); fighting against social exclusion and discrimination; orientating and giving assistance to public for employment needs and training. In comparison to PLIE and ML, MDEF targets a larger public and aspires to become a forum for the coordination of organizations intervening in both social integration and employment policies.

It is possible to notice that *Grand Lyon*'s participation in these organizations is rather limited: it contributes certainly in financing MDEF, and acts as an important employer for young people of "missions locales" (in particular in its traditional missions, i.e. waste and road management and transport), but nothing more than this. *Grand Lyon*'s engagement in the field of economic and social insertion is carried out through a small unit, called, *Mission d'insertion par l'activité économique*, which has been recently integrated in the economic development division (it was previously attached to the urban development division). This mission is still very limited in terms of financial resources and staff, and its integration in the activities of the economic department (mainly company-oriented) can be considered a "shaky" experiment for now. Economic development and social inclusion policies clearly correspond to two-separated systems of actors at the metropolitan scale. However, some timid changes are on the way, and we will analyse them herein by presenting some pilot initiatives promoted by *Grand Lyon*.

8.3.4 Aligning economic development and social cohesion objectives: new partnerships for employment promotion

A good example of articulation of economic development and social cohesion policies is the partnership established between LVE and MDEF in order to provide specific assistance to low qualified people wanting to set up a new business activity. The initiative aims at launching a policy tool (LVE), designed for experienced people, new social classes, in particular the more distant from the entrepreneurial world. This initiative is in the wake of a pilot experiment carried out in the ninth district of the city of Lyon, in a deprived neighbourhood, called La Duchère, where a *Maison de la Création des entreprises* – MCE (House of business creation) was established (2008) and is supported by both the territorial services of MDEF and of LVE's network. The MCE of Duchère provides assistance mainly to the local population (50 per cent lives in the neighbourhood), the unemployed (70 per cent), and a rather good percentage of women (38 per cent). Moreover, a political engagement to gather different LVE organizations in a restricted number of entrepreneurship poles, offering a large variety of services in a unique place has been expressed in LVE's action plan. To this regard, a good example is the association *La Coursive d'entreprise*, in the municipality of St Fons (southeast *Grand Lyon*), an incubator offering assistance for start-ups and spaces, including a cooperative association for social and economic activities. The idea of creating a "Business creation pole" in another neighbourhood (Carré de Soie), hosting both a regeneration social urban project and a cluster nearby, is under evaluation by *Grand Lyon*'s political executives and services.

Another pilot initiative is the recent association of *Grand Lyon*'s economic developers, in charge of companies' development, with the local teams of the associations involved in activation policies (in particular those managing PLIE, such as Uni-Est and Alliés). Working groups focused on training, HR problems for SMEs and mobility have been set up to share objectives and facilitate the alignment of their actions in specific territories, which explicitly manifest their intention to work with *Grand Lyon*'s services. However, they are not organized on a regular basis and they do not cover the whole metropolitan territory. Besides, for now, these partnerships are limited to the development of a common reflection, with very little direct consequences on routines and work practices. For the moment, the association of economic developers and social staff is judged not satisfactory by civil servants active in both fields.

Lyon's case study shows a large variety and richness of policy tools at the disposal of local authorities in order to foster and protect employment. However, the entanglement of different policy tools and actors have set a real problem concerning the lack of coordination, notably at metropolitan scale. The causes are multiple, both institutional and political. As stated by a state civil servant:

> There is certainly a problem of juridical competence. Moreover, the impact of the economic crisis was not strong enough to determine a sort of "sacred union", capable of overcoming existing institutional barriers and promoting large and incisive policies to foster employment. We are more in a situation of continuity with the past, introducing several small new actions. Undoubtedly there is a local dynamism, but without a strong political endorsement.
>
> (Int. n. 9)

Regional initiatives for developing local based employment strategies are limited to actors working in social integration organizations and have difficulties in involving *Grand Lyon*'s economic civil servants. To this regard, the pilot projects previously mentioned appear to be still in a very early stage, and are often linked to informal and personal factors. The policymakers, met during the interviews, highlighted the difficulties of these two public policy spheres (economic development and social integration policies) in dialoguing and sharing common objectives. This is due to cultural barriers, but also to the lack of a collective and more direct effort to introduce institutionalized procedures and routines for collaboration.

The MDEF of Lyon represents an interesting and promising initiative to federate the different actors intervening in the economic and social integration sphere. However, its action is limited to the city centre (even if it has the vocation to work with other territories of the city-region) and *Grand Lyon*'s engagement is still too limited. There are peripheral territories, which cannot benefit from centrality jobs (linked to commercial activities) or from a rich industrial and service fabric (like in the eastern part of the city-region), risking to be marginalized from the economic dynamism characterizing Lyon's economy on a whole. This situation could lead to competition dynamics among employment organizations settled in "weak territories", struggling to capture jobs, often low-qualified, in order to match NPM (new public management) criteria, imposed at both national and European level for spending control.

To sum up, a clear metropolitan economic strategy exists at Lyon's metropolitan level, whereas social integration policies are still fragmented among several organizations, acting in different administrative areas, without a shared road map. *Grand Lyon*'s economic civil servants have the information and competences to outline a development strategy based on employment at the metropolitan level. What is missing is a strong political willingness, which appears to be particularly crucial in order to overcome the effect of path-dependent institutional factors. The latter still represent an endogenous barrier for the development of an integrated employment metropolitan strategy.

8.4 Regulative efforts in the housing market focused on social housing

The economic crisis has brought social housing at the forefront of the national agenda. First of all, for social reasons: poor households are facing increasing difficulties in accessing housing. At the same time, households, that used to let social housing with regard to acquiring property see their residential trajectories blocked because of the high level of land and estate prices and the difficulty to access mortgages. Second, for economic reasons: funding social housing construction has a positive effect on unemployment. The housing policy objectives in the Lyon city-region are framed by this national agenda. The first issue is the development of the social and affordable housing stock and the dispersion of affordable housing throughout the urban region, in particular, where land, estate prices and rents are the highest, and the risk of eviction of the poorest households are the highest. The second issue is the restructuring of large social housing estates (*grands ensembles*) through the destruction of the more stigmatized ensembles and the diversification of the housing offered in the deprived neighbourhoods. The main instrument of the housing policies in the local housing programme (Programme local de l'habitat) was voted in 2011 by the *Grand Lyon*. This programme fixed construction targets (4,000+ social housings and 5,000+ other housings per year) and has a budget of €70 million per year. These general objectives have been implemented through several mechanisms.

8.4.1 Direct provision of housings for the poorest households

The demand for social housing is really important in the *Grand Lyon* area. Between 50,000 and 60,000 households have been waiting for social housing allocation since the beginning of 2015. Four applications for each social housing unit are available. Most of the applications concern households living in the most disqualified private housing, in collective structures (*centres d'hébergement*) or constrained to stay at friends' or parents' homes. The *Grand Lyon* supports the construction of social housing through direct and indirect actions. It deals with public grants to social housing authorities, either public, semi-public, or private.[15] The *Grand Lyon* controls directly the main social housing authority (*Grand Lyon Habitat*). However, the management of social housing remains an issue because the public housing stock is managed by 27 social housing authorities. A large estate may contain property owned by a dozen or more landlords.

The *Grand Lyon* has also become a very dynamic actor on the front of land management, by constituting a reserve of public-owned lands (even if the stock is decreasing now). This asset is used strategically to develop social housing. In some cases, land plots are given or sold under market price to social housing authorities to allow them to build new developments. In other cases, the *Grand Lyon* sells land to property developers but with the obligation to deliver a project integrating 20 or 25 per cent of social housing. The *Grand Lyon* has also mobilized large institutional property owners in social housing. The church or the public hospital of Lyon wants to keep its old buildings, but meets difficulties in maintaining its heritage. The *Grand Lyon* acts as an intermediary among these institutions and social housing authorities helping them establish deals. The latter accept to renovate properties that they do not own but in which they can build new housing that they can rent to poor households. The former keep their properties and find a cheap way to renovate them.

Moreover, the *Grand Lyon* uses urban planning tools to increase the share of social housing. In areas characterized by a shortage of affordable housing, the master plan has introduced a legal rule called "*servitude de mixité sociale*" that conditions the authorization of new development projects to the compliance with a minimal share of social housing in future developments. The type of social housing (classical or specific for the poorest households) that will be built can also be defined. In these spatial sectors, private estate developers build social housing that they then sell to public social housing companies for a reasonable price.

8.4.2 Urban renovation projects in the most stigmatized public housing estates

Grand Lyon is also facing a kind of mismatch between demand and supply for social housing. The city centre neighbourhoods and the west communes concentrate their demand for social housing, whereas very unpopular neighbourhoods located in "pericentral" neighbourhoods of the city centre and eastern suburbs meet a low demand for social housing. To tackle this mismatch, the *Grand Lyon* used the programme set up at a national scale in 2003 to accelerate urban renewal in the so-called "*banlieue*".[16] The national agency in charge of the national urban renewal programme (ANRU) selected 12 projects in different neighbourhoods submitted by *Grand Lyon*. They represented a total investment of €914 million between 2007 and 2011, of which the national agency brought 34 per cent, local authorities 45 per cent (*Région, département, Grand Lyon,* Municipalities) and the social housing organizations 18 per cent. The demolition and reconstruction of 5,400 public dwellings were planned for the 2007–2013 period. When the municipality in which the renewal project takes places has a housing stock made of more than 50 per cent of social housing, the latter is rebuilt in another municipality.

Results in terms of housing diversity are really different among neighbourhoods. In some of them, property developers used fiscal advantages to build affordable private housing for the middle class. These programmes allowed local households to become landlords and attracted the middle class from other sectors where they were unable to find affordable land and housings. In other estates, the stigmatization was so strong that no property developers accepted to run the risk of residential diversification. In that case, only the poorest households stayed in the neighbourhood, leading to an increase of social deprivation.

8.4.3 Results and limits of corrective housing policies

In the *Grand Lyon* metropolitan area, public policies in favour of social housing have produced tangible results but present also limits. Since 2006, the production of subsidized social housings has clearly increased. In 2009, a national programme called "VEFA 30 000" doped the public housing production by developing partnerships between private real estate developers and social housing companies. The latter bought flats built within private programmes facing difficulties to sell. From 2009 on, households have been meeting more difficulties in accessing credit due to the financial crisis. Nevertheless, the level of public subsidies for social housing has not decreased since the crisis, even if the capacity of public finances to hold this level of investment is in debate. Another source of concern is the level of private developers' activity in the near future. Will they take the risk of launching new programmes? It is likely that they will do so in the most attractive neighbourhoods of the city-region. However, in other areas, the global level of social housing provision could be stable or in decline because property developers will differ their investments.

In France, the spectrum of housings labelled as "social" is quite broad. A wide variety of public funds allows to subsidy social housing, targeting middle classes as much as highly deprived populations. A striking feature of the public housing policies within the *Grand Lyon* is that they have been progressively oriented towards the needs of the latter ... and the former at the expense of social groups in the middle. The share of PLAI (*Prêt locatif aidé d'intégration*), i.e. loans to finance social housing for the more needy population, increased from about 20 per cent of subsidized housing units in the early 2000s to 40 per cent in 2012. On the other hand, the building of social housing for households able to pay a rent just above the private market level (funded through *Prêt locatif social*) has also increased. By contrast, the share of subsidies for the upper categories of social housing (*Prêt Locatif à Usage Social*) has remained stable. Thus, the financial crisis has led to target direct financial interventions in public housing for the poorest households. As far as the territorial redistribution of social housing in the *Grand Lyon* is concerned, no clear signs of change have appeared. Most of the existing social housing stock remains mainly located in Lyon and in the municipalities of the Eastern *Grand Lyon*. However, the efforts carried out by the *Grand Lyon* administration, aimed at reinforcing the presence of social housing in the more bourgeois western part of the city, have started to produce effects. For the 2011–2017 period, the *Programme Local de l'Habitat* has set the objective to build 50 per cent of new social housing units in the centre of the *Grand Lyon*, 25 per cent in the East and 25 per cent in the West.

Nevertheless, two limits can be formulated concerning the effects of corrective housing policies. First, even if public subsidies are focused on the public housing built for the poorest households, the new flats are not accessible for the latter in financial terms. Because of land prices and building costs, the level of public subsidies is not sufficient to make the price of new public housing decrease significantly. As a consequence, the average rent in recent public housing units – between €500 and €600 – is too high for the poorest households. The only way for them to enter the social housing circuit is to accept a housing unit in the oldest and more depreciated high rise estates of the eastern *banlieues*. The result is the reinforcement of the social specialization of these neighbourhoods. Second, the increase of rents and property prices makes it more difficult for the middle class to benefit from a residential mobility. The effects of the local

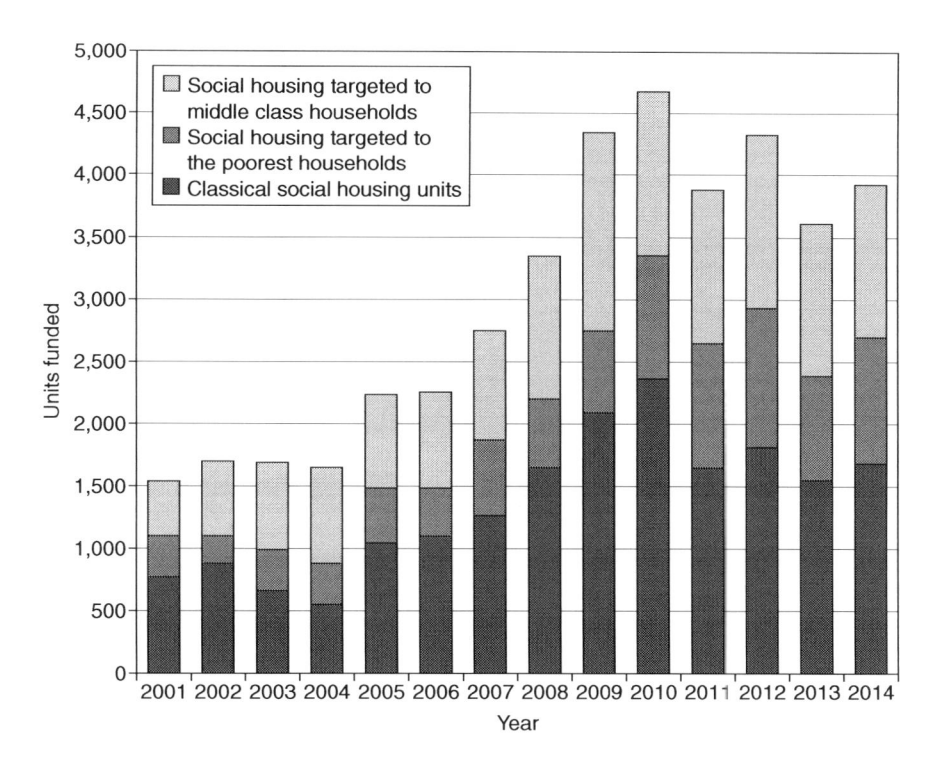

Figure 8.2 Evolution of the social housing units funded per year in Grand Lyon (2001–2014).
Source: courtesy of DDT du Rhône.

policies in developing affordable private renting are in this context really limited. Most of the landlords prefer to renounce to public subsidies for renovating their flat because they do not want to enter into agreements with public bodies that limit the rent price level and its evolution.

8.5 Conclusions

The case of Lyon shows a quite contrasted situation. On the one hand, local governments are in possession of strong legal instruments and important resources that allow them to frame the urbanization process and to make it compatible with the maintenance of the social mix. Lyon is a city-region in which the housing crisis exists but is tackled by public authorities with a commitment towards the most deprived populations. The latter are also taken care of through social and training policies in the framework of ML or PLIE. On the other hand, Lyon is a city with strong economic ambitions. The officials want to see the city-region recognized as one of the most dynamic in Europe. The objective is to attract companies and social groups that are considered in the centre of the knowledge economy. The problem is that, in-between, there is nothing or not much. No strategy to preserve and develop public employment. No strategy to preserve well (not high) qualified and paid jobs in the industry or craftsmanship. It looks like urban policies at the city and city-regional scale have been anticipating or accompanying the rise of a dual economy and a dual society, where highly qualified and mobile professionals operating in the hi-tech, rare service sectors need an army of ancillary jobs to guarantee basic needs (Krugman, 2003).

This political choice may trigger a polarization process in the labour market. Lyon is considered to be an attractive city for middle managers and young executives, looking for lower rents in comparison to Paris and for an attractive (culturally and socially) environment in which to settle down. The economic strategy combined with the economic changes of globalized capitalism have produced in the last ten years a gradual substitution of the population, in particular factory workers, with intermediary and executive workers. Something is being carried out to keep the city in competition for the localization of rare activities. Something is being done to alleviate the difficulties of the poorest. However, not much is being done for the population and the activities linking these worlds, i.e. the world of qualified but not globalized services and industries, the world of decent jobs, the world of good quality jobs. To put it bluntly, the traditional lower strata of the middle class (technicians, employees) are not the privileged targets of Lyon's metropolitan policies. As a result of this and other more global trends, income inequality has strongly increased in the last ten years. The deficiency in the supply of policies for this middle level might be explained by a historical problem linked to the national disjunction of social and economic interventions. Social interventions were historically developed within urban interventions (mainly housing and planning) in the frame of *Politique de la Ville*, and continue to be disconnected from economic development policies (cluster policies and industrial policies). This problem is reproduced at the local and urban scale, and only a strong political engagement can fix this disconnection by blending the two approaches – urban and economic – to produce true place-based employment policies.

Notes

1 We refer to the classification given by the Urban Audit (Eurostat) of "city", which corresponds to a local administrative unit (LAU) where the majority of the population lives in an urban centre of at least 50,000 inhabitants. Following the Eurostat classification in the case of Lyon, the LAU corresponds to the perimeters of the inter-municipal cooperation authority, the *Grand Lyon*.

2 The creation of inter-municipal bodies in large urban areas dates back to the late 1960s, when the central state imposed on a dozen of cities the *Communauté urbaine* (CU) formula. The CU is an inter-municipal cooperation authority endowed with an executive power (president) and a council composed of appointed municipal councillors. The CU exerts important functions such as planning, housing, transport, utilities management and economic development at the metropolitan level. Most of France's largest cities, with the notable exception of Paris, have adopted the CU model. The 2014 territorial reform created a new status of "*métropole*". The latter allows the transfer of functions from the departments and regions to this new type of cooperation body that can be created in city-regions of more than 0.5 million inhabitants. The same law created a specific status for the *Métropole de Lyon* recognizing it as a "*collectivité locale*" with a specific status even if its council is still composed of indirectly elected councillors. The most striking feature of the section of the 2014 Act concerning Lyon is the transfer of all of the *Rhône département* functions to the *Métropole* on the latter's territory. The shift from the *Grand Lyon* to the *Métropole de Lyon* occurred in 2015. Our research is based on data mainly collected in 2012. We therefore base this chapter on the *Grand Lyon* instead of the *Métropole de Lyon*.

3 This datum refers to ILO definition.

4 Claire Guélaud, "A l'usine Bosch de Vénissieux, une leçon de réindustrialisation", *Le Monde*, 20 November 2011.

5 Report, general meeting, Uni-Est Association, 5 July 2012, intervention of Jean-Luc Martinez, president of Uni-Est Association. Source: Interview n. 5.

6 The process of *territorialization* of employment policies deployed in two directions: a devolution of central state functions to state field services and agencies, and a decentralization and delegation to local governments.

7 On the uses, appropriations and operational translations by local actors in the Rhône-Alpes region of this public-policy idea, see: J. Gräbner, "La promotion de l'employabilité au défi de son opérationnalisation: une comparaison franco-italienne", Colloque du Réseau thématique 25 de l'Association Française de Sociologie, "L'employabilité et ses usages sociaux", 4–5 September 2014, Université Paris-Est Créteil (text online, available at: https://pacte-grenoble.academia.edu/JosuaGr%C3%A4bener).

8 In this chapter, we will not analyse the several measures promoted by the regional council in the field of professional training. We will concentrate on its effort to increase coordination among the different interventions promoting employment stabilization.

9 Specific measures to stabilize employment have been introduced to help subcontracting SMEs, suffering from market fluctuations.

10 The COEF initially applied to industries, which are the most subjected to seasonal cycles and new forms of temporary jobs: textile, agriculture, transport and logistic, cleaning, entertainment and audio-visual, sport, hotel and restaurant. New contracts

are currently being established in more traditional sectors, such as chemistry and the plastic industry.

11 LVE, 2011, Bilan et perspectives, Baromètre de satisfaction. Source: online, available at: www.lyon-ville-entrepreneuriat.org/.

12 "Insértion par l'économique" states for a specific set of public interventions aimed at enabling unemployed people experiencing social and professional difficulties to benefit from employment contracts, and to facilitate their social and professional integration. Two main measures can be mentioned: (1) the SIAE – *Structures d' insertion par l'activité économique* (Insertion Organizations by Economic Activity) – these organizations receive subsidies from the state in order to carry out an economic activity allowing to introduce marginalized and unemployed people in the labour market and to teach them a craft. (2) ZFU – *Zones franches urbaine*, a national law approved at the end of the 1990s that introduced fiscal exoneration (social contribution and land tax) for companies deciding to set up their businesses in ZFU areas, binding them to hire at least one-third of their employees from those areas (since 2012 increased by one half).

13 They were created during the 1980s to tackle youngsters' unemployment. There are about 500 ML in France.

14 The PLIEs were created by independent initiatives of municipalities, in Northern France during the 1990s, in order to tackle a deep employment crisis in the textile and steel industry. Since 1998 PLIEs have been integrated in the national programme against social exclusion and in the ESF OP (European Social Fund Operating Programme). They became the most widespread local device to tackle unemployment in France, in particular in urban contexts (today there are 181). Although PLIE is thought to be a municipal instrument, most of them group several communes and are managed at inter-municipal scale, by associations, public interest groups (GIP – *Groupements d'intérêts publics*) or municipal in-house services. A fusion and regrouping process of PLIEs is currently in progress.

15 In France, two types of actors act in social housing: first of all, public authorities controlled by municipalities or counties; second, private authorities that are generally controlled by the consortium collecting the compulsory contribution of large private enterprises to the housing policies (a tax corresponding to 0.46 per cent of wages for enterprises with more than 20 employees).

16 Between 2003 and 2015, €41 billion were injected by public and private actors to demolish vacant public housing, to build new social housing (in the area but also outside), to introduce housing diversity with private home-ownership, to design public spaces, to connect neighbourhoods with the rest of the city through public transport.

References

Balmary, D., Chevrier Fatome, C. and Bernard, S. (2004). *Rapport de l'instance de l'évaluation de la politique de l'emploi et recours à des opérateurs externs*. Paris: Commissariat Général au Plan, La Documentation Française.

Berthet, T. (2010). Externalisation et gouvernance territoriale des politiques de l'emploi. *Revue Française de Socio-Economie*, 6: 131–148.

Davezies, L. (2015). *Le nouvel égoïsme territorial: le grand malaise des nations*. Paris: Seuil.

Galimberti, D. and Pinson, G. (2012). Place Equality Regimes in French City Regions. Paper presented at the XXII Worlds Congress of Political Science, IPSA, Madrid, July.

Galimberti, D., Lobry, S., Pinson, G. and Rio, N. (2015). La métropole de Lyon: Splendeurs et fragilités d'une machine intercommunale, *Hérodote*, 2014, 154: 191–209.

Gräbner, J. (2014). La promotion de l'employabilité au défi de son opérationnalisation:

une comparaison Franco Italienne. *Colloque du Réseau thématique 25 de l'Association Française de Sociologie*, "L'employabilité et ses usages sociaux", 4–5 September 2014, Université Paris-Est Créteil.

INSEE (2015). Rhône-Alpes: une région riche mais des inégalités qui s'accentuent. *Insee Analyses Rhône-Alpes*, 18: February 2015.

Jouve, B. (2009). De la métropole d'équilibre à Lyon. In: Boino, P. (ed.). *Lyon la production de la ville*, Marseille: Paranthèses.

Krugman, P., (2003). Requiem per la gloriosa classe media. *Reset*, 75: 30–40.

Levy, J. D. (2008). From the Dirigiste State to the Social Anaesthesia State: French Economic Policy in the Longue Durée. *Modern and Contemporary France*, 16(4): 417–435.

List of interviews

Int. n. 1: *Grand Lyon*, Inclusion through Economic Activity Mission, 16 April 2012.

Int. n. 2: *Grand Lyon*, Ville de Lyon, *Gerland District Mission*, Director, 23 April 2012.

Int. n. 3: Rhône Alpes Region, Department of Economic Development and Employment, Mutation, Employment, Territory and Social Innovation Service, 24 May 2012.

Int. n. 4: Mission Locale Val de Saône/Plateau Nord, Director 25 May 2012.

Int. n. 5: Association Uni-Est, PLIE Lyon Sud-Est, Director, 25 May 2012.

Int. n. 6: Grand Lyon, Department Economic and International Development, *Local Development Service*, Director, 2 May 2012.

Int. n. 7: CGPME – Union Régionale, Regional secretary, 9 May 2012.

Int. n. 8: Maison de l'emploi et de la formation de Lyon, PLIE Lyon, 26 June 2012.

Int. n. 9: DIRRECTE, Territorial direction, 69, Rhône, *Employment Service*, 26 June 2012.

Websites

Aliès association. Online, available at: www.allies-plie.org.

CTEF Rhône-Alpes region. Online, available at: www.rhonealpes.fr/139-contrats-territoriaux-emploi-formation-ctef.htm.

Direccte Rhône-Alpes. Online, available at: http://direccte.gouv.fr/-accueil-18-.html.

Economic Departement Grand Lyon. Online, available at: www.economie.grandlyon.com.

INSEE, Base de données détaillés localisées. Online, available at: www.insee.fr/fr/bases-de-donnees/default.asp?page=statistiques-locales/donnees-detaillees_tableau.htm.

INSEE, CLAP, connaissance locale de l'appareil productif. Online, available at: www.insee.fr/fr/methodes/default.asp?page=definitions/clap.htm.

Lyon Ville de l'entreuprenariat. Online, available at: www.lyon-ville-entrepreneuriat.org.

Maison de l'emploi et de la formation de Lyon. Online, available at: www.mdef-lyon.fr.

Mission locales. Online, available at: www.missions-locales.org.

Uni-Est association. Online, available at: www.plie-uni-est.org.

9 Manchester

Institutional and policy innovation amidst austerity

Nicola Headlam

9.1 Introduction

The United Kingdom is a comparatively centralised nation, politically as well as economically. City-level policies must take account of actions at other levels. The present government interest in 'localism' is associated with a series of reforms, including unprecedented cuts in local government funding and the national 'capping' of local taxation, which impinge directly on local capacities to support economic and social development. In the United Kingdom, the national policy context frames resources available for local government (more than 70 per cent of funding, overall, comes from central government), with local councils funded by a combination of grants, council tax (a locally set tax based on residential property values), business rates (which are collected and redistributed to local authorities but are subject to calls for 'localisation' favouring areas with a stronger business base), and fees and charges from certain services. The proportion of revenue that comes from council tax is low, meaning that if a council wishes to increase its funding modestly, it has to increase council tax by a large amount. Central government retains the right to 'cap' council tax, or to incentivise local authorities not to raise their tax levels, if potential increases are deemed to be excessive.

This chapter concentrates on the ways in which 'The ascent of Greater Manchester' has been designed despite this political and fiscal centralism and explores the national urban and partnership policy context within which Greater Manchester has garnered significant national/international attention for the way in which it has sought to work across the administrative boundaries of the conurbation and to build partnerships for tackling key economic and social challenges with other public and private bodies and higher levels of government. It suggests that the most recent manifestation of this is the piloting of new, statutory arrangements for a 'combined authority' (the Greater Manchester Combined Authority, GMCA) providing a vehicle for the ten boroughs of the city-region to collaborate on a range of strategic issues that affect them collectively and provide the institutional basis for accepting further devolved responsibilities from national government. It then argues that the more recent phase of place-based budgeting and city dealing still lacks the requisite levers for policy inroads into either housing or skills issues.

The governance and policy development capacities of the GMCA has been addressed in this chapter in two different terms: the former as it functions deploying 'soft power' and narrative-building for the purposes of institutional innovation, which sees a trail-blazing set of governance exper mentations garnering plaudits from central government and the private sector; the latter, on the other hand, explores local innovation in housing and labour market policies to find a more mixed picture of the proceeds of governance innovation in a conurbation characterised by a north–south divide in terms of prosperity both in housing and neighbourhood quality and skills leading to employment.

It is possible to argue, as its architects do, that the institutional innovation is a prelude to a more thoroughgoing attack on the pernicious inequalities scarring the conurbation, and that a more advantageous settlement in Greater Manchester's favour would lead to the potential for further policy differentiation at the Greater Manchester scale in favour of those policies of social protection and welfare benefiting the deprived communities of the city-region.

In short, an impressive record on the institutional response to austerity has been in the making for many years in Greater Manchester. However, the deployment of these institutions in terms of their policy innovation in the fields of skills and housing, whose adverse conditions crystallise in the boroughs of the north of the conurbation, is yet to emerge, demonstrating a disconnect between the dual roles of local government in framing economic development and in containing and mitigating social issues. A focus on either side of this complex equation, it may be argued, is also a problem inherent to the centralised governance structure of the United Kingdom, which can be resolved through the devolution of further levers to the city and regional level.

9.2 Institutional context: the ascent of Greater Manchester

The formal establishment of the GMCA, encompassing the ten Greater Manchester boroughs, is the result of significant institution building and collaboration, leading to a coherent polity at this experimental scale in the UK context. Greater Manchester has weathered central government policy concerning regions (i.e. at a larger scale) and a current trend towards localism (i.e. at a smaller scale) and has interpreted a general turn within UK policy towards 'localism' in a specific way, giving way to specific experimentation both in housing and skills policies, as well as through a devolution agenda characterised by the striking of deals between local and central government. Such deals notwithstanding, it must be emphasised that general discretionary spending for local government – such as the funds allocated in special purpose programmes and initiatives – is low in a general context characterised by national restrictions on local spending. This context, which has been described as 'austerity localism', has restricted the productive spending of localities for economic development. As such, Greater Manchester exposes some of the contradictions of sub-national policy

Despite local government reorganisations ostensibly orchestrated to reduce the power of elected local government, Manchester City Council (MCC) was prominent in the promulgation of 'local socialism' during the 1980s. This movement saw the protection and growth of public employment, linked to a highly interventionist approach to the promotion of indigenous industrial growth, as a more desirable alternative to the laissez-faire economic restructuring envisaged by central government. Confidence in this municipal socialist strategy wavered following the third successive Conservative national election victory in 1987. Quilley (2000) describes the 'seeming futility of municipal resistance to national government strategy'. Nevertheless, its legacy is still felt in the ways that local politicians view their roles today. As MCC's long-time leader Councillor Richard Leese has commented, Labour politicians were looking for strategies other than simply overt resistance, which was proving electorally unpopular and (to some) economically unviable: 'I fought central government through the '80s and I can tell you – It doesn't work'. Indeed, the fact that the leader and chief executives of the city council have had such a stable tenure in charge of the core city (Councillor Richard Leese since 1994 and Sir Howard Bernstein since 1998) has led to the development of a close network of city leaders, referred to as 'the Manchester men' or 'the Manchester family'. There is no doubt that the functioning of this network over three decades is the most significant explanatory factor in the case of Greater Manchester.

The steady accretion of Greater-Manchester-wide organisational capacity would not have been possible without the stability of political and executive leadership within key local authorities that have led the process. Executive stability within Manchester has effectively been provided by the fact that – de facto if not *de jure* – the city has had a single chief executive, (now Sir) Howard Bernstein, since the early 1990s. Writing in the *Guardian* about his career, Bernstein picks out this period and the way that the city leaders 'put place before party politics':

> The Manchester story is both long and complex – but hugely exciting. Events such as the terrorist bomb in 1996 and the Commonwealth Games in 2002 were major influences in the development of the city. I think my highlight was in the early 1990s when a so-called hard left council successfully negotiated with a Conservative government a funding package for the first phase of our light rail system – the first privatised railway this country had seen for a century. *I think this showed more than anything our capacity to put place before party politics – a characteristic which applies to this day – and why we have one of the most formidable partnerships with business to be found anywhere.*
>
> (Bernstein, quoted in the *Guardian*, 9 November 2010, emphasis mine)

The leadership of the core city over time have made a case for the city to be viewed as the ten boroughs of the conurbation together, as opposed to the central city alone. The GMCA covers an area of some 2.7 million people (2011 census) and encompasses nine local authority boroughs in addition to the city of Manchester. For this collective, collaborative approach to have purchase, it has needed to be expressed through a process of narrative-building that each of the ten local authorities could support. It covers a physical territory of more than 500 square miles and, lacking formal powers has developed strategically and through the building of informal alliances, often based on combining 'brand, plan and strategy' collaboratively.

The origins of the current approach can be found in the first 'City Pride prospectus', which Manchester, along with Birmingham and London, was asked to develop by national government when it became apparent that many of the regeneration initiatives underway in that period were successful on their own terms within a small area, but did not connect effectively with the needs and potentials of other areas in the city. The city of Manchester was unique in opening the City Pride process out to other local authority areas, and coined the term 'regional centre' to draw attention to the cross-district area of high actual and potential employment growth in the centre of the conurbation. This was the first stage in the development of collaborative, cross-district planning for Greater Manchester. It spawned a number of joint initiatives between pairs of local authority areas and opened up the way for Greater-Manchester-wide economic strategising – and, eventually, the Manchester Independent Economic Review (MIER) in 2009 – which drew upon common analysis and action plans across local authority boundaries.

The key hypothesis underlying the MIER was that Manchester is the UK city, outside of London, most likely to increase its long-term growth rate, access international markets and enjoy strong connections with the rest of the world. However, it was argued, the city has for many years 'punched below its weight', given its size and scale. This was viewed as an opportunity for the city to reassert its importance within the national urban hierarchy and to influence the national policy climate to underpin the cultivation of new areas of economic growth.

Collaborative thinking and planning were given greater force and coherence by the development of institutional capacity at the Greater Manchester level. Some aspects of institutional development are peculiar to Greater Manchester. Its international airport, for example, is jointly owned by the ten local authorities. Greater Manchester was also the one conurbation in which, following the abolition in 1986 of the six, short-lived 'metropolitan counties' that were created by local government re-organisation in the mid-1970s, a standing, voluntary body – the Association for Greater Manchester Authorities (AGMA) – was created to provide some oversight of the various special-purpose, conurbation-wide bodies that continued to exist after abolition and to provide a forum for discussion of Greater-Manchester-wide issues. Over time, the AGMA has been joined by other Greater-Manchester-wide institutions that provide conceptual and delivery capacity for actions agreed by the ten authorities.

All of the above factors have contributed to the reputation Greater Manchester has gained for its capacity to deliver. This is particularly the case for the city, whose management of the completion of a succession of economic development, regeneration and transport projects over the last 20 years, across a wide range of fields, has given Manchester an unrivalled reputation, nationally and internationally, and within private as well as public sectors, for 'getting things done'. There is no absolute consensus on the iconic projects that have sealed that reputation, but those that are cited regularly include:

- The city's second Olympic Games bid, which was unsuccessful in terms of achieving Manchester's nomination but brought together the city, government, government agencies, sports bodies and the private sector in a joint effort that produced external investment in sports facilities that kick-started the regeneration of East Manchester, encouraged city leaders to see Manchester's comparators in international rather than domestic terms, and provided a popular rallying point for citizens;
- Hulme City Challenge, which is popularly seen as having transformed the city's approach to the design and management of regeneration, the lessons of which were later applied, most notably, in East Manchester;
- The reconstruction of the city centre following the IRA bombing of 1996, which drew upon many of the organisations and individuals who had contributed to the City Challenge;
- The successful realisation of the Commonwealth Games in 2002, which demonstrated the city's capacity to stage internationally-significant events as part of a broader sports development strategy, which has since had significant pay-offs;
- The development of Manchester's strengths as a 'Science City', including the successful merger of the city's two formerly-independent research-intensive universities in 2004, which has created the United Kingdom's largest higher education institution and a rival to London, Oxford and Cambridge in terms of 'research power', and more recent initiatives to build upon the discovery of graphene by the university's first modern-day Nobel Prize winners.

For all of these projects, evidence was mobilised, for a variety of audiences, including funders and partners, as part of case-making processes that won designations, triggered investment flows and encouraged continued momentum after particular milestones were reached. It is important to recognise, though, that the use of evidence in such cases was, essentially, as good as it needed to be in order to trigger the desired responses. At least as important in these cases, and in many others, was the extent of the ambition involved in project delivery and the sequencing of further activities that could be built upon them. The key to understanding and increasing the city of Manchester's commitment to good evidence is less about its utility in 'ticking boxes' designed by others, and more about persuading a variety of potential supporters that the ambitions the city and city-region wished to achieve were consistent with their own goals. In other words, evidence has been used to influence others and shift their understandings and behaviour, and not merely as a route to complying with externally imposed wishes.

This functional approach can be connected to a wide literature on the historic role of the 'Manchester men' and their role in propelling the rapid development of industrial capitalism and associated urbanisation in nineteenth-century Manchester (see Harding *et al.*, 2010 for a review; Quilley, 2000). This established modus operandi has been altered by the period in which entrepreneurial approaches to urban development began to dominate policy. Manchester embraced the idea of 'selling' the contemporary attractiveness of the city. This often involved capitalising assets such as the city's footballing and popular cultural heritage. Yet it also involved harnessing external assets, particularly Cheshire's desirable countryside and villages, as particularly Mancunian assets. Whereas previous efforts to develop metropolitan governance had been founded on a desire to enhance the city's fiscal integrity by annexing its affluent peripheries, contemporary approaches sought to claim the 'quality of life' assets prevalent in the suburbs but in short supply in the core city.

This chapter will now turn to an analysis of the recent development of selective policies for economic development and social integration in Greater Manchester. It is important, from the outset, to recognise two things that are relevant to the account we offer. First, the specific policies we have selected as case studies, chosen to reflect the needs of the overall project, have been developed in a context in which the emergence of 'bottom up', locally-determined metropolitan/city-regional forms of governance have advanced further and faster in Greater Manchester than in other parts of the United Kingdom (Metropolitan governance arrangements for London are arguably stronger, in terms of statutory underpinnings, but have been pushed more aggressively by national government). Second, recent policy innovation has developed in the midst of what might be described as 'austerity localism' in which most national government support for 'area-based initiatives' that have dominated national urban policy in the United Kingdom for over 30 years has been withdrawn, along with substantial mainstream grant support (hence 'austerity'), while at the same time greater expectation has been placed on local agencies to fill the vacuum created by dwindling national resources (hence 'localism'). The loss of national resources has been felt unevenly across Greater Manchester. The city of Manchester itself was one of the authorities that lost the maximum percentage of resources that was possible under national austerity budgeting, whereas authorities whose areas suffer fewer social problems escaped more lightly. As a whole, though, the traditional industrial areas of England – especially in the North and the Midlands but also Inner London – have faced larger cuts in central grants that were the mainstay of local initiatives in economic development and social integration than those in the South. This, along with staffing cuts within local government and amongst voluntary sector groups, has meant that the last two years have been characterised by an experimental search for low cost, non-labour-intensive alternative approaches to local economic and social development that rely much more heavily on local, and to some extent European, resources, in line with a government strategy that emphasises 'localism'.

The more recent phase of city-region institution building in Manchester, from 2006 onwards, has attracted considerable attention from academics (Harding *et al.*, 2010) and proponents (Emmerich and Frankal, 2009) as a potential model for other UK cities outside London. These two developments, at the strategic, metropolitan scale and in terms of local initiatives, are imperfectly correlated as yet. However, we consider it important to describe the context in which specific initiatives are unfolding, as it remains distinctly possible that the crisis unleashed by the global financial turbulence of 2008 will lead, in the United Kingdom, to a model of response to sub-national socio-economic challenges that relies far more on locally-generated and locally-funded than has typically been the case for the last 60 years, and that the 'natural economic areas' centred upon cities will feature heavily in new forms of mobilisation. It is only by understanding the particular machinery that has been created in Greater Manchester over the last 25 years that we can see how the metropolitan area has been positioned to take advantage of any radical redrawing of the contours of the UK state. In what follows, we contrast some of the policy prescriptions of the former government with the current situation, not least because the creation of new governance arrangements took shape during that earlier period and is often credited with having played a key role in the 'Manchester miracle', which saw parts of the conurbation experience economic growth at a scale that was comparable to areas in Southern England.

We also explore work undertaken at the level of the Greater Manchester City Region (GMCR) to track the whole spending as part of a community budgeting pilot. This provides a context for specific analyses of the 'Manchester Mortgage' and 'Manchester Apprenticeship Guarantee' schemes, which give a flavour of the way in which very different circumstances are beginning to produce small-scale policy innovations of a sort that may come to characterise a rapidly-changing urban policy landscape. Both policies are micro-level innovations being trialled with very small cohorts of citizens in unpropitious circumstances, and lack serious resourcing commitments. These two pilot policy innovations have been scaled up with the City Dealing process of 2012 into the planks of far more thorough-going approaches. On the one hand, the notion of creative use of resourcing trialled under the 'Manchester Mortgage' scheme has scaled into a new investment model, Manchester Place. On the other, the apprenticeship model policy has been also transformed into a skills hub for the city-region. It remains to be seen whether resources commensurate with the scale of these policy ambitions and the challenges of inequalities within the city-region are forthcoming. For the careful architects of this approach, then, it is the stability of a partnership model of governance that is Greater Manchester's biggest policy innovation success.

The chapter now turns towards the ways in which this ambition has been translated into action through the national urban policy agendas and partnerships and the vehicles of place-based budgeting and City Deals, before addressing the two more specific policy areas of skills policy and housing.

9.3 Shifts in urban policy

9.3.1 *National urban policy and partnerships since 1997*

Significant dates marking changes in UK urban policy orientation are 1997, with the election of the New Labour Government, 2008, the beginning of the recession, and 2010, which saw the subsequent change in government. While the period from 1997 was characterised by an overt focus on regional and neighbourhood renewal and regeneration through activist government policies (see Table 9.1 below), this period of activism at the urban scale saw a great deal of investment channelled through special-purpose vehicles and partnerships. By the onset of 'the crisis' in 2008, such approaches had fallen from favour and the incoming government in 2010 heralded the disestablishment of a series of

Table 9.1 UK government approaches to urban policy and partnerships

	Previous government 1997–2010	*Conservative–Liberal coalition 2010–2015, Conservative majority 2015 to present*
Planning reform	Development of local government partnership architecture at local authority scale and regional, spatial and economic strategies compiled by regional institutions for planning.	National Planning Policy Framework (NPPF) 'presumption towards sustainable development' – repeal of detailed Planning Policy Guidance (PPG).
Urban policy	Neighbourhood Renewal: National Strategy for Neighbourhood Renewal (2001). Holistic renewal of neighbourhoods. Sustainable Communities Plan (2006), new growth points in South East and housing market renewal (HMR) in North. English Partnerships and the HCA Homes and Communities Agency (HCA) Academy for Sustainable Communities.	Regional Growth Fund (RGF) direct to businesses. Enterprise Zones (EZs) to tackle employment land issues. 'Cull of quangos' except Homes and Communities Agency (HCA) with responsibility for social housing.
Partnerships	Regional Development Agencies (RDAs) for localities. Local Strategic Partnerships (LSPs), supply-side public sector. Multi-Area Agreements (MAAs) for cross-boundary working.	Local Enterprise Partnerships (LEPs) private sector-led partnerships at city-regional scale. City Deals with localities.
Welfare reform	Tax credits, child poverty targets.	Universal Credit Welfare Reform.

Source: authors' elaboration.

regional bodies and successive waves of tightening of local government expenditure. As we will see, there has been increased policy interest in 'total place' or 'place-based budgeting' approaches, which minimise the traditional roles of vertical accountability to government ministries. However, this radical approach has not been used to its full potential as yet.

Here we explain the significance of each area of policy to Greater Manchester in terms of impact upon housing and skills policy agendas.

Planning reform: Planning has occupied a rather vexed position within the GMCR and has been seen at times as an impediment to growth. There is some evidence that this position is changing with the development of the new spatial strategy through to 2035.

Urban housing and regeneration policy: A more activist urban policy in the period from 1997 was used very effectively by the GMCR.

Partnerships: The city-region developed a city-regional development plan, which became a multi-area agreement. These processes served to connect partnerships working within the city-region to developments in the wider regional and English context.

Welfare reform: Although not expressed in urban/spatial terms, changes to the ways in which benefits are paid and to whom has had a huge impact on budgets not least as universal credit policy shifts the payment of rental income for social housing away from registered social landlords to the tenants themselves.

9.3.2 Place-based budgeting and city-dealing

Whilst all these individual policy areas are important, an additional approach has evolved over this period, emerging in the wake of some of the previous government's enthusiasm for targeting expenditure according to deprivation data. What would be the consequences of calculating all government inputs, across all spending departments, and the way in which they impact upon a specific place? Despite the notorious difficulties associated with tracking public sector spending, this 'place-based' approach was trialled in GMCR.

Viewed as a whole over the period of austerity, there has been *no net reduction* in spending to the GMCR. There has been a critical shift, however, away from productive and economic development spending, over which local government has traditionally exercised control, in favour of welfare spending, which is paid directly to benefit recipients and over which local government has no control. This is of huge significance to the forms and functions of both traditional and aspirational local governance forms. It is in this context that a 'City Deal' was agreed between GMCR and HM Government in 2012. Both skills and housing policy are prominent within this 'City Deal' for Manchester; in fact, within its seven areas of focus we find two specific actions oriented to these areas of policy: the creation of a City Apprenticeship and Skills Hub to place apprentices with SMEs, as well as the piloting of a skills tax incentive and locally determined outcome payments to providers, and the establishment of a housing investment fund to use local and national investment to develop new housing.

The 'City Deal' has been promoted as a part of a more devolved and mature relationship between central and local government and had the authority of deputy prime minister Nick Clegg, who announced the policy in July 2012 thus:

> These *groundbreaking deals signal a dramatic power shift*, freeing cities from Whitehall control. Everyone in these eight core cities will feel the benefits – from young people looking for jobs, to businesses looking to expand. Over the coming months, we are transferring more and more power from Whitehall to these cities. They are the economic powerhouses of England – so it makes sense that the cities decide for themselves how to boost their local economies.
>
> (HM Govt, 2013, emphasis mine)

This powerful rhetoric, however, is not supported either by the resources or the promised transfers in power to cities.

A focus on these policy positions on housing and skills policy areas within the City Deal is instructive as an opportunity to dig below the city-regional narrative about the ways in which institution-building at the conurbation-level functions in the areas of real, concrete, and potentially pro-social and pro-poor policies. In the next section, we explore two very specific policies that the City Deal seeks to scale up from their early successes through the Manchester Mortgage and Manchester Apprenticeship Guarantee.

9.4 Employment policy: City Apprenticeship

> *What is important now is to* ensure there is a skills base in place *to fuel success in areas that are yet to see such benefit*, so that the full productivity and potential of the 'new-look' city-region can be realised.
>
> (Interview with a local authority leader, September 2012, emphasis mine)

This quote, which emphasises skills and their clear relationship with productivity and potential, highlights the case for the City Apprenticeship and Skills Hub from the City Deal. Efforts to regenerate Manchester have regarded attracting mobile capital and labour into the knowledge-intensive and high-value-service sector. Prior to the crisis, the MIER report in 2009 painted a bright picture of the way in which this was working:

> The city-region regularly out-performs its competitor cities with regards to offering high-skilled jobs; retaining and providing the talent required to fill those jobs; retaining graduates from local universities and providing the necessary skills support and training suited to the job opportunities available in the region. More of the Manchester city-region's (MCR) population are employed in the knowledge based industries of financial and business

services, such as legal services, than ever before. However, the *transformation of the city-region's economy has wide-ranging implications for policy makers* if Manchester is to continue to remain the dominant economic force outside of London and the South East.

(MIER, 2009a, emphasis mine)

There are those, however, who argue that this focus on highly skilled in-migration has been misguided and that city-regional policy should focus on existing resident skills profiles, while city leaders are keen to boost the image of the city and not to emphasise skills shortages and gaps among the resident population.

The MIER was very keen to point out that more of the Manchester city-region's (MCR) population are employed in the knowledge based-industries of financial and business services, such as legal services. *Understanding Labour Markets, Skills and Talent* (MIER, 2016) cites a 120 per cent increase in employment in this sector since 1981. There has also been a 49 per cent increase in the number of people employed in the information, communication and technology sectors. These increases, coupled with a 54 per cent reduction in the number of people employed in manufacturing, have transformed the economic landscape of the city-region and the opportunities available for graduates and local communities. Knowledge-based industries (KBIs) include ICT (e.g. software development), business and financial services (e.g. legal), creative media (e.g. broadcasting, publishing and advertising), knowledge-intensive manufacturing (e.g. pharmaceuticals) and elements of the public sector (e.g. health and higher education). For most sectors, a greater proportion of Manchester's workforce is employed in KBIs than in other regional UK cities. The MCR exhibits particularly high concentrations of KBI employment (compared with comparator city-regions outside London) in the ICT, business services and public sectors. Furthermore, Manchester has a greater proportion of its workforce employed in knowledge-based manufacturing than London and all other comparators.

Increased employment in KBIs has been recorded across the city-region, but has mainly been concentrated in the centre and areas to the south, as private sector investment has been concentrated where greater levels of high-skilled workers reside. This signals that the development of the MCR's infrastructure is vital to ensuring that these strong gains are replicated and built upon across the region, thereby improving the skills base and density of its labour markets.

Nevertheless, this attention paid to KBIs strongly contrasts with the following description of the situation in schools:

School results are improving but are behind the national average, and this impacts upon the ways in which young people can access both further/higher education and the workplace. In 2008, 82.1 per cent of Year 11 school leavers went on to full-time education, 2.6 per cent into Apprenticeships and 0.9 per cent into jobs without training. 6.7 per cent went on to be NEET. Many young people were leaving school without any qualifications

– in some parts of the city more than one in seven young people left school without qualifications. The issue remains a concern for the Council, as it hampers young people's ability to get on in life. In 2009 unemployment in Manchester stood at 5.4 per cent an increase of nearly two percentage points on the previous year. During the same period, available vacancies shrank by 50 per cent.

(Manchester City Council, 2009)

These figures offer a sobering contrast to the rhetoric of the MIER and the policy objective of attracting highly qualified people. In the absence of policy levers to tackle the pernicious skills shortages in the city-region, it is hard to see how the young people of the city can share in the hoped-for growth.

At the MCC level, there is an apprenticeship strategy that focuses on the role of the local authority in offering opportunities, extending the reach of apprenticeships to those on the margins of learning and work, and establishing apprenticeships as a popular and highly-regarded learning pathway.

Manchester's vision for Apprenticeships is that they will raise the aspirations both of young people in the city, and of its community and workforce. MCC has committed itself to skills development through building on the competency base of existing employees, and offering opportunities to workless residents. In December 2007 Manchester City Council signed the Skills Pledge, a public commitment to improving the quality of skills in the area. The Apprenticeship strategy, linked to the Skills Pledge, is committed to providing realistic and, crucially, sustainable training opportunities for local young people. These opportunities are focused on young people from the most deprived wards and priority schools (the top five 'NEET producing' schools), although some initiatives target specific groups such as the Young People into Construction Programme, which prioritises young people NEET, looked-after children (LAC) and black and minority ethnic groups (BME).

(Manchester City Council, 2009)

The approach and spatial targeting of the Manchester Apprenticeship Guarantee would appear to be sound. However, they have been trialled with only 20 young people to date in the media sector. This is because the apprenticeship strategy is 'sustainable' as it is not reliant on 'external funding sources'. As long as measures to tackle skills shortages and regional disparities are implemented in this 'resource-neutral' way, it is hard to see how the cycle of deprivation regarding low-skilled and low-wage employment can be broken. Skills policy at the city-regional scale, overseen by the Employment and Skills Board and with a specific objective within the City Deal is a clear example of the ways in which levers for change within the skills market are highly complex and can include pre-school, school and post-school (further and higher education), the levers of control for which are distributed over different governmental scales and across a plethora of institutions.

The Manchester Apprenticeship Guarantee measure has been innovative in that it addresses the issue of NEETs (young people not in employment education or training) and leads them into real jobs. However, the *very* small numbers of young people involved mean that it is only a proof of concept for such an approach. The City Deal does seek to scale up the approach through the 'hub' concept. However, it is clear that intervention with regard to skills must be of an appropriate scale and scope if public agencies are to affect the macro and structural issues facing the labour market. As long as the city-regional skills agenda remains focused on high-skilled jobs there is a risk that those at the bottom are unable to share in the successes of the city-region.

9.5 Housing policy

> It's grim up north – and it's going to become grimmer when we have housing policies that favour the south east.
>
> (Interview with a housing provider, August 2012)

Housing policy within the GMCA sits within a spatial expression of the conurbation's priorities, which are currently the subject of consultation for the period to 2035. This process sits squarely with the economic growth and knowledge economy strategies driven by the Manchester family of organisations.

Garnering data about housing across the city-region, for example, exposes a number of areas in which the top-line 'brochure' version of the Greater Manchester story may be challenged, not least the ways in which 'the family' have viewed the role of the planning system. In welcoming a planning strategy for the core city itself in 2012, the leader writer of the *Manchester Evening News* wrote:

> The plan includes many ideas that should impact on the lives of ordinary Mancunians. If there is one persistent criticism of the redevelopment of the city in recent times, it is that the positive effects have not always been felt across Manchester. There are parts of this city still characterised by deep deprivation. The benefits of a bustling city centre have not been shared as widely as they should have been. Rightly, this plan looks to address this.
>
> (Manchester Evening News, 19th June 2012)

As already seen, the spatial locations of the benefits of growth is characterised by a north–south divide within the borders of the Manchester area. While deprivation and unemployment still remain at their lowest-ever levels for the city-region, progress has been unevenly spread. Local authorities with a small number of deprived communities include Trafford, Stockport and Bury, while Central and North Manchester, East Salford, Wigan, Bolton, Rochdale and Tameside have a higher concentration of unemployment and deprivation.

In short, the growth story promulgated for the dual purposes of attracting resources from central government on the one hand and as an advertisement for inward investment capital on the other, stands in stark contrast with evidence of deprivation from housing data. In short, for Greater Manchester prosperity flows south, significantly into the county boroughs of Cheshire. A MIER study painted these distinctions in sharp terms. Their analysis, that city-regional policies be focused on the 10 per cent most deprived areas, has not been the driving force behind the more recent round of institution-building.

Housing policy in the United Kingdom has always struggled to constrain the rapid rise in house prices seen in the post-war period. Factors including a strong preference for owner occupation and relatively cheap access to mortgage finance have led to high levels of owner occupation. However, the housing crisis has resulted in exclusion from the housing market for many. The Labour government implemented a range of policies that 'tinkered' with housing markets, the most significant of which was the Sustainable Communities Plan, which was intended to be an area-based regeneration policy aimed at improving housing supply.

Another salient policy area is welfare reform, as it impacts those excluded from owner occupation in a context where new social housing has not been built or replaced following the right-to-buy policy introduced in the 1980s, which saw public housing tenants buy social housing at large discounts. The revival of this policy in 2015 has sparked concerns about registered social landlords (housing associations) being able to replace houses sold to tenants. Those interviewed for this research were clear that current national housing policy is insufficient in terms of meeting the specific needs of the city-region, and expressed strong concern that housing policy is skewed towards South East England at the expense of the North. 'Here housing market restructuring has been largely determined by economic deprivation, falling population and physical dereliction caused by the decline in traditional manufacturing industries. Suburbanisation has largely followed a southerly trajectory' (MIER, 2009).

Actors at the city-regional level do not have the requisite powers at their disposal to make significant interventions in the key policy area of housing. The city-regional level thematic commission for planning and housing is not well-funded and has had very limited success in acting collectively across ten local authorities with planning functions and fulfilling its task of preparing 'core strategies' for planning. Core strategies have no statutory force. They can only work if they influence the local plans of each of the individual local authorities. This makes planning for housing, potentially, highly uncoordinated. The city-region, however, has gathered evidence to support further devolution of housing policy and delivery at this scale. In addition, despite the relatively higher proportion of residents of the city-region living in social housing, this provision is no longer the direct responsibility of the local authorities themselves, as most of the homes they used to own have been transferred to independent housing associations generally regarded as private entities in that they are not owned or directly controlled by the state.

Levers for change within the housing market include planning, housing supply, affordable housing, social housing and access to mortgage finance. The previous government approach to the problem of housing market failure was at an area scale and required significant public investment. The most significant initiative was the Housing Market Renewal Programme's Manchester Salford Pathfinder (MSP). This initiative was a large public-led attempt to revitalise the most deprived neighbourhoods of the city-region according to 'worst-first' neighbourhood renewal and deprivation criteria. MSP was an informal unincorporated partnership set up by Manchester and Salford city councils, which operated between 2003 and 2011 to develop and coordinate a long-term strategic programme to restructure the housing market in parts of North Manchester, East Manchester, South Manchester and Central Salford. The goal of the MSP was to support the economic growth potential of the Manchester City Region by renewing these neighbourhoods to offer a mixture of privately-owned and rented homes of higher quality and a more diverse range of housing types, thus meeting the aspirations of both new and existing residents who might otherwise move elsewhere.

From April 2003 to March 2011, MSP received £354.11 million in funding from national government, and successfully levered an additional £244 million in complementary investment. The Audit Commission review of this scheme[1] evaluated to what extent MSP had met the targets agreed with the Homes and Communities Agency. Although fewer than anticipated, over 3,700 new homes were built – the most secured by any pathfinder. It improved over 14,500 existing homes, acquired 4,000, and demolished over 6,000 obsolete properties. Overall in the pathfinder area, developers built some 15,000 new homes, making a significant contribution to new housing supply in the city-region.

Despite these positive results, the MSP was cancelled in a wave of cuts to regeneration schemes made by the Conservative coalition government. It was relatively easy to abolish such schemes, as they were largely run by unincorporated partnerships outside of the local authorities themselves. Much of the governance of regeneration was informal and, as it turned out, vulnerable to changes in national government policy.

The delivery void left by the MSP has not yet been filled by large-scale or area-based policy interventions. More recently, however, MCC has introduced the Manchester Mortgage scheme in order to tackle the chronic shortage of affordable housing and lack of finance capital for people to obtain mortgage finance. The promoters of this scheme are MCC, the Greater Manchester Pension Fund (GMPF) and the Cooperative Group, based in Manchester. The local authority has identified five sites in the city on which it plans to build nearly 250 homes for sale or rent through a pilot scheme. As part of the plans, the council is seeking to create a mortgage guarantee scheme specifically for first-time buyers, which will underwrite up to 20 per cent of the loan. The GMPF will pay for construction costs and, if successful, the programme could be rolled out over ten years. The aim of the Manchester Mortgage scheme is to address the problem of lack of mortgage finance, which is perceived as a core reason for the housing crisis in the city-region, in the absence of large-scale, nationally-led programmes to alter the nature of the housing market and its unevenness across the city-region.

To sum up, the intervention of the Manchester Mortgage scheme is innovative in that it addresses housing issues at the household level, seeking to enable people to borrow who may not otherwise be able to get onto the housing ladder. This is achieved by leveraging hitherto inaccessible assets, such as those within pension schemes, in order to 'prime the pump' of the market itself. The very small sums involved are a proof of concept for such an approach, which is also being looked at by central government as a way of funding infrastructure in an age of declining public spending by leveraging major pension funds. This is in marked contrast to the previous government approach to the problem of housing market failure, which was implemented at the area scale and required significant public investment.

9.6 Conclusions: addressing the urban policy vacuum in housing and skills

This chapter has argued that the development of a governance model has been afforded more focus and attention than the specific skills and housing policy measures that it contains. This is despite the fact that skills policy is a core area of focus for the City Deal processes introduced by the present government. While the specificities of the governance trajectory of the Greater Manchester city-region are instructive in explaining the growth coalition that emerged in order to manage change, there remain sizeable challenges in creating a new, effective policy regime, given current circumstances.

The small-scale initiatives examined here are experimental, as are a wider range of new developments, but it remains to be seen how effective the particular brand of 'localism' being trialled in Greater Manchester will prove, in the absence of a more decisive decentralisation of power and resources to the metropolitan level.

Austerity localism and cuts in public sector funding have resulted in an extremely limited range of policies available to counter structural issues within housing and labour markets, and heavily circumscribed actions for city-regional actors in active employment policies and mechanisms. The Manchester Mortgage policy intervention is interesting in that it offers an approach to using normally unavailable classes of assets. UK government is looking to explore the loosening of regulations around the investment decisions of pension funds in order that they might fund infrastructure in a variety of 'creative ways'. This happens in the context of public money for local and city-regional government actors contracting. Another interesting approach to 'sweating' assets is the attempt to look at the spending of taxation from across different government departments. In moving towards a new statutory combined authority that provides a potential structure for devolved powers and resources and guards against difficulties in achieving metropolitan consensus on key development issues, Greater Manchester has positioned itself 'ahead of the pack' in terms of delivering 'the new localism'. Much remains to be achieved, however, if the experimental innovations covered in this chapter are to be 'scaled up' to the extent that they represent serious attempts to grapple with the challenges facing Greater Manchester, the solutions to which do not currently lie in local hands.

Note

1 See Audit Commission website, online, available at: www.auditcommission.gov.uk/ housing/marketrenewalpathfinders/reports/manchestersalfordperformancereviews/ Pages/Default.aspx

References and further reading

Barlow, M. (1995). Greater Manchester: Conurbation Complexity and Local Government Structure. *Political Geography* 14(4): 379–400.

Bernstein, H. (2010). Interview in the *Guardian*. Online, available at: www.theguardian. com/guardian-professional/2010/nov/09/sir-howard-bernstein-blog (accessed 2 April 2016).

Blakeley, G. and B. Evans (2008). 'It's Like Maintaining a Hedge': Constraints on Citizen Engagement in Community Regeneration in East Manchester. *Public Policy and Administration*, 23(1): 100–113.

Cochrane, A., J. Peck and J. Tickell (1996). Manchester Plays Games: Exploring the Local Politics of Globalisation. *Urban Studies*, 33(8): 1319–1336.

Comune di Milano (2011) La citta' come bene comune: Informativa alla Giunta Comunale in merito al Documento politico di indirizzo per il Governo del Territorio. Online, available at: www.comune.milano.it.

Deas, I., B. Robson and M. Bradford (2000). Re-thinking the Urban Development Corporation 'Experiment': the Case of Central Manchester, Leeds and Bristol. *Progress in Planning*, 54(1): 1–72.

Devine, F., N. J. Britton, R. Mellor and P. Halfpenny (2003). Mobility and the Middle Classes: a Case Study of Manchester and the North West. *International Journal of Urban and Regional Research*, 27(3): 495–509.

Durose, C. and V. Lowndes (2010). Neighbourhood Governance: Contested Rationales within a Multi-Level Setting – A Study of Manchester. *Local Government Studies*, 36(3): 341–359.

Emmerich, M. and B. Frankal (2009). Building the Manchester of the Future. *Local Economy*, 24(1): 93–97.

Evans, B. (2007). The Politics of Partnership: Urban Regeneration in New East Manchester. *Public Policy and Administration*, 22(2): 201–215.

Garcia, B. C. (2006). Learning Conversations: Knowledge, Meanings and Learning Networks in Greater Manchester. *Journal of Knowledge Management*, 10(5): 99–109.

Harding, A., M. Harloe and J. Rees (2010). Manchester's Bust Regime? *International Journal of Urban and Regional Research*, 34(4): 981–991.

Haughton, G. and P. Allmendinger (2008). The Soft Spaces of Local Economic Development. *Local Economy*, 23(2): 138–148.

Hebbert, M. and I. Deas (2000). Greater Manchester – 'Up and Going'? *Policy and Politics*, 28(1): 79–92.

Hetherington, K. (2007). Manchester's Urbis. *Cultural Studies*, 21(4–5): 630–649.

HM Government (2013). 2010 to 2015 Government Policy: City Deals and Growth Deals. Deputy Prime Minister's Office. Online, available at: www.gov.uk/government/ publications/2010-to-2015-government-policy-city-deals-and-growth-deals/.

Mace, A., P. Hall and N. Gallent (2007). New East Manchester: Urban Renaissance or Urban Opportunism? *European Planning Studies*, 15(1): 51–65.

Manchester City Council (2009). Manchester Apprentice Strategy File. Online, available at: www.manchester.gov.uk/.

MIER (2009a). 1. *The Case for Agglomeration Economies*. Online, available at MIER website, now closed: www.manchester-review.org.uk.

MIER (2009b). 2. *Innovation, Trade and Connectivity*. Online, available at MIER website, now closed: www.manchester-review.org.uk.

MIER (2009c). 3. *Sustainable Communities*. Online, available at MIER website, now closed: www.manchester-review.org.uk.

MIER (2009d). 4. *Growing Inward and Indigenous Investment*. Online, available at MIER website, now closed: www.manchester-review.org.uk.

MIER (2009e). 5. *Understanding Labour Markets, Skills and Talent*. Online, available at MIER website, now closed: www.manchester-review.org.uk.

MIER (2009f). 6. *Review of Daresbury Science and Innovation Campus.* Online, available at MIER website, now closed: www.manchester-review.org.uk.

MIER (2009g). *Reviewer Report.* Online, available at MIER website, now closed: www. manchester-review.org.uk.

MIER (2016). *Understanding Labour Markets, Skills and Talent.* Online, available at MIER website, now closed: www.manchester-review.org.uk/project_722.html.

Quilley, S. (2000). Manchester First: From Municipal Socialism to the Entrepreneurial City. *International Journal of Urban and Regional Research*, 24(3): 601–615.

Shapely, P. (2006). Tenants Arise! Consumerism, Tenants and the Challenge to Council Authority in Manchester, 1968–92. *Social History*, 31(1): 60–78.

Skelcher, C. (2005). Jurisdictional Integrity, Polycentrism, and the Design of Democratic Governance. *Governance*, 18(1): 89–110.

Stewart, M. (1994). Between Whitehall and Town Hall: The Realignment of Urban Regeneration Policy in England. *Policy and Politics*, 22(2): 133–145.

Ward, K. (2003). Entrepreneurial Urbanism, State Restructuring and Civilizing 'New' East Manchester. *Area*, 35(2): 116–127.

While, A., A. E. G. Jonas and D. Gibbs (2004). The Environment and the Entrepreneurial City: Searching for the Urban 'Sustainability Fix' in Manchester and Leeds. *International Journal of Urban and Regional Research*, 28(3): 549–569.

Young, C., M. Diep and S. Drabble (2006). Living with Difference? The 'Cosmopolitan City' and Urban Reimaging in Manchester, UK. *Urban Studies*, 43(10): 1687–1714.

10 Milan

Challenging the private interest government in times of austerity

Rossana Torri

10.1 Introduction

Milan was governed by centre–right coalitions uninterruptedly from 1993 to 2011, distinguishing it as one of the cities with the greatest continuity in terms of political rule in Italy; 2011 marked a major turning point, with the election victory of a centre–left alliance, in office until June 2016. Looking back over the last 20 years, it can be said that economic growth and social cohesion have followed independent trajectories in Milan. This situation is characterised on the one hand by weak, public regulation of dynamics connected with urban growth and competitiveness mainly oriented by neo-liberal ideas, and on the other by a lack of investment in policies in support of the most disadvantaged social groups. The recent financial crisis has further exacerbated such situation, paving the way for the development of a strong urban dualism.

Despite their various flavours, the centre–right governments that followed each other until 2011 – beginning with the Lombard League (*Lega Lombarda*), followed by Forza Italia (the party founded by Silvio Berlusconi), for three consecutive terms – played a rather passive role with regard to the economic dynamics of the city, in keeping with the neo-liberal policies that became established in Europe over the same period (Brenner and Theodore 2012). In addition they did not develop an explicit, clear strategy aimed at regulating the city's transition towards an economy increasingly based on finance and integrated into global networks, and at protecting the social groups excluded from these dynamics at the same time.

Although Milan does not exhibit a particularly segregated structure, household incomes became increasingly polarised over the period. The flip side of the rise of an urban élite concentrated in the financial and advanced service sectors was that the economic conditions of the middle class, impoverished by the crisis, gradually worsened, as did the living conditions of traditionally more marginal groups, in part as a result of the progressive weakening of the local welfare system (Giovannetti *et al.* 2014). The centre–right coalitions adopted a residual approach to social welfare, reducing public expenditure earmarked for funding existing local services (Costa *et al.* 2016).

The 2011 elections and the instalment of a new centre–left council marked a turning point in the administration of the city, which was hailed by many as a "revolution" in terms of governance principles and instruments. A vision of the city's future based on the principles of justice and social inclusion has been reintroduced into public discourse, which could lead to policies capable of constructing a possible new link between social cohesion and economic growth.

In practice, after four years of management by the new government, such change has been partly frustrated by a series of obstacles, including the onset of the economic crisis in 2008 and the tight budgetary constraints imposed by national austerity policies. Other obstacles to change have stemmed from the council's problematic financial situation, from pressures connected with Expo 2015 – with which the new administration decided to push ahead, in keeping with previous choices – and from conflicts within the governing coalition. It should also be pointed out that transition to a new development that is capable of re-establishing a link between economic competitiveness and urban attractiveness, on the one hand, and fairness and social justice on the other, requires timeframes that extend beyond those of a single term of government. The new administration has governed the city in the midst of a full-blown economic crisis and has sought to use a number of social "counter-crisis" measures as a lever for the city's economic recovery, exhibiting some capacity for social inclusion and fostering greater involvement on the part of citizens in local government decision-making.

It is argued here that the political turning point of 2011 marked a moment of fundamental discontinuity not only in terms of rhetoric but also in the development of public policy in the city. Two specific policies are analysed in order to verify this hypothesis. The first is housing policy, in which access to accommodation has become increasingly difficult for broad sections of the population. A review of public regulation is followed by a description of the dual model that characterised urban development and housing policies from the 1990s until 2007; we therefore focus on the impact of the crisis, emphasising the role played by housing policy developed at the national level. Finally, the paradigm shift that took place following the turning point of 2011 is described. The second is labour policy, affected by broad processes of "casualisation" of labour during the 1990s, which did not spare the most competitive sectors of the urban economy. Here too, it is argued that the positive growth dynamics observed until the 2008 crisis – driven by economic sectors of excellence such as fashion and design – were not accompanied by adequate policies to support and incentivise innovation and economic development; on the contrary, attention was focused on labour market deregulation and liberalisation instruments, which have built a fragile employment system, which was easy to be struck in times of crisis (Peck *et al.* 2013). As in the first case, this part of the chapter offers a reconstruction of Milan's transition towards an advanced service-based economy and the failure to develop policies for "high-quality employment"; it thus describes the crisis of 2008 and the general economic downturn, which had severe repercussions on a highly-flexibilised labour market. Finally, the new approach fostered by the centre–left to support "high-quality employment" is described.

10.2 The long cycle of urban regeneration and its impacts on access to housing

10.2.1 Milan 1993–2011: the dualism between urban growth and housing affordability

From the 1990s onwards, the face of Milan has been reshaped through a long cycle of property-led urban regeneration (Healey 2007), which can be defined as "the assembly of finance, land, building materials and labour to produce or improve buildings for occupation and investment purposes" (Turok 1992). *Property-led regeneration* involves the regeneration of an inner-city area by changing the image of the area, improving the environment, attracting private investment and improving confidence for further investment. In Milan, it involved "flagship" projects located in central areas of the city, such as Porta Nuova or Citylife. Partnerships represented a major switch of funding mechanisms towards competitive bidding. Local government came up with imaginative projects but also had to form partnerships in the local inner-city area with the private sector and the local communities.

The policy instruments that have characterised this phase of Milan's urban development are the so-called *programmi complessi* or "complex instruments", a series of negotiated planning mechanisms introduced at the beginning of the 1990s to facilitate and implement urban transformation projects promoted by private sector entities, which were also designed to satisfy significant public interests. Unlike traditional urban plans, which assigned a specific use to and regulated all land and buildings within a given perimeter, these instruments promote transformations that are incremental in nature, setting out the implementing bodies, economic resources, preliminary projects and implementation timeframes for each transformation, coordinating and integrating resources and stakeholders and assigning a reduced role to public financial resources.

The cycle of property-led urban transformations got underway in Milan in the early 1990s with a number of major urban projects to regenerate and convert industrial areas and with considerable strategic potential connected with their central position and the attractiveness of the functions put in place. This took place through sizeable investments in urban developments, which sparked some of the most rapid growth in property development in Italy in terms both of values reached and the constant growth trend. Alongside these major urban projects, several smaller-scale transformations also took place: a combination of new building projects and expansion or renovation of existing buildings, limited in scope if considered individually, but capable of significantly impacting the districts in question and the city considered as a whole (Memo 2007). The redevelopment of small industrial buildings and workshops – highly sought-after among wealthier members of the creative economy – for residential or professional purposes also received a major boost (Bruzzese 2013; Torri 2010).

A contributory factor in this increase in the supply of residential property in the city's central and semi-central areas was a 1996 regional law that encouraged the redevelopment of attic spaces for residential use. In less than ten years, around 800,000 m² of attic space was converted into dwellings, with approximately €1 billion of private investment and 15,000 new residents (La Varra 2007). Population density in the central and semi-central zones of the city was thus increased still further in the space of a few years.

Private investors were the undisputed drivers of this phase, sustained by substantial deregulation of the existing system. Essentially, against a background of extremely weak public regulation of urban and residential transformations, private investors not only earned profits and property income from independently promoted developments, but also gained from extraordinary contributions for developing services for collective public use in partnership with the local council. One of the "services" that private investors undertook to produce in exchange for planning permission, on particularly advantageous terms, was social housing. In proportion to the amount of residential property developed during this phase, the amount of low-cost housing that resulted from such public–private partnerships was nonetheless extremely modest and did little to create any form of social mix (Bricocoli and Savoldi 2010). The largest operations in central settings with well-developed infrastructure, with high expected profit ratios, produced no significant collective benefits or measures for affordably-priced housing.

10.2.2 *"Property-led regeneration" against the 2008 financial crisis and the structural weakness of housing policies*

With the onset of the economic and financial crisis, the development described in the previous paragraph became unsustainable. The crisis marked a drastic slowdown for a number of major projects that had commenced during the growth years, which became unrealistic given the subsequent contraction of resources. In several cases, this resulted in the development of a great deal of housing stock that remained largely unsold or unoccupied. According to a census of vacant non-residential property conducted by the Urban Land Institute with BNP Paribas Real Estate, at the end of 2013 some 12.6 per cent of the total stock was vacant in terms of floor area, with an increase of 1.4 per cent in the space of a year. In 2007, prior to the explosion of the financial and real estate crisis, the total vacant area was below 7 per cent. Equally significant are the 2013 figures for sales of residential units in the areas of the major transformation hubs, pending economic recovery. Only 60 per cent of residential housing stock was occupied, while the figure for the new flagship project Citylife was 35 per cent, 60 per cent for units developed by Zaha Hadid, and 49 per cent in the Portello development project area, with only 30 per cent of the 530 units on the market (Scenari Immobiliari 2012).

Another aspect of the crisis in the urban property market is represented by the halting or permanent cancellation of many of the small and medium-sized projects that form part of urban transformations of a more ordinary nature. The government in office since 2011 has returned over €20 million of development fees paid in advance by private businesses that subsequently found themselves unable to deliver the projects they had planned.

The limitations of this property-led regeneration development are all the more evident if we consider the increase in housing problems due to the lack of affordable housing for mid-to-low-income households and for business activities with low added value. The reduction in the economic resources of households and difficulty in accessing credit, combined with high house prices in Milan, account for the significant drop in the housing private market after a long positive trend that saw ownership rates increase from 33 per cent in 1971 to 70 per cent in 2001.

The effects of the crisis were exacerbated by the failure to implement publicly funded housing development in support of the weakest social groups. The trend is a national one: according to estimates made in 2007 by national government, already before the crisis the stock of public housing fell by over 20 per cent (Presidenza del Consiglio dei Ministri 2007). In Milan, too, the availability of social housing was reduced as a result of the combined effect of several factors: (a) inefficient management of the stock of public housing, which did not allow an adequate turnover of beneficiaries; (b) the poor state of repair of properties, leading to the gradual decay of a significant proportion of housing stock, which became unusable as it fell below the minimum space standards established by law; and (c) a reduction in the size of the public property portfolio as a result of privatisation policies. Of the approximately 70,000 publicly-owned dwellings located in the municipality, around 12,400 were privatised between 1991 and 2001.

Housing policies provide a number of instruments for regulating the private rental sector and monetary transfers to poor households who cannot pay high rents. Superseding the previous law, which established a fixed scheme of maximum rents, legislation enacted in 1998 liberalised the rental market and introduced a number of new types of subsidised limited-rent contracts. The impact of this policy instrument, however, was extremely limited as a result of the excessive disparity between market prices and the prices set by the reduced-tax scheme.

In addition, in 2006 a national fund for access to rented housing (the FSA) was established in order to supplement the costs borne by citizens in paying private rental charges. Nevertheless, financial resources provided annually by the government steadily reduced from €12 million in 2006 to €1 million in 2012. The fund was cancelled in 2012 and replaced by a new *Fondo sostegno disagio acuto* (FSDA) in support of households in situations of severe hardship, with a radical lowering of the maximum income threshold necessary to access the contribution (from €12,000 to €4,000 per year).

Overall, the succession of local centre–right governments between 1993 and 2011 failed to counter the decline in housing policies effectively, despite the urban dynamics – such as the long cycle of urban regeneration described above – which generated resources that could have been used for balancing policies. The economic and financial crisis of 2008 only served to exacerbate the negative social effects of a weakly regulated development path left in the hands of private real estate investors, with respect to which local policy took on a subordinate role. Several concomitant factors played their part in weakening the capacity of local government to develop a more positive action, effectively leaving the city's development at the mercy of a spontaneous free market logic. The first factor was the dominance of a liberalistic approach in local policy, while a second was the goal of "getting the city moving again" after the phase of stagnation that characterised the 1990s. Finally, the lack of strategic planning further encouraged chaotic, disorderly growth, given the failure to establish shared priorities.

10.2.3 The political turning point of 2011: towards a new paradigm for the development of the city

The change in local government that came about in 2011 marked a turning point in the approach to housing policy. In a policy guideline document entitled *La città come bene comune* (The City as a Common Good), the new government set out new guidelines for urban planning in the city (Comune di Milano 2011), in marked contrast to the previous tendency to encourage further urban densification. The new goals were now reducing building, reviving social housing, expanding green areas, reducing private traffic and boosting cycling mobility, strengthening the public transport network and above all improving public infrastructure and services within private projects. In all new dwellings, at least 50 per cent of total surface area must be given over to local infrastructure (Campos Venuti 2012).

Another key part of this strategy is represented by the establishment of a new housing policy that is capable of meeting the housing demand that has emerged during the crisis and developing a more extensive system of supplying low-cost housing for disadvantaged groups. The strategy that has been adopted is the renovation of existing but unused public and private housing stock. The Social Agency for Housing modelled on other cities has been set up to integrate various instruments and lines of action aimed at reducing housing deprivation by involving public and private resources. The agency aims to increase the stock of low-cost dwellings by proposing an "agreed rent" as a new instrument for mitigating household deprivation, and to help bring together owners and tenants interested in entering into an agreed rent contract by offering financial incentives and a series of instruments to safeguard and guide the parties signing the contract.

The paradigm change sketched out here through two main spheres of intervention – the new urban planning approach and the development of a system to offer low-cost accommodation – places the issue of urban development at the centre of political action once again with a view to repairing the dualism between economic growth and social cohesion. This transition, however, has come at a particularly difficult time, owing to a series of concomitant factors. The first is the situation of economic crisis and the severe contraction in both public and private investment in the construction sector. The second factor regards the need to make sharp budget cuts. The third factor is Expo 2015, which absorbed a large proportion of both the organisational and economic resources of the new administration in office.

10.3   Urban policies for economic development and good quality employment

10.3.1   Milan 1993–2011: points of excellence and economic dynamism in the absence of a policy to steer the city through the tertiary-sector transition

The transition towards a tertiary economy has gone through several stages in Milan. The first stage saw the beginning of a process of deindustrialisation and the rapid expansion of the economy's tertiary sectors: from services for businesses, to professional and financial services, as well as services in the social and healthcare areas. The latter two were driven by the public sector, which at this stage was still capable of absorbing labour. The transition was thus surmounted by means of a rapid development of advanced business services, and by the capacity of the sectors driving the local economy to change their organisational structure by adapting to the new global scenario. For the fashion sector, which we discuss below as an illustration of these dynamics, this has entailed a transition from a local, tangible, product-focused industry to a global, intangible, customer-focused industry that is demand-driven and willing to purchase products or delocalise production in accord with market expediencies.

Over the course of this long transition, the city concentrated a number of strategic functions connected with its role as "global network hub" (Magatti *et al.* 2005), specialising in functions to attract flows of capital, goods and people with its potential. Almost one-third of the added value produced in 2001 in the Milan metropolitan area came from the financial intermediation sector, the real estate sector and enterprise, which accounted for 27 per cent of employment. In addition, the presence of a wide range of services and facilities and a highly-developed creative milieu led to businesses typical of the "symbolic economy" in sectors such as fashion and design taking root in the city. The most evident consequences of these transformations in terms of the employment structure have been: (a) an increase in the level of higher and advanced education; and (b) a reduction in standard employment contracts and an increase in the number of fixed-term employment contracts (Torri 2007).

While during its industrial phase Milan had been able to take advantage of economic policies adopted on a national scale that had sustained its development and established its central importance for the country as a whole (Artoni 2005), these conditions evaporated during the post-industrial transition phase, which was characterised by a new production model and high growth in employment, which was nevertheless accompanied by an increase in non-permanent employment. During the 1993–2011 period, policy measures abandoned the attempt to regulate the complex balances between stakeholders and interests while seeking to reposition the economy within the transformed economic scenario (Bolocan

2009). The "city of fashion" is a case in point, as it offers a good illustration of the difficulty encountered by policy during the period in question in rooting one of the economic activities of excellence on a global scale in the city.

10.3.1.1 The case of the "city of fashion"

Milan, as is well known, is home to some of the world's most important fashion companies, such as Giorgio Armani, Versace, Prada, Valentino, Trussardi, Ferrè, Gucci, and Dolce and Gabbana. Fashion is not only one of the mainstays of the "Made in Italy" brand, but is also an integral part of the city and its very identity in the collective imagination. Its "Fashion Weeks" are spread over several periods of the year and attract buyers and journalists from all over the world. During these events, Milan hosts over 200 fashion shows, hundreds of presentations and other major events, as well as some of the industry's most important trade fairs. Around the Spiga-Monte Napoleone urban district of high fashion in the heart of the city, Milan boasts around 12,000 businesses involved in the sector, 800 showrooms and 6,000 retail outlets (Jansson and Power 2010).

The global transformation of the fashion industry has strongly affected Milan, where the textile, clothing, tanning and leather industries have experienced a contraction in employment. Moreover, temporary, low-paid employment has spread throughout both the rapidly expanding intangible sector and the more traditional tangible sector (Arvidsson 2010).

The policy response to these issues has been extremely weak. In 2000 the centre–right government decided to launch an urban planning project designed to create a "City of Fashion" and set in motion procedures for the construction of one million cubic metres of office space, hotels and residential buildings located in a huge vacant lot of the city centre and with a high environmental impact. The idea was to foster the economic and entrepreneurial vocation of Milan's fashion industry, with an estimated cost of €2 million and the establishment of a number of central functions representing the activities of Milan's fashion sector and its global profile: a museum, a centre of excellence for training and exhibition spaces dedicated to the fashion houses. However, the extremely weak capacity to anticipate the needs of the players in the sector by understanding their location strategies within the urban fabric was at the root of the project's rapid demise due to the lack of interest of Milan's most important fashion designers, who in the meantime had made alternative arrangements and found spaces elsewhere. Fashion had long pursued selective location strategies based on highly-selective principles, favouring small "islands" that are often excellent in terms of global relations but poorly interconnected or separated by invisible barriers (Boeri 2003). The "City of Fashion" project constituted the failure of a project characterised by a high degree of public sector input, which represented the local government's contribution to stronger synergies between the spontaneous, self-sustaining processes typical of Milan's fashion economy and the public aspect of regulating such dynamics, including through the production of goods and services that can be enjoyed by the community.

10.3.2 The Milan model of development put to the test by the economic crisis

The onset of the 2008 financial crisis revealed the fragility of Milan's economy. First of all, the large amount of non-permanent employment produced as part of the processes of the tertiarisation of the economy proved to be highly vulnerable to attack during times of crisis. Milan's labour market, previously distinguished by a low unemployment rate (3.8 per cent in 2007), experienced a progressive rise in unemployment, with a higher increase than was seen at the national level.

The effect of this was additional flexibility in the labour market. In 2012, at the provincial level, for each new permanent job created there were 4.5 new temporary employment contracts. At the end of 2014 this ratio had become 1 to 5.7.

In response to the economic crisis, new national unemployment benefits were introduced for employees of small and medium-sized enterprises, as they were previously excluded from traditional forms of protection against unemployment. While responsibility for employment protection is basically centralised at national level, active labour market policy has been under the responsibility of regional governments. In Lombardy, the onset of the crisis has not significantly altered the previous policy approach, which was dominated by a "quasi-market" approach in which private agencies perform the main functions of training, employment activation and intermediation between labour demand and supply. This policy hinges around a system of vouchers (called "*Dote Unica Lavoro*"), which provides recipients with access to personalised "service packages" (such as training courses, demand and supply matching, career counselling or coaching services) provided by accredited public and private sector organisations. The limitations of this approach are those of a highly-centralised funding system on the part of the regional government, which is also extremely individualised and fragmented in terms of implementation of the measure, with problems of consistency, efficiency and continuity (Sabatinelli and Villa 2011).

Moreover, the province of Milan manages vocational training and careers guidance services with retraining programmes for workers laid off as a result of company crises, atypical workers and unemployed foreign workers. These measures are nevertheless underdeveloped with under-qualified personnel and little dialogue with enterprises. To counter rising unemployment, since 2010 the municipality of Milan has allocated an "anti-crisis" fund to a broad target of beneficiaries (such as young couples, the unemployed, workers receiving only

Table 10.1 Unemployment rate in Milan, NUTS 1-NUTS 2 and NUTS 3 level (2004–2014)

	2004	2005	2006	2007	2008	2009	2010	2011	2012	2013	2014
Milan	4.8	4.5	4.0	3.8	4.2	6.1	5.7	5.2	6.9	6.4	–
Province	4.7	4.2	3.9	3.8	3.8	5.6	5.8	5.9	7.7	7.7	8.4
Lombardy	4.1	4.1	3.7	3.4	3.7	5.3	5.5	5.7	7.4	8.0	8.2
Italy	8.0	7.7	6.8	6.1	6.7	7.7	8.4	8.4	10.7	12.1	12.7

Source: authors' elaboration on ISTAT.

temporary and limited income support) with a maximum one-time payment of €5,000.

As the measures implemented at the various levels of government have had an extremely limited impact, non-state actors have taken up the slack: for example, the Catholic Church of Milan, traditionally committed to policies of combating poverty and social exclusion, set up a fund to support poor families of unemployed people. The fund raised €19.5 million between 2011 and 2014 and was used to help 11,500 families, involving over 600 volunteers. In the face of the inertia of local government policy, therefore, protection against poverty and unemployment came to a large extent from the action of private religious philanthropy, which historically is particularly active in Milan.

10.3.3 The political turning point of 2011 and the new vision of development for the city, at the nexus between crisis and innovation

The political turning point of 2011 came during a phase that was profoundly affected by the global economic and financial crisis, demanding the implementation of innovative policies that were capable of tackling the already-visible effects of the crisis. With regard to jobs and development, the local administration approved a policy document entitled *Linee guida per le politiche del lavoro, lo sviluppo economico, l'università e la ricerca a Milano* (Policy Guidelines for Employment, Economic Development, Universities and Research in Milan), which set out a range of measures on several fronts, based on support for microenterprises and self-employment, attracting and training human capital and support for innovation. On the first front, the new government has sought to foster the development of a web of microenterprises operating in various sectors yet sharing an orientation towards creativity and social, economic and technological innovation, through services to facilitate the start-up phase. On the second front, it has fostered cooperation between universities and enterprises by supporting new training services, setting up work start programmes and providing help for highly-qualified young Italians and foreigners in finding accommodation. The last front has targeted the creation of local "clusters" of innovation, taking already existing specific local aspects and specialisations as a starting point.

Even taking the measure's limited room for manoeuvre at the municipal level, the new approach has shifted the focus of action and redefined its purpose. By reversing the logic that had essentially entrusted the task of job creation to the capacity of private enterprise to make efficient investments, the new government has made skills support and self-employment – especially among young people – a central focus of its action.

The initiatives that have trialled include a series of experimental "active labour policy" measures. The first measure regards microcredit, with the granting of loans of up to €20,000 under favourable conditions to individuals working in Milan or starting a business on a self-employed basis. A second line of action has been the establishment of a number of specialised business incubators in different zones of the city, with the aim of recreating links between residential and productive functions. Some of these incubators are dedicated to supporting the start-up of innovative enterprises capable of providing employment for highly-qualified young people, while others are dedicated to developing businesses that provide social services characterised by a high degree of occupational and social inclusion. Milan is currently home to the largest number of innovative start-ups in the country (470 out of a total of 3,200 surveyed in Italy in 2014). Milan, together with Lombardy, also heads the rankings in terms of areas with the largest number of start-ups with a social purpose. Finally, funds have been allocated to sustaining the organisational infrastructure necessary for new forms of work, such as co-working spaces, which, in addition to representing physical work-sharing spaces, in some cases foster the development of innovative business projects.

Another area in which the local government has invested resources to support mechanisms of economic innovation fostering inclusion and employment is digital manufacturing workshops (so-called "fab labs" or "makerspaces"), which are home to experiments with new forms of connections between digital innovation and manufacturing and artisan traditions in Milan and Italy. In the light of experiences in other countries, the idea is that the apparently marginal phenomena that develop in peripheral spaces may in reality conceal processes that might also shape mass production in the future.

A certain emphasis has been placed on Milan's leading role in the nascent sharing economy, which by its nature tends to overturn traditional economic categories and sectors by building new kinds of relations between producers and consumers and including broad sections of society in the processes of production of collective goods and services. In recent years, Milan has seen a proliferation of examples of the sharing economy, often sustained by digital platforms, not only in the area of mobility but also accommodation/hospitality, food, services and even finance, with numerous crowdfunding platforms or the so-called "social street" experiments. They are examples of a new collaborative economy that generates new markets and calls into question existing regulations yet which also builds new kinds of community and solidarity "circuits". The local government's policy documents do not define the sharing economy as a temporary reaction to the crisis but rather a new developmental approach, in which private actors are not only considered stakeholders in conflict or in contrast with the public interest but also "solution holders" capable of co-planning and co-managing procedures, spaces, goods and services. As with co-working spaces, the municipality of Milan has instituted a "list of actors in the sharing economy" with the purpose of raising the profile of a phenomenon that is underrepresented in public discourse and in policymaking, and offering a chance for forging links between economic actors and local government.

The picture painted hitherto illustrates a number of significant developments at the level of policy governance, with the building of strategic partnerships between government and a broad platform of public and private stakeholders called upon to make an active contribution to the construction of a shared project for the city. Previous centre–right administrations were distinguished by an approach that aimed to remove any restrictions on spontaneous economic processes in the city and to provide incentives for the economic and production sectors that had played a part – at least until the crisis struck – in reducing unemployment. This approach, however, also led to specific forms of social and economic inequality as a result of the increase in non-permanent and low-skilled employment. The city's new political government in contrast has focused on soft regulation of spontaneous economic dynamics with innovation potential and supporting forms of enterprise that are capable of combining added value and innovation, on the assumption that they can produce not only high-skilled employment but also occupational inclusion for broad sections of the population.

10.4 Conclusions

This chapter has described two fields in which local policy has developed over the space of 20 years. The aim was to examine, on the one hand, the policies that accompanied the processes of radical (physical and economic) transformation that have left their mark on the city since the 1990s and, on the other hand, to analyse how the consequences of the 2008 crisis have been tackled.

From the former perspective, the accent has been on the lack of an overall vision of local governance that can protect specific local interests while favouring far-reaching transformations by private stakeholders with specific, fragmentary interests. It has been shown how, during the period under consideration, the local governments at the helm of the city did not invest resources in constructing a "social" housing policy capable of mitigating the effects of rapidly rising prices in one of the most dynamic residential property markets in Italy and in Europe until the crisis was well underway. On the contrary: the stock of affordable rented housing was reduced and its quality steadily deteriorated.

On the other hand, what has also emerged is the absence of an explicit urban policy for creating "high-quality employment", along with the weak capacity of local politics to take the reins of development processes driven by spontaneous market forces and by the capacity of private actors and functional bodies to self-organise and influence the decision-making arenas of the city. This situation has especially benefited economic sectors in which unstable, low-qualified jobs are most common, that is, the intangible part of the fashion and design industries and the creative economy in general, as well as basic services for businesses.

Taking stock of this phase of urban policies, the first consideration to make is that the policy areas referred to are regulated by a multi-level system of governance characterised by a high degree of institutional fragmentation.

Although nominally all different levels of government (from the European Union all the way down to the local municipal level) participate in public policy building, policymaking suffers from highly centralised regulation, which in practice limits skills and operational capacity at the local level.

Second, the trajectory traced by Milan has evidenced an urban development mechanism of a dual nature. On the one hand, a property development dynamic has worked mainly to the advantage of private operators, who have benefited substantially from the injection of public resources in various forms (direct financing, tax incentives, fast-track building permits and streamlined regulations, etc.), which has produced social polarisation. In turn, housing policies, traditionally based on ownership for increasing shares of the population and public housing as a residual policy measure only for those individuals who are excluded from this possibility, have been exposed in all of their weakness in the context of the strong unmet housing demand created in Milan as a result of the property market dynamic described above and the crisis in employment and household income.

The rapid growth dynamic in economic sectors and activities characterised by high added value has also created low-quality employment and highly unstable occupational pathways, leading to an ever-widening gap between workers who, even within the same sector, experience extremely unequal conditions in terms of occupational stability, continuity and pay. In this case, the instruments adopted to protect workers and provide support and incentives for businesses have proven ineffective in the face of the explosion in unemployment brought about by the economic crisis. The measures put into action to cope with the crisis have been dominated by short-term monetary benefits limited to specific targets, based on limited resources, with contributions mainly coming from the private philanthropic organisations that are traditionally active in the city in the fight against poverty and social exclusion.

Essentially, the direction of the policies developed in Milan between 1993 and 2011 was characterised by a limited vision of the city's public interests. The style of governance that characterised the city until 2011 was one of ordinary, short-term administration strategies, which were also reflected in a ruling class made up of second-level leaders with little motivation to renew local politics and institutions. The centre–right mayor Albertini, in office from 1997 till 2006, stood for office as a "good property manager" to represent his style of government, bringing in a decision-making practice defined as "modernisation without responsibility" (Aleotti 2008: 17) based on a neo-liberal ideology. The result was an objective impoverishment of the city and the weakening of its fabric of social cohesion.

The vacuum left by this policy meant that the crucial challenges for the city's future were managed according to exclusively private sector principles, dominated by élites who were completely removed from politics and who opted instead to pursue action of their own accord or with the aim of acquiring the public resources that they required. This situation opened the way to an ever greater divergence between dynamics geared towards urban competitiveness (characterised by a marked imbalance in favour of specific, private interests) and policies geared towards mitigating the less sociably desirable effects of these dynamics (Bolocan 2009: 13).

A new connection between economic and social innovation on the one hand and public policy on the other has been one of the fundamental policy aims of the new administration, which starting from this vision has implemented new instruments of governance designed to bring about greater openness in decision-making procedures and to reunite the plural, fragmentary interests expressed by the city, and recognising this pluralism as a positive asset to be governed.

At the present time it is difficult to evaluate the results of the policies put to the test over the last four years of government, all the more so given the substantial financial and organisational demands of Expo 2015, the difficult financial situation and above all the profound economic and social crisis that has resulted in increased poverty and unemployment. The spheres and scope of application of the new administration's policy approach remain partial as yet. It will only be possible to evaluate the results of the largely experimental policies and projects implemented thus far in the medium-to-long term, and on condition that a number of them take on a more structural character.

It remains to be seen whether the policies currently being trialled, which are heavily geared towards innovation as a lever for local development, will be able to act in synergy and conjunction with the more traditional measures implemented at other (regional and national) levels of government, in view of a picture that remains critical, characterised by a broad section of the population with problems of housing affordability and the rise in unemployment, in particular among young people.

References

Aleotti, A. (2008). Da Milano a Milania, Milano: Creative Commons Italia. Online, available at: www.milania.it (accessed 7 September 2012).

Artoni, R. (2005). Alcune considerazioni sull'economia Milanese. In: M. Magatti *et al.*, *Milano nodo della rete globale*, Milan: Bruno Mondadori.

Arvidsson, A, Malossi G. and Naro, Serpica (2010). Passionate Work? Labour Conditions in the Milan Fashion Industry, *Journal for Cultural Research*, 14(3), 295–309.

Boeri, S. (2003). Le tre anime di Milano [The City with Three Souls], *Domus*, 859, 72–77.

Bolocan, M. (2009). *Geografie Milanesi*, Santarcangelo di Romagna: Maggioli.

Brenner, N. and Theodore, N. (2002). *Spaces of Neoliberalism: Urban Restructuring in North America and Western Europe*, Oxford: Wiley-Blackwell.

Bricocoli, M. and Savoldi, P. (2010). *Milano Downtown: Azione pubblica e luoghi dell'abitare*, Milan: et al. Edizioni.

Bruzzese, A. (2013). Centralità a tempo: Industria creativa, trasformazioni urbane e spazio pubblico a Milano. In: *Planum, Atti della XVI Conferenza Nazionale Società Italiana degli Urbanisti "Urbanistica per una diversa crescita"*, Napoli, 9–10 May, 1–6.

Campos Venuti, G. (2012). Nuovo Pgt: Endorsement di un urbanista militante, *Arcipelago Milano: Settimanale milanese di politica e cultura*. Online, available at: www.arcipelagomilano.org/archives/17168 (accessed 18 June 2012).

Costa, G., Cucca, R. and Torri, R. (2015). Milan, towards a Governance of Social Innovation in the Local Welfare, ISTR Working Papers. Online, available at: www.istr.org.

Giovannetti, M., Gori, C. and Pacini, L. (2014). *La pratica del welfare locale: L'evoluzione degli interventi e le sfide per i Comuni*, Santarcangelo di Romagna: Maggioli Editore.

Healey, P. (2007). *Urban Complexity and Spatial Strategies: Towards a Relational Planning for our Times*, London: Routledge.

Jansson, J. and Power, D. (2010). Fashioning a Global City: Creating and Maintaining Global City Status in the Fashion and Design Industries: the Case of Milan, *Regional Studies*, 44(7), 889–904.

La Varra, G. (2007). Abitare in un sottotetto. In: Multiplicity Lab (ed.), *Milano: Cronache dell'abitare*, Milan: Mondadori.

Magatti, M. *et al.* (2005). *Milano nodo della rete globale: Un itinerario di analisi e proposte*, Milan: Bruno Mondadori.

Memo, F. (2007). Nuove caratteristiche del sistema immobiliare e abitabilità urbana: Alcune evidenze a partire dal caso di Milano, *Sociologia Urbana e Rurale*, 84, 103–123.

Peck, J., Theodore, N. and Brenner, N. (2013). Neoliberal Urbanism Redux? *International Journal of Urban and Regional Research*, 37(3), 1091–1099.

Presidenza del Consiglio dei Ministri – Unità di analisi strategica delle politiche di Governo (2007). Le politiche abitative in Italia: ricognizione e ipotesi di intervento, Roma.

Sabatinelli, S. and Villa, M. (2011). Shifting in Power Towards a New Centralized Regulation of Labour Policies in the Lombardy Region, Paper for the Espanet Conference *Innovare il welfare: Percorsi di trasformazione in Italia e in Europa*, Milan, 29 September–1 October.

Scenari Immobiliari (2012). *Osservatorio Nazionale Immigrati e Casa*, IX Rapporto. Online, available at: www.scenariimmobiliari.com.

Torri, R. (2007). Milano tra eccellenze e nuove polarizzazioni. In: Ranci, C. and Torri, R. (eds), *Milano tra coesione sociale e sviluppo*, Milan: Bruno Mondadori.

Torri, R. (2010). Nuove linee di divisione spaziale. In: Ranci, C. (ed.) *Città nella rete globale: Competitività e disuguaglianze in sei città europee*, Milan: Bruno Mondadori.

Turok, I. (1992). Property-led Urban Regeneration: Panacea or Placebo? *Environment and Planning A*, 24 (3), 361–379.

11 Munich

The struggle to combine competitiveness and social inclusion

Alain Thierstein, Irina Auernhammer and Fabian Wenner

11.1 Introduction

'Munich has been able to anticipate, withstand and recover from different economic shocks and weighed the relative contribution to resilience of its indigenous assets, economic structure and other contextual factors and governance and policy' (Evans and Karecha, 2013: 1275). Munich is a city that, during the last three decades, has created an urban agenda strongly focused on developing social cohesion as an asset to succeed in the post-industrial transition. In this chapter, we focus on two particular policies that help shed some light on the abovementioned 'phenomenon'. First of all, housing policies have long been the key priority of the city of Munich. For decades, politicians and the municipal administration have perceived providing sufficient affordable housing as their key task. Housing helps to guarantee social blending, safeguard public security, create quality oriented housing, provide social infrastructure in the city districts and the effective use of land plots in the central city area associated with the process of re-densification (Thierstein *et al.*, 2010).

Second, a strong tradition of social democratic housing policies goes hand-in-hand with a long lasting concern of the strong industry trade unions for labour qualification and corresponding initiatives concerning manufacturing hotbeds. Therefore, this chapter argues that Munich combines a series of interventions in the fields of both housing and labour market policies that are supported by different levels of government.

At the core of such approach there is an overarching strategic urban policy framework: the *Perspective Munich*, a strategic plan developed by the city of Munich in the late 1990s. The *Perspective Munich* was initiated by the planning department of the city of Munich in order to bring together the variety of space-related policy fields of the municipality in a more comprehensive way. The intermediate evaluation of the *Perspective Munich* in 2007 stated that strategy develops over time like a 'breathing' mechanism, adjusting to the city's new external and internal challenges.

With 2.7 million inhabitants, the city-region of Munich is regarded as the most densely populated region in southern Germany, and more than half of the inhabitants live in the actual city of Munich (Bavarian State Office for Statistics and Data Processing, 2015). The administration of the municipality of Munich is organized in ten sectoral departments. At the sub-city level, district committees act as an important link between the citizens and the municipal administration. Rather late, the city became aware that a number of challenging issues are not confined solely to the city-regional limits but are at the core of the future development of the entire functional metropolitan region. The Munich Metropolitan Region (MMR) was established formally in 2007 as a private association, a territorial approach with a fixed demarcation followed suit (EMM e.V., 2015). The Munich city-region forms the heart of the MMR, surrounded by the major regional centres of Augsburg, Ingolstadt, Landshut and Rosenheim. Altogether almost half of the population of the German federal state of Bavaria lives in the MMR, in total 5.8 million inhabitants (EMM e.V., 2015). Currently, the interregional cooperation within the MMR only acts in a sectoral and small-scale dimension.

The chapter is structured as follows. Sections 11.2 and 11.3 present Munich's development strategy. Section 11.4 deals with the housing market and social mix. Section 11.5 talks about the promotion of employment, while Section 11.6 presents final considerations.

11.2 The *Perspective Munich*

The *Perspective Munich* is the urban development policy tool established in 1997 and since then developed into 16 binding thematic guidelines. Four 'strategic guidelines' and a 'common leitmotif' overarch the 'thematic guidelines'. When the city of Munich started to formulate future challenges, it considered issues concerning far-reaching strategies for urban development. Strategies translate into measures, which are inseparably linked with the process of customizing social infrastructures for childcare, the care of the elderly and for other social services as well as many other key aspects.

These strategic guidelines were implemented in the core activities of urban planning. Within *Perspective Munich* they interconnect the leitmotif (Figure 11.1) and the thematic guidelines. 'Fields of activity' have the task to translate the strategic guidelines into spatial strategies (Thierstein *et al.*, 2010).

The guideline called 'governance and cooperation' transcends all other strategic guidelines by serving basic premises of action within the urban development, whereas another strategic guideline titled 'open-mindedness and attractiveness' aims at stimulating the exchange with other cities and city-regions in Europe and all over the world. As a counterpart to social polarizations, the guideline 'solidarity and active civil society' has been inserted in order to balance the potentials and consequences of growing civil societies and to strengthen the responsibility and cohesion within the urban community, the equality of opportunities and possibilities to participate. In a more practical way, the last of the four strategic guidelines called 'urban spaces and quality' focuses on Munich's urban traditions on the one hand, and the creative and responsible use of land reserves on the other, summarized in the slogan 'urban, compact, green' (Thierstein *et al.*, 2010).

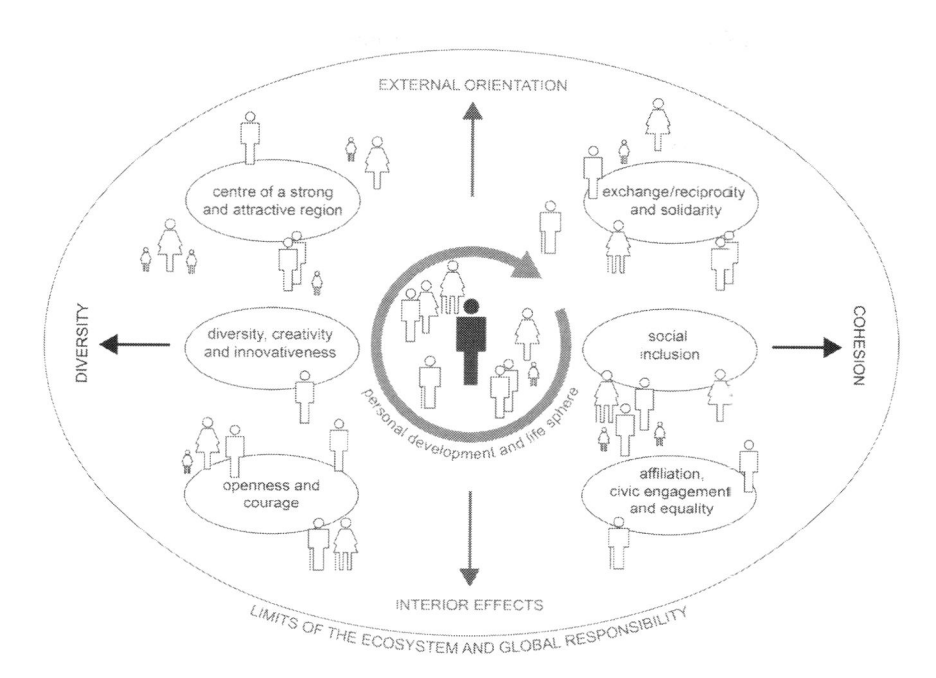

Figure 11.1 Leitmotif, the *Perspective Munich*.
Source: Thierstein *et al.*, 2010: 37.

In contrast to the strategic guidelines, 16 thematic guidelines are moreover oriented in a functional and specific direction. These thematic guidelines shall be part of the political daily life of the city departments determining the full year target of their particular field of responsibility.

While the guidelines of the *Perspective Munich* described above must be considered as a meta-level between functional and spatial views, the 'areas for action' enable to locate targets of urban development selectively. Being amorphous and diffuse, they are able to spread over the administrative borders instead of covering the whole urban area like a land-use plan does (Thierstein *et al.*, 2010).

In April 2012 the updated *Perspective Munich* was publicly debated during three citywide conferences. The municipality launched a public consultation process under the slogan 'Thinking together. Talking together. Planning together'. Among other issues, participants addressed their fears and reservations about urban growth. How could they be dispelled, noting the fact that according to citizens' surveys (City of Munich, Department of Social Affairs and Department of Urban Planning and Building Regulation, 2010), the housing supply and the level of renting cost are the greatest problems for the inhabitants of Munich? The city council approved an updated *Perspective Munich* in June of 2013, shortly after the forming of the new coalition by the Social Democratic Party and the conservative Christian Socialist Party. The Christian Socialist Party replaced the Green Party as the Social Democratic Party's coalition partner, which had been governing the municipality consecutively since the early 1990s. A strong socio-ecological consensus developed also allowing to establish the unique instrument of the 'Sozialgerechte Bodennutzung' (SoBoN) – the socially equitable land use scheme, which is described in more detail below. It must be kept in mind that for decades the Free State of Bavaria was governed by the Christian Socialist Party, while the city of Munich tended to vote for a Social Democratic Party-led coalition. The Christian Socialist Party's policy traditionally gears towards their constituencies in rural and semi-rural urbanized areas, renouncing to the active support of the larger cities, and the emerging of the metropolitan regions of Munich and Nuremberg in particular.

11.3 A local development approach

The strategic document *Perspective Munich* indicates the current priorities of Munich's urban development. Mainly, the approximation on the objective of social stability and integration takes place on the municipal level. The local level of policies – welfare, education, health and public safety – is regarded to be the appropriate level for finding solutions for the consolidation of social cohesion.

According to the strategic plan, Munich's particular position has been defined by continuous development dynamics up to 2030. Munich is expected to stay in the leading position as business location, and will profit furthermore from national and international immigration. As a result, the civil society will progressively be characterized by intermixed socio-cultural identities. This development will require new adaptations in various fields of economic and social life and will also be visible and perceived in the spatial structure of the urban agglomeration. A further differentiation of people's circumstances and lifestyles will induce the creation of new types of – patchwork or temporary – families, housing demands (living and working together, multi-generation housing) and consumption behaviours (use value instead of ownership, sharing and caring economy). This process will be followed by a change in the demand for infrastructural and social services. Closely connected is the increasing individualization of values and lifestyles that will reach up to old age, which reinforces the needs of these groups for long-term autonomy. At the same time, traditional family structures might be changed. Thus, demands will increase for age-related assistance services and housing typologies, appropriate mobility systems, sufficient local supply in the district and social meeting points (Thierstein *et al.*, 2010).

Considering social milieus, according to the strategic document, the 'bourgeois middle class' is clearly underrepresented in the city compared to the national average. In contrast, the number of persons assigning themselves to the milieu of 'post-materialists' and 'hedonists' is significantly above national average (City of Munich, Statistical Office, 2006). The average net household income in Munich is €2,500 on the median referring to the year 2010 – the figure for Germany this year was about €3,000 (City of Munich, Department of Social Affairs and Department of Urban Planning and Building Regulation, 2010; Destatis, 2012: 12). It must be kept in mind however that this figure is still high compared to other German cities, and strongly surpassed by the household income in the municipalities surrounding the city, resulting from Munich's economic strength. Also evident is the presence of patchwork families and single-child families (City of Munich, Statistical Office, 2014a). This pushes demand for childcare outside the family, as well as financial support for single parents and appropriate housing solutions. Short travel distances among housing, working places and childcare facilities characterize suitable residential environments. The significant changes in the family and parental structures will also affect the sizes of households undergoing the upward trend for single-households (Thierstein *et al.*, 2010).

Social groups such as low-income families with children, single parents and their children, non-German households and persons with poor qualifications will mainly be affected by the abovementioned developments. These groups of inhabitants will have to face the challenges caused by disparities in the income sector, social polarization and increasing impoverishment, especially among the elderly.

These facts have been acknowledged in the strategic document *Perspective Munich* and have been addressed through a comprehensive planning activity involving local districts in defining goals and their implementation. The main approach intends to join the existing resources with the local potential, which is not already sufficiently exploited. For this process a close cooperation between the public and the private sectors becomes increasingly important, including the fields of adult education and training, work with children and the youth, and social inclusion interventions for immigrants (City of Munich, Department of Urban Planning and Building Regulation, 2005).

Programmes for local employment and health promotion are provided on a citizen-oriented basis. Thus, citizens' participation is considered as an indispensable element in the planning process in order to promote the potential for self-help and to use existing facilities and institutions. According to the district management of Munich, various forms of participation are to be developed on a targeted basis. The several projects seek to consolidate the essential functions of local districts in order to reinforce social integration (Schächtl, 2012).

An example of such an approach is the implementation of the urban development programme 'Towns and cities with special localized development needs' and 'The Social City', jointly launched in 1999 by the German federal government and the regional government. The priority of this action programme was to face overarching social and economic problems by initiating the process of self-renewal on a local scale (City of Munich, Department of Urban Planning and Building Regulation, 2012a). In this programme, municipalities nominate districts that require assistance with respect to, for example, living conditions, economic base or education or work opportunities, and apply for funding.

The programme 'Social City – Hasenbergl' in Munich exemplifies this concept of urban management. The district 'Hasenbergl' was formerly constructed as an extensive mono-structural residential area in the 1960s. At that time, available housing was urgently required for the accommodation of socially disadvantaged social groups. Later, in the 1990s, this urban district started to cause serious problems, such as the increased ageing of the older population, the increase to above average numbers of immigrants and the rise in unemployment (City of Munich, Department of Urban Planning and Building Regulation, 2012a). The high percentage of poverty and the stigmatization of the inhabitants caused by the poor image of the district were equally significant.

Public initiatives are the result of the city's own efforts, multiplied and sometimes even initiated by the availability of federal programmes. Within ten years, funds in the amount of €15.6 million were invested in several projects for the city district refurbishment (City of Munich, Department of Urban Planning and Building Regulation, 2012a). The funds were provided by public authorities, private organizations and public–private partnerships (Schächtl, 2012). Encompassing all, the district refurbishment programme consisted of two parts: the basic programme for urban development funding (1993–1999) and the programme 'Social City' (1999–2012). Within the latter, the inhabitants of the district and local actors were asked to be involved at an early stage in the refurbishment measures. Even future user groups were intended to participate as early as possible, considering their ideas for the implementation of the project (Schächtl, 2012). The development process was characterized by a strategic and target-oriented procedure, meaning that time frames and short-, medium- and long-term objectives had been communicated to all the relevant actors right from the beginning. Marketing concepts were designed to strengthen local activities and communicate the shift in the image of the district (Schächtl, 2012).

11.4 Keeping the housing market affordable and promoting the social mix

11.4.1 Current trends in the housing sector

In Munich, the housing market has become ever more important as a location factor – it has long been so in quantitative terms, but it is increasingly becoming so in qualitative terms. As a result, a strategic development is required within the city limits in terms of re-densification, due to the rising scarcity of land plots. At the same time, demands for housing units are increasing, thus compensating the impact on increasing immigration, especially with the knowledge workers who on their part are predominantly affected by the international economic crisis (Rode *et al.*, 2010).

As a contrast, the economic capacity of Munich could be regarded as constantly positive and resistant to the crisis in a national and international comparison. Indirectly, the stable economic situation in Munich encourages young couples to start a family, as exemplified by the growing number of newly born babies in recent years (City of Munich, Statistical Office, 2015). Summarizing all these effects, the demand for appropriate housing remains high, followed by constantly rising costs in rent and property prices (City of Munich, Department of Urban Planning and Building Regulation, 2012b).

The price level could be considered as an indicator of the situation in the housing market. In the German national comparison, Munich's 164 residential rental index exceeds by far the national average of 100. Munich's housing stock counts the highest rental costs in all categories of age groups. Thus, Munich is classified as the most expensive rental property market in Germany (F+B, 2014). The high level of rent prices on the privately financed housing market also intensifies the demand for social housing. Simultaneously, the socio-spatial segregation seems to be intensifying due to varied price trends in the several districts and housing quarters.

These trends occur in a city where the rent sector still plays a relevant role in the housing system. According to the last census in 2011, of the approximately 730,000 dwellings in Munich, 23.8 per cent were owner-occupied, while 73.7 per cent were rented. The comparable figures for Germany are 42.6 per cent and 52.3 per cent, respectively, indicating a strongly above-average proportion of renters in Munich. Of all residential buildings in Munich, 64 per cent were owned by private landlords and a further 19.6 per cent by landlord associations or groups. Some 7.1 per cent of the buildings (with approximately 110,000 dwelling units) were held by private (housing) associations, while 4.9 per cent (with 60,000 units) were in ownership by municipal housing associations. Federal or state organizations on the one hand and non-profit bodies like the church on the other, held only 1 per cent of the buildings (Destatis, 2011).

These figures indicate an above-average share of publicly held housing stock in contrast to more rural parts of Germany. The figures are also comparable to those of other German cities like Berlin, which show a somewhat higher share of flats owned by private housing organizations and a lower share of private landlord associations. It is important to note here, however, that a considerable share of the privately owned dwellings are in fact rented social housing, as described later.

The trend of the rising housing prices was not really reversed by the financial crisis. Since 2006 secure and reliable investment forms such as the real estate sector have experienced an appreciation. Persistent low interest rates on all forms of investments, combined with a rather strong German export-led economy, has created a situation in which huge amounts of free flowing capital make real estate investments very attractive – for decades a rather neglected asset that seldom experienced a 'bubble' in Germany. Thus, prices for residential real estate have grown rather incessantly in the last five years. In 2009, the average price per square meter was €3,500–€4,400 in the case of newly constructed condominiums, and therewith ranked top in Germany (Sparkassen Immobilien GmbH & Co KG, 2010). Since then, prices have risen to €6,000 for average locations and almost €7,000 in very good locations, and are still increasing (Gutachterausschuss München, 2015).

11.4.2 Housing policies

To date, housing remains Munich's top political priority, and thus the creation of housing units capable of satisfying the users' varied needs falls within its key social policy interests. The action programme 'Living in Munich WiM' plays an important role in the *Perspective Munich* plan (City of Munich, Department of Urban Planning and Building Regulation, 2005). Embedded in strategic guidelines, Munich's housing policies give a high profile to the issue of housing supply and social spatial mix (Thierstein *et al.*, 2010). In recent decades, the city of Munich has often been involved in debates about the national regulation of subsidies for the construction of owner-occupied housing and rental properties.

Munich's housing policy includes the concept of the 'Munich social mix', the unique – and, among German planners, famed – instrument of the SoBoN, that is the socially equitable land use scheme, local housing programmes, the wide range of local housing funds and the instruments for the protection of the housing stock.

In the period 1990–2010, four 'Living in Munich' plans were sequentially implemented (WiM I–IV, Wohnen in München I–IV) with the aim to promote the construction of new housing units. Since the programme's launch in 1990, the construction of 125,000 housing units was officially permitted, 115,000 housing units were realized, 22,000 of which were financially supported (City of Munich, Mayor, 2011). This socially oriented development in the housing programme was possible thanks to the funding of the SoBoN. The SoBoN obliges property owners to set aside 30 per cent of the value added generated by the building permit. This money is used for technical and social follow-up costs of planning, such as the construction of children's facilities, nurseries, social housing units, green spaces, and the development of public roads (City of Munich, Department of Urban Planning and Building Regulation, 2009).

The WiM programme encompasses the local promotion programme the 'Munich Model'. This financing model consists of three types of housing subsidies. The 'Munich Model for Rental Housing' – since 2001 – promotes the housing rental sector, whereas the 'Munich Model for Property Housing' – since 1996 – promotes residential properties. Another strand, the 'Munich Model for Cooperatives' was launched in 2001 (City of Munich, Department of Urban Planning and Building Regulation, 2006). The 'Munich Model for Rental Housing' addresses mainly families with children belonging to the lower middle-income sector. On the other hand, the city of Munich governs the subsidy of home-ownership with financial resources of the federal state by granting loans at affordable rates. Moreover, it subsidizes housing units for rent, starting with favourable rents in the price range of $7.50 €/m^2$ to $11 €/m^2$ (City of Munich, Department of Urban Planning and Building Regulation, 2015).

'Living in Munich V' (WiM V) was launched in November 2011. The core of the programme remains, but the current challenges in the housing market required that new priorities be set, including to supply affordable housing units in sufficient numbers and to establish concepts for a middle and long-term settlement development. The 'Initiative for Housing' aims at granting new building permits for 3,500 housing units a year, whereof 1,800 housing units per year will be subsidized: 900 rental units for low income households, 300 rental units for middle income households, 300 property housing units for middle income households, 100 rental units for occupancy rights within the private housing market – 'Belegrechtsprogramm' – and 200 housing units for cooperatives and housing associations. The distribution of the promoted housing units is based on a classification in low and middle income groups, in which the applicants are categorised (City of Munich, Department of Urban Planning and Building Regulation, 2012c).

11.5 Promoting new employment

11.5.1 Munich's economic success

German economic policies are based on the principle of subsidiarity, which has characterized the entire political orientation of the Federal State of Germany since the post-war period. The tasks of local governments in economic terms comprise employment policies, the promotion of business development and the investment management of shareholdings (Eller, 2012). Also the tourism sector and activities in European networks fall within the local level responsibilities (City of Munich, Department of Labour and Economic Development, 2012d). In particular, when establishing company contacts, the municipality consults on site issues and aims. The focus is on project development, management of commercial premises, city marketing and the promotion of the economy at the city level (Eller, 2012).

Success in maintaining Munich's economic position depends also on these following aspects: (1) its future attractiveness for sustained foreign investments, particularly in innovation and firm networks; (2) its relative wealth of human capital supported by investments in the education sector; (3) its interaction among different cultures, and thus attracting and keeping talented people in the region, such as highly skilled workers or students. This development requires also a powerful knowledge and innovation environment and the support of developing industries. As a result, the settlement of young and innovative companies in the region is expected to act as the driving force of a regional economic development (EMI, 2011).

The economic structure of the region of Munich is regarded as a centre of future industries (EMI, 2011), particularly the information and communication industries as well as the media, finance and insurance sectors. In addition, in Munich a comparatively high proportion of employees work in the innovation, research and development sectors (City of Munich, Department of Labour and Economic Development, 2012c). Numerous public and private research institutes and universities have established bases in the urban area. Thus, Munich is also regarded as a strong location of higher education and high-tech innovation (Rode *et al.*, 2010). This raises Munich's attractiveness to highly skilled workers, which has led to a growing influx of such workers.

One of the main reasons that Munich has remained comparatively resilient to the financial crisis is the diverse economic base of its region, referred to as the 'Munich Mix': The economic structure of Munich is multi-sectoral with strong positive effects on the diversity and flexibility of the local labour market. A wide range of sectors, including SMEs and global players, define the composition of the 'Munich Mix'. Medium-sized businesses are present in various branches or market niches and have a stabilizing impact on the local market (Bavarian Ministry of Economic Affairs, Infrastructure, Transport and Technology, 2011).

Since 2011 the national average unemployment rate has decreased and the situation for the German labour market has significantly improved. In Munich the unemployment rate at the beginning of 2015 was 4.7 per cent. Those mainly affected by the positive developments of the labour market have been to a large degree young people and groups of people over 50 years of age (City of Munich, Department of Labour and Economic Development, 2012c).

11.5.2 Employment policies: supply-side measures

Munich's economic policies aim at accommodating the urgency of employment and at developing skills for growth and social stability. These policies comprise measures and projects for reinforcing employment as well as fighting against discrimination and inequalities in the labour market, and can be differentiated into supply-side (workers and employees) and the demand-side (economic sectors and entrepreneurships) policies (City of Munich, Department of Labour and Economic Development, 2012d).

On the supply-side, despite the significant decline in unemployment in recent years and thanks to the economic upturn, the municipality still focuses vigorously on labour market integration. The responsible institutions seek to dismantle obstacles that inhibit people from integrating or re-integrating in the labour market. Regardless of professional qualifications, certain restraints may prevent people from entering the labour market, such as age, health conditions or migrant backgrounds (City of Munich, Department of Labour and Economic Development, 2011a).

The local labour market policy rests on three pillars, which are all based on the principle of collaboration with partners, supporters or institutions, headlined with the principle 'innovation through cooperation' (City of Munich, Department of Labour and Economic Development, 2011a). This sheds light on a sustainable employment strategy, which is characterized by dialogue with the stakeholders involved in the local labour market. At first, the municipality seeks to found cooperation with local and regional institutions and to establish supporters and partners. To this end, the closest partners are the 'Munich Job Placement Agency' (Agentur für Arbeit) and the 'Jobcentre Munich'. Other important partners are the trade unions, the business lobbies and the Department of Social Affairs. Concerning the second pillar, the city of Munich intends to pool experience with European partners, for example with other European metropolitan regions of comparable size. The third pillar is the promotion of innovative labour market projects summarized in the 'Munich Employment and Qualification Programme' (City of Munich, Department of Labour and Economic Development, 2012a). The city of Munich offers about 110 promotion and educational programmes to disadvantaged persons. In 2011, the city council of Munich provided about €29 million in order to supplement the services of the 'Jobcentre' and the 'Job Placement Agency', stemming from funds at national level (City of Munich, Department of Labour and Economic Development, 2011a).

The municipality offers more than just aid programmes against unemployment when implementing local employment policies. Policies tend to simplify and to accelerate structural transitions by sponsoring support to those companies currently are affected by these changes. This field of activity covers three levels of issues: job creation in companies; industry-specific training; consulting and advice (City of Munich, Department of Labour and Economic Development, 2012b). The process for generating jobs within companies focuses on the branches of the construction industry, ancillary trades, hotels and gastronomy. The method for creating jobs is characterized by the founding of production and service cooperatives. The promotion of industry-specific training includes adult education programmes or consulting programmes on training and education for employee council members. The promotion area for consulting and advice, for example addresses those companies confronted with forthcoming adjustments with regard to personnel issues. Here we also find the advisory service on vocational training at the Munich adult education centre as well as the women experts consulting network on career orientation (City of Munich, Department of Labour and Economic Development, 2012b). Between 2006 and 2011, the annual job growth in Munich was approximately 1.5 per cent, and even higher in the surrounding municipalities (City of Munich, Statistical Office, 2012).

One of the most relevant programmes directly addressing Munich's inhabitants by activating people and enabling them to work is the 'Munich employment and qualification programme' (Münchner Beschäftigungs- und Qualifizierungsprogramm, MBQ), which targets people 'who are able to work and of employable age, but whose employability and/or chances of being placed in employment are impaired due to social, health or personal factors'. This programme seeks 'to overcome structural barriers to labour market integration and fight against (long-term) unemployment' (City of Munich, Department of Labour and Economic Development, 2011a: 1). It is the most extensive local government programme on employment in Germany: its budget runs at €28.7 million for 2011.

The core of this programme was launched in 1993 and is based on the former Labour Development Initiative (AFI), existing since 1984. Given its declared objective to shape appropriate labour market policies, the city of Munich decided to supplement the statutory promotion programmes on employment offered at the federal level on a voluntary basis. In the following, three supply-side projects will be presented, each focusing on special target groups (City of Munich, Department of Labour and Economic Development, 2011a):

- reduction of long-term unemployment;
- equal opportunities for women and men;
- development of skills and expertise.

Reduction of long-term unemployment. The target groups in this area are socially disadvantaged people affected by long-term unemployment. They are often burdened by multiple problems and therefore require a high level of support. These people in many cases receive social security benefits to guarantee a minimum subsistence level, the so-called 'Unemployment Benefit II – ALGII' (Arbeitslosengeld II). The goal of the projects within this area of support is to improve the personal conditions of the people affected in order to provide social stability and to increase their possibilities of entering or re-entering the labour market (City of Munich, Department of Labour and Economic Development, 2011b). For this purpose, the city of Munich has established employment schemes providing long-term unemployed people with work experience and the chance to improve their skills and qualifications. These projects offer real-world conditions, which allow participants to progress into real jobs. The net pecuniary flows generated by the programme are reinvested in employment projects.

Equal opportunities for women and men. Mothers and fathers who intend to return to their working life after a three-year interruption for childcare are the target groups of this promotion project. Within the childcare period they may not have been able to sustain regular employment or to pursue self-employed economic activities. The project promotes equal opportunities for women and men in the labour market. Measures comprise advisory services and assistance for re-entry into employment (City of Munich, Department of Labour and Economic Development, 2011b). The model-project 'power-m' launched in 2009 exemplifies this area of intervention in a comprehensive manner. The projects are based on the prediction that by 2025 Germany will face a shortage of 6.5 million skilled people. The aim is to exploit all latent potential, which includes women who intend to return to their working life after a period of childcare but who are often hindered by psychological barriers despite their high qualifications and skills (City of Munich, Department of Labour and Economic Development, 2011c). About 48.1 per cent of all employed people working in Munich are female, signalling a high rate of female participation in the labour market when compared to the German average of 46 per cent (City of Munich, Statistical Office, 2014b; Bundesagentur für Arbeit, 2014).

Development of skills and expertise in companies and industries. Immigrant entrepreneurs are expected to create jobs and to stimulate economic growth through the establishment of small and medium-sized enterprises. In turn, they often engage in providing employment for other immigrants. From this point of view, they have the potential to promote social cohesion within their own entrepreneurship (City of Munich, Department of Labour and Economic Development, 2011b). As a result, the municipality offers a wide range of support for stabilizing companies and for improving the ability to integrate and to compete within the business arena.

Finally, one of the issues vigorously discussed at the local, state and federal level is the issue of childcare facilities. All levels of government seem to be aware of the close interconnection between promoting quality oriented childcare and the resulting positive developments on the labour market. A new federal law, the 'Childcare Funding Act KifoeG' ('Kinderförderungsgesetz'), which entered into force at the end of 2008, holds that from the year 2013 every child in Germany has a legal claim to childcare services. Overall €12 billion are being invested to implement the objectives of the KifoeG on the local level, of which about one-third will be financed by the central state (Federal Ministry for Family Affairs, Senior Citizens, Women and Youth, 2012). Moreover, the Free State of Bavaria has decided to invest €185 million per year in further developing child-care services (Bavarian Ministry of Work and Social Order, Family and Women's Affairs, 2012). Local authorities also have to fulfil their obligations. In fact, burning issues are the scarcity of available land plots and the lack of trained personnel. In response to this situation, Munich has launched the 'Agency for day-care supervision' in order to cope with the increasing heterogeneous composition of Munich's children and youth (City of Munich, Department of Education and Sports, 2012). In 2010, 40 per cent of Munich's children under the age of three were provided with childcare services. Responding to actual demands, the municipality decided in 2012 to increase this objective to 60 per cent. Furthermore, 82 per cent of Munich's children attend kindergarten (for children aged between three and five) while the goal remains 90 per cent (City of Munich, Department of Labour and Economic Development, 2012c).

11.5.3 Employment policies: demand-side programmes

The MBQ programme includes measures aimed at fostering 'Creative Economy' as a location factor. The 'Art and Creative Economy' in the MMR in 2010 generated about €20 billion revenue, with a 3.9 per cent contribution to the regional economic performance. Especially prominent are film and broadcasting businesses. This is considerably above the German average of 2.6 per cent. More than 115,000 people in the MMR are employed in the Art and Creative Economy (Söndermann, 2012). The means for influencing the 'Creative Economy' depend on how specific situations within this economic sector can be shaped and how the different needs of the actors involved can be fulfilled. This is a great challenge because of the high degree of complexity and small-scale organizations. As a result, measures for governing and supporting the 'Creative Economy' are characterized by decentralized and network-like structures.

On the local level, the crucial challenges are to bundle the creativity of all the actors involved and to improve communication and cooperation between the actors of the 'Creative Economy' and the local authorities. As such, the model-project Platform3 was launched by the city of Munich. As an integral part of the MBQ, this project seeks to combine artistic and cultural activities with training programmes, as well as the provision of event areas, laboratories and office spaces. This particular combination of support within the areas of culture, economy and floor space management, characterizes the innovative approach of the project (City of Munich, Department of Labour and Economic Development, 2011b). Indeed, the 'Creative Economy' in many sub-sectors is characterized by small companies and single entrepreneurs that interact mostly in network-like, project-based manners. Thus, physical proximity – being located door-to-door in the same street, in the same premises – facilitates the mutual exchange of information.

Furthermore, in order to improve the working conditions within the 'Creative Economy' in Munich, the municipality has launched open dialogues between the Department of Culture and the 'creative class'. As a result of the dialogues, integrated action plans are required in the future, so as to combine the capacities of all of the branches of the city's administration for bundling creative potential. In this perspective, even the marketability of the 'creative class' is considered to be improved. The city of Munich is still not much known for its creative potential, which from now on should be promoted much more actively as a brand. Munich is constantly concerned in battling against rising land and real estate prices that only seem to follow simple market rules. The city of Munich expects municipal property managers, housing associations, urban planners, as well as the real estate industry to be much more sensitive with regard to facilitating temporary uses of idle premises (Küppers, 2010).

An example of such strategy is given by two competitions launched by the city of Munich for the conversion of a former military complex of about 20 ha. The area is located near the centre of Munich and is an example for the process of urban re-densification (Förster, 2014). The brief of the competition asked for spaces aimed at housing, working, knowledge and culture for a life in the urban community. Two listed industrial halls are located on the site, which are intended to accommodate various future uses, for example commercial or cultural uses and uses for the 'Creative Economy'. The area is located near the Munich University of Applied Sciences as well as to other cultural and economic facilities. Thus, high expectations spur the municipality to develop in the centre of Munich an outstanding knowledge, culture and business location. The future 'Creative Quarter of Munich' may create a genuine new impetus for the whole city district (City of Munich, Department of Urban Planning and Building Regulation, 2012d).

11.6 Final considerations

The case study on Munich demonstrates the comparative strengths of the city and the region. Unemployment is low, Munich's economic mix is thriving, public debt per capita seems to be manageable. However, social integration remains a challenge, and affordable housing is considered to be the most pressing issue in public political debate. Still, underneath the gloomy surface, the same structural problems that challenge other city-regions in Europe are present in Munich: demographic change, lack of qualified workforce, diminishing options of public policy to effectively intervene and deploy results on the ground, an old building stock that needs to be made more environmentally friendly and more suited to the inhabitants' shifting needs.

The need for higher qualification and more 'creative' workers has been addressed by developing a large range of local policies aimed at supporting both the demand-side and the supply-side of the labour market. Some of these programmes address the need for the re-qualification of poorly educated individuals, or those ethnic social groups traditionally excluded from core employment.

The main challenge for the city comes from the expectation that rising prices will decrease the supply of affordable housing and weaken the policy strategy adopted so far. Here again, the city's administration has looked ahead, and in the year 2010 had already launched the key 'long-term perspective for urban development' project. This project started from the following questions: What is the long-term urban development prospect for the city after the years 2025–2030 when all the public, non-built-up land has been used? Which levers does public policy still have in order to implement its basic ideas, especially on affordable housing, social integration, open spaces, public transportation and other infrastructure? Strength always bears the seed of weakness. The provision of social and affordable housing as well as related social infrastructure has been fairly successful so far due to the financing mechanism – the socially equitable land use scheme –, which makes mandatory for property owners to put to one side the 30 per cent of the value added created by the building permit. When all the publicly owned non-built up land has been used, this mechanism will also lose its impact. Thus, while pushing ahead with proposals for new strategies in densification, urban transformation and regional cooperation, it remains to be seen how social inclusion through the provision of affordable and social housing and the like can be secured into the longer future.

While the focus of public policies is highly concentrated on the quantitative issue of housing – particularly against the backdrop of the most recent influx of refugees – the qualitative aspect (e.g. diversity of multi-purpose housing across all income levels) is not centre stage at all. But the availability of high quality, diverse and mixed-used housing, at accessible locations, is a key requirement for keeping and attracting well-qualified people and skilled workers. Human capital thus is the key for maintaining the competitive edge of Munich's economy.

Finally, the strong and persistent influx of new inhabitants puts enormous pressure on real estate prices, which in turn do not allow to let any property sit unused, idle or under-utilized. Exactly such premises and buildings are often breeding grounds for creative industries and cultural activities. While many German cities look towards Berlin with envy – Berlin's awkward slogan goes: poor, but sexy – Munich rarely is the object of such envy. The renewal of the economic structure requires unexpected activities, keen entrepreneurs and fertile soil to let ideas flourish. Still, Munich has most of these ingredients ready: ideas, financial capital, seed money, nurturing milieus, challenging competition. However, Munich lacks some of the necessary idle spaces that also form the breeding grounds of urban renewal. Less utilized plots, in-between spaces, disused warehouses usually offer cheaper and more stimulating environments.

Thus strengths and weaknesses seem to be closely tied together in Munich, which does not make it any easier to identify and to disentangle the key driving factors of sustainable urban development.

References

Bavarian Ministry of Economic Affairs, Infrastructure, Transport and Technology (2011). *Initiative for Medium-Sized Businesses*. Online, available at: http://goo.gl/J5PHGd (accessed 30 April 2015).

Bavarian Ministry of Work and Social Order, Family and Women's Affairs (2012). *Das neue BayKiBiG, Entwurf der Staatsregierung für eine Reform des Bayerischen Kinderbildungs und-Betreuungsgesetzes*, Munich.

Bavarian State Office for Statistics and Data Processing (2015). *GENESIS*. Online, available at: https://goo.gl/glaLWm (accessed 29 April 2015).

Bundesagentur für Arbeit (2014). *Beschäftigungsstatistik*. Online, available at: http://goo.gl/r9IWBa (accessed 4 August 2015).

City of Munich, Department of Education and Sports (2012). *Kommunales Bildungsmanagement: Die Münchner Serviceagentur für Ganztagsbildung*. Online, available at: http://goo.gl/CU7yDk (accessed 17 September 2012).

City of Munich, Department of Labour and Economic Development (2011a). *Munich Employment and Qualification Program (MBQ): In Touch with the Labor Market, In Touch with People*, Munich.

City of Munich, Department of Labour and Economic Development (2011b). *Projektehandbuch, Münchner Beschäftigungs-und Qualifizierungsprogramm (MBQ)*, Munich.

City of Munich, Department of Labour and Economic Development (2011c). *Wiedereinstieg erfolgreich gestalten, power m, Erfahrungen aus einem Modellprojekt*, Munich.

City of Munich, Department of Labour and Economic Development (2012a). *Labour Market Policy*. Online, available at: http://goo.gl/0lZxjN (accessed 17 September 2012).

City of Munich, Department of Labour and Economic Development (2012b). *Labour Market Policy, Structural Transition, Background Information and Fields of Activity*. Online, available at: http://goo.gl/sw5CHX (accessed 17 September 2012).

City of Munich, Department of Labour and Economic Development (2012c). *Münchner Jahreswirtschaftsbericht 2012*, Munich.

City of Munich, Department of Labour and Economic Development (2012d). *Referat für Arbeit und Wirtschaft, Leitbild*. Online, available at: http://goo.gl/hzdfho (accessed 16 September 2012).

City of Munich, Department of Social Affairs and Department of Urban Planning and Building Regulation (2010). *Perspektive München I Analysen, Münchner Bürgerinnen- und Bürgerbefragung 2010, Soziale Entwicklung und Lebenssituation der Münchner Bürgerinnen und Bürger, Kurzfassung*, Munich.

City of Munich, Department of Urban Planning and Building Regulation (2005). *Development Report 2005 – Shaping the Future of Munich – Perspektive München – Strategies, Principles, Projects*, Munich.

City of Munich, Department of Urban Planning and Building Regulation (2006). *Perspektive München I, Konzepte, Wohnen in München IV*, Munich.

City of Munich, Department of Urban Planning and Building Regulation (2009). *Die Sozialgerechte Bodennutzung, der Münchner Weg*, Munich.

City of Munich, Department of Urban Planning and Building Regulation (2012a). *Stadtsanierung und Wohnungsbau, Stadtteilsanierung Hasenbergl, Vielfältig – Ganzheitlich – Quartiersbezogen*, Munich.

City of Munich, Department of Urban Planning and Building Regulation (2012b). *Wohnungspolitisches Handlungsprogramm Wohnen in München V, Wohnungsbauoffensive 2012–2016*, Munich.

City of Munich, Department of Urban Planning and Building Regulation (2012c). *Ausstellung: Zukunft findet Stadt, München: einfachwohnen? Wohnraum schaffen – Spielräume nutzen*, Munich.

City of Munich, Department of Urban Planning and Building Regulation (2012d). *Stadt kreativ denken – das Kreativquartier an der Dauchauerstaße – Ergebnisse des städtebaulichen und landschaftsplanerischen Ideenwettbewerbs*, Munich.

City of Munich, Department of Urban Planning and Building Regulation (2015). *Das Programm 'München Modell' für Mieter*. Online, available at: http://goo.gl/RJDUjP (accessed 30 April 2015).

City of Munich, Mayor (2011). *Wohnungsbau: München verstärkt sein Engagement*, Press Conference, Grütznerstube, Munich.

City of Munich, Statistical Office (2006). *Milieus in der Stadt München*, Münchner Statistik, Fourth Quarterly Edition, Munich.

City of Munich, Statistical Office (2009). *Das Zusammenleben zwischen Ausländern und Deutschen in München*, Fourth Quarterly Edition, Munich.

City of Munich, Statistical Office (2012). *Pendlerverflechtungen der Stadt München*, Fourth Quarterly Edition, Munich.

City of Munich, Statistical Office (2014a). *Die Privathaushalte mit Kindern in den Stadtbezirken zum*. Online, available at: http://goo.gl/wyoqyq (accessed 27 August 2016).

City of Munich, Statistical Office (2014b). *Die Sozialversicherungspflichtig Beschäftigten in München am Arbeitsort nach Wirtschaftsbereichen 2014*. Online, available at: http://goo.gl/RK2cF4 (accessed 4 August 2015).

City of Munich, Statistical Office (2015). *Mehr Geburten, weniger Sterbefälle: Die Geburten- und Sterbefällestatistik 2014*, Münchner Statistik, First Quarterly Edition, Munich.

Destatis (2011). *Zensus 2011 – Gebäude und Wohnungen*. Online, available at: https://goo.gl/zuXoRf (accessed 13 August 2015).

Destatis (2012). *Einnahmen und Ausgaben privater Haushalte*, Subject Series 15, 1. Online, available at: https://goo.gl/Dem6ui (accessed 13 August 2015).

EMI (European Metropolitan Network Institute) (2011). *The Economic Vitality of the Munich Metropolitan Region, Case Study*, The Hague: NICIS Institute.

EMM (Europäische Metropolregion) e.V. (2015). *Die Metropolregion München*. Online, available at: http://goo.gl/qntW9F (accessed 29 April 2015).

Evans, Richard and Jay Karecha (2013). Staying on Top: Why is Munich so Resilient and Successful? *European Planning Studies*, 22(6): 1259–1279.

F+B (2014). *F+B Mietspiegelindex 2014*. Online, available at: http://goo.gl/fncQBK (accessed 30 April 2015).

Federal Ministry for Family Affairs, Senior Citizens, Women and Youth (2012). *Kinder und Jugend, Kinderbetreuung*. Online, available at: http://goo.gl/k7cMoK (accessed 17 September 2012).

Förster, Agnes (2014). *Planungsprozesse wirkungsvoller gestalten – Wirkungen, Bausteine und Stellgrößen kommunikativer planerischer Methoden*. Dissertation at the School of Architecture, Chair of Urban Development, TUM Munich. Online, available at: https://goo.gl/0ea2Op (accessed 13 August 2015).

Gutachterausschuss München (2015). *Quartalsbericht*. Online, available at: http://goo.gl/8eFoKe (accessed 4 August 2015).

Küppers, Hans-Georg [Cultural Advisor of the City of Munich] (2010). *Die Stad tals Dienstleister für freischaffende Künstler, Autoren, Designer*, Fourth Workshop in the Context of the Conference 'Cultural and Creative Industries Initiative of the Federal Government' in Dusseldorf, 26 October 2010.

Rode, Philipp, Max Nathan, Anne von Streit, Peter Schwinger and Gesine Kippenberger (2010). *Munich Metropolitan Region, Staying Ahead on Innovation*, Paper for the Conference 'The Next Urban Economy' in Chicago, 7–8 December 2010.

Söndermann, Michael (2012). *1. Teilbericht Kultur- und Kreativwirtschaft in der Europäischen Metropolregion München (EMM)*, Köln: Büro für Kulturwirtschaftsforschung.

Sparkassen Immobilien GmbH and Co KG (2010). *Marktspiegel für Oberbayern 2010*, Munich: Datengrundlage Geodatenpool.

Thierstein, Alain, Christof Abegg, Joelle Zimmerli, Michael Droß, Anne Langer-Wiese, Barbara Zibell, Franz Eberhard, Ernst Basler and Partner Zurich, and Munich University of Technology (2010). *Perspektive München 1 Konzepte: Fortschreibung Perspektive München*, commissioned by the City of Munich, Department of Urban Planning and Building Regulation, Zurich/Munich.

Interviews

Eller, Bernhard [City of Munich, Department of Labour and Economic Development] (2012): Interview, 14 June 2012 in Munich.

Schächtl, Thomas [District Manager for the 'Social City' programme at the city district Hasenbergl] (2012): Interview, 3 May 2012 in Munich.

Part III

Final considerations

12 Disconnected cities

Dealing with competitiveness and social integration

Costanzo Ranci

12.1 Introduction

European cities have been generally considered as characterized by high inter-dependence between competitiveness and social integration (Préteceille 2000; Häussermann and Haila 2005; Kazepov 2005). Specific factors, such as the solid tradition of national welfare systems and the weight of the middle classes in the occupational structure of European cities, explain the fact that in Western Europe the issue of social equity is only relatively distinct from the dynamics of economic competitiveness and growth. Such factors, notwithstanding their progressive erosion, still anchor the West European population to a base of social rights and public protections that is able to attenuate economic and social disparities. Welfare policies, mainly organized at national level, still perform a crucial role in defending the urban population of such cities against the new risks deriving from globalization (Letho 2000; Kazepov 2005).

In this book we hypothesize, however, that today European cities face an increasing *disconnection* between global competitiveness and social integration. In some EU countries, such as the United Kingdom, this disconnection started to increase during the 1980s as result of the retrenchment of the welfare state. In the new century the same trend has gradually characterized most of the EU countries as the effect of neo-liberal policies and the globalization of the economy. Finally, the current financial crisis and austerity measures have exacerbated this disconnection in many countries, especially in Southern Europe. Whereas high urban competitiveness and strong social integration were tightly interwoven in the age of Keynesian development that characterized West European cities for several decades after the Second World War, today these two elements are much less interdependent (Ache *et al.* 2008; Ranci 2011; Novy *et al.* 2012).

Partly in contrast with traditional interpretations of the integration/competitiveness nexus in European cities (Häussermann 2005), this chapter analyses the interdependency between these two aspects in the six big West European cities considered in this book on the basis of the evidence gathered in the previous chapters. The chapter will highlight how, before the economic crisis, in these cities globalization and economic restructuring have offered new opportunities for growth and success to those enterprises that have been operating in the leading sectors, making these cities more competitive and attractive on both a continental and worldwide scale (Musterd and Murie 2010). On the other hand, the same trends have contributed to the spread of new social problems and tensions, which are related to transformations occurred in the labour market, in the housing market, and in the composition and spatial distribution of the urban population. The chapter will show how the increase in the level of global competitiveness of such cities has been matched by an increase in their levels of inequality or social exclusion and will argue that the most recent economic crisis and austerity measures have worsened this already ongoing trend of disconnection.

We will look at *the specific mechanisms whereby social integration and economic growth have become disconnected* in such cities. Four aspects were considered in previous chapters in order to analyse connections and disconnection:

- conflicts and synergies between spaces of flows and spaces of places (Castells 1996) in these cities: what are the most important local factors contributing to make these cities competitive and attractive and what are the main local impacts of such attractiveness;
- local patterns of post-industrial transition and their impact on social inequalities: what is the impact of the local path of economic development on the inequality structure of such cities;
- urban transformations and their contribution to spatial inequalities: what have been the spatial consequences of the extensive urban regeneration processes and changes in the housing market taking places in such cities;
- the challenge of multi-ethnicity: what have been the integration problems of the recent increase in the multi-ethnic composition of the urban population.

12.2 Competitive cities

The six cities analysed in this book are, albeit to different extents, fully integrated into the contemporary global economy. They are equipped with advanced economic, infrastructural and logistical systems, and they are endowed with an abundance of financial and productive resources, human and social capital. They are all major players in the international market, and they have invested in their capacity to compete, substantially completing their transition to post-Fordism.

According to available statistics (see Table 12.1), these cities are ranked as prominent global centres, both in their own national contexts and in Europe, being included within the top 30 most globalized cities in the continent. Moreover, with the only exception of Manchester, each is ranked as the first or second most innovative and richest city in their own country, showing the capacity of these cities to attract the most relevant economic resources and the most innovative business activities.

In point of fact, they are not cities in competition *as such*. Not all of their productive and social components take part in the global market. Nor are their urban politics exclusively geared to economic competition. The six cities considered

Table 12.1 Ranking of the six cities for indicators of economic competitiveness (2006)

	Ranking of the cities in Europe (over 158 cities)			Ranking of the cities in their own country		
	Globalization index	Innovation index	GDP per capita (over 244 EU cities)	Globalization index	Innovation index	GDP per capita
Munich	5	2	4	2	2	1
Milan	10	54	15	2	1	1
Manchester	17	81	85	3	5	10
Copenhagen	18	16	24	1	1	1
Lyon	19	30	36	2	1	2
Barcelona	29	99	56	2	2	3

Source: Urban Audit, 2006; author's elaboration from D'Ovidio and Ranci (2014).

are highly complex, only partially globalized, urban systems. More than economic entities defined by boundaries and identifiable assets, they are what Amin and Thrift describe as "assemblages of more or less distanciated economic relations, which will have different intensities at different locations" (Amin and Thrift 2002: 52). Their global importance depends primarily on the fact that they *attract resources and promote exchanges.* That is to say, their importance depends on their attractiveness, and on their capacity to intercept and relaunch flows of people, capital and information. In this perspective, Turok uses the concept of "city competitiveness" to indicate the combination of three elements: trade (the ability of a city's firms to sell their products in contested external markets), productivity (the value of these products and the efficiency of their production), and the use of resources (the extent to which local human, capital and natural resources are utilized) (Turok 2005: 26).

Again according to Amin and Thrift (2002), contemporary cities are places of sociability helping to strengthen economic transactions. Here the significant point is that such places of sociability must be organized and maintained if they are to yield long-term benefits. Global flows must be organized within cities, and they must be combined with local relationships (Castells 1996). In the Fordist age, competition and social integration were two elements in strong equilibrium. Cities were simultaneously the principal places of both production and consumption. Economic growth was fuelled by strong demand for consumption, to a large extent concentrated in the cities. At the same time, if the production functions were to be efficient and stable, they required the organization of social reproduction through stable industrial relations, housing policies able to make residence in the city affordable, measures to protect the vulnerable and to support consumption. The strong need for stability of economic systems found its pivot in the industrial city, and it was supported by high growth rates and by the generosity of welfare systems.

Today, by contrast, social stability is less economically important than flexibility, and this entails that the search for greater competitiveness no longer requires a high level of social integration. Indeed, social integration may become an obstacle, a social superstructure that hampers the development of the new, post-industrial economy. The disconnection observed between social integration and competitiveness, therefore, is not so much a problem as an economic necessity (Buck *et al.*, 2005).

However, the issue of the relationship between social integration and global competitiveness is not entirely irrelevant. International interconnectivity must be matched with a certain level of internal organization. Our cities have to organize their flows, both inside and from/to outside, consistently both with their international positioning and with the interests and structure of local society. The existing connection between interior and exterior is therefore one of the main fields of analysis on the local impact of globalization on cities; but also the internal conditions that foster, or hinder, the development of cities' global competitiveness have to be considered.

12.3 Cities that attract

The six cities considered are specialized, in various ways, as *poles of attraction*. Numerous initiatives, policy measures, infrastructural projects and schemes for the localization of services, are undertaken to enhance the cities' attractiveness to foreign direct investments and high-quality human capital (see Table 12.2). These flows are governed only in part by the allocative decisions of global players; they also depend on the capacity of cities to attract them on the basis of the quality of places or specific factors. All the cities analysed have made investments in this regard, not only through the usual urban marketing strategies, but also through specific projects aimed at improving accessibility and at encouraging the location of new productive activities.

Such cities have promoted initiatives in order to attract flows of tourists (Barcelona), travellers (Copenhagen), factories and other economic activities (Munich and Lyon), financial services (Manchester and Milan).

As already explained in the previous chapters of this book. Barcelona has invested in attractiveness through prolonged policies of "great events" and through the strong promotion of arts and tourism. Copenhagen has developed a large-scale project (Oresund), promoting the international airport and the surrounding area, with which to catalyse the knowledge economy by enhancing links with nearby Sweden and other Scandinavian countries. Munich has developed various programmes to support the installation of new productive activities in brownfield areas through generous financing policies and infrastructuration (also promoted by the *Länder* and the German state). Lyon has mounted numerous cultural initiatives and has profited from the infrastructuration obtained from government investments in high-speed railway lines. Manchester and Milan have invested in the attractiveness of specific financial and knowledge economy areas.

Although these policies have had different outcomes (the most successful cases being those of Munich, Barcelona and Copenhagen), some problems are nevertheless shared by these cities. These problems mainly concern the *capacity to balance inside and from/to outside flows*. All the cities considered have had to deal with the internal effects provoked by the growth of flows and mobility, and they have had to adjust their urban transport systems accordingly, especially investing in new underground lines and systems for sustainable mobility (car sharing, bike sharing, etc.). Moreover as city-attractors, they have had to develop their capacities as city-organizers of flows. We now discuss the main problems that have emerged in this regard.

One of the principal issues has concerned new areas for the installation of advanced economic activities. Knowledge-intensive services tend, in fact, to concentrate internally to cities, whence they are attracted by the benefits of physical proximity (easier coordination, access to social capital, synergies in the use of services, accessibility, etc.) and by the availability of human capital. Moreover, the demand for centrality produces large flows of people and private vehicles towards the centre of metropolitan areas, causing traffic congestion and the strong growth of commuting. Some cities have reacted to this tendency by decentralizing advanced economic activities to peripheral areas of the metropolitan region. The most evident cases are those of Copenhagen (Oresund), Munich (massive investments in brownfield areas), and Barcelona (upgrading of working-class districts). This strategy has been accompanied by aggressive policies of urban marketing focused on cultural and symbolic actions (in the case of Barcelona and of Lyon), the explicit promotion of new local production clusters through the offer of good public incentives (Munich and Lyon), the building of large infrastructures (for instance, the bridge between Copenhagen and Malmö). In general, it seems that policies aimed at promoting diffused localization of new attracting economic activities in the urban region have achieved good results, especially when interconnections and the mobility of people (both radial and transverse) have been simultaneously enhanced. This has made it possible to aim at not only productive diversification, but also at the distribution of the population across a broad area, thereby partly decongesting the central areas.

Infrastructures, transport, services to businesses, and logistics constitute the most relevant "hard factors" of attractiveness (Musterd and Murie 2010). All the cities considered have made substantial investments in both long and short distance transportation infrastructures (see Table 12.2). One crucial issue has been the capacity to invest in public transportation in order to reduce the concentration of private traffic and to make it sustainable. But also high speed interconnections have become of crucial importance. This has required a larger and effective multilevel governance on a metropolitan scale. Some cities have made progress in this direction by creating strategic plans for the urban region and by introducing policies for decentralizing the location of new firms of excellence (Munich and Barcelona).

A further aspect of urban attractiveness concerns the development of "soft factors". "Soft factors" are related to the quality of urban life in order to attract skilled workers and to influence the location decisions of multinational companies. The six cities analysed have developed specific soft factors: Barcelona has promoted culture by emphasizing the city's creative identity; Munich has promoted green spaces and the quality of life in decentralized areas; Copenhagen has concentrated on its image as a "city of knowledge" and on environmental sustainability; Barcelona and Milan have promoted large-scale events; and Lyon has relied on cultural programmes. While the efforts have been diversified, the results in terms of attracting high-skilled workers have not been particularly satisfactory so far. The amount of foreign high skilled workers or foreign students is still low in many of the cities considered, with the exceptions of Munich, Barcelona and, partly, Manchester (see Chapter 3). More than contributing to the attractiveness of the city to talented workers and students, soft factors have played an important role in the urban marketing strategies by enhancing the public image of the cities and increasing tourist flows (see the cases of Barcelona, Copenhagen and Munich, but also Milan to lesser extent). Moreover, soft factors are important positional goods for the new urban elites that live in the cities, increasing the prestige and desirability of specific areas, as explained in Chapter 3.

In general, therefore, the growth of an urban economy based on international flows has required the development of urban policies able to act systemically on the internal and external linkages of the metropolitan area. The growing demand for centrality by advanced services and high-skilled workers, as well as the centralization of economic activities of excellence, have increased the congestion of urban centres and have deteriorated their habitability. Consequently public intervention aimed at improving mobility and enhancing soft factors has become necessary. The capacity of these cities to compete in attracting global flows of capital and talent is grounded also on these aspects.

In this respect the case of Milan is emblematic of the persistence of conflicts between the external attractiveness and the quality of the "space of places" (Castells 1996). The strong international attractiveness of Milan is mainly favoured by the multi-sectorial nature of the local economic system and by the strength of its financial sector. Nevertheless, external attractiveness is off-set by various obstacles: the still limited adequacy of the urban public transportation system; its scant endowment with soft factors; the absence of multilevel governance on the scale of the urban region. These three aspects instead explain the competitive strength of cities like Munich and Barcelona, which have launched processes of political innovation and have invested massively in these aspects.

Governing large urban regions is one of the main challenges facing the urban policies of our cities. At the level of the urban region, locational dynamics and commuter flows show that the dominant dynamics at present do not assume the features typical of urban sprawl. Rather than creating an indistinct urban continuum around the main urban centre, new productive and residential locations have occurred in areas where local centralities already existed, or they have contributed to creating new ones. The six urban regions are characterized, in fact, in their urban continuity, by the existence of "decentralized centres" specialized in specific productive functions and offering distinct residential quality. These urban regions include a plurality of territories with specific identities and do not merge into a magmatic "diffused city".

In these regions the relationship between the main urban centre and the surrounding area has become highly complex. In some cities an integrated regional pattern is strongly evident. It results from specific policies aimed at transferring high-quality productive and residential urban functions to the regional government: this is the case of Munich, Copenhagen and, to a lesser extent, Barcelona and Lyon (see Chapter 3). This *refocusing* (*recentrage*) of metropolitan areas has had generally very positive effects because it has reduced central congestion (Munich), has eased commuter flows and the consequent traffic problems (Lyon), and has revived former industrial areas at strong risk of decay (Barcelona). Where this process has not been pronounced, as in Milan and Manchester, a traditional dualism persists between the core city, which is hyper-specialized in advanced tertiary services, and the peripheries, increasingly characterized by scant attractiveness, in which industrial areas remain. This failure to *refocus* is responsible for persisting problems of traffic congestion, but also for the increasing social and economic dualism between centre and periphery.

Table 12.2 Main projects of urban regeneration in central and/or peripheral areas

City	
Copenhagen	• Kongens Enghave in Vesterbro • Holmbladsgade in Amager • Femkanten in the north-west – and later extended to the Nørrebro Park neighbourhood and Kvarterløft North-west
Milan	*Central areas:* • Garibaldi-Repubblica • Milan City Life *Peripheral areas:* • Santa Giulia (stopped because of the bankruptcy of the real estate company managing it) • Rho-Pero: new space for the Milan Fair
Barcelona	*Central areas:* • requalification of the Old City (Ciutat Vella) in the 1980s • Olympic Village in the 1980s • Diagonal Mar and Forum area in the 2000s Programme of upgrading of the peripheries ("monumental peripheries")
Munich	*Micro-projects* *Soziale Stadt*: regeneration programmes in many peripheral distressed urban areas, integrating social, occupational, mobility and environmental intervention: • Milbertshofen (2004) • Hasenbergl (2007) Since 2001 regeneration programmes have been started also in District 14 (Berg am Laim), District 16 (Ramersdorf – Perlach), District 17 (Obergiesing), District 18 (Untergiesing-Harlaching) *Big urban projects* *Messestadt Riem*: a public area close to the previous airport. The new plan locates a new fair, new spaces for manufacture, high tech industry and advanced services (13,800 new jobs), residences (14,500 new residents) and an urban park
Manchester	Several regenerations programmes in East Manchester, including demolishing or refurbishing of old buildings, erection of new flats as well as the creation of a business park

Source: see Chapter 3, data gathered on the basis of local investigations.

But even when policies are introduced to create a multipolar and reticular regional system, the chances of improvement and the resources invested are not equally distributed across the urban region. Some areas have such large amounts of resources (in terms of human capital, productive system, spaces available and connections) to put them in the best conditions to develop new regional centralities. Where marked differentiations already exist in the urban region, the pressure to refocus tends to radicalize them and to create strong territorial imbalances if urban policies do not intervene: this is the case of the territorial disparities along the north–south axis of Manchester, but also of the inequalities arising along the east–west axis of Lyon. Areas strongly industrialized in the past, or with major problems of accessibility, may therefore fail to grasp the new opportunities and remain marginal, while other areas will acquire the status of new urban or metropolitan centralities.

12.4 Unequal cities

The positioning of cities in the international economy has relevant impacts on their occupational structures, and therefore on the distribution of the opportunities and risks that are connected with the labour market. There is in fact a close relation between the characteristics of the local production system of the cities and the structure of social inequalities, as we have shown in Chapter 2.

European cities have been historically characterized by the presence of a large middle class, mostly employed in the public administration or in highly stable professional or white-collar occupations. This presence of a large middle class has long been an important factor in social stabilization and political consensus. The stability of the middle class has been a source of attractiveness and internal equilibrium.

The pattern predominant in the six cities analysed is characterized by professionalization (Hamnett, 2003), consisting in the growth of high-skilled jobs matched by a decrease, or immobility, of low-skilled ones. Over the five years before the economic crisis (between 2000 and 2005), all our cities, especially Copenhagen, Milan and Barcelona, had seen a significant increase in highly-educated workers, as shown by the variation between 2000 and 2005 in the education level of the active population (see Table 12.3). As described in Chapter 2, the professionalization process has come about in different ways, creating professional elites mainly in some cities (Copenhagen, Munich and Barcelona), while in other cities (Milan, Lyon and Manchester) professionalization has been less intense because of persisting mismatches between the training system and the labour market, or an inadequate capacity to exploit talents. The theory of the dual city, anyway, did not seem applicable to these cities, at least until the crisis.

After the crisis, however, the situation has changed, especially in cities such as Milan and Barcelona that have lost considerably occupation in the manufacturing professions, public administration and other white-collar professions.

In cities where the labour market has been less affected by the crisis, the tendency to professionalization has therefore gone hand-in-hand with the rise of a new urban elite driven by the capacity of new professions to grasp the opportunities offered by economic globalization and ongoing changes in the urban production system. However, this growth has not affected many other layers of the urban population, including a substantial section of the middle class. Professionalization is therefore a process that creates new inequalities and new forms of social stratification, as explained in Chapter 2.

Table 12.3 Education level of the active population (2002 and 2005) (%)

	2000 (percentages by city)			2005 (percentages by city)			2000–2005 variations		
	Mandatory school	High school	Academic degree	Mandatory school	High school	Academic degree	Mandatory school	High school	Academic degree
Munich	18.0	52.0	29.7	15.6	53.3	31.1	−15.3	2.5	4.9
Copenhagen	22.4	52.3	25.3	20.2	47.5	32.3	−9.7	−9.1	27.4
Barcelona	48.8	22.6	28.6	43.3	23.5	33.2	−11.4	4.0	16.1
Lyon	27.8	45.7	26.5	25.4	47.1	27.5	−8.6	3.0	3.7
Milan	42.6	45.8	11.6	38.7	46.7	14.6	−9.1	2.1	25.2
Manchester	14.1	58.6	27.3	23.4	48.0	28.6	66.6	−18.1	4.5

Source: FOCI database, 2000 and 2005.

One of the most serious problems, especially before 2008, was related to the impact of the growth of this new urban elite on the housing market. Higher demand for elite housing, together with the financialization of the housing market, has given rise to a marked increase in the house prices in all six cities, which has gradually pushed a section of the middle class towards peripheral areas (see Chapter 3). While on the one hand this process of substitution may have increased the city's attractiveness to the outside, on the other it has widened the gap between the urban elite and the urban middle classes. This is a phenomenon reported especially in Milan, Barcelona and Copenhagen, although after the economic crisis the housing market has become more affordable, opening opportunities for new buyers and new problems for the households that have bought before the downturn (see Chapter 7 on Copenhagen).

A further consequence is that inequality in these cities is quite high if compared with other European cities. Notwithstanding the high economic performances of our six cities, their high level of wealth and economic success has not turned into a fair distribution of social opportunities in the population. As shown in Table 12.4, our cities (with the only exception of Copenhagen) have very differentiated rankings concerning gender parity, educational equity and inclusiveness of the labour market. In their own countries, our cities are ranked in a low position on most indicators, to confirm that the prominent position achieved in economic performances is not followed by equivalent equity in resource distribution and access of the population to social opportunities.

A consequence of that situation is the creation of a huge gap between the top elite and the middle class, and the urban middle class suffering a relative deprivation in respect of the most affluent social groups. As explained in Chapter 2, this is a phenomenon especially evident in the cities of southern Europe (Milan and Barcelona), where the size and stability of the middle class were already lower.

Finally, while until 2008 the development of low-cost sectors (for instance, construction and tourism in Barcelona, in-home care provision and construction in Milan) has contributed to reducing unemployment in all the cities studied, it has created a marginal sector of the labour market characterized by low skills, modest incomes and occupational insecurity (see Chapter 2). This marginal labour market has caused higher social polarization insofar as it exposes workers in these sectors to the risk of entrapment in precarious and low-paid occupations. More recently, especially in Barcelona and Milan, this trend has worsened as result of growing unemployment, especially among the youngers.

The professionalization of the middle class has therefore had some negative effects: the expulsion of a significant portion of the middle-low class from the central city; an increase in income disparities; the growth of job precariousness; and the risks of occupational segregation on ethnic bases. These dynamics are apparent in all the cities considered, though to different extents and with different features. The impacts of these phenomena on the urban middle class is under scrutiny because of the possible consequences on local consensus and social stability.

Table 12.4 Ranking of the six cities for indicators of social equity (2006)

| | Ranking of the cities in Europe (over 314 cities) | | | Ranking of the cities in their own country | | |
	Gender equity in activity rate	Inclusiveness of the labour market	Equity in education	Gender equity in activity rate	Inclusiveness of the labour market	Equity in education
Munich	130	33	76	9	1	13
Milan	216	38	218	7	11	5
Manchester	81	40	94	4	14	15
Copenhagen	11	8	–	1	1	–
Lyon	56	136	20	19	9	7
Barcelona	184	178	207	7	11	9

Source: author's elaborations of the Urban Audit database, 2006.

Some specific aspects have contributed to mitigate these dynamics, as we have shown in the second part of the book. One of the most significant is the preservation of a substantial industrial system able to offer job security and average wages to medium-skilled workers. Some cities have intentionally developed this strategy. For example, as already shown, Lyon and Munich have adopted a model of urban economic development centred on sectors of excellence, complementary to which new industrial investments have been fostered by ad hoc local and national policies.

An alternative aspect has been the maintenance of a generous welfare system able to guarantee adequate incomes for low-paid workers. In Copenhagen the introduction of work flexibility has been accompanied by the development of generous income-support policies aimed at developing a flexicurity system.

Social inequalities are much more widespread in cities where international competition has led to the development of highly attractive production sectors (finance, tourism, high-tech) in greatly weakened local productive contexts. These cities have seen the growth, in parallel with the new advanced sectors, of a low-skilled service sector in which workers at high risk of poverty are concentrated. In these cities the tendency to professionalization has given rise to a new urban elite, but in parallel it has not created a general upward shift of the whole population. This is a pattern that characterizes cities like Milan and Barcelona: a model of the Mediterranean city characterized by the co-presence of excellences and traps that configure an urban dual development.

12.5 New social morphologies

All six cities considered have been affected by relevant changes in the housing market and in the social morphology.

This increase in house prices and rents, until 2008 has been accompanied by several other phenomena that can be only partially grouped under the heading of "gentrification": urban renewal; the embellishment of working-class districts, the creation of commercial services of various kinds catering to gentrifiers, renewed attractiveness of urban centres for affluent social groups and new professionals. All the cities considered, though with considerable differences among them, have had part of their territories markedly transformed by these processes. Gentrification has also gradually spread, in the case of Munich for instance, through the urban region, affecting specific districts and residents in the metropolitan area (see Chapter 3).

The main factors responsible for this general increase in house prices have been the capitalization of the real estate market, the growth of demand for high-cost properties and the partial privatization of the public housing stock.

Before 2008, the increased demand for housing of the new urban elite has been matched by a larger supply of high-priced properties driven by capitalization of the real estate market. Supply-side and demand-side factors have coincided, therefore opening the way for incremental gentrification. This process has not only generated replacement effects but has also gradually changed the urban environment.

Second, the property market has received a considerable boost from the sell-off of the public housing stock in several cities (Manchester, Copenhagen, Milan) in order to reduce the deficits of the municipal agencies managing such properties, or from a relaxing of public control over rents (as has happened in Copenhagen and in Milan). The privatization of the public housing stock has been particularly relevant in some cities. In Copenhagen, since 1995, 20,000 public apartments have been sold to cooperative housing agencies. In Milan the public housing stock (45,000 units) is constantly decreasing: 800 units are sold every year on average. In Manchester the impact of the "right to buy" scheme has been huge. Privatization has been extolled as salutary not only for the finances of the public institutions managing it, but also for the large number of middle and lower-class people who have become home-owners at subsidized prices. In several cities, however, the concentration in social housing of the poorest classes, unable to purchase homes because of insufficient income or job precariousness, has generated new processes of social segregation, progressively turning some working-class districts into marginal ghettos. This has been particularly visible in cities such as Copenhagen and Manchester.

The most marked social effect of these processes has been, in various cities, the gradual expulsion from the centre of low-to-middle class families, especially those with children, who have increasingly moved to the outlying areas of the urban region in search of affordable housing. This process is very evident in Milan, where in recent years several tens of thousands of people have been expelled from the core city. Only Copenhagen, by virtue of its strong endowment with welfare services and the development of ad hoc urban policies, has been able to attract new families to the gentrified central areas, thereby reversing the progressive ageing of the population. Copenhagen is therefore no longer a city of elderly people, students and welfare recipients, as perceived in the past. This has nevertheless caused the partial substitution of the population to the detriment of medium/low income groups. The other cities have lost part of their capacity for generational exchange because of the exodus of families with small children. As shown in Table 12.5, Munich and Barcelona are ranked very poorly in the young-age dependency ratio, with the percentage of the population aged

Table 12.5 Young-age dependency ratio (population aged 0–19 to population 20–64 years) (2010)

	Percentage	Ranking (over 808 EU cities)
Lyon	42.1	118
Manchester	42.1	119
Milan	27.4	665
Copenhagen	27.3	666
Barcelona	25.3	742
Munich	25.3	740

Source: author's elaboration from the Urban Audit database, Eurostat 2014.

0–19 compared to the population 20–64 years reaching 25 per cent (in respect of a European average of 34 per cent). Even Milan and Copenhagen are below the average level (27.3 per cent), while only Lyon and Manchester are ranked above the average level (42 per cent).

This process has been paralleled by the growth of a new urban elite that progressively has moved into the most valued areas of the urban centres. The substitution nevertheless has come about gradually and with limited social impacts. The potential disruptive effects of gentrification have been dampened by various factors, including the role played by public policies. In fact most of the substitution effects have been harmful mainly because of the mitigation policies adopted by local administrations. As better explained in the second part of the volume, these policies have taken a wide variety of forms: the introduction of measures providing economic support for house purchase; new forms of regulation of the rental market; public rent support schemes for needy families; a role attributed to non-profit organizations or housing cooperatives to enable protected house purchases or controlled forms of leasehold.

A further factor working in favour of *mitigated gentrification* has been the mixed nature of the urban territory of the cities. Gentrification in these contexts has contributed more often to the creation of new urban social mixes than to the wholesale replacement of lower-class groups by wealthy ones.

However, despite their mitigation, some effects of these processes are still problematic. First, as already pointed out, the effects on the distribution of the population across the territory are not equal. While gentrification has created privileged urban areas, it has also produced, or expanded, marginal areas that remain extraneous to the positive dynamics in progress. Second, the privatization of the public housing stock, though accompanied by public measures to support purchases by tenants, has created areas of degraded social housing in which the poorest social groups are concentrated, with high risk of social segregation. In Copenhagen, municipal housing has increasingly become a tenure for marginalized groups: from 1994 to 2002 the share of ethnic minorities in the social housing sector increased from 12 per cent to over 20 per cent, with uneven concentration of immigrants over 50 per cent in specific areas. In Barcelona, there is a high concentration of immigrants/ethnic groups in a few social housing areas (like La Mina with a high concentration of Spanish gypsies) or in deprived areas (Raval). In many cases, these spatial polarization effects have proved to be very difficult to remedy with public intervention.

12.6 Multiethnic cities

Multiethnicity may prove damaging to the social integration of the cities analysed. While on the one hand the mobility and the migration of skilled workers have increased in all the cities, on the other this seems to be at the price of the progressive marginalization of certain ethnic minorities.

In our cities two different situations have been identified. On the one hand, some cities have already experienced large immigration inflows during the 1950s and 1960s. These cities have therefore long had large ethnic populations, to a large extent constituted by second-generation immigrants born in the city: this is the case of Lyon, Munich and Manchester. In these cities, ethnic minorities represent at least 20 per cent of the overall population (up to Munich's record level of 24 per cent). On the other hand, there are the cities where immigration is a more recent phenomenon (Milan, Barcelona and in part Copenhagen), and where in recent years immigrant numbers have risen to represent between 15 per cent and 20 per cent of the population. In these cities, immigration has been very rapid, and has constituted an unprecedented phenomenon, reaching a percentage of the ethnic population close to that of the cities of older immigration within only one decade. More than the amount of immigration, therefore, it is the timing that matters. Moreover, the experiences of the cities of long-standing immigration illustrate what the trends of the cities of more recent immigration may be.

In cities where immigrants have formed a stable component for 50 years, there are persisting situations of disadvantage and discrimination in the labour market, which assume a substantially more ethno-racial nature in the case of Lyon and a socio-economic one in Manchester. In these cities, ethnic groups are more affected by unemployment and employment precariousness, and they have been the social groups most damaged by the recent economic crisis. This form of long-lasting discrimination is due both to ethnic and racial factors and the cumulative effect caused by time itself. Ethnic minorities, in fact, are subject not only to discrimination because of their ethnic identity or race, but also because of the social reproduction of economic disadvantages from generation to generation. These groups are *today* discriminated by a mixture of factors whereby ethnic identity interweaves with other factors, such as lower education levels, low skills, a strong concentration in economic sectors ethnically connoted. They therefore suffer discrimination due to ethnic membership but also to more traditional mechanisms of social reproduction of inequalities.

However, in these cities of long-standing immigration some forms of mitigation of labour-market discrimination have arisen over time, also as a result of policies implemented by city governments. Ethnic discrimination, therefore, has not necessarily been inevitable for all immigrants. For instance, in these cities the stratification by occupational category of ethnic groups has increasingly come to resemble the stratification of the native population, to indicate that stable entry into the labour market creates more equal opportunities. In the cities of long-standing immigration there has slowly formed an ethnic-minority middle class, while the concentration of ethnic groups in specific sectors of the labour market has gradually decreased. Finally – and this is the most interesting finding – striking differences among ethnic groups have emerged across generations (see Chapter 5). While some ethnic groups have been highly hit by unemployment, others have gained entry into better occupational sectors. Some ethnic groups, in specific cities, have moved into crucial professional positions operating in the global network.

More severe ethnic discrimination is instead manifest in the cities of recent immigration. Here the immigrant labour force is strongly concentrated in those low-skilled sectors (domestic services, construction, tourism, cleaning services, small trade and so on) at high risk of unemployment and precariousness. There are signs of discrimination on racial bases. In these cities, a notable discrepancy is also emerging between the education levels of numerous immigrants – which are not particularly low for some ethnic groups – and their chances of labour-market entry. The gap between education level and occupational position shows that discrimination, in the initial phases of immigration, depends both on factors inherent to the immigration process itself (such as difficulties in obtaining regularization), and on ethnicity (cultural differences, language difficulties, difficulties of social and cultural integration) as well as, in some cases, on racism (see Chapter 5).

Finally, the territorial concentration of ethnic minorities has a significant impact on their segregation in the labour market. As supposed ethnic-based or racial-based territorial segregation is not so apparent. The concentration of ethnic groups in the urban areas (considered on different territorial scales according to the city) almost never exceeds 30 per cent. This does not mean, however, that immigration has spread uniformly in the six European cities. Some effects of concentration are in fact clearly visible, which are driven by mechanisms such as house prices or migratory chains. Even though these mechanisms are not so powerful to create outright segregations, they nevertheless distribute the ethnic population across space. Moreover, on a very detailed territorial scale, some urban districts in various cities have assumed an overt ethnic character even though they are embedded in mixed urban contexts.

The scant residential concentration of ethnic groups (paralleled by their concentration on a micro scale) has therefore created mixed districts that are typical of multi-ethnic cities. The social mix has long been an explicit objective of most urban social inclusion programmes in many cities. In some examples, however, the social mix has generated, besides positive effects, also local conflicts. Milan and Lyon exhibit various foci of racial or inter-ethnical tensions. But the proximity of diverse ethnic identities has caused problems in numerous other cities as well. In these cities, in fact, multiethnicity has given rise to social boundaries on ethnic bases that have significantly hindered access to the labour market or public services by ethnic minorities. A reaction in many cities has been the growth of avoidance practices among the middle-class native population. These practices consist, for instance, in educational choices that exhibit marked ethnic discrimination and foster the reproduction over time of discrimination in the labour market.

Multiethnicity is therefore an outcome that the six European cities find difficult to achieve. Over time, they reproduce forms of discrimination that resist elimination. These European cities do not produce strong ethnic segregations, but they indubitably fuel considerable disparities on ethnic bases. The notable territorial contamination that seems characteristic of European cities does not help remove these disparities. Indeed, it often increases discrimination, provoking local conflicts or social avoidance practices.

Moreover, discrimination in the labour market receives a partial solution that often does not depend on the social mix, but rather on the mobilization of economic resources and social capital that is present within ethnic relationships. In some cases, the use of these resources facilitates the integration into the labour market – through ethnic entrepreneurship, for instance. While on the one hand ethnic entrepreneurship is a partial solution to the problem of ethnic segregation in the labour market, on the other it is a selective process that requires substantial start-up resources and involves mainly individuals with higher education levels.

12.7 Conclusions

The classic theories on urban development have always considered the city as an organized system endowed with specific forms of internal coordination and a certain degree of functional interdependence. The idea that the city is a specific form of local society has been proposed (Bagnasco and Le Galès, 2000; Le Galès 2002) to point out that the economic and social organization of the city is founded upon a variety of elements that have adjusted to each other over time. Situated within this framework is the interdependence between competitiveness and social integration on which this volume has concentrated.

That cities have since long ceased to constitute unitary local societies it is unanimously acknowledged. Unitariness and internal coherence are by now exceptional features that occur only in specific temporal phases and under very particular conditions. Predominant today are differentiation, fragmentation and the diversification of logics and interests.

On applying these general considerations in the more circumscribed field of analysis addressed by this volume, it can be concluded that the global European cities that we studied have generally exhibited a pattern of weak internal coherence and a modest ability to confine economic logics within a socially acceptable framework. In these cities incongruity and fragmentation seem largely to increasingly prevail over the capacity to organize and coordinate urban development. Although they belong to diversified systems of welfare capitalism, all the cities analysed exhibit a certain degree of entropy and a lack of coordination.

This lack of organization may indicate that the economic growth of these cities, before the economic crisis, came about on parameters increasingly less dependent on the social quality of places. If globalization requires the high mobility of capital, commodities and people, it may be concluded that our analysis has shown that this view of globalization (Friedman, 2005) has also gained ground in traditional Europe.

While the purpose of this study has been to determine the links between social integration and competitiveness in six European cities, the conclusion to be drawn is that today social integration and economic competitiveness are two distinct dimensions, and that greater competitiveness does not lead to greater social well-being or to better chances of social mobility for the most disadvantaged social groups.

To sum up, the European cities that we have considered emerge as urban systems characterized by tensions that reduce their internal coherence. The nodal economic function performed by these cities is juxtaposed with others, and it develops independently from the interests of the social actors embedded in the local setting. Success as a global node does not depend, except for some functional aspects, on the quality of the local social system.

Nevertheless, some coordination functions, even if they are not decisive for their nodal activities, are still important. These cities represent the functional platform of resources, spaces and capacities on which global players draw in their competitive strategies. But at the same time, these cities must organize their internal flows, create linkages among different economic actors, and reconcile the dominant exogenous interests and the multiple local ones. Also social and territorial inequalities, to the extent that they are deeply rooted and radicalized, require the development of urban policies aimed at softening the trends towards polarization. With respect to the functions connected with the activities of a global node, these maintenance and coordination activities may seem weak. But they are crucial not only for social integration but also for the maintenance of internal consensus. Alongside the nodal activities situated in the space of flows, in fact, there still survive localized economic activities absorbed in the space of places (Castells, 1996). Even if the six European cities are constructed on these two different spaces, the logics that are inherent to these spaces require ad hoc policies. Sometimes the two functions may act in synergy, when investment in the global competitiveness of the city helps to improve also the living standards of the urban population. It is sometimes social integration policies that are economic investments by spurring the start-up of new businesses and improving the international attractiveness of cities.

The connection between competitiveness and social integration has been addressed in various ways by urban policies. In fact, there are still some urban policies oriented to protect the middle class or to create new opportunities for the most vulnerable population. However, this requires not only a high capacity for resources mobilization and coordination, but also a systemic vision that is able to see interdependence where neither the dominant economic interests nor local ones are interested or able to perceive it. This is a difficult task, in the accomplishment of which the cities analysed in this research differ greatly in their performances. Not all the cities, in fact, are endowed with similar capacity. The futures of the heterogeneous communities that live and work in these cities will depend greatly on this strategic capacity.

References

Ache, P., Anderson, H. T., Maloutas, T., Raco, M. and Tasan-Kok, T. (eds) (2008). *Cities between Competitiveness and Cohesion*, New York: Springer.

Amin, A. and Thrift, N. (2002). *Cities: Reimagining the Urban*, Cambridge: Polity Press.

Bagnasco, A. and Le Galès, P. (eds) (2000). *Cities in Contemporary Europe*, Cambridge: Cambridge University Press.

Buck, N., Gordon, I., Harding A. and Turok, I. (eds) (2005). *Changing Cities: Rethinking Urban Competitiveness, Cohesion and Governance*, New York: Palgrave.

Castells, M. (1996). *The Rise of the Network Society, the Information Age: Economy, Society and Culture Volume I*, Cambridge, MA: Blackwell.

D'Ovidio, M. and Ranci, C. (2014). Social Cohesion and Global Competitiveness: Clustering Cities. In: Ranci, C., Brandsen, T. and Sabatinelli, S. (eds). *Social Vulnerability in European Cities: The Role of Local Welfare in Times of Crisis*, London: Palgrave Macmillan, pp. 31–63.

Friedman, T. L. (2005). *The World is Flat: A Brief History of the Twenty-first Century*. New York: Farrar, Straus and Giroux.

Hamnett, C. (2003). Gentrification and the Middle-class Remaking of Inner London, 1961–2001. *Urban Studies*, 40(12): 2401–2426.

Häussermann, H. (2005). The End of the European City? *European Review*, 13(2): 237–249.

Häussermann, H. and Haila, A. (2005). The European City: A Conceptual Framework and Normative Project. In: Kazepov, Y. (ed.). *Changing Contexts, Local Arrangements, and the Challenge to Urban Cohesion*, Malden, MA: Blackwell, pp. 43–63.

Kazepov, Y. (ed.) (2005). *Cities of Europe: Changing Contexts, Local Arrangements, and the Challenge of Urban Cohesion*, Malden, MA: Blackwell.

Le Galès, P. (2002). *European Cities: Social Conflicts and Governance*, Oxford: Oxford University Press.

Letho, J. (2000). Different Cities in Different Welfare States. In: Bagnasco, A. and Le Galès, P. (eds). *Cities in Contemporary Europe*, Cambridge: Cambridge University Press, pp. 112–113.

Musterd, S. and Murie, A. (2010). *Making Competitive Cities*, Oxford: Wiley-Blackwell.

Novy, A., Coimbra Swiatek, D. and Moulaert, F. (2012). Social Cohesion: a Conceptual and Political Elucidation. *Urban Studies*, 49: 1873–1889.

Préteceille, E. (2000). Segregation, Class and Politics in Large Cities. In: Bagnasco, A. and Le Galès, P. (eds). *Cities in Contemporary Europe*, Cambridge: Cambridge University Press.

Ranci, C. (2011). Competitiveness and Social Cohesion in Western European Cities. *Urban Studies*, 48(13): 2789–2804.

Turok, I. (2005). Cities, Competition and Competitiveness: Identifying New Connections. In: Buck, N., Gordon, I., Harding, A. and Turok, I. (eds). *Changing Cities: Rethinking Urban Competitiveness, Cohesion and Governance*, New York: Palgrave, pp. 25–43.

13 Conclusions
Life and death of the "European city"?

Costanzo Ranci and Roberta Cucca

13.1 Introduction

Scholarly research of current trends occurring in European cities has been mainly influenced by different and often conflicting interpretations, in spite of the general lack of comparative analysis providing empirical evidence for such theories. This volume contributes to fill this gap by providing a comparative analysis of the social and policy trends occurring in six big European cities belonging to different welfare regimes. Though some geographical limits and analytical restrictions (Robinson 2011), the empirical elements obtained in this research are useful to provide a more general interpretation of current trends. In this concluding chapter, we discuss our results in respect of more general theories about the fate of the so-called "European city model" (MacLeod *et al.* 2003; Sapir 2006).

This discussion has been mainly shaped by two different theoretical approaches: (a) a structural neo-Marxist approach, which considers economic dynamics as the most relevant driver of change and sees a neo-liberal turn in contemporary cities as functional to the post-industrial and global restructuring of capitalist society (Peck and Tickell 2002; Brenner 2004; Brenner *et al.* 2010); (b) a neo-Weberian approach highlighting the great capacity of European cities to govern social and economic transformations and combine strategies to promote competitiveness with consideration for locally-based, collective interests (Bagnasco and Le Galès 2000; Le Galès 2002).

In spite of their different theoretical assumptions, both approaches have actually converged empirically, acknowledging the continuous rise of socioeconomic inequalities and socio-spatial segregation in European cities (Tammaru *et al.* 2015) and the growth of urban policies explicitly aimed at promoting the cities' attractiveness and global competitiveness (Camagni 2002)

The recent crisis that started in 2007 has operated as a "stress test" in this context (Hemerijck 2012). Squeezed between reduced state financial support and increasing social needs (mainly due to higher unemployment), cities have had to innovate their policy initiative in order to reduce the gap between emerging problems and financial constraints. Their capacity to close/reduce this gap could be interpreted as a measure of the actual resilience (Fainstein 2015) of the "European city model".

If scholars basically agree on the current trends occurring in European cities (see Chapter 12), still controversial is the general interpretation of such trends and the role played by urban policy in this respect (van Kempen 2007; Scott 2008). Do rising inequalities show a substantial "Americanisation" of the European city (Häußermann 2005)? Should we explain this trend as being due to the supremacy of global players over local and urban ones? Is there still room for European cities to develop their own policy agenda leaning to address local and urban interests or mitigate emerging risks? Or do these facts disclose the weakening capacity of European urban cities to govern the huge social and economic transformation occurring in the last decades?

Our study is positioned within such broader theoretical context. Indeed, current trends can be interpreted as a critical rupture in the functional and programmatic link between competitiveness and social integration (Pahl 2001), which is one of the main features of the "European city model" (see Chapter 1). Alternatively, trends can be understood as challenges that put the European city model under strong pressure, requiring systemic adaptation and resilience capacity (Maloutas and Pantelidou Malouta 2004; Matznetter and Musil 2012).

Two aspects of the "European city model" are especially challenged by concomitant trends towards stronger austerity policy and increasing social pressure due to the rise of unmet social needs: (a) the capacity of state intervention to provide the regulatory framework and financial resources necessary to support place-based economic growth and welfare policies (Andreotti *et al.* 2012; Ranci *et al.* 2014) through institutional multi-level coordination (Kazepov 2010); (b) the capacity of urban governments to elaborate local policy strategies aimed at mediating market logics and the pursuit of public interest (Van Kempen and Murie, 2009; Body-Gendrot *et al.* 2012).

In this concluding chapter, we will consider these two aspects as crucial criteria to evaluate the resilience vs. rupture of the "European city model" thesis on the basis of our previous analysis. We will analyse the peculiarity of the state–city relationship on the one hand, and the capacity for cities' policy action on the other. Our general hypothesis is that a progressive dissociation between social protection and pro-growth policies has occurred in European cities. As the competitiveness–social integration nexus is one of the most important peculiarities of the "European city model", an analysis of such dissociation will eventually show the extent to which European cities have differently distanced themselves from this original pattern, which has been considered as unitary and largely encompassing different social welfare regimes.

13.2 The crucial role of nation states in shaping urban policy

Nation states have greatly contributed towards shaping European cities through a number of nation-wide, inter-scalar policies (Van Kempen and Murie 2009; Kazepov 2010). In the 1980s and 1990s (with different timing among countries) the overwhelming regulatory role played by the state in many European countries has weakened as a consequence of welfare retrenchment strategies, progressive decentralisation of responsibility, liberalisation and privatisation policies (Brenner and Theodore 2002, Brenner 2004). National policies aimed at preserving or promoting territorial equity have been increasingly replaced by selective state place-based intervention aimed at fostering the competitiveness of specific targeted cities (Brenner 2004; Crouch and Le Galès 2012). New inter-scalar arrangements have been therefore developed within a more selective entrepreneurial strategy (Jessop and Sum 2000). At the same, responsibilities for social cohesion and spatial equity have been progressively decentralised and jointly managed by central, regional and local intervention (Brenner 2004).

According to some authors, leading European cities have not decreased their autonomy and capacity for collective action in this new scenario (Le Galès 1998; Borraz and Le Galès 2010; Crouch and Le Galès 2012). Nation states have become more selective in their support and have increasingly concentrated their financial and political efforts in the most competitive and globalised cities, contributing to rising spatial and social inequality but also to foster the resurgence of many European cities during the 1990s and the early 2000s (Scott 2008). On the other hand, welfare state retrenchment has not been so extensively achieved across Europe due to policy resistance by welfare-state stakeholders and the strong stickiness of welfare public institutions (Pierson 2001). In the end, the state seems to have played a relevant role in supporting the resilience of the "European city model" even in more constraining structural and institutional circumstances.

Nevertheless, some authors have found an increasing differentiation between cities as a consequence of the new inter-scalar setting and economic restructuring of post-industrial capitalism (Van Kempen and Murie 2009). Reduced state intervention, combined with increasing economic globalisation, have paved the way not only for increased territorial inequality, but also for higher localism and place-based path dependency. Local traditions have emerged as a source not only of home-grown activism but also of increasing differentiation among localities and local policy orientations. As a result, European cities have become more divided than before (ibid.). At the same time, the significance of different welfare regimes across Europe has become even more relevant for cities affected by rising inequality and lower central funding. According to Van Kempen and Murie, cities embedded within weak welfare regimes moved forward as an "American city", while cities embedded within strong welfare states were able to maintain their own identity as a "European city". In this perspective, therefore, state retrenchment and downward rescaling of social welfare have paradoxically reinforced the multi-scalar interdependence between cities and nation states, since cities have simultaneously become less dependent on central funding, more responsible for social cohesion and local competitiveness, but also more constrained by tighter national austerity rules.

In this context, multi-level institutional governance (MLIG) settings are found in our research to be highly differentiated across Europe. Following Kazepov (2010) and Barberis *et al.* (2010) we can identify two main dimensions characterising MLIG: (a) *political and legal vertical regulation*, which is related to the extent to which urban policy is subjected to central regulation through specific laws or direct political decisions; (b) *financial dependence on the state*, which is related to the level and amount of local public funding that is provided by the state, and/or the degree of central limitation in sub-national financing and/or expenditures.

As far as the first dimension is concerned, the range of situations found in our research goes from cities where urban policy is embedded within strong and over-encompassing state constraints (Copenhagen, Lyon, Manchester) to cities where regulation and decision-making are more decentralised, devolving strong regulatory power to regional (Barcelona, Munich) or urban (Milan) governments. In the last decade, institutional decentralisation has taken place in Lyon and Manchester. According to Kazepov (2010), downward rescaling of competencies to local and regional authorities in the European context are better understood as "subsidiarisation", a process by which a central authority performs only tasks that cannot be performed effectively at a more immediate or local level.

The second dimension is related to different degrees of centralisation–decentralisation in the financial relations among territorial levels. Starting from the 1970s and 1980s (though with different timing across Europe) reforms increased the overall financial autonomy of sub-national governments in all continental countries: a trend that was understood as part of a neo-liberalisation process (Keating 1998). In countries previously characterised by higher financial decentralisation, such as Scandinavian countries and the United Kingdom, a strong fiscal re-centralisation took place at the same time. However, the implicit convergence in the level of state financing responsibility has been contrasted by the persistence of huge differences in the multi-level financial relationships across Europe. In generous and extended welfare regimes (in universalistic and continental regimes, using the Esping-Andersen typology), urban policies have been strongly fostered by large amounts of central funding, while in more residual welfare regimes (in liberal and South-European regimes) local governments face lower state financial support. More generally, however, and different to widespread opinion that cities in Europe have gained a great degree of autonomy in respect of state financing, evidence shows that central funding is still the main source of finance for place-based social cohesion policy carried out in all Western European countries (Kazepov 2005).

Combining the two criteria discussed above, Table 13.1 identifies four peculiar MLIG settings within which specific urban policies have developed in the six cities examined in our study:

- An *active subsidiarity setting* is characterised by large local and regional autonomy in setting urban policy rules and goals with strong state financial support. Locally-based programmes get funding from central programmes with ample room for setting specific goals and methodology, and with high involvement of local stakeholders in the planning activity. Within a subsidiarity system, therefore, local stakeholders enjoy generous, and not highly restrictive, support from the state. Munich represents the city-case closer to this type: most urban programmes (such as *Munich Perspective*, a strategic master plan established in 1997) have been implemented by the municipality with strong cooperation at the city-region scale and generous funding provided by national state programmes. In such cases, the German government's strong orientation to invest in place-based competitiveness by supporting high value-added programmes in attractive urban areas (Mazzucato 2015) has successfully matched with the vision and strategic capacity of the city government. Moreover, Germany's federalist structure has strongly helped to coordinate local, regional and national efforts.

- A *passive subsidiarity model* is characterised by high local governing autonomy, eventually reinforced by a national federalist institutional structure, but very poor financial support by the state. In this situation, central constraints are very limited since the responsibility for urban competitiveness, welfare protection and social integration is basically devolved to local and/ or regional levels. As opposed to the previous situation, central funding and financial decentralisation are very limited. The result is that urban policy heavily depends on the capacity of local governments to carry out large-scale planning relying on locally-funded or European programmes. This is the case for Barcelona and Milan. Even though these cities are embedded in very diverse institutional settings (Spain is a federalist state while Italy has historically been a highly centralised country), they both reflect, in different ways, a situation characterised by high autonomy and very limited development of social welfare policy at the national level. In Italy, a constitutional law introduced in 2001 shifted regulatory and financial responsibilities for housing, employment and social services away from the state. The result was very poor development of such policies on an urban scale, as shown in Milan's case. Moreover, weak inter-institutional cooperation and lack of strong political vision at the urban scale together with lack of available financial resources, have driven urban policy towards a classic managerial model rather than to a more innovative "entrepreneurial city" model (see Chapter 10). On the other hand, in Barcelona, a strong long-standing cooperation between regional and local governments has paved the way for the success of the so-called "Barcelona model" (see Chapter 6). In this case, weak state financial support has for a long time been supplemented by a strong urban governance system, with high integration of social and political forces and local institutions. High local institutional coordination has made an intensive strategic planning activity and frequent use of public–private partnership possible. The economic crisis has, however, shown how weak the Barcelona model's financial basis was, opening the way to a deep political and social change. To sum up, the high differentiation in these cities' trajectories shows that the passive subsidiarity model can be only partially, and temporally, supplemented by urban activism and the capacity of local policymakers to build horizontal, place-based coalitions.
- *Constrained localism*: this setting is characterised by highly-centralised regulatory power but weak financial support from the central state. Cities embedded in this MLIG setting deal with strict financial and sectorial regulation on

the one hand, and relatively scarce funding on the other: a difficult situation, which, in the case of Manchester, has solicited a closer cooperation among municipalities within the same metropolitan area in order to provide supplementary place-based programmes addressing specific local needs. Manchester is closer to this type as a consequence of the strong financial re-centralisation that occurred in the United Kingdom in the 1980s and 1990s, coinciding with the abolition of the Greater Manchester Council in 1986. In this city more than 70 per cent of total funding came from central government, with local councils funded by a combination of central government grants. Despite this regulatory and fiscal centralism, Manchester has garnered significant attention for the way in which it has sought to work across the administrative boundaries of the conurbation to build partnerships for tackling key economic and social challenges through horizontal and vertical alliances with other public and private bodies and higher levels of government (Gordon *et al.* 2012). In spite of these efforts, the structural situation that is distinctive of a "constrained localism" setting explains why the huge economic growth experienced by the city in the last decade has come together with a general poor capacity by the local government to address its large territorial and social disparities.

- *Place-based urban entrepreneurialism*: this setting is characterised by strong central interventionism combined with generous financing. In this case local governments have a limited functional and institutional autonomy and hugely depend on state interventionism. Lyon and Copenhagen experience a similar situation, by which they received huge state funding aimed at promoting the development of internationally competitive, highly-specialised, locally-based economic functions. In Lyon, state economic investment has come with partial decentralisation of public responsibility for planning, housing and local initiatives. Moreover, a relevant aggregation of local authorities in an inter-communal body, the *Grand Lyon*, has been developed to deal with large-scale tasks (such as mobility). This has paved the way for the creation of master plans on a large scale, and of a local housing programme (Programme local de l'habitat) at an inter-municipal scale. In Copenhagen, since the 1980s the Danish state has strongly enforced the adoption of a local neo-liberal agenda to reverse the city's serious financial condition, and focused the intervention on economic development and the support of private initiatives. On the other hand, while the generous Scandinavian welfare state provided the poorest population with a large range of public social services and social benefits, local housing programmes and planning activity have been severely blocked by state constraints. In these cities, therefore, urban governments have had little room for autonomy but have enjoyed the generous support of nationally-framed interventionist policy aimed at fostering place-based competitiveness and attractiveness. However, the turn towards "state entrepreneurialism", if this was a crucial lever for urban development in both these cities, has also meant an important shortage of policies effectively addressing new locally emerging social needs.

Table 13.1 A typology of multi-level institutional governance settings

Degree of funding centralisation	Degree of regulatory power concentration	
	Low	*High*
Low	Passive subsidiarity (Barcelona, Milan)	Constrained localism (Manchester)
High	Active subsidiarity (Munich)	Place-based state entrepreneurialism (Copenhagen, Lyon)

Source: authors' elaboration.

The typology presented here shows that multi-level institutional settings have been highly differentiated across Western Europe. General assertions about the capacity of European cities to act as "collective actors" or about their role as mere "transmission belts" of centrally/globally-framed entrepreneurial strategies run the risk of greatly over-simplifying actual facts. Even in very rich, globalised cities, urban policy is embedded within highly-differentiated and complex institutional contexts, where the capacity for urban government action is limited by central regulatory or functional constraints. On the other hand, central state support is crucial in fostering complex and innovative urban policy strategies, while extended local and regional autonomy without state support is hugely vulnerable to changes in local favourable conditions.

13.3 Shifts in state–city relationships due to the crisis and the new urban policy trilemma

Since 2007 onwards, MLIG arrangements had been under strong pressure due to the financial crisis, paving the way for new configurations (see Table 13.2). On the one side, austerity policies caused severe cuts in local policy national funding in a number of countries. Local welfare programmes were placed under stricter control by national governments, which imposed budget caps or stricter balance between local tax revenues and expenditures. Austerity contributed to retrenchment and the privatisation of welfare state programmes. In this context, MLIG settings faced a general reduction in state support and a progressive shift of policy responsibility from central to local authorities. Cities, though to a different extent, increasingly managed social programmes and pro-growth strategies autonomously while simultaneously relying on reduced financial resources and less discretionary power (Kearns and Forrest 2000). Austerity policy and economic recession, therefore, jointly acted as a stress test, challenging the capacity for positive action and strategic planning of cities (see Table 13.2).

In this context, only Munich and to a lesser extent Copenhagen did not suffer a big deterioration in respect of the previous situation. A significant reason was that both Denmark and Germany recovered quickly from the crisis, and in 2009 already showed positive trends in GDP and employment. In Munich, the large institutional and financial autonomy of the city-region allowed a higher economic and demographic growth than that which occurred in other German cities, consolidating the economic supremacy of this city in the country. In Copenhagen, the strong state control over city policy was not basically altered.

In all the other cities examined, the crisis had stronger effects and contributed towards modifying the previous multi-level institutional setting. In Lyon, fiscal austerity decreased state interventionism and direct support of local programmes, and enhanced the previous trend towards the decentralisation of responsibility for urban planning, social housing and social integration. During the crisis, the city had to deal with increasing social demand, lower financial resources, and increased responsibility to carry out a direct response to social problems simultaneously: a hard-to-solve trilemma showing how much local policy was still dependent on state support.

Southern Europe cities – Barcelona and Milan – experienced the most dramatic change. Harsh austerity policy, mainly inflicted by the European Union, drove local authorities to heavy cutting and targeting of social expenditures. Reduction in welfare state programmes and economic recession caused a large increase in unemployment and poverty rates. In the absence of adequate nationwide minimum income protection, local authorities were unable to effectively curb the increase in inequalities and poverty risk and lost political legitimacy. In both cities, strong budgetary control by the state imposed strict caps both on expenditure and local taxation. While responsibility for social integration and economic development remained in the hands of local authorities, the crisis drastically diminished the fiscal and financial autonomy of the cities, driving them into a regime of strongly-centralised budgetary control. From a passive subsidiarity system Barcelona and Milan shifted towards a new "austerity localism", in which strong financial constraints by the state drastically limit the chance of local government to carry out long-term strategies. It was, therefore, not accidental that both Barcelona and Milan faced, after a prolonged phase of political stability, a huge political turn at the onset of the crisis, even though in opposite directions.

Finally, Manchester showed a similar path. The limits of its "constrained localism setting" became very clear in austerity times. While in the late 1990s and early 2000s Manchester was able to foster impressive economic growth thanks to state investments and a very active local governance system, austerity programmes imposed by central government inflicted huge cuts in urban programmes as well as the closure of local flagship social programmes. Strong financial dependency on central funding and limited political autonomy conspired to strengthen the limits of a system where localism was not supported by adequate state financing.

To conclude, in all the cities analysed, state–city relationships were characterised by high functional and institutional interdependence. Functional state–local interdependence and vertical multi-level coordination were the keys for the development of active, effective urban policies. Cities could effectively operate as

Table 13.2 Changes in different MLIG settings due to the financial crisis and austerity measures

	Financial relationships	*Vertical coordination*
Active subsidiarity (Munich)	Temporary austerity measures by the state	No relevant changes; state provided new forms of social protection against the crisis
Passive subsidiarity (Barcelona, Milan)	Heavy cuts in national programmes due to austerity measures; reduction in state financing of local programmes	Stronger restrictions to the fiscal and financial autonomy of local and regional governments
Constrained localism (Manchester)	Heavy cuts in national programmes due to austerity measures; reduction in state financing of local programmes	No changes in the regulatory setting preventing local government from taking initiatives
Place-based state entrepreneurialism (Copenhagen, Lyon)	France: cuts in national programmes due to austerity; lower financial support to local programmes	France: decentralisation of responsibility to local governments
	Denmark: temporary austerity measures by the state	Denmark: no relevant changes

Source: authors' elaboration.

collective actors only within this multi-level institutional setting. Decentralisation of regulatory powers without full, persistent financial support from the central state, limited the capacity of cities to carry out long-term, coherent strategies.

The observation of our case studies shows that optimally-balanced state–city interdependence is very rare and only temporary: cities are embedded within hugely different institutional configurations. In crisis times, such configurations often contributed to increase the cities' financial difficulties and to lower their capacity of direct action. The "stress test" experienced by cities has, therefore, revealed how vulnerable the institutional arrangements on which their economic success was previously based have often been. The crisis has caused a triple move towards: further downward rescaling of public responsibility, loss of central financial support, and harsher central budgetary control. In the next section, we will see how cities have acted in this complex, turbulent trilemmatic situation.

13.4 Urban policies fostering competitiveness and protecting employment

13.4.1 Policies towards competitiveness

The cities analysed in this study have shown great economic performance in their capacity to generate and intercept global flows of capital and people (see Chapters 2 and 3). Barcelona, Copenhagen, Milan and Munich are the major global nodes and the richest cities in their respective countries, while Lyon and Manchester represent the greatest second cities in their countries, after London and Paris respectively. The economic success of such cities depends on a number of factors, on which urban policy has played an important role in connection with national intervention (Turok 2004). However, the extent to which urban policies aimed at improving competitiveness have been able to also care about social integration is disputable.

Economic trends in these cities had been mainly positive from 2000 (first year for which data are available) until the 2007 crisis. In terms of GDP per capita, all cities showed a great positive trend, with some beneficial impact on labour market participation (see Table 13.3). Contrary to the auspices of the Lisbon strategy, however, income inequalities also grew, mainly as a consequence of the high increase in temporary, low-paid jobs (see Chapter 2). In all the cities, GDP growth was higher than the increase in employment rates, with the only exception being Milan.

This positive economic trend was completely reversed by the financial crisis. In 2008–2009, GDP per capita values suddenly collapsed in all the cities, and recovered only in some of them. In Munich the after-crisis growth rate was even higher than the previous one, while in all the other cities the GDP performance was negative in the 2008–2014 time span. Trends in the employment rate reflected the GDP performance, with Munich showing a positive trend, and Lyon and Manchester in a steady situation (close to zero); Copenhagen, Barcelona and Milan faced a strong decrease in labour market participation. In short, while in the first part of the 2000s there was a convergence in the cities' economic performance (with Barcelona and Milan showing the highest growth in employment), the crisis has increased the gap among cities with positive development, cities in a steady situation, and cities with a dramatic, negative trend.

How have cities reacted in this shifting scenario? In general, while most of the responsibility for employment protection was held by national or regional governments, cities were more active in supporting their own local economic development and attractiveness.

Table 13.3 Yearly variations in GDP per capita (current price 2015) and employment rates, before and after the crisis

	GDP per capita		Employment rate	
	2001–2007	*2008–2013*	*2001–2007*	*2008–2014*
Copenhagen	2.6	−0.5	n.a.	−0.9
Munich	0.4	0.9	0.1	0.8
Barcelona	2.4	−3.1	1.4	−1.7
Lyon	1.8	−0.6	0.2	0.2
Milan	0.6	−2.1	1.1	−0.4
Manchester	0.9	−2.0	−0.3	0.1

Source: Eurostat Urban Audit online database.

This goal was achieved by adopting two different strategies. In Lyon and Munich (and in Copenhagen to some extent), urban policies have channelled public and private investments to specific areas of the city, linking economic development with territorial planning in the attempt to concentrate economic innovation in strategic areas. Economic development has, therefore, been used as a driver for the requalification of suburban, de-industrialised, or deprived areas, by promoting infrastructural and ad hoc training, and giving incentives to private companies localising their business in such areas. While in Lyon innovative sectors (such as biotech and clean-tech) have been supported through the institution of *pôles de competitivité* aimed at fostering publicly-financed cooperation between local universities and private companies (see Chapter 8), in Munich the main strategy was the promotion of the "Munchen Mix", an action aimed at fostering several local poles of economic development with strong positive effects on the diversity and flexibility of the local labour market (see Chapter 11).

In the other cities, the dominant approach was shaped by the liberal idea that public funding should not alter market dynamics. Urban policy was, therefore, limited to providing incentives to specific sectorial, highly competitive, companies without any steering capacity. In Milan, for example, urban policy was limited to providing some globally-integrated sectors (such as design, fashion, bio-technologies, high-quality medical services and research) with financial incentives (see Chapter 10). The main investments were focused on huge real estate developments that were supposed to increase the city's attractiveness, while only a few interventions addressing the economic development of deprived areas were launched thanks to state funding. After the big political turn in 2011, a partial re-orientation of the city's policy is found, based on the new goal to offer infrastructures for innovative start-ups and spin-offs. In Barcelona, local public investment was aimed at promoting the region's international attraction through support to touristic activities and innovative clusters, but all these actions were disrupted with the financial crisis. Finally, the efforts to regenerate Manchester after the previous difficult de-industrialisation phase were focused on attracting mobile capital and labour into the knowledge-intensive and high-value service sector. Today, Manchester is a city where financing and support activities, such as banks, insurance companies, law firms, labour supply companies and accounting agencies, are the main engines of the local economy.

To sum up, all the cities made relevant efforts to sustain their competitiveness and attractiveness through financial support to the most competitive and globalised economic sectors. The distinctive productive specialisation of the cities was therefore promoted and supported through injections of public money. This action, largely developed in the 1990s and early 2000s, paved the way for a crucial diversification in the productive structures of our cities (see Chapter 2). While Copenhagen, Lyon, Manchester and Munich followed a "high way" to international competitiveness by fostering sectors characterised by high productivity and capacity for innovation, Barcelona and Milan ran the "low way" to competitiveness and invested in low-productivity sectors, such as tourism and constructions, which gave immediate economic returns due to low labour costs, but with less chance for innovation and technological development.

13.4.2   *The protection of the unemployed in times of crisis*

Since the onset of the financial crisis, cities faced increasing occupational and poverty problems. Here, the specificity of state–city relationships played a relevant role in explaining our cities' different capacity of reaction. Generally speaking, unemployment protection has been a traditional field for direct state intervention, while cities have played a complementary role in providing active labour market services. This division of labour, however, has been differently shaped in different MLIG settings, paving the way for a different role played by urban policy.

To synthesise these distinctions, cities were identified in different situations according to two criteria: (a) whether the national state provided (or not) a generous protection against the risk of unemployment reinforced by a substantial active labour market policy; (b) whether local urban policy was significantly active in this field (see Table 13.4).

Some cities have enjoyed strong state intervention aimed at protecting the unemployed and/or promoting activation measures. Copenhagen represents the clearest example of a state-led strategy towards employment protection, which left little room for local intervention addressing the needs of low-skilled workers and migrants. Lyon basically followed the same pattern: no employment policies were introduced at the local level as most of the responsibility was retained by the state. As a consequence, with the sole exception of urban policies at the city scale, they were unable to contrast the increasing dualisation of the labour market (see Chapter 2). Only in Munich, were state social programmes providing unemployment protection complemented by local intervention addressing low-qualified workers. Within the "Munich employment and qualification programme", for example, special programmes for young people were launched to reduce long-term unemployment, to provide care–work balance and apprenticeship for young unemployed, and to support ethnic businesses. To sum up, while a state-led strategy aimed to comply with unemployment emerged in Copenhagen and Lyon with very limited local intervention, in Munich a more complementary strategy was carried out by which the needs of specific groups of workers were met through place-based special programmes.

In the other three cities considered here, national states developed less generous forms of unemployment protection. In Italy, until 2015, national social programmes providing unemployment protection only covered workers employed in medium to large firms. A residual emergency programme was introduced during the crisis covering temporary unemployment of workers employed in small firms. In Spain, national unemployment benefits were very modest and did not adequately protect the unemployed from the risk of poverty. In the United Kingdom, unemployment protection is traditionally a residual programme covering the needs of poor workers only. This fact partially explains why these cities were so hugely affected by the crisis and did not show any recovery in employment rates after 5–6 years from the onset of the economic depression. In this situation, urban policy played a minor role in Manchester and in Milan, while it was relevant in the case of Barcelona.

In Manchester, a "city deal" agreement was signed between the Greater Manchester Association and the government to promote a skill-learning programme, including a specific Apprenticeship Guarantee addressing the issue of NEETs. However, only a very small number of young people were involved. Apart from this example, the local policy agenda was basically focused on high-skilled jobs, and this fact increased the risk of labour market exclusion for those at the bottom (see Chapter 9). In Milan, no specific local programmes addressed unemployment problems since the onset of the crisis. The lack of public intervention was only supplemented by the new activism of traditional social forces (the Church and local trade unions.).

Only Barcelona had started a specific urban policy addressing the huge increase in unemployment for some years and lately almost removed. In the first phase of the crisis, a local pact ("Barcelona Activa") focusing on the "quality of employment" was signed between the local administration, local trade unions and entrepreneurial organisations. This programme included measures to attract creative and innovative talent, to include drop-outs and people affected by the reconversion of sectors in difficulties, to start up new activation policies including training programmes and itineraries of personalised insertion. With the crisis, however, the city's public budget was drastically reduced and severe cuts were introduced in employment policy. The big political turn that occurred in 2011 put an end to *Barcelona Activa*, while a new liberal approach by the city's new government was introduced, focusing on subsidising part of the costs of hiring unemployed workers for a short-term period.

To conclude, policies aimed at strengthening the competitiveness of cities were mainly characterised by a neo-liberal approach, based on the distribution of public economic incentives to competitive firms and/or sectors, and scarce attention paid to dynamics in the labour market. Manchester and Milan (and Barcelona after the

Table 13.4 Different employment protection models

Urban policy to stabilise the local labour market	State unemployment protection and active labour market policy: degree of generosity	
	Low	*High*
Weak	Local residual/state dualistic policy (Manchester, Milan)	State-led centralisation (Copenhagen, Lyon)
Strong	Local activism substituting poor state intervention (Barcelona)	Complementary intervention (Munich)

Source: authors' elaboration.

political turn of 2011) were the most significant examples of such an approach. In Copenhagen and Lyon, the neo-liberal approach adopted at the city level was complemented by generous social protection offered by the national welfare state which, in both Denmark and France, retained most of the responsibility in unemployment protection. The consequence was the creation of a dual system, where local public incentives for the most competitive sectors were combined with state assistance provided to workers excluded from the labour market. Further attempts were made to break such dualism by promoting activation programmes addressing low-skilled workers and specific categories of unemployed people, especially in Copenhagen.

In Barcelona, urban policy played a more active role, but it was mainly cancelled by the municipality's fiscal crisis and the political turn towards a liberal approach that occurred in 2011. Local activism in the lack of state funding and central responsibility showed to be highly vulnerable to changes in the local economic and/or the political scenario.

Only Munich was able to develop a locally-based programme of protection complementing national unemployment benefits in the search for a new compromise between local pro-competitiveness policies and initiatives supporting higher participation in the labour market. In Munich, the policy solution found was based on a "social investment strategy" (Hemerijck 2012), in which social expenditures in training and childcare services were seen as public investments generating future returns in terms of higher participation to the labour market and higher labour productivity.

Policies specifically addressing the issue of "good employment" must be understood within this broader scenario. To summarise our results, cities did not develop specific responsibilities in employment policies and labour market regulation while they were very active in promoting their economic competitiveness. In some cities, however, policies aimed to support the employability of the weakest labour force, to re-qualify low-skilled workers, or to foster new entrepreneurship initiatives, were developed with different results. This is the case of Barcelona (for a limited time) and especially Munich. In other cities, employment policies were simply not activated because of the lack of institutional competencies and resources (as in the cases of Copenhagen and Lyon) or because the dominant neo-liberal orientation of the political elite was not considering this as a priority (as in the case of Manchester and Milan).

13.5 Urban policies addressing housing unaffordability

Housing affordability problems have been emerging in the last years in all cities, mainly as a consequence of a re-commodification process[1] in housing taking place in most European countries over the last three decades (Doling 1999; Aalbers 2013). Since the 1970s, home-ownership became largely accessible to the majority of households, finance started to be liberalised and governments began to reduce direct housing supply in the face of the need to reduce public expenditure (Turner and Whitehead 1993). The pressures to redirect public resources were found even in those countries with a tradition of social rented housing. In many places this led to large-scale shifts away from public owner- ship and funding as well as to greater targeting of both people's needs and local areas. The next decade was, therefore, a period of rapid change in the organisa- tion of social housing, both in the demographics of its residents and in the scale of provision.

This process of re-commodification of housing has gradually reduced housing affordability, reinforced by the residential sector's increasing costs and the intensi- fication of economic vulnerability of a large share of the population due to the crisis (Ranci *et al.* 2014). Gradually, increasing difficulty towards paying housing costs have not only affected the poorest population groups, but also a relevant part of the middle class, including families with children, pensioners, and youths in transition towards adulthood. Finally, the crisis has especially reduced the afford- ability capacity of the most vulnerable groups, while opening new windows for profitable investment and increasing inequalities between landlords and renters.

These trends have been established, even in our cities, as a partial result of the policies developed at the local level. In fact, programmes fostering urban requalification and real estate investment in the attempt to support the city's eco- nomic competitiveness, have indirectly contributed to the contraction of the rental sector. While in some cities (Manchester, Copenhagen, Barcelona) the percentage of home-ownership has decreased as a result of increasing difficulties in accessing mortgages schemes, the affordability of the rental sector has become critical in all cities, promoting an acute crisis in the housing sector, and increas- ing evictions as well as social exclusion. More severe impacts have been experi- enced in cities (such as Barcelona and Milan) where the size of the public–social housing sector was very small and there was less chance to accommodate the households that were more affected by economic recession and unemployment.

In general, two dynamics define the scenario of housing policy in our six cities (see Table 13.5):

1   Housing re-commodification processes, obtained through the privatisation of the municipal housing stock and/or programmes supporting home- ownership; although re-commodification has been important in all the urban contexts analysed, in Copenhagen, Milan and Manchester this dynamic has been particularly affected by the policies of municipal housing stock privati- sation, while in Barcelona the public housing sector has always been resid- ual and has even been reduced through policies oriented towards home-ownership.
2   The development of local programmes directly addressing housing afforda- bility; three types of programmes with different aims have been found: (a) programmes designed to increase the direct production of public/social housing managed by municipal authorities; (b) programmes producing new social housing through public/private partnerships in land use management; (c) programmes providing private affordable housing, usually by rent- control strategies after neighbourhood renewal.

Table 13.5 Different scenarios of housing policies

Programmes addressing with housing affordability	Process of re-commodification fostered by national/local policies	
	Lower	Higher
Increase public/social housing by direct provision	Lyon	Copenhagen
Increase public/social housing by public/ private partnership	Munich	Milan
Neighbourhood requalification and incentives to private provision of affordable housing		Barcelona Manchester

Source: authors' elaboration.

Lyon and Munich have been less affected by housing re-commodification than the other cities, although starting from very a different point in terms of the relevance of municipal/social housing stock on the total housing stock. In fact, the most positive situation in terms of housing affordability is registered in Lyon, a city located in a national context presenting a good diffusion of public and social housing, and where housing policies have recently been sustained by different levels of government. However, Lyon has been characterised by a twofold, contradictory, policy orientation. On the one hand, urban planning has mainly supported the gentrification of central areas through the restoration of historic neighbourhoods, improvement in the quality of public spaces and concentration of prestigious equipment in central neighbourhoods. Moreover, demolition and rebuilding of buildings in the most distressed areas have diminished the available resources for social housing policy, and the upgrading of the public stock contributed to an increase in rental prices. On the other hand, a large range of housing affordability policies was introduced, which allowed approximately 50 per cent coverage of demand for low-cost housing. Among these, the "*servitude de mixité sociale*" in areas with a shortage of low-cost housing is worth mentioning, a rule imposing a minimal share of social housing for each future real estate development (20 or 25 per cent of social housing).

In Munich, affordable housing has been an important issue in the public debate as the local housing market is one of the most expensive ones in the country, and is characterised by a low provision of social housing (10 per cent). The main task of housing policies at the urban level has been to provide affordable housing, and maintain an adequate quality of life in all the urban districts. These measures have been interestingly linked with an attempt to customise social infrastructures for childcare, care for the elderly and for other social services, and has been promoted through a socially equitable land-use approach, which, however, does not seem to be sufficient to mitigate increasing housing market costs.

In Copenhagen, housing affordability has been strongly reduced in the last two decades mainly as a result of important changes in housing market regulation and the housing policy sector. For many years, the city government promoted home-ownership in an attempt to capture high income groups and solve the financial crisis of the local public budget. Public intervention aimed at renewing deprived neighbourhoods (e.g. Vesterbro) and fostering private investments in new development areas (Oresund) worked out as drivers of gentrification and increasing costs of housing. Moreover, during the 1990s, a massive sale of municipal housing was accepted in order to cover the city's public debt. In recent years, local authorities implemented a new social-housing masterplan, aimed at providing 5,000 new dwellings at an affordable price. The houses should have been located on publicly-owned land in order to reduce total costs. However, government decided that the sale of publicly-owned properties under the market price was illegal and consequently, the plan was aborted.

In recent decades, Milan has mainly invested in big real estate development, with the aim of attracting financial investors to the city. The dominant orientation was to give greater incentives to high-value private investments and to very profitable private housing rather than enlarging the affordable housing sector. Affordability problems have been mainly addressed through public and private partnerships aimed at increasing the supply of low rental houses, with very poor impact. In recent years, the new administration initiated a new agenda for housing policies. However, the lack of public funds has only enabled programmes that are still based on private intervention, such as the provision of public land properties to be made available for a few new public housing projects, or the setting up of a small public fund reserve to increase the low rental social housing sector.

In Manchester, the housing crisis is very acute. Despite the current round of institution-building undertaken, the city's regional stakeholders do not have the requisite powers at their disposal to make significant interventions in the key policy area of housing. In addition, despite the relatively high proportion of residents living in social housing, this provision is no longer under the direct responsibility of local authorities and has been largely "stock-transferred" to independent bodies outside of public control. Though many housing interventions have been launched by the Greater Manchester City Region (GMCR) in the last decade, mainly through public–private partnerships and private finance initiatives (PFI), many of them have been more recently cancelled in a wave of cuts for regeneration schemes by the national government.

Barcelona, finally, experienced a huge increase in housing prices before the crisis (between 1995–2006 an increase of 500 per cent). In the same period, there was a significant decrease in public housing stock for rent and in public expenditure for housing (only 0.5 per cent of GDP devoted to the housing policy). State housing regulation was directed towards fostering ownership, with low development of social housing and other forms of tenure. These trends were contrasted through a policy intervention aimed at regenerating peripheral neighbourhoods and lately, at supporting the rental sector (i.e. State Plan for Housing and Rehabilitation); however, with a very low budget. The housing crisis has been particular sharp in this city. With regard to urban regeneration and housing, *Poblenou* and the 22@ exemplify the difficulties of changing the general framework of the housing market given the preponderance of ownership and the poor social-housing provision. Moreover, rental grants to support housing access were introduced in Barcelona without solving the issue of housing affordability. Paradoxically, following the housing crisis that developed with the collapse of the housing bubble in 2008, thousands of empty housing units were repossessed by banks. This housing market mismatch has become central in the debate on housing in Barcelona as well as in the rest of Spain, while housing renewal as a strategy for social cohesion has lost priority in the political agenda at the national, regional and local level.

To sum up, the most relevant evidence from our investigation is that quite recently all the municipal governments have tried to reframe their local policies in favour of conditions promoting increased housing affordability. Lyon and Copenhagen have tried mainly to foster programmes to increase the social/municipal housing stock, but in Copenhagen the programme failed due to conflicts at the national level; Munich and Milan have invested more in projects based on private–public partnership, although in Milan the experiments were very small in comparison to the huge housing crisis affecting a large part of the population. Finally, Manchester and Barcelona have oriented a large part of their efforts towards tools to promote housing affordability in the private stock. However, these programmes have produced very limited results, not being able to contain the long-term trend effects of the re-commodification process in housing, fostered by the same local and national governments in the decades just before the crisis.

13.6 Departures from the "European city model"

As already argued, the economic crisis that started in 2007 represented an important "stress test" (Hemerijck 2012) for the European cities analysed in this research. It worked to accelerate the deep transformations that occurred in previous decades. The economic recession, together with austerity measures, has revealed the fragile status of these urban governments (Brenner 2010). Their ability to govern social and economic transformations has become increasingly limited faced with the trilemma due to: growing social needs, increasing responsibility in key policy areas, and stronger financial constraints. In this situation, the traditional capacity of urban governments to combine the protection of the weakest social groups with the promotion of the city's economic development (Bagnasco and Le Galès 2000; Le Galès 2002) has weakened. In the framework of rapidly emerging social needs and severe budget constraints, all these cities have developed specific programmes with some level of innovation. However, this intervention has only been partially able to address social and economic criticalities in an effective way. Neither have urban governments been able to institutionalise the most effective policy tools that they have experimented with.

Urban policy in these cities has been fundamentally contradictory in dealing with the competiveness-social integration nexus (Brenner *et al.* 2010). All these cities were extremely successful in obtaining a dominant position in the global economy before the crisis (Musterd and Kovács 2013). The capacity of such cities to attract new investment was not only grounded in their economic solidity, but was also driven by urban policies able to support the most attractive and innovative specialised sectors. Local policies played an important role in this respect, providing financial support, infrastructures and investment opportunities to both local entrepreneurs and global players. Nevertheless, although an important divide has emerged between cities developing a "high road" to post-industrial transition and cities oriented towards a "lower road", in both these patterns social and economic disparities increased as a consequence of two main trends: the decline of housing affordability and the dualisation of the labour market.

In all our cities, urban policies have actually contributed to this trend. Inequalities are, therefore, not only the result of socio-economic transformations, but also of urban policies directed towards inter-city competitiveness and attractiveness. Cities have shown different approaches towards this issue relatively independently from the national welfare regimes and the political orientation of their urban governments, but as result of a complex entanglement of factors, such as the general multi-level governance system and the specific distribution of power among institutions in specific policy areas, as already reported in Sections 13.2 and 13.3.

This inability to govern change is the result of a number of factors already considered in previous research, including specific policy orientation and capacity of local governments, the public resonance obtained by the neo-liberal discourse, the lack of public funds due to national and/or European austerity policy, and the weakened role played by traditional social stakeholders in setting the urban policy agenda. In this study, the state–city relationship has shown to be crucial in enabling local governments to act as "collective actors" (Le Galès 1998, 2002). In crisis time, the capacity of urban governments to carry out effective policy has been substantially reduced by a three-fold dynamic: state delegation of further responsibility for local economic development as well as social integration, strong cuts in central funding and tighter constraints on local budgets. Urban governments had therefore to deal with a new trilemmatic situation: addressing increased social needs with reduced financial resources and more limited political autonomy. It is in this situation that the challenge to follow the so-called "European city model" collapsed for most of these cities. And this fact has shown how much this model was vulnerable, financially unsustainable, and largely dependent on state support.

It is paradoxical that the departure from this model has been mainly caused by the tightening of the state–city relationship under the auspices of austerity policy. In the countries where state austerity was not a prolonged pervasive strategy, state financial support for urban policy persisted over time, and the MLIG setting gave more room for local policy autonomy, where the challenge had more chance to be strategically met by cities. In countries where austerity was strongly dictated by national and/or European authorities, state financing to local authorities was significantly reduced, and local autonomy was limited and even further reduced, cities were unable to meet the challenge.

On the other hand, as a consequence of these factors the crisis has magnified the emergence of different patterns of departure from the "European City Model". Combining the results of our investigation, three different patterns can be identified.

A neo-liberal strategy. Before the crisis, cities such as Copenhagen and Milan had already applied a policy agenda that was mainly based on a neo-liberal approach, although with some relevant differences in the local government style. Until 2011, the municipality of Milan's political agenda was strongly oriented towards major investment in the regeneration and redevelopment of urban areas, by running major international events (Expo 2015) and strongly promoting the interests of private operators in these issues, in a sort of *private interest government pattern* (Streeck and Schmitter, 1984). In Copenhagen, national and local programmes addressed the issue of economic growth through housing renewal projects and new infrastructure projects. The aim was to improve the long-term balance of the city's budget through the privatisation of public housing stock and requalification programmes aimed at attracting high-income groups. The concept of the *entrepreneurial city* (Hall and Hubbard 1996; Jessop 1997; Jessop and Sum 2000) is quite effective in defining the pattern followed by this city. In both these cities, social integration was left to the responsibility of third parties: to private, charitable initiatives in the case of Milan; to the strong welfare state intervention in the case of Copenhagen. These two options obviously generated very different outcomes for the most vulnerable groups of the population. After the crisis (and a political turn in the case of Milan in 2011), both local governments tried to re-orient their neo-liberal approach to mitigate the harsh social effects of the recession, but huge budget constrains in Milan or governance conflicts in Copenhagen have strongly limited their ability to dramatically change the previous pattern.

A social investment strategy. In some cities, measures were promoted to obtain a stronger social integration as an important asset for urban development, applying a "social investment strategy" (Hemerijck 2012) at the city level. This is the case of Munich (still current) and Barcelona before the onset of the crisis. In Munich, the huge emphasis on local economic growth has come with attention being paid to create the social preconditions for the attraction of both high and low-skilled workers. "*Perspective Munich*" especially focused on urban development as a flexible and process-related way to promote socially-sustainable economic, demographic progress. In Barcelona, global competitiveness objectives (promotion of culture, tourism, arts, real estate investments) were associated with social programmes aimed at improving the conditions of the most deprived areas and to improve the skills of lower-educated people in order to support the professionalisation of the workforce. In both these cities, the capacity to develop an integrated network of public and private stakeholders played a relevant role. However, the long-term sustainability of such a strategy stems from a favourable economic trend and a multi-level governance system supporting local autonomy. These two factors explain why in Munich this pattern has long been developing while in Barcelona the crisis has actually stopped any further development.

A mitigation strategy. In Lyon and Manchester, local governments have prioritised interventions for economic development but at the same time have tried to mitigate the possible negative effects for the most vulnerable social groups, showing a more traditional approach towards social policy. In Lyon and Manchester, this pattern is mainly the result of a lack of coordination between different institutional levels. In Lyon, the local government is in possession of strong legal instruments and important resources to frame the urbanisation process and to make it compatible with the maintenance of social integration. In fact, the rise of the crisis has been tackled through special programmes, both in housing and training, addressing the most deprived population. On the other hand, Lyon is a city with strong economic ambitions, fostering policies oriented towards competition for the localisation of foreign direct investment and high-skilled workers. As a result, dualisation in the labour market and income inequality have been increasing in the last ten years. A traditional administrative disjunction between social and economic intervention may explain this dualism. In Manchester, this disconnection has mostly been due to multi-level governance conflicts. This city has pursued an urban policy agenda that is strongly oriented towards economic resilience, urban planning and branding as the city of finance and ICT. However, weak attempts have been made to support local residents to gain skills for accessing good quality jobs and to get affordable housing. Besides the large-scale privatisation of municipal housing stock, some few experimental programmes for housing affordability have been pursued, while major housing renewal programmes have been blocked by the central government's austerity policy. In this case, the high level of disconnection between pro-growth and social integration strategies does not lie in local hands.

To sum up, a general process of "Americanisation" of the European city (Häußermann 2005) has not emerged from our analysis. At the same time, the so-called European city model has almost completely vanished in our cities. The present institutional, social and political conditions do not support this model any more. We identified different paths of departure in this study, which need to be further explored over the coming years.

The departure from the "European city model" towards new urban patterns shows three main aspects. First, urban policies are still intrinsically contradictory in their orientation: although they have largely contributed to sharpen social inequalities in our cities, in many contexts they are still crucial to preserve social integration. It is through this paradoxical and contradictory aspect that urban governments still play a relevant role in Europe. Second, the policy capacity of European cities has significantly decreased when compared to previous periods characterised by strong state support and fostered by positive, permanent economic growth. The instability of the MLIG systems in which urban governments are today embedded not only makes it difficult for urban policy to pursue long-trend effective strategy, but it also takes substantial power and influence out of

270   *C. Ranci and R. Cucca*

local control. The inability of urban governments to deal with rising inequalities is based on resources, regulatory power, and actual responsibility that are predominantly out of local control, embedded in a complex multi-level governance system. Third, and finally, the departure paths from the European City model are found in a piecemeal agenda, much more fragmented by function and geography in comparison to the institutional settings that characterised European cities just a few years ago (Kazepov 2005; Body-Gendrot *et al.* 2012). This fragmentation represents an additional element of instability. It is not guaranteed, therefore, that cities still represent a crucial asset for a possible resilience of the balance between economic development and the social integration that has characterised European cities until recently.

Note

1 Hoekstra (2010: 35) defines commodification as the "extent to which households can provide their own housing, independent of the income they acquire on the labour market".

References

Aalbers, M. B. (2013). Debate on neoliberalism in and after the neoliberal crisis. *International Journal of Urban and Regional Research*, 37(3), 1053–1057.

Andreotti, A., Mingione, E. and Polizzi, E. (2012). Local welfare systems: a challenge for social cohesion. *Urban studies*, 49(9), 1925–1940.

Bagnasco, A. and Le Galès, P. (eds) (2000). *Cities in Contemporary Europe*. Cambridge: Cambridge University Press.

Barberis, E., Sabatinelli, S. and Bieri, A. (2010). Social assistance policy models in Europe: a comparative perspective. In: Kazepov Y. (ed.) *Rescaling Social Policies: Towards Multilevel Governance in Europe*. Farnham: Ashgate, pp. 177–202.

Body-Gendrot, S., Garcia, M. and Mingione, E. (2012). Comparative social transformations in urban regimes. In Sales, A. (ed.), *Sociology Today: Social Transformations in a Globalizing World*, London: Sage, pp. 359–380.

Borraz, O., Le Galès, P. (2010). Urban governance in Europe, the governance of what? *Metropoles*, 1 (32), 137–151.

Brenner, N. (2004). Urban governance and the production of new state spaces in Western Europe, 1960–2000, *Review of International Political Economy*, 11(3), 447–488.

Brenner, N. and Theodore, N. (eds) (2002). *Spaces of Neoliberalism: Urban Restructuring in Western Europe and North America*. Cambridge, MA: Blackwell.

Brenner, N., Peck, J. and Theodore, N. (2010). Variegated neoliberalization: geographies, modalities, pathways. *Global Networks*, 10(2), 182–222.

Camagni, R. (2002). On the concept of territorial competitiveness: sound or misleading?. *Urban studies*, 39(13), 2395–2411.

Cattacin, S., Evers, A. and Zimmer, A. (eds) (2016). *Social Innovations in the Urban Context*, New York, Springer Verlag.

Crouch, C. and Le Galès, P. (2012). Cities as national champions? *Journal of European Public Policy*, 19(3), 405–419.

Doling, J. (1999). De-commodification and welfare: evaluating housing systems, in *Housing, Theory and Society* 16(4): 156–164.

Fainstein, S. (2015). Resilience and justice, *International Journal of Urban and Regional Research*, 39(1), 157–167.

Gordon, I., Harding, A. and Harloe, M. (2012). *Leadership, Legitimacy and the Uncertain Development of Metropolitan Governance: Comparing England's First and Second City-regions*, paper presented at conference "Governing the metropolis: powers and territories: new directions for research", Paris, 28–30 November.

Hall, T. and Hubbard, P. (1996). The entrepreneurial city: new urban politics, new urban geographies? In *Progress in Human Geography* 20(2): 153–174.

Häußermann, H. (2005). The end of the European city? *European Review*, 13(02): 237–249.

Hemerijck, A. (2012). *Changing Welfare States*. Oxford: Oxford University Press.

Hoekstra, J. (2010). *Divergence in European Welfare and Housing Systems*, Delft: IOS Press.

Jessop, B. (1997). The entrepreneurial city: re-imaging localities, redesigning economic governance, or restructuring capital. In Jewson, N. and MacGregor, S. (eds). *Transforming Cities: Contested Governance and New Spatial Divisions*. Hove, UK: Psychology Press, pp. 28–41.

Jessop, B. and Sum, N. L. (2000). An entrepreneurial city in action: Hong Kong's emerging strategies in and for (inter) urban competition. *Urban Studies*, 37(12), 2287–2313.

Kazepov, Y. (ed.) (2005). *Cities of Europe: Changing Contexts, Local Arrangements, and the Challenge of Urban Cohesion*. Malden, MA: Wiley-Blackwell.

Kazepov, Y. (ed.) (2010). *Rescaling Social Policies: towards Multilevel Governance in Europe*. Farnham: Ashgate.

Kearns, A. and Forrest, R. (2000). Social cohesion and multilevel urban governance. *Urban Studies*, 37(5/6), 995.

Keating, M. (1998). *The New Regionalism in Western Europe, Territorial Restructuring and Political Change*, Northampton, MA: Edward Elgar.

Le Galès, P. (1998). Regulations and governance in European cities. *International Journal of Urban and Regional Research*, 22(3), 482–506.

Le Galès, P. (2002). *European Cities: Social Conflicts and Governance*. Oxford: Oxford University Press.

MacLeod, G., Raco, M. and Ward, K. (2003). Negotiating the contemporary city: introduction. *Urban Studies*, 40(9), 1655–1671.

Maloutas, T. and Pantelidou Malouta, M. (2004). The glass menagerie of urban governance and social cohesion: concepts and stakes/concepts as stakes. *International Journal of Urban and Regional Research*, 28: 449–465.

Matznetter, W. and Musil, R. (2012). The European city in the age of globalisation. *Belgeo: Revue belge de géographie*, (1–2).

Mazzucato, M. (2015). *The Entrepreneurial State: Debunking Public vs. Private Sector Myths*. London: Anthem Press.

Musterd, S. and Kovács, Z. (eds) (2013). *Place-making and Policies for Competitive Cities*. Malden, MA: John Wiley & Sons.

Pahl, R. (2001). Market success and social cohesion. *International Journal of Urban and Regional Research*, 25(4), 879–883.

Peck, J. and Tickell, A. (2002). Neoliberalizing space. *Antipode*, 34(3), 380–404.

Pierson, P. (2001). *The New Politics of the Welfare State*. Oxford, Oxford University.

Ranci, C., Brandsen, T. and Sabatinelli, S. (eds) (2014). *Social Vulnerability in European Cities: the Role of Local Welfare in Times of Crisis*, Basingstoke: Palgrave Macmillan.

Robinson, J. (2011). Cities in a world of cities: the comparative gesture. *International Journal of Urban and Regional Research*, 35: 1–23.

Sapir, A. (2006). Globalization and the reform of European social models. *Journal of Common Market Studies*, 44(2), 369–390.

Scott, A. J. (2008), Resurgent metropolis: economy, society and urbanization in an interconnected world. *International Journal of Urban and Regional Research*, 32: 548–564.

Streeck, W. and Schmitter, P. (1984). Community, market, state and associations? In *European University Institute Working Paper*, No. 94, Florence.

Tammaru, T., van Ham, M., Marcińczak, S. and Musterd, S. (eds) (2015). *Socio-economic Segregation in European Capital Cities: East meets West*. London: Routledge.

Turner, B., Whitehead, C. (eds) (1993). *Housing Finance in the 1990s*. Research report National Swedish Institute for Building Research, Gavle.

Turok, I. (2004). Cities, regions and competitiveness. *Regional Studies*, 38(9), 1069–1083.

Van Kempen, R. (2007). Divided cities in the twenty-first century: challenging the importance of globalisation. *Journal of Housing and the Built Environment*, 22(1), 13–31.

Van Kempen, R. and Murie, A. (2009). The new divided city: changing patterns in European cities. *Tijdschrift voor economische en sociale geografie*, 100(4), 377–398.

Index

Page numbers in *italics* denote tables, those in **bold** denote figures.